Owing to the antiquity and rarity of this book, certain pages are regrettably absent, and readability is compromised due to the blurring of the original text. If you possess any insights regarding the availability of these missing sections, kindly inform us. Your assistance is crucial in ensuring the completion of this significant work for the benefit of future generations.

INDIA'S NORTH EAST FRONTIER IN THE NINETEENTH CENTURY

VERRIER ED. ELWIN

Published by

FacsiMile Publisher
12 Pragati Market
Ashok Vihar, Ph-2
Delhi - 110052, India
Phone: 011-47034999
Email: www.facsimilepublishers.com
info@facsimilepublishers.com

Distribution Network
gyanbooks.com
India, USA, Canada, UK, Australia

ISBN: 978-93-3333-650-5 (HB)
First Published, 1915

2nd Impression 2025

Printed at: Gyan Press, Delhi.

INDIA'S NORTH EAST FRONTIER IN THE NINETEENTH CENTURY
Author: VERRIER ED. ELWIN

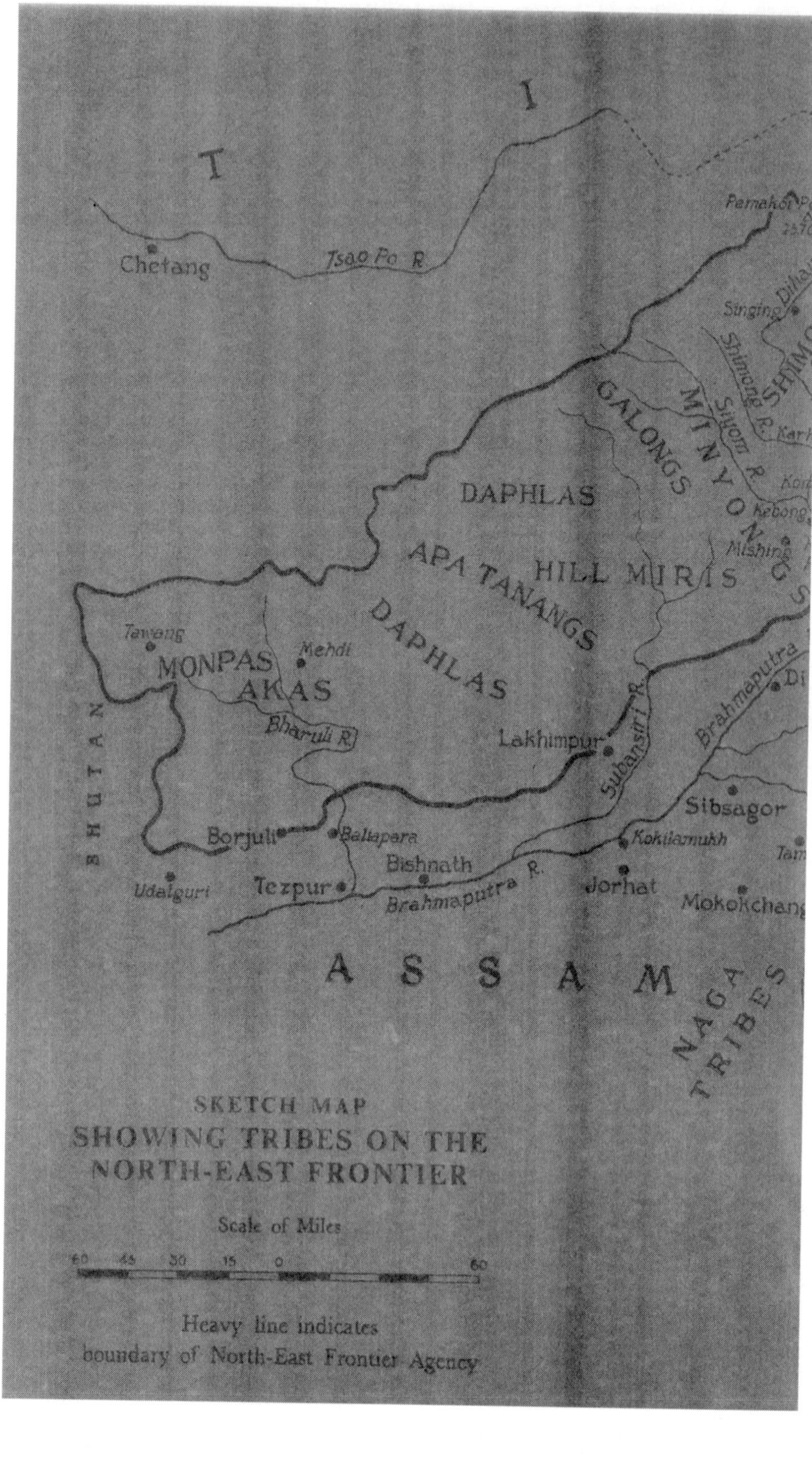

SKETCH MAP
SHOWING TRIBES ON THE
NORTH-EAST FRONTIER

Heavy line indicates boundary of North-East Frontier Agency

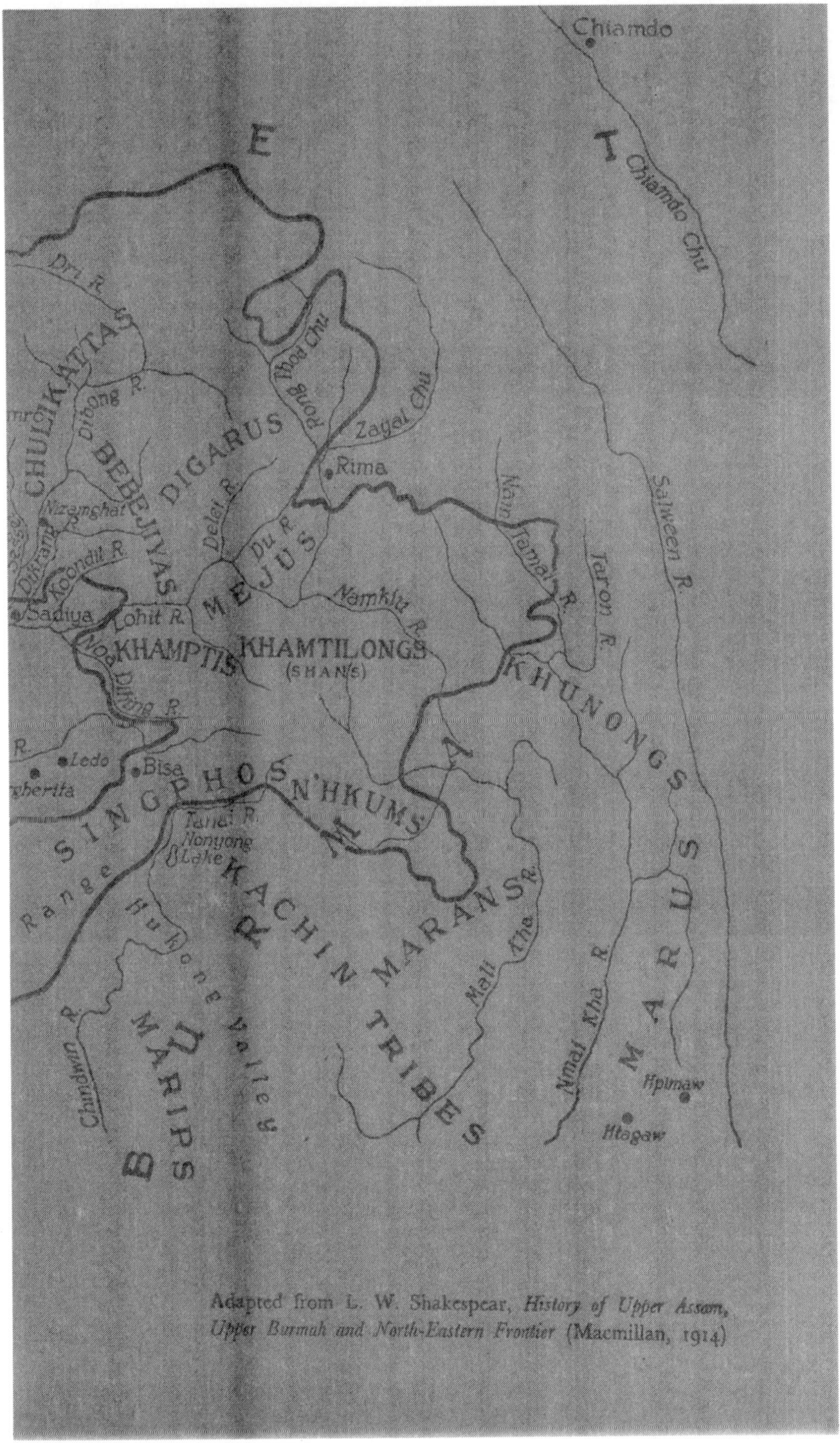

Adapted from L. W. Shakespear, *History of Upper Assam, Upper Burmah and North-Eastern Frontier* (Macmillan, 1914)

INDIA'S NORTH-EAST FRONTIER in the Nineteenth Century

ALSO BY VERRIER ELWIN

MONOGRAPHS

The Baiga (Murray, 1939), out of print
The Agaria (O.U.P., 1942), out of print
Maria Murder and Suicide (O.U.P., 1943, second edition, 1950)
Folk-Tales of Mahakoshal (O.U.P., 1944), out of print
Folk-Songs of Chhattisgarh (O.U.P., 1946), out of print
Myths of Middle India (O.U.P., 1949), out of print
The Muria and their Ghotul (O.U.P., 1947), out of print
Bondo Highlander (O.U.P., 1950)
The Tribal Art of Middle India (O.U.P., 1951)
Tribal Myths of Orissa (O.U.P., 1954)
The Religion of an Indian Tribe (O.U.P., 1955), out of print
Myths of the North-East Frontier of India (NEFA Administration, 1958)
The Art of the North-East Frontier of India (NEFA Administration, 1959)
Nagaland (Adviser's Secretariat, Shillong, 1961)

GENERAL

The Aboriginals (O.U.P., 1943, second edition, 1944), out of print
Motley (Orient Longmans, 1954)
Leaves from the Jungle (Murray, 1936, second edition, O.U.P., 1958)
A Philosophy for NEFA (NEFA Administration, 1957, third edition, 1961)
When the World was Young (National Book Trust, 1961)

NOVELS

Phulmat of the Hills (Murray, 1937), out of print
A Cloud that's Dragonish (Murray, 1938), out of print

WITH SHAMRAO HIVALE

Songs of the Forest (Allen & Unwin, 1935)
Folk-Songs of the Maikal Hills (O.U.P., 1944), out of print

INDIA'S NORTH-EAST FRONTIER
in the Nineteenth Century

Edited with an Introduction by

VERRIER ELWIN

OXFORD UNIVERSITY PRESS

Oxford University Press, Amen House, London E.C.4

GLASGOW NEW YORK TORONTO MELBOURNE WELLINGTON
BOMBAY CALCUTTA MADRAS KARACHI LAHORE DACCA
CAPE TOWN SALISBURY NAIROBI IBADAN ACCRA
KUALA LUMPUR HONG KONG

FIRST PUBLISHED 1959
SECOND IMPRESSION 1962

PRINTED IN INDIA BY V. M. PHILIP AT THE DIOCESAN PRESS, MADRAS 7 BY PHOTO OFFSET, WITH BLOCKS MADE AT THE SUN PROCESS WORKS, BOMBAY, AND PUBLISHED BY JOHN BROWN, OXFORD UNIVERSITY PRESS, APOLLO BUNDER, BOMBAY 1

To

Minnie and Lindsay Emmerson

ASSAM is naturally a beautiful tract of country, and enjoys all the advantages requisite for rendering it one of the finest under the sun—though at present, owing to its very thinly populated state, by far the greater portion of it is allowed to run to waste with luxuriance of vegetation. Notwithstanding, it occasionally presents a scenery comparable perhaps to the richest in the world. Its plains decked with a rich verdant robe, and abounding with numerous crystal streams, which winding along the base of a group of beautifully wooded hills, covered to their very summits with trees, interspersed with dark and deep glens, and heaving their swelling ridges into a bright blue sky, constitute altogether a scene of extraordinary magnificence and sublimity, and display a regularity and softness of feature that beggars description. On the other hand, to such as find satisfaction in contemplating nature in her rudest and most gigantic forms, what an inexhaustible fund of delight is here likewise displayed! Mountains beyond mountains hurled together in wild confusion, seem to the spectator like the wrecks of a ruined world; and whilst the eye is gratified with the pleasing panorama, a series of hills innumerable is presented to view, retiring far away in fine perspective, till their blue conical summits are relieved by the proud pinnacles of the Himalaya towering their lofty magazines of tempests and snow midway up to the vertex of the sky, and exhibiting scenes calculated to animate the mind with the sublimest sentiments, and to awaken the most lofty recollections.

W. ROBINSON
1841

CONTENTS

IX VISITORS TO MEMBU

X THE ABORS AT THE END OF THE CENTURY

XI THE MISHMIS

XII THE KHAMPTIS

XIII THE SINGPHOS

ILLUSTRATIONS

INTRODUCTION

I

VERY little has been written on the tribal peoples of the north-east frontier of India. In J. P. Mills's ethnographic bibliography of Assam only about one in ten of the items listed has anything to say about them. And these items are mostly articles or notes in periodicals now impossible to obtain and difficult to consult, or they are official publications which have been indifferently preserved. The few books of the early period, such as those by Robinson, Butler and Dalton, are today collector's pieces. Yet these elusive records contain much that is of absorbing interest.

In this book, therefore, I present a selection of passages from the older literature, down to 1900, which has a bearing on the history, people and problems of what is now known as the North-East Frontier Agency. These passages are of unusual value, for they give us a picture of the country as it was before it had suffered any external influence, and although the reader may sometimes regret that the writers did not use their opportunities for exact observation more fully, he must be thankful for what he has. He should remember that the administrators, soldiers, missionaries and explorers represented in these pages were not anthropologists. Even Dalton was not an anthropologist in the modern sense. Their information is not always correct; it is sometimes heavily marked by personal bias; some of it is obviously guess-work. But they were fresh to the country and their eyes were open; from them a general idea of what the tribal people were like sixty, eighty, a hundred or even a hundred and twenty years ago, does emerge, and despite all the faults both of fact and of taste their work is of value to scholars and administrators alike.

In contrast to both an earlier and a later age, the European travellers of the nineteenth century were under no illusions about the Noble Savage; in the main their opinion of the tribes was a low one and their attitude was all too often patronizing or scornful. In 1865, declared a leading article in the *Pioneer* of the day, 'the only idea which most men had, with reference to the hills and forests [of Assam], was that they were the habitat of savage tribes, whose bloody raids and thieving forays threatened serious danger to the cause of tea'.

The people were not even interesting: Lord Dalhousie pronounced the Assam frontier to be a bore, and even as late as 1911 we find the wife of an officer attached to the Abor Expedition of that year expressing herself in a series of puns: 'It is such a bore that my husband has to go off on that silly Abor Expedition to fight those stupid aborigines with their queer arboreal habits.'[1]

Even the serious writers took the same view. Butler declares that the troops of his command 'wish for nothing better than an opportunity of contending with the Singphos, or indeed with any of their treacherous neighbours (whom they hold in the utmost contempt) in a fair battle in the open country'. He speaks of the 'general degeneracy' of the Assamese people who are emaciated by their predilection for the 'pernicious opiate', opium, even though under British rule 'we may yet regard Assam as a rising country'. He calls the Khamptis 'a discontented, restless, intriguing tribe'; the Singphos are 'a rude treacherous people'; the Abors are 'as void of delicacy as they are of cleanliness'; the Nagas are 'a very uncivilized race, with dark complexions, athletic sinewy frames, hideously wild and ugly visages, reckless of human life'. Among such, says Butler in 1847, we might reasonably expect missionary zeal would be most successful. For the last eight years, however, two or three American Baptist missionaries had in vain endeavoured to awake in them a sense of the saving virtue of Christianity.

Rowlatt, who explored the Mishmi hills in 1844, describes the Mishmis as 'disgustingly dirty: with the exception of a few of the Chiefs, they are seldom washed from one year's end to another. . . . They seem to have but a very faint idea of any religion'. M'Cosh, who included a chapter on the hill tribes in his *Topography of Assam* (1837), says of the Miris that their manners and habits are 'wild and barbarous and their persons filthy and squalid'. Robinson, though he speaks well of the Abors, describes the Daflas as having ugly countenances and a 'somewhat ferocious' appearance. The Mishmis are 'in general excessively filthy'. Beresford speaks of the

[1] P. Millington, *On the Track of the Abor* (1912), p. v.

Abors as 'truculent and aggressive . . . like all savages, the only law they know or recognize is that of force and in the ability of awarding prompt and speedy punishments'.

Even J. F. Needham, who was once criticized by authority for allowing himself to be 'cheeked by the men and pulled about by the young women', spoke on occasion in the most uncomplimentary terms of his people. 'Notwithstanding that they [the Abors] are most hospitable,' he writes in 1886, 'their manner is so rough and they are so provokingly impertinent (unmeaningly, I admit, for it is nothing but ignorance, coupled with self-conceitedness, that makes them so) and familiar, as likewise possessed of such monkey-like inquisitiveness, that their society very soon palls upon one, especially after the first novelty of being amongst them has worn off. They are so excessively suspicious too, that one shirks even asking them questions about their manners and customs, except in the most casual manner.' He also calls the Mishmis 'treacherous and cowardly curs'; they are 'blustering' and leniency is as little understood by this tribe 'as by any other similarly uncivilized and savage'.

Dalton's attitude, however, is very different, and he foreshadows the new attitude of respect, interest and affection that in the main governs the relations of literates and pre-literates in the modern world. Not only does he never speak of the tribal people with contempt or scorn, but he never misses an opportunity of recording instances in their favour. Even the Chulikata Mishmis, to whom he gives a bad character (adding, however, that 'I would not venture to have done so on any authority but their own'), have many virtues and are the 'most ingenious of the family'. He is impressed by the 'practical utility' of the Abor dormitory and by 'the ready alacrity and good feeling and discipline' of its member . Of Miri women he says that they make faithful and obedient wives and cheerfully bear the hard burden imposed upon them. The Tanaes (Apa Tanis) make war both effectually and honourably, fighting only men and inflicting no injury whatever on non-combatants. 'If this be true,' adds Dalton, 'the Tanae may claim a hearing as the most humane of belligerents at the next International Congress.'

Unhappily, such an attitude was rare and a lack of sympathy with the people accounts for many mistakes of the earlier writers. In no field are our old records more imperfect than in that of religion. We must remember that it was not easy, at that date, for the majority of European officers to take seriously any religion other than their own. The outlook of Sir James Johnstone, as expressed in his book *My Experiences in Manipur and the Naga Hills* (1896), is typical: 'I strongly urged the advisability of establishing a regular system of education, including religious instruction, under a competent clergyman of the Church of England. I pointed out that the Nagas had no religion; that they were highly intelligent and capable of receiving civilization; that with it they would want a religion, and that we might as well give them our own, and make them in this way a source of strength, by thus mutually attaching them to us.' Dalton also did his utmost to aid Christian missions among the Kols, when he was Commissioner of Chota Nagpur, his argument being, so Johnstone says, 'that they wanted a religion, and that were they Christians, they would be a valuable counterpoise in time of trouble to the vast non-Christian population of Bihar. In the same way it cannot be doubted that a large population of Christian hillmen between Assam and Burma would be a valuable prop to the State.'

This belief that the tribal people of Assam had 'no religion', or alternatively that what religion they had was (as Butler said of the Singphos) 'a mixture of all the various idolatries and superstitions' ever invented, did not encourage unbiased and scientific inquiry. Thus even Dalton says that 'the religion of the Mishmis is confined to the propitiation of demons', and of the Chulikatas he observes, 'I have met with no people so entirely devoid of religious feeling as are the Chulikatas. I had long conversations on the subject with several of the Chiefs, and they utterly rejected all notions of a future state or of immortality of any kind'. Of the Miris he declares that 'the religious observances of the Miris are confined to the slaughter of animals in the name of the sylvan spirits and vaticination by the examination of the entrails of birds'. Of the Nagas he says, 'they have no temples and no priests, and I never heard of any form of worship amongst them, but I do not doubt that they sacrifice and observe omens like other tribes'.

Yet this was not the last word of the older writers and a fine passage by T. H. Lewin, written in 1869, anticipates the attitude and policy of modern India:

> This I say, let us not govern these hills for ourselves, but administer the country for the well-being and happiness of the people

dwelling therein. What is wanted here is not measures, but a man. Place over them an officer gifted with the power of rule, not a mere cog in the great wheel of government, but one tolerant of the failings of his fellow-creatures and yet prompt to see and recognize in them the touch of nature that makes the whole world kin, apt to enter into new trains of thought and to modify and adopt ideas, but cautious in offending national prejudice. Under a guidance like this, let the people by slow degree civilize themselves. With education open to them and yet moving under their own laws and customs, they will turn out not debased and miniature epitomes of Englishmen, but a new and noble type of God's creatures.

II

ON the whole, very little is known about the men whose writings are reproduced in this book: only two of them find a place in the *Dictionary of National Biography*, and I have had to collect what information there is from chance references in journals and occasional autobiographical passages. The following notes, scanty as they are, will however give some idea of who our authors were and what they did.

John Butler

John Butler, author of *A Sketch of Assam* (1847) and *Travels and Adventures in the Province of Assam during a Residence of Fourteen Years* (1855), first visited Assam in 1837, when he spent three months at Goalpara. He was a soldier, belonging to the 55th Regiment of the Bengal Native Infantry, and in November 1840 he was appointed second-in-command of the Assam Light Infantry. His journey from Calcutta to the 'desolate and remote' station of Saikwa took no less than sixty-five days, of which thirty-seven were spent travelling up-stream to Gauhati, 'the metropolis of Assam'. On this second visit, Butler found that Gauhati had been greatly improved; roads had been made, many brick bungalows had been erected, the jungle had been cleared, while 'the view of the river, the islands, temples, and verdant foliage of the trees' made the place 'one of the most picturesque scenes to be met with in India'. From Gauhati he travelled in a canoe (formed of a single tree hollowed out and propelled by eighteen 'merry paddlers') up the Brahmaputra to Saikwa, 'the north-eastern frontier military post in Upper Assam'. Saikwa had been established in 1839 after the station of Sadiya on the opposite bank had been surprised and burnt in a tribal attack. Here at Saikwa the Light Infantry was posted 'to afford protection to the Tea Gardens from the sudden aggressions of the numerous wild, fierce, border tribes'.

Here Butler settled down in a mat-and-grass cottage plastered with mud 'in comfort and solitariness'. He had many adventures; one night his house was invaded by a great python, and he was constantly in trouble with the Brahmaputra.

His stay did not, however, last very long, for in the following year he was appointed to the civil branch of the service as an Assistant to the Agent to the Governor-General, North-East Frontier; and after a residence of about three years in Lower Assam, in the month of February 1844 he was placed in charge of the hill tribes subject to the Political Agent of Upper Assam. Now again he had to go to Saikwa, this time with his family, and in June of that year his house was washed away by the 'merciless river'. But Butler was never left in one place for long; indeed, as he says, 'during a period of twenty-seven years' service it has seldom been my lot to enjoy, at one place, an undisturbed residence of more than a few months', and the 'perpetual motion' in which he lived now took him to Nowgong in charge of the Cachar Levy. In 1846–7 he visited the Naga Hills and received tribute of ivory and hand-woven cloth from the Angamis who took solemn oaths to stop their raids on the villages of the plains, and in 1848 he again visited Khonoma. He founded a small Levy Post and a market at Samaguting and opened cart-tracks to Dimapur. He came to the opinion, however, that Government should abandon any attempt to administer the hills, considering that official intervention in internal disputes had been a failure, and for a time his advice was followed, though a different policy was, of course, adopted after a few years.

Butler, in the fashion of the day, describes Assam as 'a wild, uncivilized, foreign land' and he suggests that 'to those accustomed only to the comforts of civilized life, or to the traveller who is indifferent to the beauties of scenery, the monotony, silence and loneliness of the vast forests of Assam will present few features of attraction'. But Butler clearly was attracted by this wild country, especially by its people, and he wrote his first book 'to make Assam better known, to remove some prejudices against it, and preserve the memory of many remarkable scenes'.

Butler was evidently what we would now call a 'character'. Wherever he went he carried with him two glass windows, one for a sitting-room and another for a bedroom, which he used to insert in the reed walls of the thatched houses which were usually allotted to him. Once, finding himself being carried down the Brahmaputra in the middle of the night with only one servant to attend him, he was not dismayed but hastily donned his red woollen nightcap and a pea-coat, seized a paddle and rowed most heartily until the skin peeled off his hands. Many other adventures make entertaining reading.

Major Butler retired in 1865. His son, also a John Butler, became Deputy Commissioner of the Naga Hills and was killed in a Lhota Naga ambuscade in 1875.

T. T. Cooper

Thomas Thornvill Cooper, from whose book, *New Routes for Commerce: The Mishmee Hills*, a number of extracts are given in Chapters XI and XII, has been described as 'one of the most adventurous of modern English travellers'. He was born in 1839, the son of a coalfitter and shipowner, and from his boyhood showed a desire for travel. While still in his teens he was sent on a sea-voyage to Australia for the good of his health, and on the way the crew mutinied; young Thomas, pistol in hand, mounted guard over the captain's cabin. In Australia he made several journeys into the interior and thought of settling down permanently there. But in 1859 he came to India and was employed by the mercantile firm of Arbuthnot and Company in Madras. This, however, was far too tame for his adventurous spirit, and after two years he resigned from his position, visited Sind and Bombay, and finally found himself in Rangoon.

He learnt Burmese, but even now could not settle down and in 1863 went to Shanghai to join a brother who was in business there. He was almost immediately involved in a rebellion and had to help in the protection of the city against the Taiping insurgents. The problem of expanding trade now became an urgent one, and at the age of only twenty-nine Cooper was invited by the Shanghai Chamber of Commerce to attempt to travel through Tibet to India. At the beginning of 1868, therefore, he left Hankow for Batang, whence he hoped to reach the first point on the Lohit Brahmaputra in eight days. The Chinese authorities, however, refused to let him proceed, and he went instead south to Bhamo, reaching Tse-ku, a splendid achievement for that period. Here he was less than a hundred miles from Manchi on the Upper Irrawaddy, which had been visited by Wilcox in 1826.

He now ran into serious trouble, for on passing Weisi-Fu, he was prevented from going further by a tribal Chief, and had to return to the city, where he was imprisoned for five weeks by the local authorities on suspicion of being involved in a rebellion at that time in progress in Yunnan. For a while he lay under the threat of death, but in August was permitted to depart. He had now been eight months on his journey, but it was not until the middle of November that he finally came back to Hankow. He returned to England and wrote an account of his adventures in his excellent book *A Pioneer of Commerce*.

In 1869, Cooper decided to try again. He had failed to reach India from China; he would now try to reach China from India. In October 1869, accordingly, he set out from Sadiya and worked up the Brahmaputra to a village called Prun, some twenty miles from Rima. But here again he was greeted with determined opposition and was compelled to return. It is this journey which he describes in his *New Routes for Commerce*, which contains a number of shrewd observations on Mishmi and Khampti life.

Later, he went again to Rangoon and was appointed Political Agent at Bhamo. But he was soon compelled by ill health to return to England, where he was attached to the India Office. In 1876 he was sent to India with dispatches for the Viceroy and was soon afterwards re-appointed Political Agent at Bhamo. Captain Gill, who was received here by Cooper after his remarkable expedition through China, describes their meeting in his book *The River of Golden Sand*. Only a year later, while still under forty years of age, Cooper was murdered at Bhamo in August 1878 by a sepoy in revenge for some minor punishment.

Cooper, says the *Dictionary of National Biography*, from which many of the above facts are taken, was a 'man of great physical powers, and was endowed with the calm courage essential for a successful traveller. Under a somewhat reserved demeanour he possessed a warm and generous nature, and won the regard and affection of all who knew him by his singleness of heart and his unaffected modesty'.

E. T. Dalton

Of all the works on the North-East Frontier written during the last century, there can be no doubt that pride of place must be given to the thirty-five pages on the subject in Dalton's great *Descriptive Ethnology of Bengal*, and to the remarkable 'lithograph portraits copied from photographs' with which the book is adorned.

Edward Tuite Dalton was born in 1815 and in due course joined the Bengal Staff Corps, of which he was a colonel in 1872 and a major-general three years before his death on the 30th of December 1880. His name appears but seldom in the histories, but we know that in 1845 he visited the hills in the neighbourhood of the Subansiri River, that he went to Membu in the Abor country in 1855, and that about the same time he was having official dealings with the Singphos. In 1851 he was Political Assistant Commissioner in charge of Kamrup and wrote in that year for the Asiatic Society on the 'Mahapurushyas, a sect of Assamese Vaishnavas', in which he praises the 'general respectability and intelligence of the disciples', and gives an interesting and sympathetic account of Sri Sankardeo. A little later he wrote on the ruined temples of Assam.

In 1855 Dalton was Principal Assistant to the Governor-General's Agent in Assam. Three years later he was transferred to Chota Nagpur as Commissioner of the area and took part in an expedition to put down a rising in Palamau. He also accompanied the Field Force against the Singhbhum rebels in 1858–9. His period of duty in this part of India was as fruitful as his years in Assam, for some of the best passages in his book deal with the Juangs, Hos and Santals.

The *Descriptive Ethnology* was a direct sequel to the Ethnological Congress which was proposed early in 1866 to be held in Calcutta. The Congress, which was to have been an adjunct to a general industrial exhibition, was dropped on account of the practical difficulties of bringing the 'strange shy creatures', the tribesmen of the hills, to a great city. The Commissioner of Assam stated his conviction that even twenty typical 'specimens of the hill tribes of his province' could not be conveyed to Calcutta and back at any time of the year 'without casualties that the greatest enthusiast for anthropological research would shrink from encountering'. If any of the more independent tribes were to die on the way, 'it might lead to inconvenient political consequences'.

Before the scheme had been dropped, however, the Government of Bengal and the Supreme Government had called on all local authorities to furnish complete lists of the various races to be found within their jurisdictions, and Dalton was asked to edit this information and to draw up a 'descriptive catalogue' which would serve as a guide to the ethnological exhibition. Dalton, however, found that there was insufficient material even for a catalogue and it was then suggested that he should write an account of all the tribal peoples of what was then 'Bengal' and which included Assam and Chota Nagpur, 'the most interesting fields of research in all Bengal'. Many persons assisted Dalton in this project, and in particular he was able to collect a few photographs taken for the London Exhibition of 1862. A Dr B. Simpson, 'one of the most successful of Indian photographers', was deputed to the valley of the Brahmaputra, 'that most prolific of ethnographical fields', to take photographs, while the skill of Dr Brown, Political Agent at Manipur, was also utilized for illustrations of Manipuris and the neighbouring tribes.

For the publication of the work, the Government of Bengal contributed a sum of Rs 10,000—an enormous sum for those days—and the book was printed under the direction of the Council of the Asiatic Society of Bengal, which from the first had done everything possible to encourage the project.

Dalton claims that he was himself responsible for the accuracy of a large proportion of the descriptions given. Unhappily a number of his manuscript tour diaries perished 'during the mutinies', and it is doubly unfortunate that these were the earlier diaries, referring to his travels in Assam, as a result of which his notices of some of the Assam tribes 'were not as full as he should like to have made them'.

Dalton's work did not escape criticism. It is curious, moreover, that it was not reviewed by any of the journals of the day, not even by the *Indian Antiquary* or the *Journal of the Asiatic Society of Bengal*. Captain John Butler, son of the author of *A Sketch of Assam*, was particularly critical and in a diary of March 1873 he writes:

> Amused myself by reading some of Dalton's work on the Ethnology of Bengal and was much surprised to find that the letterpress, at all events as far as the Naga Tribes are concerned, is not in my humble opinion worth very much and yet this is the very portion of the book for the accuracy of which he states in his preface that he himself is alone responsible. It seems strange that he should not apparently ever have considered it worth his while to refer to any of the Frontier Officers in Assam, for I notice that although he concludes his preface with a long list of officers to whom he is indebted for their contributions, there is not a single Assam Officer among the list.

Captain Butler also questioned the identification of some of the illustrations, though these were not those reproduced in this book. It is a pity that Butler did not elaborate his criticisms, for to say that a book is not 'worth very much' does not lead us anywhere. It is true that Dalton borrowed freely from his predecessors; that in some cases, he was writing up material gathered a quarter of a century earlier; and that in his day there were few anthropological precedents to follow and no anthropological training to be had. But his sympathy, his observation, and above all the elegance and purity of his style render his book one of the outstanding achievements of the anthropology of India.

J. Errol Gray

J. Errol Gray was a tea planter who was interested in extending the trade of Assam beyond the frontier. In 1891 he was invited by the Government of India to explore the Bor Khampti country in a semi-official capacity on their behalf, and on the 24th of November 1892 he left Saikwa in an attempt to cross into western China through the mountains first explored by Wilcox in 1827, and later by Woodthorpe and MacGregor in 1884–5. But Gray went further than any of his predecessors, crossing the Nam-Kiu and entering the valley of the Tisang, an important affluent of the Irrawaddy.

Gray travelled unarmed and with a comparatively small party of thirty-eight Khasi and eight Khampti porters, two military surveyors and one private servant. His diary is one of the most interesting of the early travel documents, and is enlivened by a controversy between himself and J. F. Needham about the behaviour of a Singpho Chieftain named Ningro who, annoyed at not receiving a political present, seems to have done all he could to hamper Gray's progress. Gray returned to Sadiya on the 23rd of April 1893.

Although part of Gray's journey was beyond the frontier of what is now the North-East Frontier Agency, some of his most interesting observations were made within the Indian border, and his account of the Singphos is of special value.

Gray travelled hard and his relations with the people were friendly, though his journey was overshadowed by the behaviour of Ningro which led him to exclaim: 'There is no getting to the bottom of a Singpho.'

William Griffith

Dr William Griffith, M.D., F.L.S., was born in 1810 and died at an early age in 1845. He came to India in 1832 as an Assistant Surgeon on the Madras establishment of the East India Company. But he was essentially a botanist and a few years later he went with Dr MacClelland, the geologist, to explore Assam with the special aim of developing the cultivation of tea. This gave him the opportunity to make the expeditions for which his name became rightly famous. In 1836 he went into the Mishmi Hills 'from the debouching of the Lohit to about ten miles east of the Ghalums'. He explored the tracts between Sadiya and Ava and once marched right through from Assam to Ava and Rangoon. He fell ill and was given an opportunity to recuperate as surgeon to the Bhutan Embassy. On his way to Bhutan he visited the Khasi Hills. He also travelled to Khorassan and Afghanistan. In 1842 he took charge of the Botanic Gardens at Calcutta. He was a great collector, a daring traveller, bravely endured many hardships and illnesses, but he had a very bad temper. He has been called 'the acutest botanist who ever visited India'. His diary of the visit to the Mishmi Hills, from which we quote, first appeared in the *Journal of the Asiatic Society of Bengal* for 1837. After his death, there was published in Calcutta a large book of some 550 pages in which his friend MacClelland edited the many journals he had kept of his travels in Assam,

Burma, Bhutan and Afghanistan. Although the interest of this work is largely botanical, it contains references to the Khasis, Singphos, Mishmis and Konyaks.

Father Krick

Father Nicholas Michael Krick, who, with his friend Father Bourri, was murdered in October 1854 in the Mishmi Hills, was born in 1819 at Lixheim in France, so that he was only thirty-five at the time of his death. After entering the priesthood and becoming a member of the *Société des Missions Etrangères*, he came to India in 1850 as Superior of the South Tibetan Mission, and proceeded to Gauhati on the banks of the Brahmaputra with the intention of making his way into Tibet through the Mishmi Hills. He was not the first, even at this early date, to think of doing so, though the reports he must have heard at Gauhati can hardly have been encouraging. Thirty years earlier, a soldier, Lieutenant Burton, had reported that the Mishmis 'were very averse to receive strangers'. In 1827, Wilcox made his way into the Miju country, as far as the point 'where the Brahmaputra after flowing nearly due south from Tibet suddenly changes its course and flows in a westerly direction', but the notorious Chief Jingsha forced him to retreat. Ten years later, Griffith succeeded in penetrating as far as the village of Ghalum on the Lohit, but was unable to enter the Miju hills. In 1845 Rowlatt went up the Du river as far as Tuppang, where he met a number of Tibetans. Early in 1848, a Hindu ascetic, Parmanand Acharya, whose name may be remembered with the Christian ascetics who suffered after him, was killed by Miju followers of Jingsha.

Father Krick, however, was undismayed, and alone and on foot, with his cross, his flute, sextant and medicine-chest, worked his way up the Brahmaputra and part of the Lohit. At Saikwa he obtained the services of a Khampti Chief as guide and pressed on through the 'rugged, grand but uncultured' mountains of the Mijus. After passing through the friendly villages, so Dalton tells us, he appears to have been guided so as to avoid the hostile clans, but on passing near the home of the formidable Jingsha, a young girl significantly pointed out to him the spot where the pilgrim from India had not long before been massacred, and intimated that a like fate awaited him if he were caught.

However, Father Krick succeeded in reaching the Tibetan settlement of Oualong, and was well received there, and was able to go forward to Sommeu or Samar, in a well-watered and well-cultivated valley not far from Rima, a small Tibetan administrative centre. All went well at first, but presently the Father's resources were exhausted and the people, once the novelty of his arrival was over, were not inclined to support him gratuitously and he was asked to leave the country. On the way back, he stopped at Jingsha's village, where he was roughly treated, but was fortunately able to cure a sick member of the family and was allowed to leave without injury.

After returning to the plains, Father Krick paid a visit to Membu, an important village of the Padam Abors, and then in January 1854 he set out again for Tibet, this time accompanied by Father Bourri, and, escorted by a friendly Mishmi Chief, reached Samar within seven months. The travellers successfully crossed the pass at the head of the valley to Zayul, but had to turn back from Makonglang as the weather was against them and their Mishmi guides refused to go further. They returned down the Du river and went up the Tellu instead.

Unhappily, the Fathers managed to offend a powerful Digaru Mishmi Chief, whose name is spelt variously in the records as Kaisa, Kahesha and Kai-ee-sha. This was not, apparently, their fault. They had invited Kaisa to take them over the Tho Chu Pass and had promised him money and guns as reward. But another Chief double-crossed Kaisa and got the reward instead, at the same time ensuring that the Fathers did not pay the expected friendly visit to Kaisa's house. The angry Chief followed the Fathers into Tibet and killed them as they came up the Tellu path by the mouth of the Tho Chu. He carried off their property and took their Singpho servant as a slave.

The following year, under orders from Lord Dalhousie, a small party of the Assam Light Infantry, with Khampti volunteers and porters, led by Lieutenant F. G. Eden, set out from Sadiya. 'For eight days,' says Mackenzie, 'this little band pressed on by forced marches, swinging across dangerous torrents on bridges of single canes, climbing for hours at a time without water and in bitter cold, till in the grey dawn of a misty morning Kaisa was surprised and captured in his village on the Du, his elder sons slain in open fight, his people dispersed and the murdered Frenchmen to the full avenged.' Kaisa was tried and hanged at Dibrugarh (Dalton says it was Calcutta, but appears to be mistaken), but not before he had killed two of the guards who were watching him in the jail.

Father Krick's own account of his first Tibetan journey and his visit to the Abor Hills was published in Paris with the title *Relation d'un Voyage au Tibet* in 1854. The parts of it relating to the Abors were translated into English and published in the *Journal of the Asiatic Society of Bengal* for 1913, and selections from this are reproduced later in this book.

In this relation Father Krick reveals himself as a witty, kindly person, a keen observer, a vivid and entertaining writer, and a man of unusual devotion and courage.

Father Krick claims that he was the first person to penetrate into the Abor country, although several agents of the East India Company had tried to do so. For the Padams were not anxious to receive visitors, especially English visitors. If once we allow Englishmen to enter our country, they said, they are sure to have an army at their heels. Father Krick entertains himself over his efforts to prove that he is a perfectly good Frenchman, a priest with no territorial ambitions, who has nothing to do with the English. But in tribal opinion, he observes, 'any white skin, any nose somewhat protruding, is of English make'.

Father Krick was not correct in supposing himself to be the first foreigner to visit the Abor area. Bedford and Wilcox were there in 1825–6, and in 1847 there had been a friendly conference of Padams and British Officers. But he was correct in stressing the tension between the Abors and Government, for from 1850 onwards there were a number of outrages and punitive expeditions. It is curious that in 1855, only two years after Father Krick, Colonel Dalton should have visited Membu in the company of Lieutenant Eden. He has left an account of it which differs in several particulars from that of the priest.

Father Krick was evidently a very human as well as a very courageous person. When we read his summary of the character of his hosts (and his impressions are far more sympathetic than those of many of his contemporaries) we cannot help suspecting that he himself had the same sort of virtues. 'The Padam,' he says, 'is very active, jolly, a lover of freedom and independence, generous, noble-hearted, plain-spoken, more honest than the average Oriental, not over-moderate in eating and drinking, at least as far as quantity is concerned.... He seems to possess much of the child's simplicity, and Membu is undoubtedly less corrupt than Paris.'

J. F. Needham

J. F. Needham had the unique distinction of serving for no less than twenty-three years in Sadiya. Belonging originally to the Bengal Police, he was posted to Assam as Assistant Political Officer in Sadiya in 1882 and did not leave the place until the end of 1905. In time he came to be regarded as the earliest of the advisers to Government on tribal affairs. He made many expeditions, though not so many as he desired, for he was considered rather too adventurous—'he had a dash', it was said—and a little too free with the people. In 1885–6 he visited the Mishmi Hills and nearly reached Rima, travelling without escort and following the route of Fathers Krick and Bourri who had been murdered in the Zayul Valley thirty years before. The following year he visited the Hukong Valley. In 1891 he crossed the Patkoi Range to Burma. In 1893 he went as Political Officer with the military expedition into the Abor Hills, and was blamed for a lack of foresight and a spirit of over-confidence which led to the disastrous massacre at Bordak. In 1899, he again accompanied an expedition (the Bebejiya Mishmi Expedition) which came in for severe criticism, this time from Lord Curzon himself, though he himself was praised.

Needham was a voluminous, lively and careless writer. The reports on his various expeditions are always worth reading. He was interested in linguistics and wrote outline grammars of the languages spoken by the Sadiya Miris, the Singphos, the Khamptis of the Sadiya area, and he made brief studies of the Digaru and Moshang Naga vocabularies.

William Robinson

William Robinson, an educationalist of the Gauhati Government Seminary, published his first work on Assam in 1841. In the fashion of the day it had a long and sonorous title: *Descriptive Account of Asam: with a sketch of the Local Geography, and a concise*

History of The Tea-Plant of Asam: to which is added, a Short Account of the Neighbouring Tribes, exhibiting their History, Manners and Customs. Robinson was very interested in philology, and during the next fifteen years he published, on each occasion in the *Journal of the Asiatic Society of Bengal*, a series of articles on the Abor, Khampti, Konyak, Singpho, Dafla and Mishmi languages.

The *Descriptive Account* is well written and its picture of the frontier tribes is lively and informative, though most of Robinson's contemporaries were probably more interested in his chapter on tea, that 'polyandrous plant of the natural order Ternstiomicae'. Indeed Robinson declares in his preface that the subject is one of acknowledged interest. 'The daily increasing importance of Asam, and the conspicuous position it begins to hold as the scene of great commercial advantages to British India' render an account of the province a 'great desideratum'.

But Robinson's literary objective was not merely to bring 'this highly valuable province into more general notice'. Should his book 'even in the most distant manner lead to an improvement in the moral, as well as the temporal condition of the people, he will consider the labour bestowed on it, more than repaid'. The *Descriptive Account* is, in fact, one of the first of the gazetteers; it devotes chapters to climate and to the effect of climate on man, to geology, botany and zoology, to historical and political geography, to productive industry and to the civil and social state of the Assamese. The hill tribes are discussed in a separate and final section.

Robinson's knowledge was fullest for the Mishmis and Nagas. Except for a brief account of the Khasis and Garos, he confines himself largely to the frontier tribes. He frankly admits his ignorance, however, and indeed the general ignorance, of such tribes as the Akas, and he has likewise little to tell us of the Daflas.

R. Wilcox

R. Wilcox carried out a number of surveys in Assam during the four years 1825 to 1828 and gave an account of them in a *Memoir* which was published in the 17th volume of *Asiatic Researches* (1832). This was reprinted in *Selections from the Records of the Bengal Secretariat*, No. 23, in 1855. Wilcox was an intrepid explorer and in his 1826 expedition succeeded in penetrating the Mishmi country three-quarters of the way to Rima; fifty years later Cooper did not get so far. Sir James Johnstone describes him thus:

> Wilcox was one of the giants of old, men who with limited resources did a vast amount of work among wild people and said little about it, being contented with doing their duty. In 1828, accompanied by Lieutenant Burton, and ten men belonging to the Sudya Khamptis (Shans), he penetrated to the Bor Khamptis' country, far beyond our borders, an exploit not repeated till after our annexation of Upper Burmah.

III

In editing these extracts I have preserved as far as possible the original spelling, even though this results in many inconsistencies, and punctuation in order to emphasize the fact that they come from another age, which looked on tribal people with a different eye to ours. Very few of our writers indulged in the luxury of footnotes, and I have not included any of the originals; all footnotes should, therefore, be regarded as my own contribution.

Some confusion may be caused by the indiscriminate use of tribal names by the earlier writers, who used words like 'Abor' or 'Naga' as if they meant 'hillman' or 'tribesman'. This is specially true of the word 'Naga', which they applied to a number of tribes which we do not classify as Naga today.

I must express my obligation to the *Bibliography of Ethnology of Assam*, compiled in 1952 by J. P. Mills, on which I have inevitably drawn in the compilation of the select book-list at the end of this volume. I received every possible assistance from my friend B. S. Kesavan, Librarian of the National Library, and his staff, and from L. N. Chakravarty. I am grateful to the Asiatic Society for permission to reprint the extract from Father Krick's writings, translated into English by Father Gille, which appeared in the *Journal of the Asiatic Society of Bengal* in 1913.

V.E.

Shillong
October 1955

Chapter I

THE FRONTIER OF ASSAM

1

PREGNANT WITH SILVER, PERFUMED WITH TEA

(J. M'Cosh, *Topography of Assam*, 1837, pp. 132 f.)

FEW nations bordering upon the British dominions in India are less generally known than those inhabiting the extreme N. E. Frontier of Bengal; and yet, in a commercial, a statistical, or a political point of view, no country is more important. There our territory of Assam is situated in almost immediate contact with the empires of China and Ava, being separated from each by a narrow belt of mountainous country, possessed by barbarous tribes of independent savages, and capable of being crossed over in the present state of communication in ten or twelve days. From this mountain range, navigable branches of the great rivers of Nankin, of Cambodia, of Martaban, of Ava, and of Assam derive their origin, and appear designed by nature as the great highways of commerce between the nations of Ultra Gangetic Asia. In that quarter, our formidable neighbours, the Burmese, have been accustomed to make their inroads into Assam; there, in the event of hostilities, they are certain to attempt it again; and there, in case of its ever becoming necessary to take vengeance on the Chinese, an armed force embarking on the Brahmaputra, could be speedily marched across the intervening country to the banks of the greatest rivers of China, which would conduct them through the very centre of the celestial empire to the ocean.

This beautiful tract of country, though thinly populated by straggling hordes of barbarians and allowed to lie profitless in impenetrable jungle, enjoys all the qualities requisite for rendering it one of the finest in the world. Its climate is cold, healthy, and congenial to European constitutions; its numerous crystal streams abound in gold dust, and masses of the solid metal; its mountains are pregnant with precious stones and silver; its atmosphere is perfumed with tea growing wild and luxuriantly; and its soil is so well adapted to all kinds of agricultural purposes, that it might be converted into one continued garden of silk, and cotton, and coffee, and sugar, and tea, over an extent of many hundred miles.

2

THE GRAND FIELD OF INQUIRY AND INTEREST

(J. B. Neufville, *On the Geography and Population of Assam*, 1828)

THE existence of a very large river called the Sri Lohit, (or sacred stream) running at the back of the mountainous ranges, appears to be too generally asserted to be altogether void of foundation, but I am totally unable to ascertain the direction of its course, and can only reconcile the contradictory accounts by supposing it to separate into two branches taking opposite channels; one of these flowing from East to West, is said to discharge its waters into the Dihong, periodically with the rainy season, and the arguments in favour of this statement are supported by very strong data. The opening in the mountainous ranges through which the Dihong issues, is sufficiently defined to authorize the opinion of its being the channel of a river, and that there is a communication with the plains of the North, as has been shown by fatal experience.

In the reign of Hajeswar, little more than half a century ago, a sudden and overwhelming flood poured from the Dihong, inundating the whole country, and sweeping away, with a resistless torrent, whole villages, and even districts: such is described to have been its violence, that the general features of the country, and the course of the river, were materially altered by it. This flood continued for about fifteen days, during which time various agricultural and household implements, elephant trappings, and numerous articles belonging to a race, evidently social and civilized, of pastoral and agricultural habits, were washed down in the stream.

This circumstance, which does not seem to admit of any doubt, must establish satisfactorily the existence of a passage from the North to a stream connected with the Brahmaputra, and its communication, either perennial, periodical, or occasional, with a considerable river of the northern plains. All the accounts received by me, concur in calling this river the Sri Lohit, and that it takes its original rise from the upper or inaccessible Brahmakund, (as recorded in their sacred traditions,) at the same spot with the Buri Lohit, or Brahmaputra. It must be a stream of great importance, as it is familiar to all the various tribes with whom I have held intercourse. The Dihong River, therefore, as being supposed to unite with it, I consider as the point of keenest interest in the extension of geographical knowledge.

The post of Sadiya is nearly encircled, at a distance of from thirty to fifty miles, by lines of mountains, behind which are more lofty ranges covered with eternal snow—from which the Dihong and Dibong Rivers flow from the North, the Lohit East, and the Theinga and Now Dihing, more to the southward, where the hills decrease in height, and present the pass to Ava.

The portion of hills of the lower ranges, between the heads of the Dihong and Dibong, I have already described as the territory of the Abors; more to the eastward of them, on the line of hills including the opening of the Brahmakund, is the district of Mishmis, another numerous hill tribe, differing only in name from the others.

Beyond this mountainous region extends the grand field of inquiry and interest, if any credit be due to the opinion universally prevalent here respecting the nations inhabiting those tracts. The country to the eastward of Bhot, and the northward of Sadiya, extending on the plain beyond the mountains, is said to be possessed by a powerful nation called Kolitas, or Kultas, who are described as having attained a high degree of advancement and civilization, equal to any of the nations of the East. The power, dominion, and resources of the Kulta Raja are stated to exceed by far those of Assam, under its most flourishing circumstances, and in former times, a communication appears to have been kept up between the states, now long discontinued.

To this nation are attributed the implements of husbandry and domestic life, washed down by the flood of the Dihong before mentioned. Of their peculiar habits and religion, nothing is known, though they are considered to be Hindus, a circumstance which, from their locality, I think most unlikely, and in all probability arising merely from some fancied analogy of sound, the word Kolita being used in Assamese to signify the Khaet caste. There is said to be an entrance to this country from Upper Assam, by a natural tunnel under the mountains; but such is obviously fabulous, at least to the assumed extent. All accounts agree in stating, that a colony of Assamese, under two sons of a Bara Gohein, about eight generations back, took refuge in the country of the Kolitas, on the banks of the Sri Lohit, whence, till within about two hundred years, they, at intervals, maintained a correspondence with the parent state. They were hospitably received by the Kulta Raja, who assigned lands to them for a settlement, and they had naturalized and intermarried with the inhabitants. Since that period, however, no trace either of them, or of the Kultas, had been found until the flood of the Dihong exhibited marks of their existence, or of that of a nation resembling them in an acquaintance with the useful arts.

The plain to the eastward of the Kulta country, beyond the Mishmis, is well known as the country of the Lama, or the Yam Sinh Raja, a nation also independent, and said to be frequently engaged in hostility with Kultas. The inhabitants are described as a warlike equestrian race, clothed something after the European manner, in trousers and quilted jackets, and celebrated for their breed of horses. There is a pass to the Lama country, through the Mishmi hills, a little to the northward of the Brahmakund, a journey of twenty days, which was described by a man who accomplished it in seventeen: it is practicable only to a mountaineer, and appears to present almost insuperable difficulties. He states, that on two occasions, the traveller is obliged to swing himself across precipices by the hands and feet, on a rope of cane stretched from rock to rock.

3

A VERY EXTENSIVE FORTRESS

(H. Vetch,[1] Political Agent, Upper Assam, in a letter dated 3rd January 1848)

It may not here be altogether out of place, or uninteresting to you, my observing that a more intimate acquaintance with these Border

[1] Later General, Hamilton Vetch founded the cantonment at Dibrugarh and led a number of expeditions on the Frontier: in 1848 he rescued some Hindu gold-washers who had been carried off by the Abors above Sadiya.

tribes may lead to the discovery of antiquities now hid in the jungle which may throw light on the early History of Assam at present so involved in obscurity. For in my late tour, in company with Major Hannay and Captain E. F. Smith, we visited the ruins of what appeared to be a very extensive Fortress, situated between the gorges of the Dikrong and Dihong Rivers, about twenty-four miles North of Suddyah. Want of time, and the thick jungles with which these ruins were so over-grown, prevented our exploring more than a part of the walls which we traced for several hundred yards, and which appeared to encircle some low hills and tableland abutting from the mountains. The walls were of no great height, but in a wonderful state of preservation, and consisted of from six to nine courses of hewn stone (chiefly granite) surmounted by a breastwork of excellent bricks loopholed, but without any binding of cement. Tradition assigns to this Fort the name of Bishuck, while another extensive Fort, some miles to the eastward, is said to be that of Sissoopaul; the former the brother of Rukmuine, and the latter her betrothed, as also cousin of Krishna, who carried her off. If this tradition can be relied on, it would make these ruins of great antiquity, but to whatsoever age they belong, they must, I think, be prior to the Ahum conquest of Assam. If inferences can be drawn from the form of the stones and style of architecture, it probably belongs to the same era as the copper temple, a small square building of granite (the roof of which was formerly sheathed with copper) situated on a rivulet which falls into a branch of the Digaroo River, and which was for the first time visited by any European about two years ago, when I went there on my way to the Brahmakund.

When up the Dihong, we heard of a temple or some other building surrounded by a tank or canal, which was said to have been discovered by some Khanyans when out elephant-hunting, but of which they could give no very particular account, as they could not approach the building for the water with which it was surrounded, and its existence yet remains to be fully ascertained.

The remains of a stone temple have lately been discovered at the foot of the Abor Hills near the gorge of the Sisee River, and from the carving on some of the stones brought to me, it would appear to be of Boodhist origin.

4

THE BRAHMAKUND

(J. Bedford, in the *Government Gazette*, 21st September 1826)

After some ineffectual attempts to open a passage to the supposed head of the river, the Deo Pani, or Brahmakund, the divine water, or well of Brahma, which it was known was not remote, and after some unsuccessful efforts to reach the villages, the smoke of which was perceptible on the neighbouring hills, a communication was at last effected with the Meeshmees of Dilli, a village of about a day's journey from the left bank, as well as with the Gaum, or Chief of the village near the Brahmakund, in whose company a visit was paid to the reservoir on the 4th of April. This celebrated reservoir is on the left bank of the river; it is formed by a projecting rock, which runs up the river nearly parallel to the bank and forms a good-sized pool that receives two or three small rills from the hills immediately above it. When seen from the land side, by which it is approached, the rock has much the appearance of an old gothic ruin, and a chasm about half way up, which resembles a carved window, assists the similitude. At the foot of the rock is a rude stone seat: the ascent is narrow, and choked with jungle. Half way up is another kind of seat, in a niche or fissure, where offerings are made. Still higher up, from a tabular ledge of the rock, a fine view is obtained of the Kund, the river, and the neighbouring hills. Access to the summit, which resembles gothic pinnacles and spires, is utterly impracticable. The summit is called the Deo Bari, or dwelling of the deity. From the rock the descent leads across a kind of glen, in the bottom of which is the large reservoir, to the opposite mainland, in the ascent of which is a small reservoir, about three feet in diameter, which is fed by a rill of beautifully clear water and then pours its surplus into its more extensive neighbour below. The large Kund is about seventy feet long by thirty wide. Besides Brahmakund and Deo Pani, the place is also termed Prabhu Kuthar, in allusion to the legend of Parasurama having opened a passage for the Brahmaputra through the hills with a blow of his *kuthar* or axe.

5

THE MOUNTAIN SCENERY OF SADIYA

(R. Wilcox, 'Memoir of a Survey of Assam and the neighbouring Countries, executed in 1825–6–7–8', *Asiatic Researches*, Vol. XVII, 1832)

THE mountain scenery of Sadiya would form a noble subject for a panorama, though the distance of the hills is rather too great for the larger features required in a detached picture. To the south the high Naga Hills bordering Assam beyond the Bori Dihing lift their heads above the tree jungle of the opposite bank of the Brahmaputra; to the west and south-west the ranges are too distant to be visible; but in the north-west they rise to a considerable height, where the mountain Reging of the Abors towers above the Pasi village; thence there is a sudden fall, and in the opening of the Dihong the hills diminish to a comparatively small size, over which, however, a cluster of remarkable peaks, clothed in heavy snow, are occasionally to be seen in the very clear weather of the winter months, bearing about 310°, or nearly north-west. They are evidently south of the Dihong in its course from west to east, and are very distant. On the opposite side of the banks rises a conical mountain (which at the mouth of the Dihong, and in the river, forms a most conspicuous object). The Abors call it Regam, and declare that it is the residence of a sylvan deity. The range continues round to the north, overtopped near Regam by a high-peaked ridge of six or seven thousand feet high, retaining its snowy covering only during the colder months. Nearly north the tops are sometimes to be distinguished of a range at a considerable distance, which, from more favourable points of view, is seen to be a continued line of heavy snow. The opening of the Dihong is marked by a corresponding fall of the hills immediately to the north. Turning to the north-east a more interesting group presents itself. The first and highest in the horizon is the turret-form, to which we have given the name of Sadiya Peak; its base extends to the Dibong on the left, and to the right it covers a considerable extent, allowing a more distant class of mountains to peep above its sloping sides. The next is the huge three-peaked mountain called Thigritheya by the Meeshmees, a magnificent object from the singular outline. It is succeeded by a wall always streaked with the pure white of its beautiful mantle, after one or two minor yet interesting peaks. Thathutheya, a high round-backed ridge, rises high above the ranges near the Kund, or Prabhu Kuthar. There is then a fall, but the gap is filled with mountains low in appearance, because they are distant, and the channel of the river is not there as has been supposed, though that is the place of its issue to the plains, but in fact winds round the group situated in this gap and running first to the north-west till it washes the base of Thathutheya; it then traverses back to the southward. Immediately to the east the ranges at the distance of forty-five miles are high, and snow is seen on some of them throughout the cold season, but the last peak in that direction is the loftiest to be seen (of those whose heights have been ascertained); and so remarkable and magnificent a tower it is, that it has been ever known amongst us by the name of Beacon, and it has been seen at the distance of one hundred and thirty miles. Turret Peak is also remarkable—near to Thathutheya in the horizon, but distant—that it ought not to be forgotten. Beyond Beacon, or Dapha Bhum as it is called by the Singfos, the lofty mountains suddenly retrograde to a considerable distance, and form a deep basin, the southern and eastern sides of which are alone visible; through the centre of this basin the Dihong winds, having its sources in the most distant point.

6

TRADE WITH TIBET

(A. Mackenzie, *History*, 1884, pp. 15 f.)

MANY interesting facts regarding the state of commercial intercourse between Assam and Thibet are collected by Pemberton in his Report on the North-East Frontier. There we find quoted the following description of the trade as given by Hamilton: 'At a place called Chouna, two months' journey from Lassa, on the confines of the two States, there is a mart established, and on the

Assam side there is a similar mart at Geegunshur, distant four miles from Chouna. An annual caravan repairs from Lassa to Chouna, conducted by about 20 persons, conveying silver bullion to the amount of about one lakh of rupees, and a considerable quantity of rock salt for sale to the Assam merchants at Geegunshur, to which place the latter bring rice, which is imported into Thibet from Assam in large quantities; Tussa cloth, a kind of coarse silk cloth, manufactured by the Native women in Assam from the queen downwards; iron and lac found in Assam, and other skins, buffalo horns, pearls, and corals, first imported from Bengal.' In 1809 this trade amounted in value to two lakhs of rupees, even although Assam was then itself in a most unsettled state. The imports from Thibet, in the shape of woollens, gold dust, salt, musk, horses, *chowries*, and Chinese silks, were especially noticeable. The protracted troubles of Assam ultimately affected the traffic, but even in the year before the Burmese invasion, the Lassa merchants were said to have brought down gold amounting in value to Rs 70,000. The Burmese occupation put a stop to this annual fair for a time. In 1833 a successful attempt was made to revive it by Lieutenant Rutherford, who then had charge of Durrung. Of all this trade the Kuriapara Dwar is the principal channel. Udalgiri is now the place where the fair is held, and a very interesting spectacle may be seen there annually. Traders from all parts of Thibet, from Lassa and places east, west, and even north of it are present in crowds, some of them clad in Chinese dresses, using Chinese implements, and looking to all intents Chinese. Many have their families with them, and carry their goods on sturdy ponies, of which some hundreds are brought down to the fair yearly. In 1852 the Government sanctioned a proposal to move the site of the gathering to Mungledye which was expected to be more convenient for the Bengal and Assam traders. It was found, however, that such a change would not be popular. The hill caravans would not venture so far into the plains, and existing arrangements were left undisturbed.

Chapter II

THE EASTERN TRIBES IN THE NINETEENTH CENTURY

1

HISTORICAL PRELUDE

(A. Mackenzie, *History*, 1884, pp. 88 ff. and 91 ff.)

I HAVE first to notice a group of Nagas living on the northern slopes of the Patkoi mountains with whom we first came in contact about 1835. In the correspondence of that period regarding the Singpho Chief, the Duffa Gam, mention is made of raids committed upon villages under our protection by Nagas of the Upper Patkoi Hills. The first impression among our local officers was that we had now in this quarter to reckon upon frequent incursions by Nagas as well as by hostile Singphos and Burmese; and orders were given by Government to retaliate sharply and severely upon all villages concerned in such outrages. But it was shortly afterwards discovered that these Nagas were themselves most peaceably inclined, and that if any of our villages had been attacked by them, it was only in mistaken retaliation for wrongs done to the Naga tribes by Singphos either of Assam or Burma. The Singphos seem in fact to have sought by conquest of the Nagas to supply the deficiency of slave labour following on the annexation of Assam. In 1837 when a party of British officers was sent across the Patkoi to negotiate with Burma regarding the Duffa Gam, they encountered a war party of Singphos fresh from the sack of Naga settlements and dragging along gangs of captives. In those days we considered all upon this frontier that was not Burmese to be actual British territory, and our officers had no scruples about interfering to deliver the Naga captives. Subsequently it was proposed to give permanent protection to these Naga clans by establishing a post under a European officer on the upper waters of the Bori Dehing. It was hoped that such an officer would be able to take efficient political charge of all this Singpho-Naga tract. The Government, however, felt doubtful of the expediency of assuming active charge of this sparsely-peopled wilderness; and indicated its preference for the plan of deputing an officer from headquarters occasionally to visit the tribes and settle disputes as they arose. A further series of Singpho outrages shortly after led to the temporary occupation of a military station on the Bori Dehing and to the deputation of Captain Hannay to report more fully as to what was feasible to give protection to the Naga tribes. But the result of his inquiries was to show that Government had taken the correct view, and that, unless the Nagas would remove their settlements within the circle of our posts we could afford them no effectual protection. Their communities were few in number and reckoned in all at under 5,000 souls. To protect by military defences a mountain territory ninety miles long by forty miles deep inhabited by such a mere handful of people was clearly more than Government was warranted in attempting.

From this point the notices of these Patkoi Nagas are few and unimportant, and in later years their very existence seems to have been lost sight of or to have been confusedly merged in that of the greater tribes to the west who are ordinarily communicated with through the officials of Seebsaugor. At any rate in 1871 the Deputy Commissioner of Luckimpore reporting specially on the Nagas of his district stated their numbers at 14,383 living in 2,865 houses and belonging to seven different clans, but the names of the clans as given by him are certainly most of them names of Seebsaugor clans, viz. Namsingia, Bordwaria, Dadum, Juboka, Banfera, Toopigonuja, and Holagonuja. The fact is that the Eastern clans of the Seebsaugor Nagas trade both with that district and with Luckimpore.

The tribes occupying the low hills to the south of the Seebsaugor district have been in close communication with our local officers ever since the first annexation of Assam. The Assamese Government had at times indeed claimed them as its subjects, and Purunder Sing is known to have asserted successfully his right to share with the Nagas the produce of the salt manufacture of the lower hills. The hill Chiefs, when the Native Government was strong, came down annually bringing gifts, that may perhaps have been considered to be tribute. It has in fact been conjectured that the inhabitants of this tract are descended from settlements of hill mercenaries of various tribes planted here by the ancient Ahom Kings, and the variety of the tribal dialects is adduced to support this theory. However that may be, it is certain that several of the Chiefs had received grants of *khats* or lands, and of *bheels* or fishing waters on the plains, and enjoyed assignments of *paiks* like the ordinary Assamese nobility.

The tract occupied by the clans of whom we have any knowledge may be taken to extend back for thirty miles from the frontier of Seebsaugor to the Patkoi Range, and to run for sixty miles from east to west. The tribes in this tract are termed Boree or dependent; beyond them in the recesses of the Patkoi are many Abor or independent clans, of whom we know little save from some one or other of them occasionally figuring in a raid. The Abor trade is chiefly conducted through the medium of the Boree clans, which last, in spite of their title, are really more powerful than those beyond them.

In the years 1840–4 our dealings with the Boree villages became more direct and intimate. Captain Brodie, then Principal Assistant to the Governor-General's Agent, drew attention to the fact that the perpetual quarrels subsisting between the different villages and clans showed a dangerous tendency to boil over, as it were, into the plains, where our revenue-paying villages offered themselves a tempting prey to savages already armed for internecine strife, and when in fighting humour not very particular as to the precise direction of their raids. Brodie, therefore, suggested that he should be allowed to bring them all under formal agreement to the British Government, and exact a small annual tribute as token of submission, and the course of events led very shortly to the acceptance of his proposals.

From the records of 1840 it appears that the Nagas living near Jaipur, the Namsang, Pani Dwar, and Bor Dwar Nagas, lived chiefly by manufacturing salt, which they retailed to the people of the plains. There were in the lower hills eighty-five salt wells in all of which the Government was allowed to be absolute owner of only three, enjoying merely a right to a certain number of flues or fire-places at each of the others. These rights Purunder Singh had regularly asserted, but our officers had contented themselves with levying a duty of twenty per cent on all salt brought down to the regular markets for sale. Early in 1841 the Government abolished these duties, thereby giving a great stimulus to the intercourse between the Nagas and the plains.

A missionary, Mr Bronson, had for some years resided among the tribes, teaching them Christianity and the art of cultivating tea.

The Governor-General's Agent thought so highly of this gentleman's work, that he asked Government to give Rs 100 a month towards his Naga schools. Government, however, at this time thought it improper to give direct aid to missions, even when working among savage tribes, forgetting perhaps that it had made grants in 1829 to the Garo missions with very fair results, but it agreed to pass for a year any small sums shown in the Agent's contingent bill and not exceeding a monthly maximum of Rs 100, 'for objects of practical utility connected with the improvement of the Naga country, and spent with the view of leading its population into habits of industry'. The mission school was kept up till Mr Bronson was compelled, by illness, to leave the place. While it lasted it was very successful, as many Chiefs of the eastern tribes sent their sons to him for instruction. It is interesting to note that Mr Bronson, who knew these Nagas better than any European before or since, was all in favour of Brodie's plans of direct and active control. He reported that the only effect of our tacit surrender of our rights in the salt mines had been to make the tribes independent and insolent as they had never been before. His prognostications were certainly supported by subsequent events, for in March 1841 the Nagas of Teeroo and Kapung Dwars attacked a party of Assamese on the road to Borhath; and the Chiefs refused to attend when summoned to explain their conduct. Guards had therefore to be posted to close the passes to trade and so to coerce the hillmen into submission. This being done during the rains, when there is little traffic between hill and plain, had not much effect, and in the cold weather Brodie was ordered to enter the hills with a party of troops to compel all the Chiefs to enter into engagements, such as had already been taken by a few of the clans, binding them to keep the peace towards one another and towards our subjects.

In January 1842 Captain Brodie began his tour for the pacification of the Naga Frontier between the Dikho and the Bori Dihing. He found in this tract ten different clans—

1	The Namsingias with	8 villages
2	,, Bordwarias with	8 ,,
3	,, Panidwarias with	10 ,,
4	,, Mutons or Kooloongs with ..	4 ,,
5	,, Banferas with	4 ,,
6	,, Jubokas with	4 ,,

7	The Changnois with	8 villages
8	„ Mooloongs with	5 „
9	„ Jaktoongias with	8 „
10	„ Tabloongias with	13 „

The Mooloongs Raja, head of the Teroo Dwar, was the most powerful of the Naga Chiefs, and the Changnoi Raja, of Namsang, ranked next to him. To the latter all the Nagas from the Dikho to Jaipur paid tribute.

Brodie took engagements from all the Chiefs to abstain from outrages in the plains, to be responsible for the surrender of offenders within the limits of their Dwars, to discontinue hostilities with other tribes, leaving Government to punish any attacks made on them, and, finally, to abstain from importing Naga children as slaves to British territory. All existing feuds he settled. The villages in these parts were found situated on high hills surrounded by ditches and barricades indicating an ever present fear of attack. Each village had a large building or *morung*, where hung a hollow tree that was beaten to give the alarm of an enemy's approach. In the *morungs* the skulls of slain foes were also kept. In one *morung* Brodie counted 130 of these trophies. The arms used were spear, *dao*, and cross-bow. All the men went nearly naked, a thin rattan passed twice round the loins being the prevailing fashion among a large section of the people. The Chiefs were distinguished by girdles of brass-plates. An Assamese, Neeranye Deka Phokon, who had been an officer under Raja Purunder, gave much assistance to Brodie in his tour, and was made Superintendent of the Naga Frontier on Rs 30 a month. The whole population was estimated at between 40,000 and 50,000.

The agreements thus accepted by the Chiefs were not in every case or all at once successful in preventing raids by subordinate sections of tribes. In November 1842 the Khettree Nagas, a clan owning some sort of fealty to the Changnoi Raja, attacked a friendly village, and when Captain Brodie, attended by the Namsang and Bor Dwar Nagas, to whom the village belonged, went up to inquire into matters, they even attacked him; and he was compelled to retire till troops came to his assistance. The Khettrees then deserted their village and withdrew to the inner hills.

In January 1844 Captain Brodie made a tour through the western clans lying between the Dikho and the Doyeng. His report mentions in detail the villages visited and gives the title of Chief to the head of each; but from other papers it would appear that on this side the tribes arranged themselves in six groups; the Namsangia (not the same as the Namsangias of the east), with four villages; the Dopdaria, with twelve villages; the Charmgaya or Asringaya, with six villages; the Hatheegurhiya,[1] with seven villages; the Doyengiya or Torphatia, with eleven villages; and the Panihatia, with ten villages. The Panihatias and Doyengiyas are described as branches of the Lhota Naga tribe. No information is given by Brodie as to the probable strength of these western clans. He was met on his tour by the Chief of the Seema Nagas, a powerful clan of the inner hills, ruling over fourteen villages, who desired to open a trade with the plains; and he obtained a certain amount of information regarding the names of various Abor communities, of which we hear nothing nowadays. They are probably now known under other appellations. Generally he remarked that the Boree Nagas to the east of the Dikho seemed more powerful than those to the west, and were more under a settled form of government by Chiefs. They held also apparently a somewhat effective control over the Abor tribes of the interior—a state of things which did not obtain between the Dikho and the Doyeng. The western communities were found to be disorganized and democratic, and their principal men being ordinarily drunk had no authority in the villages, and could not be trusted. Still Brodie cherished hopes that, 'though no absolute confidence could be placed on such vile people as the Nagas', the arrangements made by him, and which were similar to those effected in the eastern tract, would prevent their disturbing the peace of the plains.

To each of the Dwars in this quarter was attached a Kotokie or clan representative to be the channel of communication between the Government and the tribe ordinarily using that Dwar. These men were paid by a remission of the poll tax, and under our revenue system received a remission on their land equal to the amount of the old remission of poll tax. Some of the Kotokies also managed the *khats* or grants held by different Naga Chiefs on the plains, and from reports of 1871 it may be gathered that they, being generally Assamese, have in most instances succeeded in appropriating these lands altogether. One of these *khats* still claimed by the Nagas

[1] A synonym for Ao.

is Bhitur Namsang, and their rights over this were acknowledged in 1871.

The total number of Kotokies in Seebsaugor was eighty-eight, and the total revenue remission on account of Nagas (Kotokies and *khats*) was Rs 797. Government agreed on Brodie's suggestion to give the Lhota Nagas some lands on the Dhunsiri, and to compensate some other Chiefs for lands formerly held by them, but which had become lost to them.

In 1846 an attack upon the Boree Naga tribes of Changnoi and Tangroong by some Abor Nagas (called Longhas), accompanied by Singphos or Shans, took Brodie again into the hills. It was supposed that the Singphos had come from the valley of the Kyendwen in Burma, and some anxiety was felt locally as to the possibility of a Burmese inroad, but nothing more was heard of them, and the thing died out.

The plan that Brodie proposed for future management was that every village should be visited periodically by an officer with a strong escort to prove to the people that they could easily be got at. Then he meant uniformly to insist on their referring all quarrels to the Seebsaugor officials, and he intended to punish contumacy by fine, occupation, or otherwise. Where an Abor tribe attacked a Boree clan, he did not propose retaliatory expeditions, but trusted to negociation to bring in the Abors to submit themselves to our officers. In brief, the policy proposed here as elsewhere on the north-east frontier during the early days of our occupation of Assam was one of active control, and tolerably vigorous interference in tribal matters.

It was at first found necessary from time to time to prove to the Chiefs by show of force that the Government intended them to keep to their engagements.

In April 1844, for instance, the Bor Mootuns attacked the Banferas, and Brodie had to send up troops to enforce his demand for the offenders. The expedition brought down the Chief of the offending tribe a prisoner to the plains. Again, in April 1849, the Namsang Nagas committed a murder on the plains, and a similar plan was adopted to compel obedience. The offenders were, however, in this case given up as soon as the troops showed themselves at any of the villages reached by Captain Brodie. Generally it was inferred that the Nagas in this part were too entirely dependent on the plains to afford to quarrel with us. It was Brodie's opinion that only a little time was required to make them see that we were determined to stop outrages, and in fact the frontier settled down and became perfectly tranquil. As a rule no difficulty was found in getting the tribes to act up to their engagements.

The events of the next few years were unimportant.

In April 1851 some Banfera Nagas committed a cruel murder in Seebsaugor on the Dhodur Allee (the frontier road running along the foot of the hills and at that time representing the line of our revenue jurisdiction), and then fled to the Juboka villages. On our closing the Dwar the Juboka Raja gave them up. . . .

In the cold season of 1853-4, there was an outbreak between the Namsang and Bor Dwar Nagas. The Seebsaugor Principal Assistant, however, brought about an amicable settlement.

Other cases of murders by Seebsaugor Nagas are reported in 1854-5, but the Chiefs always gave up the accused on demand.

Soon after this the policy of Government with reference to these tribes was radically changed. Non-interference became the rule, and our officers were not encouraged to visit the hills or keep up intercourse with the hillmen. The Boree Nagas, however, on the Seebsaugor frontier continued to be generally well-behaved. They frequented the plain markets regularly and combined to exclude therefrom the Abor Nagas of the upper hills. The charms of trade appeared indeed to have taken so strong a hold on the clans in this quarter, both Boree and Abor, that it was almost the only frontier on which the policy of closing the markets on occasion of a murder or outrage by hillmen was speedily followed by surrender of the guilty parties. In April 1861 the Dwars were closed to Naga traders by order of the Commissioner of Assam, in consequence of the murder of one Tonoo Cachari in the Gelaki Dwar, used by the Namsang and neighbouring clans. In February following, the Nangota Abor Nagas, who were not known to us to be the guilty tribe, surrendered five of their number as those who had committed the murder. This surrender, it appeared, they made under pressure brought to bear on them by the Boree Nagas of Tabloong, Jaktoong, Kamsang, and Namsang, who being much distressed by the closure of the Dwars threatened to attack the Nangotas if they did not give up the offenders. In March 1863 a murder was committed in Mouzah Oboipore of Seebsaugor by Banfera Nagas: and at the close of the same month the guard-house in Gelaki Dwar was burnt down by a raiding party belonging apparently to some of the Abor tribes. It was never distinctly brought home to any of them, and the Government did not on this occasion order the closing of the Dwars.

Some alarm was, however, felt at these disturbances on a usually tranquil part of the frontier; and when in 1866 it was reported that Naga trading parties were wandering about Seebsaugor armed, contrary to custom, with spears and *daos*, stringent orders were given for disarming temporarily all Nagas who passed the police outposts. In November 1867 the Gelaki guard-house was again attacked at night, and some of the constables killed. The outrage created much excitement among the European settlers of the neighbourhood, which was not certainly lessened by a subsequent attack upon a village not far off. Every possible motive was suggested to account for the outbreak. Every known clan was suspected in turn. One officer thought the prohibition to carry spears to market had something to do with the raid. Another was convinced that the encroachments of tea-planters in the hills were unsettling all the frontier tribes. A third thought survey operations had excited their suspicion. The Dwars were at any rate closed to trade; the outposts strengthened; and neglected stockades hastily repaired. The stoppage of trade again proved a successful policy. The Tabloong, Namsang, and other Nagas, who were now carrying on a most profitable traffic with the tea-gardens, which they could not afford to lose, speedily combined, and in a few months' time they succeeded in tracing out the raiders, and arresting by force or strategy two of their leaders, who were delivered over to the British authorities for punishment. These men proved to belong to the Yungia Abor Nagas, a remote clan in the upper hills, who actuated by a love of plunder and a craving for skulls had led a stealthy war party through the trackless jungles to the plains below; and had, as they said, attacked the police station under the notion that it was a settlement of *ryots*—a mistake not very creditable to the discipline of the post.

In 1869 the Changnoi Nagas were charged by a tea-planter with carrying off three labourers from his garden on the pretence that they were escaped slaves. The Nagas were communicated with by the Deputy Commissioner and denied the charge, declaring that the men had left the garden because they did not get their wages.

The Nagas were warned not to take the law into their own hands, and the planters advised to cultivate a good understanding with their savage neighbours and to avoid engaging hillmen unless they were prepared to face difficulties arising from such relations.

The rapid extension of tea cultivation along this frontier gave rise to considerable correspondence between 1869 and 1873. The limit of the revenue jurisdiction of Luckimpore and Seebsaugor to the south was, as above noticed, the old frontier road called the Dhodur Allee and Ladoigurh road. Although the Government claimed as British territory the whole country up to the boundaries of Manipur and Burma, it had hitherto treated the Naga tract as outside Assam for all civil purposes. The tea-planters had long since in many places, both in Luckimpore and Seebsaugor, taken up lands south of the revenue line, in some instances paying revenue to us, and in others to the Naga Chiefs. The earlier settlers found it to their interest to conciliate the Nagas, and troubled themselves little about Government protection. But now the fashion of claiming police assistance in every little difficulty came into vogue, and the Government had to consider what course it should adopt. The question acquired prominence from a quarrel between a planter and some Changnoi Nagas in Luckimpore early in 1871, which led to serious apprehension of Naga raids.

At length in 1872, the occurrence of a massacre of Borlangia Nagas perpetrated by Kamsingias within two miles of a tea-garden showed that measures for defining clearly the limits of Naga territory towards the plains could no longer be deferred. Under the provisions of the Inner Line Regulation already described, such a boundary was accordingly laid down, compensation being paid to the Nagas for the area occupied by those tea-gardens which lay beyond the Inner Line.

The later references to the Seebsaugor Nagas contain an account of differences between them and one Mr Minto, tea-planter, which do not seem to have been of any great importance. There appear also to have been certain intestine quarrels brought to the notice of our officers. With the tribal disputes of Nagas beyond the Inner Line the Government does not now interfere, save so far as the good offices of the Deputy Commissioner of Seebsaugor may serve to bring about peace.

In 1875 an attempt made to complete the survey of the Eastern Naga Hills led to serious results. Lieutenant Holcombe, Assistant Commissioner of Jaipur, and the Survey Party under Captain Badgeley, were on the 2nd February treacherously attacked at Ninu, a Naga village four days' march from the plains. Lieutenant Holcombe and eighty men were butchered, while Captain Badgeley and fifty men were wounded. Captain Badgeley succeeded in bringing off the remnants of the party, and a military expedition sent up promptly to the hill (in March 1875) destroyed the offending villages, and recovered the heads of the murdered men, and nearly all the arms and plunder taken by the Nagas. In 1876 a small force again escorted a survey party through the hills, and again burnt Ninu which refused to surrender some of those concerned in the massacre of 1875.[1]

Since then the Nagas on this frontier have given no trouble directly; but the Namsingias and Bordwarias have for years been at feud among themselves, and there is always some danger of a collision between the members of these or other warring clans taking place within our border. Petty occurrences of this description have indeed more than once been reported, but the offending villages have hitherto readily submitted to the fines imposed on them by our officers for violating our territory. An American Baptist missionary, the Reverend Mr Clarke, has for some years past been settled in the Naga village of Molong Kong, south of Amguri, and his labours are apparently bearing fruit in leading to the settlement of blood feuds, and a desire on the part of these villages which have come under his influence to live at peace with their neighbours. They are, however, exposed to attacks from the outer tribes, against which they desire to have the assistance of Government. They have been told that they must depend upon themselves, show a firm front, and avoid all provocation to quarrel. The local trade with the Nagas is largely developing, and even the remoter Lhota Nagas are now found visiting our markets and showing a wish to maintain commercial intercourse with the plains. Altogether the state of the South Luckimpore and Seebsaugor frontier is at present satisfactory.[2]

[1] For a full account, see Chapter III.

[2] The people described in this and the following chapters as 'Nagas' or 'Abors' are people of varied origin whom we now classify as Wancho, Nocte and Tangsa. The Namsingias and Bordwarias to whom reference is made in

2

THE ORIGIN OF THE NAGAS

(W. Robinson, *Descriptive Account of Asam*, 1841, pp. 380 ff.)

THE origin of the word Naga is unknown;[1] but it has been supposed by some to have been derived from the Sanskrit word नग्न, and applied in derision to the people, from the paucity of their clothing; but there seems little foundation for this etymological derivation, as the term has never been known to be applied by the Bengalees to either the Khassias or Garos, with whom they were far better acquainted than with the Nagas; and besides, the Garos especially are habitually accustomed to a greater degree of nudity than any of the Naga tribes with whom we are acquainted. Whatever be the origin of the word Naga, it appears that the appellation is entirely

these extracts, are now called Noctes. In 1884 it was estimated that these two groups numbered six thousand and three thousand respectively. There was a certain amount of enmity between them and in 1888, for example, a party of men from Namsang carried off six people from Dilli village and put two of them to death.

'The development of the coal mines near Margherita, and the opening of the Makum garden offered a fair field for the employment of Naga labour on jungle cutting and similar rough work, of which the hillmen were not slow to avail themselves: and in 1893 one company had more than 2,000 Nagas working at one time. They caused, however, considerable annoyance by their petty thefts of cattle, iron implements, and similar articles; and in order to check these depredations, the strength of the guard at Ledo was raised in 1897 from 11 to 20 men, and an outpost of 10 men was stationed at Tikak.'—B. C. Allen, *Assam District Gazetteers: Lakhimpur* (1905), pp. 76 f.

On the whole, however, few of the tribes of NEFA have been more closely in contact with the outside world than the Noctes. Even in the nineteenth century they are recorded as speaking Assamese and as having embraced a simple form of Vaishnavism. They earned considerable sums of money by trading or labouring in the plains. The Wangham of Namsang was paid Rs 450 a year on account of the tea garden at Hukanjuri.

[1] The meaning and derivation of the word Naga has long been disputed. Our chief authority on the Naga tribes, J. H. Hutton, originally thought that it was a corruption of the Assamese *Naga* (pronounced *Noga*) probably meaning 'a mountaineer', from the Sanskrit *nag*, a mountain or inaccessible place. Later he 'reluctantly' recanted this opinion in view of the fact that Ptolemy in the third century and Shyahbu'ldin Talish in the sixteenth both speak of Nagas as *nanga*, or 'naked'. This does not seem a very strong argument. Waddell on the other hand explains Naga as meaning 'hillman' and Peal derives it from *nok*, a word used by some Eastern Naga tribes for 'people'. See J. H. Hutton, *The Angami Nagas* (1921), p. 5; J. P. Mills, *The Ao Nagas* (1926), p. 1; S. E. Peal, *Fading Histories* (1894), p. 14.

unknown to any of the hill tribes themselves. The inhabitants of these hills are divided into numerous communities or races; and they know themselves by the designations of their respective tribes only, and not by any name common to all the races.

There, however, appears to be some mark by which these tribes are distinguished from their neighbours, and some common ties by which they are all bound together as one people, though possibly at present divided into tribes by a diversity of dialects. In all probability, this common tie may have descended to all the present tribes from the great aboriginal stock by which the hills were first peopled. Other races may from time to time have entered, and taken refuge in the hills, bringing with them their own dialects; but they may have probably amalgamated with the old stock in habits and manners, and above all, in religious superstitions; and these last especially, may form the great connecting link of all the Nagas, and the cause of separation from other hill tribes.

Though constantly at war amongst themselves, and using dialects so different that two adjoining tribes cannot converse together, except through the medium of a third dialect common to both, yet they are said to intermarry and form connexions and alliances with each other, which they do not do with tribes not belonging to the Naga community.

The Nagas also appear in general to be distinguished from their neighbours by physical conformation; for though there is much difference in this respect amongst them, yet they are in common remarkable for extremely coarse, savage countenances, and dull, timid, heavy dispositions.

In some of their habits, all these tribes have a common resemblance. They are, moreover, all distinguished by their weapons, which consist solely of javelins or spears.

So little is known of the dialects of the Nagas, that our present information will not permit us, from this source, to form any judgement respecting their descent. From the apparent diversity in their languages, it may with probability be inferred, that many of the tribes have not sprung from one common origin. And further researches may yet prove, that while a number of the Naga tribes have emigrated from the north-west borders of China, probably during the sanguinary conflicts for supremacy, which took place between the different members of the Chinese and Tartar dynasties in the thirteenth and fourteenth centuries, others may from like political causes, have been driven into the fastnesses of these hills from Asam and Bengal, and brought with them languages very different from each other. Thus whilst some of the tribes may have dialects derived from a common source, others speak languages of a perfectly distinct stock.

A more general acquaintance with the people, and a more diligent attention to their languages, it is hoped, will not long be wanting to throw light on these interesting races. Already have two or three members of the American Baptist Board of Foreign Missions established themselves on the Naga hills, and have become so far acquainted with the language of the tribe amongst whom they have located themselves (the Namsangiyas) as to have been able to get up a few elementary books in the dialect, and to open a school for the education of the children. To the perseverance of these exemplary men, in the great cause to which they have devoted their lives, we shall soon be indebted for much and valuable information regarding the Naga tribes in general, and the products of the hills which they inhabit. It is further to be hoped, that by the blessing of Divine Providence, through the efforts of these excellent men, the Nagas, who from time immemorial have been the scorn and the prey of their more civilized neighbours, may shortly begin to emerge from that dark barbarism which now renders the tribe of each hill an enemy to that of the next, and has hitherto prevented an Alpine tract of great natural resources and high fertility, from supporting more than a very scanty population of savages, in a state of discomfort and privation.

3

A PROPRIETY UNKNOWN TO THE MORE CIVILIZED

(W. Robinson, *Descriptive Account of Asam*, 1841, pp. 389 f.)

In all unpolished nations, the functions in domestic economy, which fall naturally to the share of women, are so many, that they are subjected to hard labour, and must bear their full portion of the common burden. Among the Nagas this is more particularly the case, owing in a great measure, perhaps, to the anarchical state of the country; or rather to the number of independent Chiefs, who formerly, for the slightest offence, were disposed to wage war against each other, and the worst of all wars—that which is covert and unsuspected. This made it necessary for the men to be always ready for an assault; and hence the custom that the women should cultivate the fields, and the men prepare for and fight in battle. In regard to the connexion of the sexes, the Nagas may boast of a propriety unknown to their more civilized neighbours. The men confine themselves to one wife, to whom they are strongly attached, and of whose chastity they appear very jealous. The women, on their part, are said to be distinguished for the correctness of their behaviour. They are in general treated with considerable kindness by the men, and are allowed to participate with them in their festivities and social amusements.

Marriages among the Nagas are not contracted in childhood, as among the Hindoos; nor do the men generally marry young. This probably arises in a great measure from the difficulty of procuring the means of paying the parents of the bride the expected *douceur* on giving the suitor their daughter as wife. Hence the youth, who wishes to espouse a girl, if accepted, agrees to serve her father for a term of years, generally limited to the period at which she may be considered marriageable. At the end of his servitude, a house is constructed for the young couple by their parents, who also supply them with a small stock of pigs, fowls, and rice. A long previous training has fully qualified the young bride to enter upon the duties of her new station; and the value of her services is generally so well appreciated, that nothing is more prompt than the vengeance of a Naga for any insult offered to his laborious partner; his spear gives the ready reply to any remark derogatory to her honour.

4

DANCES EXPRESSIVE AND ANIMATED

(W. Robinson, *Descriptive Account of Asam*, 1841, p. 395)

AMONG rude tribes in every part of the globe, the love of dancing is a favourite passion; and we find it to be the same case with the Nagas. As during a great part of their time they languish in a state of inactivity and indolence, without any occupation to rouse or interest them, they delight universally in a pastime which calls forth the active powers of their nature into exercise. All the Naga dances are imitations of some action; and though the music by which they are regulated is extremely simple and tiresome to the ear by its dull monotony, some of their dances appear wonderfully expressive and animated. The war-dance is perhaps the most striking. In this the women dance in an inner circle, whilst the men holding up their weapons in their hands dance round them, beating time and singing in strains of wild and plaintive melody. The women on such occasions are neatly dressed in long dark blue or black garments, ornamented with all their finery of beads and brass rings about their necks. They move in slow and decent movements, but the men, arrayed in their full war-dress, enter with enthusiastic ardour into their several parts; they exhaust themselves by perpendicular jumps and side leaps, in which they exhibit considerable agility. On the whole their gestures, their countenances, and their voices are exceedingly wild, and well adapted to their various situations.

5

THE GREAT SOURCE OF CONSOLATION

(W. Robinson, *Descriptive Account of Asam*, 1841, pp. 395 f.)

THE human mind, formed, as it is, for the reception of religious truths, is even in the rudest and most uncivilized state provided with certain ideas, which are destined, when corrected and refined, to be the great source of consolation amidst the calamities of life. Thus among the Nagas, we discern apprehensions of some invisible and powerful beings. These apprehensions, however, seem at first to be suggested to the mind rather by the dread of impending evils, than to flow from gratitude for blessings received. Hence probably originated the worship of evil spirits. Amongst the Nagas there also appears to be some feeble pointing towards more just and adequate conceptions of the power that presides in nature. They seem to have a perception that there must be some universal Cause to whom all things are indebted for their being. They appear also to acknowledge a Divine Power to be the Maker of the world, and the Disposer of all events: Him they denominate the Great Spirit. Their ideas of him, however, are faint and confused; and of his attributes, they are entirely ignorant. Of the immortality of the soul they have some faint notions. The human mind, even when least improved and invigorated by culture, shrinks from the thought of annihilation, and looks forward with hope and expectation to a state of future existence. This sentiment of soothing consolation, resulting from a sacred consciousness of its own dignity, from an instinctive longing after immortality, is universal, and may be deemed natural. From their imperfect ideas concerning the invisible world, they suppose that they shall continue to feel the same desires, and to be engaged in the same occupations as in the present world. The Nagas have no established form of worship; they have no temples erected in honour of their deities, and no ministers peculiarly consecrated to their service. They have the knowledge, however, of several superstitious ceremonies and practices handed down to them by tradition; and to these they have recourse with a childish credulity, when roused by any emergence from their usual insensibility, and excited to acknowledge the power and to implore the protection of superior beings.

6

A NAGA FUNERAL IN 1839

(Reverend M. Bronson, in an article in the *Missionary Magazine* of the Baptist General Convention for Foreign Missions, Boston, 1839)

THIS day was the completion of the sixth month after the death of a wife of one of their Chiefs. Their custom is to allow the corpse to remain six months in the house; at the expiration of which time, the ceremonies I have this day witnessed must be performed. In the morning two large buffaloes, several hogs, and a great number of fowls were killed for the occasion. About noon, numbers of Nagas from the neighbouring villages, dressed in a most fanciful manner, and equipped for battle, arrived. After beating several gongs of different sizes, so arranged as to form a sort of harmony with the music of drums, they marched to the house where the decaying corpse lay, each man bearing a shield, a spear, and a *daw*. They then commenced singing and dancing, with such a regularity of step and voice, as surprised me. They sang in the Abor[1] tongue, and my interpreter informed me, that all their songs are borrowed from the Abors, with whom they hold daily intercourse. I was allowed to attend, in company with two of the Chiefs, who inter preted to me the song, the substance of which is as follows: 'What divinity has taken away our friend? Who are you? Where do you live? In heaven or on the earth, or under the earth? Who are you? Shew yourself. If we had known of your coming, we would have speared you.' The above was first pronounced by the chorister. The whole company then answered it by exclaiming, 'Yes,' at the same time waving their huge glittering spears towards heaven, in defiance of the evil spirit who was supposed to have occasioned the death. The chorister continues: 'We would have cut you in pieces and eaten your flesh.' 'Yes,' responded the warriors, brandishing their *daws*, as if impatient for the battle. 'If you had apprised us of your coming, and asked our permission, we would have reverenced you; but you have secretly taken one of us, and now we will curse you.' 'Yes,' responded the warriors. This is the substance of what they sang, though varied, and repeated many times. The noise of music and dancing continued nearly all night. During the greater part of the following day the same ceremonies were repeated. At the setting of the sun, a large company of young women came around the corpse, and completely covered it with leaves and flowers, after which it was carried to a small hill adjacent, and burnt amid the festivities of the people. Thus closed this painful scene.

[1] At this time there was no clear distinction made by observers between Abors and Nagas.

7

THE COMET

(John Owen, *Notes on the Naga Tribes, in communication with Assam*, 1844, pp. 25 f.)

THE appearance of a comet spreads alarm and despair around; during its presence, the Nagas abstain from their usual levity, and feastings, and some from even the actual necessaries of life. It is not uncommon amongst them to go into the forests during its exhibition, and remain there until report reaches them of its disappearance. The last one was supposed to be the prognosticator of a cessation of the Company's government over the plains of Assam—it indicating, in their opinion, the approach of the Mauns or Burmese from the eastward, who on their march were, in overwhelming forces, to cut up their tribes, and fire every village within their reach. On this occasion these hardy mountaineers certainly evinced a degree of cowardice, which former boastings, and certain chivalrous qualifications, would not have induced one to expect that they were capable of displaying.

Some amongst them have no settled place of residence, but like the Meerees, and others on this frontier, migrate after a certain period's stay, from one hill to another. When this is the case, the whole village moves together, men, women, children, hogs, buffaloes, and oxen, the former bearing their children, stock, and other domestic appurtenances—nothing but the habitations remain, amongst which vegetation rapidly rises, and in the course of a year or two its remains, and the paths around it are closed, encumbered with jungle. On the unanimous selection of a new spot, they halt and settle, and clear away for the first night or two, a portion of the forest which they appropriate to their women and cattle, surrounded by spears. Such a scene is very romantic, and reminds one in some degree of a gipsy camp. Their conversation on the occurrence is replete with fun and good humour, varied by singing and shouts of laughter all the night. On these occasions, it is not an unfrequent occurrence for them to lose one or more of their party by tigers—and it is to prevent such losses that they remain awake until the dawn. As soon as clearance has been effected they erect their dwelling places, and with an incredible degree of quickness a village is formed. Their motives for removing every five or six years is believed to be on account of the supposed exhaustion of the soil, for the repeated gathering of crops and the process of manuring is not esteemed by them a profitable one, although for such purposes they are plentifully supplied with means.

8

SINGULAR PRACTICES

(John Owen, *Notes on the Naga Tribes, in communication with Assam*, 1844, pp. 8 ff.)

It has been asserted, and is generally admitted in the plains of Assam, that the Nagas have no religion—which will undoubtedly bear a contradiction, for, in common with many savage tribes who worship some particular orb either of day or night, so it is with the Naga, who imagines the sun to be his presiding deity. Should any of their tribe meet a sudden death, the body is that instant committed to the flames, such party, according to their idea, having incurred the displeasure of the deity.

Moreover, the existence of a singular practice amongst them negatives the idea of their being without religious feelings, for to what can we ascribe the following observance if it be not intended as devotional. At every cross-path they meet on a march, each, whether man, woman, or child, breaks off a branch or leaf of a tree which is thrown on a heap whilst passing—and these continue accumulating until an eclipse takes place, when the whole are removed by fire. The motive for so strange a practice I could never ascertain, with any nearer approach to correctness than my interpreter's knowledge could afford me, viz. that their Supreme One might see their observance, and reward them accordingly. But putting on one side this explanation of the custom, which, in all probability, being an Assamese, he did not take the trouble to inquire into minutely—it is evidently an act of religious respect which is sufficient to confute the hitherto acknowledged absence of all religious feeling on the part of the Naga tribes.

Missionary labours have proved sorely unproductive, although the Reverend Mr Bronson, an American missionary, compiled a small vocabulary with a view to establish a school for the education of the children. The novelty at first created uncommon inquisitiveness. Younger branches of their families intimated a desire to read and learn, but all interest ceased on finding, after some days, a discontinuation of the presents that had been given in the first instance to win their attention—such as beads, looking-glasses, and other baubles.

Each class being governed by independent Chieftains, they see but few strangers, and these are principally Mohungeeas, or Assamese traders from the plains, who, with a view to obtain salt, carry up for barter quantities of grain and opium, together with a few cocks, as a present for the Khoonbow or Chief. It is a singular fact that they have such an aversion to the flesh of any female, as, in the absence of those of the male kind, to refuse this description of food altogether. They however eat of fish, snakes, etc. without endeavouring to make the same distinction.

Their manner of cooking is performed in joints of bamboos, introduced into which are as much rice, chillies, and flesh, with water, as each will hold, all mixed together and thrust tightly in by the aid of a stick; a couple of bamboos placed in the ground, with a third connecting them at the top horizontally, constitutes a fire-place, against which those holding the food rest; by continual turning it soon becomes well roasted without splitting the bamboos, a circumstance which rarely occurs, and served up on leaves from any neighbouring tree, they sit down to their simple repast with as much real enjoyment as those of more civilized habits.

In their domestic condition, both sexes on many of the hills are found *in puris naturalibus*; but before the Assamese, who are generally well clothed, if possessed of a piece of cloth they will wear it. No people perhaps in the world are more alive to the preservation of matrimonial honour than the Nagas, and any offer of insult to the wife or daughter of another, would meet with deadly satisfaction from either the battle-axe or spear.

As compared with the more refined Assamese, their dwelling-houses and appurtenances appear filthy in the extreme, and the farmyards under their houses, which are supported on posts or bamboos are none of the cleanest. Still, many of them are remarkably

neat, and display a degree of care in the interior arrangements seldom the case with their Eastern neighbours. Thatched with *toka pat*, a very large leaf indigenous to their hills, and the sides covered with mat, grass, and mud, their houses are rendered impervious to wind and rain; each has generally three different apartments, which are respectively appropriated to the purposes of sleeping, cooking, and general business. Having no windows, the smoke escapes through the roof and doors, which answers two purposes—the preservation of the thatch, and impossibility of their manufactured salt becoming injured. Vessels of any kind are not eagerly sought for by them, the bamboo answering every purpose. Large mats made of the aforenamed leaves constitute their sleeping-places, which, in wet weather, placed near a large fire, continually kept up in the chamber, is not an uncomfortable place of rest.

The unmarried men are not allowed under any consideration to sleep at night in the family residence.

They are extremely hospitable according to their own method, and after a little mutual accommodation, are ever ready to relieve the wants of a traveller by the offer of house, village supplies, and attendants. . . .

Both sexes in some instances delight in ornamenting their naked bodies with rattan, amber, and glass beads. And the warriors, with the addition of human hair, strings of teeth extracted from the jaws of their fallen enemies, tusks of boars as ear-rings, wear a hideous war-like aspect, the greater part of which articles remain on them working, bathing, and sleeping.

A remarkable feature in the Naga is the deficiency of hair. On the face it is seldom or ever found—either in the shape of beard, whisker or moustache, and on the head it is deficient in quantity, is knotted on the crown and fastened with a rude semi-circular comb, manufactured by themselves either from the wood of the Jack, or of the *tetahapa*. The average height of them is about five feet ten inches and they are seldom inclined towards obesity.

Their manner of putting to death a wild ox or buffalo is as barbarous as novel. The animal is fastened to the stump of a tree, housepost, or other secure holding-place, by rattans passed through the nostrils—the warriors of the village surround it, and on the Chief approaching, all utter a shrill piercing cry, with the intention of stupifying it, when the headman, advancing from behind,

hamstrings, and very often severs at one blow the leg in halves, under the joint. It is immediately knocked down, the spine bone separated in an instant into innumerable pieces—spears dance in the body—wild halloos echo in the distance—and the display of savage delight on such an occasion, is not perhaps in any part of the world to be equalled. Literally alive, so far as the muscular action of the flesh is perceptible, the several parts are torn from the body and borne away to their respective habitations. But this is not the most animated part of the scene—if animation it be—for immediately the hacking commences, *choongas* or joints of bamboos are placed by the multitude at each incision, with the view of catching the blood, using while warm the same as an actual bedaubment for their persons. To the spectator unaccustomed to such scenes, the exhibition is a fearful one, while the passions of the excited Naga become to an extensive degree overbearing and disgusting. Dances and sham fights follow, but too often mirth is speedily converted into deadly combat.

But the sun sets—individuals are seen collecting into groups, each having brought with him from the neighbouring forest some huge tree or load of firewood, which one would have imagined a human being scarcely capable of bearing. The whole is collected in a pile and fired; the Nagonees (their females) bring their portions, join, and preparations are made for cooking the flesh, which, by the bye, the writer was rather surprised at witnessing, taking into consideration their savage-like preliminaries. The skin is not removed, but the flesh, cut into two- or three-ounce pieces, is thrown amongst the ashes at the foot of the fire;—the hair, scarcely singed, is removed from it, and with the addition of a forest yam, or wild kind of potato, the repast commences, occasionally varied by a song or war-dance. As buffalo meat is an unusual, or rather not common, entertainment amongst them the festivities are prolonged to beyond midnight; the men, as of other countries, to promote mirth freely partake of an intoxicating drink distilled from rice—and overcome by its effects, instead of retiring to their habitations, they sleep around the fire—not, in the cold weather, an unenviable place of rest.

The compiler of these notes would consider that, supported as he has been, by that enterprising body of merchants—The Assam Company—he would commit an act of injustice were he to omit recording any information that would be of service to them, his chance of obtaining every acquaintance connected with these particular Nagas having been, strictly speaking, at their expense. He would therefore suggest, that on the discovery and purposed clearing of an indigenous tea tract on these hills, every possible invitation should be encouraged.

Other suggestions may be introduced as they occur—but the foregoing subject led to the idea—that on such occasions, from the fact of their love of forest incendiarism, the Nagas are really useful auxiliaries towards clearances—independent of the smart smash they can when willing, exercise in the jungle, and when entertained in the day-time on pay, or remuneration as labourers with their ever-ready-toned weapons.

Their both rude and singular method of swearing to keep the peace with one another is on record, and deserving of notice. Each Chief, supplied with a dog and a few cocks, meets at a Morang, or village hall, in presence of their respective warriors and a large assembly of villagers. At a signal from the administrar of the oath, with one blow from the battle-axe each dog's head is severed from the body, and blood, stirred up with the forefinger beforehand, is thrown on their weapons, by which they pledge themselves to suffer death, rather than break the peace. The birds form flesh for a repast, after which a mutual good understanding is supposed to exist. Such fact is on record, and brought to notice by our Government having sent a deputation to the Nam Sangeea and Bur-d-wareea Chiefs, between whom incessant quarrels were taking place, detrimental to the preservation of tranquillity on our frontier. . . .

Of all crimes, they consider theft the greatest, and the punishment follows immediately on detection. The wrists and ancles, fastened with rattan, are brought together by an additional binding, and in this shape the detected is carried to the top of a high summit; and rolled down the side. Meeting in its fall, short stumps of trees, and other temporary checks, the body is generally torn to pieces, before reaching the bottom. . . .

Hunting forms a favourite amusement with them, and the flesh of the elephant is esteemed a delicacy. It is captured by them entirely through stratagem. A large hole capable of receiving it is dug on a track-way, covered over with a little grass and earth. They then trace it, and with screams and shouts frighten it back, but although the animal is sufficiently sagacious to see its trap, not being able to get into the jungle on either side of the track with ease, in its fright, trumpeting alarm, plunges headlong into it, and is thus secured. As in the murdering of a buffalo, so is it with the elephant—spears pierce the body, the trunk raised in agony is separated with the battle-axe, and thus is this noble animal, powerless, left to expire by loss of blood—when it is taken from the pit in pieces and carried to their villages. Sometimes they capture males with tusks weighing half a maund each, which are disposed of to the Marwarrees, merchants of the plains, for the exchange of a few beads and shells.

Their dogs have a peculiar dexterity in catching deer for them. They go out into the woods at daybreak, set together on one or more, which they kill, return home, making the circumstance known by a continual howling, with an inclination to return, when the delighted Naga follows them in the rear, and if a tiger has not been in the way he soon finds the slain, and at once removes it to his habitation. The stratagem rarely fails, and the dogs never leave until they are satisfied of actual death.

Except in one or two instances, the Naga people have not been known to associate in marriage with any others, or even between tribe and tribe; the exceptions having been invariably with a view to strengthen the power of their own tribe by a foreign alliance that shall insure it the assistance of some powerful neighbouring Chief. They are not usually contracted until both parties have reached the age of puberty—few instances of earlier betrothal having been known; at the same time a difference of opinion prevails as to the form of contract, although in either way little solemnity is exhibited.

In the writer's opinion the following is the generally accepted marriage ceremonial so to speak—primitive it is true, nevertheless characteristic of this people. Chance of course never permitted him the opportunity of watching a pair through the tedious period of courtship, but they elope together for this purpose, to some wild retreat, where all fear of pursuit is out of the question. After the expiration of three or four days, they return to their respective families and if each be satisfied with the other the marriage is consummated; but if, during the period of this wild suit, any impropriety on the part of the lovers should have been detected by the parents, both suffer by order, instant decapitation. Should, however, mutual satisfaction be wanting, the young people are allowed to make other selections, and the former unsuccessful attempt is scarcely considered worthy even of mention in conversation. The principal part of the ceremony, as in all others, amongst these in common with the general races of mankind, consists in feastings and rejoicings, and hence arises a disinclination on the part of a Naga to marry a man who may not have it in his power to afford a suitable entertainment.

9

SLEEPING IN A MORUNG

(John Owen, *Notes on the Naga Tribes, in communication with Assam*, 1844, pp. 83 f.)

It has been before noticed that the unmarried men are not allowed to sleep under the parental roof, if female relations dwell in the same abode; but in every village there is a Morang, or large house, with high gable ends and eaves reaching down to the ground; and inside this building are a series of bamboo bed-places covered with coarse mats elevated two or three feet from the ground, and upon which the young men repose. They rise early and usually retire from eight to nine o'clock in the evening. In one of these Morangs, the writer of this has slept.

With the exception of one or two individuals, who remain on guard all night, and make a little noise, the place was very quiet until sunrise, when we were awakened by a shrill scream from the party on guard, in which all soon joined. It may be imagined that I was a little startled, and my first impulse was to look for my gun. It appeared, however, upon inquiry, that it was merely the customary morning call for each to pursue his respective occupation. A descent to the rapid below immediately followed this call, and in less than five minutes not a single person was to be seen. The guard is always stationed during the night on a high perch, overtopping all the houses; and the punishment is very severe when any remissness of duty is detected. In case of fire in a neighbouring village, or signs of an attack in any shape, a password is given, and every man is instantly on his legs, carrying his battle-axe and spear; and a large hollow tree, which is invariably kept in the Morang, is struck by large pieces of wood, which noise, in the dead of night, may well be imagined to rouse up the whole village. The brief period of time in which they all muster is incredible. The kind of tree referred to is, of itself, when scooped out, capable of producing a tremendous noise, and is on certain occasions used as a musical instrument.

On the young men attaining the age of manhood, or when about twenty years of age, they are tattooed, declared servants of the Chief, also eligible for marriage, and are compelled to wrestle with, and often to fight with weapons, a corresponding sized villager.

10

FANTASTIC BUT PICTURESQUE

(E. T. Dalton, *Descriptive Ethnology of Bengal,* 1872, pp. 41 f.)

MANY of the Naga Chiefs, as the Namsangya Raja or Kumbo, dress respectably as Hindus when they visit the plains, like highlanders putting on the trews, but at home they wear the national dress of a Naga Chief or warrior, which is very fantastic but very picturesque.

They wear singular coronals made of pieces cut out of large shells, and on the crown of the head a little periwinkle-shaped basket-work cap, black with a scarlet border with peacock's feathers and goat's hair dyed scarlet. Necklaces, bracelets, armlets of beads, shells, brass, and of cane-work, are worn in profusion, but no drapery to speak of. The girdle is of polished plates of brass with a kind of double stomacher above and below. A very small apron of black cloth decorated with small shells is seen below this in most of the tribes, but I have seen tribes who wore nothing of the kind. The legs are also ornamented with bands of cane coloured red. The arms are a gleaming pole-axe with a short black handle, decorated with a tuft of red goat's hair; a broad-headed barbed spear, the shaft of which is covered with coloured hair like a burst, and a shield of buffalo hide from four to five feet long.

The women's costume is simpler, consisting of necklaces and an apron, or sometimes without the apron.

The great Chiefs have chairs or rather stools of state on which they and their sons sit; the ruler's stool being the highest, that of the heir apparent a step lower, and the other members of the family lower still. On one occasion we had been for some time waiting for the attendance in camp of the Chief of Sangnoi, and the officers had left the camp to view some part of the adjoining country. On our return, we found within the beat of our sentries, a scaffolding of bamboos twenty or thirty feet high, on the top of which was seated the Sangnoi Chief's son prepared to receive our homage! He was made to descend very rapidly and accommodated with a stool.

In all these Naga villages of the interior there is, at each of the fortified entrances, a large building well raised as a look-out or watch-house in which a band of young men keep guard at night. They have huge drums composed of trees hollowed out, which are sounded to give the alarm, and they have also fire signals.

The young Chiefs are sometimes fine looking men, and it is not an uncommon occurrence to find the Chief himself a very portly personage; but the physique of the Nagas generally is very inferior to that of the northern tribes. They are smaller boned and have much less muscular development, and are of darker complexion.

Their faces are very lozenge-shaped, features flat and eyes small. They have amongst them many Assamese who have taken to the Naga costume. They are at once recognizable by the difference of feature: nothing can make them look like Nagas. Of the Naga females my recollections are, they are short, ugly, and waistless; too hard worked perhaps to be beautiful.

11

A TOPOGRAPHER ON TOUR

(R. G. Woodthorpe, 'Notes Descriptive of the Country and People in Western and Eastern Naga Hills', in *General Report on the Topographical Surveys of India, 1874–5*, 1876, pp. 65ff.)

The area of the country passed through being necessarily limited, and our opportunities of observing the natives of the villages which our troops were sent to punish being few, I can only describe with any minuteness the men of the Mutan, Bor-Bansang and Senua villages, premising, however, that the men of Ninu and Nisa,[1] judging from what we were able to note, do not seem to differ materially from them, and that they are all probably members of the same tribe. We were accompanied by a small detachment of Borduarias and Namsangias, of whose personal appearance and decorations I am therefore able to say something, though I had no opportunity of seeing their villages or country except from afar.

The men are of average height and nearly all well made and well developed, and, as is the case among most hill tribes, their complexion comprises every shade of brown. These would be good-looking as a rule often, but for the tattooing on their faces which in some makes it appear perfectly black where the tattooing has been heavily done: in others the tattooing is blue, and then the bare portion of the face, especially in those of fair complexions, appears pink by contrast. The tattooing on the face, called in Naga language *ak*, consists of four continuous lines carried across the forehead, round and underneath the eyes up to the nose, back over the cheeks and round the corners of the mouth to the chin; rows of spots follow the outside lines and two fine lines mark out the nose in a large diamond space. The Mutan and Senua men do not tattoo very much on the body, but their thighs are tattooed in several places with lines and spots, or diamond and egg-shaped patterns, the upper portion of the tattoo being continued round to the back.

The Namsangias and the Borduarias do not tattoo the face at all, but their shoulders, wrists, bodies and thighs are very much covered.

The men of Voka, Khanu, &c., in addition to the tattooing of the Senua men, frequently cover their chest with fine lines, either horizontal or zigzagged; all the men dress their hair apparently in the same fashion, i.e. shaving that just above the ears, and taking the remainder back off the forehead and face, and tying it behind in a knot through which are passed curved strips of horn carrying waves of red and white or black hair. Some men have a small moustache, but very few show anything like a beard.

[1] The people of these villages are not 'Nagas' but Wanchos.

The dress and decorations of all the men we saw were essentially the same, the only differences perceptible being in the style of ornamentation, differences due to the various tastes of individuals rather than to any attempt at distinction of clan or village. The helmet is conical in shape and made of plaited cane, either plain, or having patterns of coloured straw worked over it. A large plume of black or red hair passes over the helmet from front to rear, and long horns carrying toucan feathers or tufts of hair spring from the sides; some helmets are covered with leopard or bear skin, and have a wreath of red or black hair round the base. Another head-dress is a circular band of coloured cane and straw, ornamented with bits of a large shell and a fringe of hog's hair, which lies on the forehead. Their ear ornaments are generally strings of beads pendant from a piece of shell, and terminating in long tufts of hair, which fall over the chest. They have a very pretty one made of alternate tufts of red, white, and black hair, radiating from a centre of yellow straw work, which is fixed in the lobe of the ear. The necklaces are beads, some of which, of a yellow opaque colour, are highly valued by the Nagas. From the shoulders to the elbows the men encase their arms in many rings of red and yellow cane, very large at the shoulder, gradually decreasing to the elbow; these give an appearance of great breadth to their shoulders, an effect which is further heightened by the bands of black or yellow cane which are drawn very tightly round the waist, and this effect is still further increased by the lines drawn by the Borduarias from their breasts to their navels. One man had as many as nineteen turns round his waist, giving a total length of cane of over forty feet. It is amusing to see them winding this cane round them, and it is a matter of time to get it all properly twisted on. Large belts, very broad at the back, fastening in front, and made of plates of polished brass or of coloured cane and cowries, are also worn. A broad piece of blue cloth hangs from the waist, ornamented with red fringes and rows of white seeds; a portion of the cloth is taken up between the thighs and secured at the back as an extra piece of decency by those who visit the plains most frequently. On the wrists are worn deep bracelets of cowries, and below the knee, strings of the same are also tightly tied. These Nagas are very skilful in devising little adornments from palm leaves, making coronets, wristbands and anklets of them. Those have a most picturesque appearance. A curious custom prevails at Voka, and I fancy also in the neighbouring villages; it is this, that till a young man is married, he goes perfectly naked, and he at once adopts a waistcloth when he takes a wife to himself. Every Naga carries about with him a small basket or bag for his food and *pan*, &c. In wet weather he has a cloak made of grass on a small string foundation. The large cloths worn in the cold weather are generally of Assamese silk; but at Khanu I saw a cloth of black and orange stripes, identical with those we saw last year in Thetchumi on the Lanier.

The women are short in stature generally, and their figures are remarkable rather for strength than beauty, to which very few have any pretensions. They tattoo a good deal on the shoulders, body and legs, but not on the face. The shoulders are tattooed with diamond patterns, three horizontal lines are taken across the body above the breast, between which eight lines go down to the waist narrowing gradually to a point; the navel is the centre of a Maltese cross; each arm, about five inches long, consists of three lines with a pointed finial. The leg tattoo is done with an admirable sense of fitness, that on the thighs consisting of close vertical lines and on the calves of horizontal lines, a small break occurring in each on the shin bone; this has the effect of increasing the apparent rotundity of the legs below the knees. The women wear their hair braided and tied in a knot at the back, or else gathered up and tied into a small bamboo tube covered with particoloured cloth or beads, the lower end decorated with a red fringe, or a long tuft of hair.

The dress of the women consists principally of a very small petticoat, two feet two inches long and six inches deep, ornamented occasionally with bells, beads and shells; this only comes a little more than half way round the body, leaving the right thigh bare,—it is attached at the ends and middle to a string passing round the waist. Sometimes a small cloth is worn round the shoulders. Many strings of beads fall low down over the breasts. Small fillets of coloured straw adorn their brows, and several massive white-metal rings are worn above the elbow. Their ear ornaments are principally small strings of beads passed through various holes in the ear.

The arms of this tribe are the *dao*, spear and cross-bow. The first is a most formidable weapon, the blade is generally triangular;

about eight inches long, straight at the back, and four inches wide at the top, narrowing gradually with a slightly convex edge towards the handle, which is two feet long and ornamented with tufts of coloured hair; sometimes, instead of being straight all the way up, the back of the blade swells out towards the top in a semi-circular projection. The spears are not by any means such handsome or formidable weapons as those used further west, and this is due, I fancy, to the fact that with the eastern tribes the *dao*, and not the spear, is the principal weapon of offence. The spear-heads are small and resemble very similarly in shape and ornamental workings those found at Thetchumi and Primi; the shaft, though short and slender, is strongly made of bamboo and decorated with red and black hair in various fashions. The cross-bow is exactly similar to that... used by the Lhota Melomi and Primi Nagas. The shield is small, about four feet long by two feet wide, and made of buffalo hide decorated along the upper edge with a fringe of red hair, and on the face with two or four tassels of grass. Every man carries with him on the war-path a large supply of *panjies*,[1] which he plants in the road to cover his retreat. These are carried in a horn suspended at the back, or in a small basket to which is attached a long tail of bearskin; sometimes this *panjie*-holder is the skin of a bear's foot with the claws remaining, the skin sewn up to form a large bag, a little figure of a sitting man, dressed and painted after life, being affixed to the upper part. Some men wear a skin of defensive armour in the way of a leather corset which overlaps on the chest, and is kept up by means of straps which pass over the shoulders. The Voka men also wear a leather corset, but without shoulder-straps.

We found among these men a large number of gongs which they probably get indirectly from Burmah. They cast bells themselves very well in little clay moulds, the material being apparently a kind of gun-metal, and occasionally brass. A woman's walking staff is a long, thin, iron rod foliated at its upper end.

The country we passed through was fine and open except for the first march from Buruarchati in the plains, to Khulan, Mutan, the path lying through dense forest and following the course of sluggish

[1] *Panjies* are pointed bamboo stakes, hardened by fire, which are driven into the ground to repel invasion or pursuit.

streams with muddy bottoms. But on reaching Bor-Mutan the first extensive view of the country beyond is obtained. It is well watered by several large tributaries of the Delhi or Disang river as it is called in the plains, and Tisa as it is called by the Nagas themselves, meaning the 'large stream'; *te* being the prefix of all river names, and *sa* an affix signifying large. It was the largest stream we had to cross, and to the strength and velocity of its current when angry we owe the loss of a good sepoy. Water was abundant along our route, specially beyond Ninu, where the undulating, park-like character of the slopes, backed up by tall, dark wooded cliffs, suggested itself as an admirable site for a station. Methna[1] grazed about the grassy slopes in large numbers, and herds of hill buffaloes were seen at several villages; deer were seen here and there, and about Nisa, partridges flew up from the grass on either side of the path at every turn. Near most of the villages and in the deep ravines are seen tree-ferns, sago, and *toko pat* palms; the latter are carefully preserved, as they are most valuable for thatching purposes.

The villages are not always well placed for defence against rifles, being commanded from some neighbouring height; but others, such as Bor-Bansang, Senua, Niao, &c., are exceedingly well placed, occupying the highest points of the ridges on which they stand and commanding all the approaches to them. The defences consist of double stockades made of interlaced bamboo and cane, and *panjied* ditches. The houses are generally scattered up and down without any attempt at order, and are half hidden among the trees, which are not as elsewhere cut down to clear a village site, such only being felled as interfere with the houses; these are built on the unlevelled ground, the floor being carried out to the rear on bamboo piles, the back veranda being frequently a great height above the ground. These are not railed round at all, and on my asking if the small children never fell off, the reply was 'of course they do, many are killed in that way', in a tone conveying the impression that my informant looked upon it as an ingenious mode of giving effect to Malthusian theories. The house is divided into an entrance hall, as it were, where the owners' weapons hang, also skulls of animals taken in the chase, and beyond into several small apartments

[1] The earlier writers spelt the name of the splendid animal, *Bos frontalis,* which we now call *mithan* or *mithun,* in a variety of ways.

terminating with a large open veranda. Trays are suspended over the fire-places (of which there is generally one in each apartment) on which flesh, fish, vegetables and wood are dried. The walls of the houses are of bamboo matting, the roof being thatched with palm leaves or grass; the principal uprights project through the ridge some two or three feet, this portion being thatched also to keep the rain from running down the post into the house; the thatching is ingeniously worked into figures of men or animals very often. The reason given for this projection of the post is, that as the part below the ground decays, it can be cut off and the post lowered without damage to the house. The Vangam's, i.e. headman's house is always very large, and built on the most level site in the village. It is generally about 200 feet long by 40 or 50 broad, and contains two large halls, one at either end, the intervening space being divided up into several apartments and store-rooms arranged on either side of a central passage. Each of the women's apartments has its own door of exit and veranda. On one side of the entrance hall stands the drum, a large tree hollowed out and carved roughly at either end; it is played upon with clubs shaped like large dumb-bells. A large number of men perform at once on the drum, and though each seems to hammer away entirely on his own account, the effect is harmonious and pleasing. They have several tunes as it were, each being ended by a shout from the leader, responded to by the rest, when a fresh one at once commences. Opposite the drum is the rice-pounder, of great length, giving occupation to nine operators. The other hall is kept as an audience hall, where the Chief receives his friends. It has a raised and matted floor, the rest of the building having as a floor the bare ground. This hall opens into a veranda. Every house is furnished with a few small stools on four short legs, and one or two large beds which, with their legs, and a slight attempt at a bolster, are each cut out of one log. Tables made of cane-work, shaped like an inverted wineglass, and about two and a half feet high, are used on which to place their food at meal times. In each village are one or two *morangs*, or bachelors' houses, in which a drum is kept, and also the collection of heads taken in battle; these are placed in rows of about twenty-five each in a large sloping tray placed in the veranda, just within the shelter of the roof. At Bor-Mutan there were 210 bleached skulls arranged in this way.

The villages are remarkable for their sanitary arrangements, small raised houses in which calls of nature are obeyed being built in various parts of the village, and fenced round. Look-outs are built at all the gateways and in front of the *morangs*, and here watches are always kept. These are also erected in the fields. At Kamhua I saw some watch-houses in the fields surrounded by a double stockade enclosing a passage all round, and over the outer gateway a small platform was erected. Between Senua and Niao, by the roadside was a small table raised about eight feet from the ground, approached on either side by a broad wooden ramp. We were told that here peace is concluded between those two villages after a war. The Chiefs walking up, each from his own side meet face to face on opposite sides of the table, and, exchanging *chungas* of wine, drink to each other, and thus declare that peace is made. On the road to Niao, also, was a curious mud figure of a man in bas-relief, presenting a gong in the direction of Senua; this was supposed to show that the Niao men were willing to come to terms, if possible, with their enemies. Another mode of evincing a desire to turn away the wrath of an approaching enemy and induce him to open negotiations, is to tie up in his path a couple of goats, sometimes also a gong, with the symbolical palm leaf planted in the ground hard by.

The mode of disposing of the dead is the same in all these villages in its main point, viz. wrapping up the corpses in cloths and mats and placing them on platforms under small roofs. The shape of these roofs differs in different villages slightly, but all are decorated with various coloured cloths and streamers, and have at each end a tall figure of wood, dressed, painted and tattooed after the manner of the men of the village, and carrying imitation spears, *daos* and shields; gourds, baskets, &c., are suspended about the tomb. At Khanu the tombs were enclosed in small sheds with doors. Each shed contained several tombs of adults and children, being, in fact, regular family vaults. These tombs are all arranged on either side of the principal entrance to the villages. Cairns of stones are also erected, where the heads of the departed villagers, decorated with shells, beads, and bells, are collected, and earthen *ghurras* filled with the smaller bones, are ranged among them. Each head is decorated in a slightly different way from the others in order that they may be recognized by their surviving relatives.

12

THE EASTERN TRIBES IN 1875

(Narrative Report of W. F. Badgley, in *General Report on the Topographical Surveys of India, 1874–5*, 1876, pp. 50 ff.)

THE hills rise in successive and parallel ranges from the plains to the Burmese watershed, and the rivers naturally following between them take the same north-east or south-west direction, breaking out through the ranges to empty themselves after crossing the plain into the Brahmaputra, the only exception of any note being the southern branch of the Diku, which drains a long valley between high ranges of hills as yet unsurveyed and runs directly northwards. The ridges of the hills and the bottoms of the valleys are narrow; there are not throughout more than four or five level spaces either above or below, and those are of very limited extent, the most level being the place at which we were encamped when attacked at Ninu, which was not only the most level and best watered, but also the most beautiful place I saw in the hills. The lower and outer ranges are covered with wood and undergrowth, but without any fine timber, and the tops of the highest range being uncultivated, are also covered with forest. The rocks throughout are sandstone or shale, the latter being accompanied by tepid salt springs, and the former in several places overlying coal deposits which have this year been explored by the Geological Survey. The rivers are not navigable within the hills.

The climate of the eastern half of the tract surveyed was, as far as I experienced it, remarkable for rain. I find from a reference to my notes that we were constantly having rain which lasted for several days at a time, and during the time that the military expedition against Ninu was in the country, it was almost constant. This altogether embraces a period from December to the middle of April. The weather in the winter was otherwise very pleasant, the sun, as usual in these latitudes, often hot, but the air cold and enlivening, and occasionally after a fall the forest on the summits of the Patkai from frozen rain appeared as if covered with snow.

The low outer ranges are not, as a rule, inhabited or cultivated, but from beyond these to the watershed the hills are well populated and bared by cultivation, except in the valleys (the village always being built on the hill-tops or points of spurs) which it would be toilsome to cultivate, and besides dangerous among such treacherous and blood-thirsty people. The villages are more numerous in the eastern half of the tract, and smaller than among the Angamies and other tribes to the west, the average number of the houses in each being about sixty, though the number of inhabitants must not be judged from this, as the houses are larger, and more than one family inhabit each. The houses of the Chief are always very large and hold many persons. That of the Chief of Mulong, for instance, is more than 360 feet long by 100 broad, and has a balcony at one end; and several of the other Chiefs' houses seen were of equal size, and the population is as large as can be well supported with their *jhoom* method of cultivation. Most of the eastern tribes cultivate but little rice, their chief stand-by being a sort of yam (*katchu*). They have cattle in some places, and pigs, goats and fowls everywhere, and eat besides a great variety of wild produce, animal and vegetable, some of which, e.g. what are commonly called garden-bugs, appear abominably nasty to us. I did not notice that they cultivated cotton anywhere, which may be either the result or origin of their habit of dress, the tribes generally being distinguishable from one another by the greater or less scantiness of their clothing, or by the entire absence of covering. Among the tribes I first saw inhabiting Tablung, Kongan, Jaktung, etc., the males went entirely nude; the females, however, were well clothed, which made the dress of the females to the eastward the more remarkable, for there, though the men were decently dressed with broad aprons reaching to the knees, the women's only clothing, except beads and ornaments, was a strip of cloth five inches broad round the buttocks, which to our eyes made their nakedness more naked, and indeed, excepting in the case of the very young, produced a strong feeling of disgust. Some of them went quite naked.

I saw altogether four tribes in my tour, distinguished by tattoo and language as well as dress. At Kangching the people struck me at once as resembling the Semas, whom I had seen the year before to the west, and they said that they had come several generations before from that side. The men do not tattoo, have the hair cropped round as if a bowl had been put on the head, and wear a black apron ornamented with beads. The men of Tablung, Jaktung,

&c., tattoo a single line down the forehead and nose, and two broad bands from the outer parts of the arms over the shoulders to meet in a point at the waist, wear no clothes and shave the head, except a broad tuft brought forward and a small one behind. At Mulong, and east to Lungva and Joboka, they wear aprons, usually of Assam silk; tattoo the face with small dots and lines and the body with bands, as at Tablung, and wear nearly all their hair in front cut short over the forehead, the back hair being tied in a pigtail over a bamboo about nine inches long. East of these from Uto to Bansang and Ninu, they wear an apron, often of blue stuff, tattoo the face so heavily with broad lines and dots as to give them at a little distance the appearance of being blackened, and wear nearly all their hair, the front part cut short over the forehead, the back twisted into a knot fastened by a large pin of buffalo horn. The women of all the tribes tattoo slightly on the body and from the knee to the ankle, and at Kangching have three broad lines on the lower lip and chin. The men, except at Kangching, wear a belt of a long spiral cane wound round them so tightly, that the waist is sometimes compressed to twenty inches, a habit perhaps the result of the spare and poor diet they put up with, notwithstanding which, however, they are strong and active and excel in tree-climbing. No tree is too tall to go up, and if too thick to clasp, it is still to be climbed either with notches cut with their ever-handy *dao*, or by a bamboo pegged against the stem. The women wear no belt; to the men it gives a decidedly smart look, and with the gay helmets they wear, a party of young warriors has a most picturesque appearance.

There are minor differences of dress and arms among the eastern tribes, and their language differs, but of this I made no notes, leaving it to Lieutenant Holcombe, who, had he lived, would have furnished a very thorough account of them. There were two points, however, on which he made particular inquiries: the attack on the Gileki outpost in 1867, and the routes to Burmah, and from what he said to me, I believe he came to the conclusion that the Tablung, and probably Kongan men were the perpetrators of the first. His inquiries as to the routes to Burmah, though not conclusive, as all his informants (some of whom seemed jealous of our knowing anything about it, and some ignorant) did not give precisely the same information, seemed to point the following as the route *par excellence*, and the survey, as far as it went, confirms it, namely, to enter the hills by the Towkok river, ascend to Changnoi by Changsa, and cross to Lungva, from whence in three marches southward, over a distance equal to that from the Assam plains, a broad navigable river could be reached. Men from Lungva had seen the river, but the route was little used, as the tribes are inimical to strangers, who stand but a poor chance of keeping either their property or their heads. This abominable practice of taking heads, which is always carried on in a treacherous and usually cowardly way, and in which no distinction of age or sex is made, though doubtless of use in keeping down the population, must always, if allowed, prevent communication and commerce among the tribes; but they would, I believe, themselves prefer its being put down.

There is a peculiarity of these eastern tribes which cannot fail of being remarked by a visitor to their villages, as it is usually called attention to by the nose as well as the eye—their mode of disposal of their dead. These are placed at the entrances to their villages. At Tablung and the villages near it the body covered with cloth and matting is laid in a canoe-shaped coffin ornamented with red and black paint and placed on the lower branches of a tree. More eastward the coffin is of mat and supported on a small bamboo frame; is covered by a narrow roof often with one end produced into a long, tapered beak, and sometimes ornamented with wooden figures or cloth, the arms and belongings of the deceased or imitations of them, being hung on posts near it. What is more remarkable, however, is that the whole of the corpse is not in these coffins. The head is invariably removed after death. It is twisted off after decomposition has sufficiently advanced (to cut it off would be a supreme insult to both the dead and living relations), and is then disposed of elsewhere. About Tablung it is placed in a cylindrical vase of stone, and then (so they told us) cast into the most out-of-the-way part of the forest which is to prevent its ever being used as a trophy by an enemy. About Joboka and eastward it is placed (evidently previously cleaned) on a little platform outside the gate and ornamented with beads and brass ornaments.

13

A POLYGLOT COMMUNITY

(S. E. Peal, 'Notes on a Visit to the Tribes inhabiting the Hills south of Sibsagar', *J.A.S.B.*, 1872, Vol. XLI, pp. 27 f.)

BOTH physically and linguistically, there is a good deal of difference in the tribes bordering each other. The Naga vocabulary compiled by Mr Bronson at Jaipore in 1840, is of no use here, but sixteen miles west, though some words are known; but the numerals are different, and they here only count to ten.

When once with a number of Banparas on the road, a large party of Nagas passed, and as neither party spoke, I asked who they were. I was pointed out their hill, and on asking why they did not speak, they said they would not understand one another. This I thought a good opportunity to try them, and told them to call them in Naga and ask who they were. On being called to, they all turned round, and stopped, but said nothing; I then made them call again; but to no purpose, the other party simply jabbered together in twos and threes, and on calling them a third time as to where they were going, they shouted out a lot of Naga which my fellows could not make out. Both parties passed on, unable to exchange a word, though living within a few miles of each other. A few words did pass, but they were Assamese. I asked how they knew the men, and they said 'by their *ak*' or tattoo marks. There is more lingual variation among the remote tribes, I believe, than those bordering Assam as the latter frequently meet in the plains on a peaceful footing, while the Abors are shut out from all intercourse.

The physique also varies with the tribe. I can as a rule tell a Joboka man from a Banpara, and these from a Muton, or Namsangia, and Assamese. Those who are familiar with the tribes can easily do so, without seeing the *ak* to guide them, simply judging by their general physique and colour. Of course there are exceptional cases, such as small stunted men, or others unusually tall or well made.

Practically, the extraordinary confusion of tongues opposes a serious obstacle to the explorer, and the sooner we set to work to reduce the confusion by inducing apposite causes, the better for us and our successors, and for them and their successors. Tattooing as a decoration, or prize for committing murder, is at the bottom of it all, I fancy, and is so deeply rooted that it may take a long time to eradicate by peaceful means.

14

A FIRST EXERTION OF HUMAN INGENUITY

(W. Robinson, *Deseriptive Account of Asam*, 1841, pp. 390 f.)

THE agriculture of the Nagas is neither extensive nor laborious. Among some of the tribes, however, every portion of culturable land is most carefully terraced up the hills, as far as rivulets can be commanded for the irrigation of the beds; in these localities, rice forms the only object of cultivation. Arums and yams the Nagas have in great abundance, but are for the most part found wild about their villages; they have also some large capsicums, good ginger, and a few cardamom plants. Cotton is frequently grown on the sides of the hills; and with it is often seen a species of grass (*lachryma jobi*) from the grain of which the Nagas extract an intoxicating liquor by an operation that closely resembles brewing. It seems to have been one of the first exertions of human ingenuity, to discover some composition of an intoxicating quality, and there is no tribe so rude or so destitute of invention, as not to have succeeded in this fatal research. The Nagas seem as much addicted to the use of intoxicating liquors as any of the neighbouring tribes. Pigs, fowls, and ducks are abundant in all the villages, and some of the more wealthy, keep herds of cattle procured from the plains. They make no scruple of the use of beef, and in fact are by no means particular in their diet—dogs and cats, as well as reptiles and insects, are equally partaken of as food. In general, the Nagas do not use much vegetable food, and the consequence is, that most of the old people shew great and disgusting symptoms of cutaneous eruptions, scurvy, and leprosy.

15

A GRATEFUL BEVERAGE

(John Owen, *Notes on the Naga Tribes, in communication with Assam*, 1844, pp. 49 f.)

THE measures which have now been in progress for the cultivation of the plant and the manufacture of tea, lead eventually to the anticipation of very favourable results, and the immense wealth which has flowed for a century and a half from Great Britain and her colonies to a foreign country will, it is hoped, henceforth be distributed amongst British subjects, and a new source of lucrative employment opened up to thousands.

The Nagas are beginning to look on tea, manufactured according to Chinese style, as a grateful beverage; notwithstanding they still entertain the impression that our wandering over their forests in search of the plant is a mere pretext to see their country, and if found to be plentifully supplied with valuable productions that appropriation will follow. The idea may be indulged, that years hence both Assamees and hillrangers will leave off the use of opium and other intoxicating drugs for the better substitute of an indigenous, and easily manufactured article.

16

SALT-MAKING

(W. Robinson, *Descriptive Account of Asam*, 1841, pp. 384 ff.)

EAST of the river Namsang, and between it and the boundary of Asam, are several small Naga communities, who are now almost reduced to the state of slaves by the more powerful Singphos, by whom they appear to be greatly oppressed. Of late, however, the progress of our paramount authority has interposed for their relief. We are not aware, whether any Nagas are found further east; but it seems probable, that the Khunungs, who inhabit those mountains whence the Irrawadi takes its rise, may also be Nagas, though this general term is not applied to them.

Among those Naga tribes in communication with Asam, and who deserve more particular notice, are the Namsangiyas, the Borduriyas or the Borduwarias, and the Panidawarias. These tribes are in possession of brine springs of considerable value, and further, were always supposed to pay allegiance to the Rajas of Asam.

The circumstance of the Asam government having always raised a revenue from the imported salt of the hills, and the dependence of the Nagas on the Asam markets for the exchange of salt for grain and other articles, has contributed to a mutual good understanding between the two people. The Naga hills have in consequence been always accessible to the people of the plains; whilst the Nagas have on their part, been always permitted access to the markets on the frontier.

The taxes that have been till lately levied on the Naga salt have been exceedingly heavy, and the manner in which they were imposed, led to numerous exactions on the part of the tax-gatherers. The individuals appointed to the collection of the taxes were in attendance at the springs on the hills, as well as the markets below, and tolls were levied by them both on the salt itself, and on the articles the Nagas obtained in barter for the salt.

Lieutenant Brodie, now in charge of the Sibpur district, finding the old system very oppressive to the people, abolished all the duties to which they were subject, that on the salt excepted. The tax now levied upon it consists in kind. The present receipts amount to 652 maunds 38 seers and 11 chittacks of salt, which at five rupees a maund, the rate at which it has been sold, yields rupees 3,264:13:4. Deducting from this the monthly expenses, which amount to 120 rupees, or rupees 1,440 annually, and the net return is rupees 1,824:13:4.

The salt wells in the hills are for the most part the sole property of the Nagas. In some of the wells, the former Asam government obtained a joint property, the Nagas having a right to draw the brine for a certain number of hours, and the government for an equal period. Raja Purunder Sing found this right a very profitable one, and a certain portion of his Pykes were allotted to the works. As the Pyke system has since been abolished, and it would not in all probability be so profitable under a system of hired labour, at least without some more profitable method of boiling the brine than is now in use, the British government have not yet exercised their prerogative in these wells. To some springs below the hills the government have an exclusive right; but the jealousy of the Nagas induced them, during the weakness of the late Asam government, to fill up the wells and forcibly to prevent their being re-opened.

The Naga mode of manufacturing the salt is exceedingly rude, and the process both slow and wasteful, so that the salt manufactured by the Nagas, can scarcely compete with that imported from Bengal. It is, however, to be hoped, that European speculators will shortly be able to introduce a far more profitable mode of manufacturing the salt, which is the more likely to succeed, as the vicinity of several coal beds will offer the means of evaporating the brine with greater facility. The Nagas themselves are at present averse to any innovations, and it is difficult to see what measures are to be taken even for their own advantage, without giving them offence.

Chapter III

TRIBAL WARFARE IN THE NINETEENTH CENTURY

1

NAGA WARFARE

(W. Robinson, *Descriptive Account of Asam*, 1841, pp. 391 ff.)

We have already observed that the various tribes dispersed over the Naga mountains are not only independent and unconnected, but engaged in perpetual hostilities with one another. Interest is not either the most frequent, or the most powerful motive of their incessant hostilities. They must in a great measure be imputed to the passion of revenge, which rages with such violence in the breast of savages that eagerness to gratify it may be considered as the distinguishing characteristic of men in their uncivilized state. The maxims by which they regulate their military operations, though extremely different from those which are adopted among more civilized and populous nations, are well suited to their own political state. They never take the field in numerous bodies, since such a measure would require a greater effort of foresight and industry than is usual among them. On approaching the enemy's territories, they collect their troops and advance with great caution. Even in their hottest and most active wars, they proceed wholly by stratagem and ambuscade. They place not their glory in attacking their enemies with open force. To surprise and destroy is the greatest merit of a commander, and the highest pride of his followers. If no straggling parties can be intercepted, they advance towards the villages; and if so fortunate as to remain unobserved, they set on fire the enemy's huts in the dead of night, and massacre the inhabitants as they fly naked and defenceless from the flames. When the enemy is caught unprepared, they rush upon them with the utmost ferocity, and tearing off the scalps of all those who fall victims to their rage, they carry home these strange trophies of their triumph, These they preserve as monuments not only of their prowess, but of the vengeance which their arm has inflicted upon the people who were objects of public resentment. On the death of a warrior, all the scalps taken by him during his lifetime are burnt with his remains.

Such a mode of warfare may be supposed to flow from a feeble and dastardly spirit, incapable of any generous or manly exertion.

But when it is considered that many of these tribes, on occasions which call for extraordinary efforts, not only defend themselves with obstinate resolution, but attack their enemies with the most daring courage, and that they possess fortitude of mind superior to the sense of danger or the fear of death, we must ascribe their habitual caution to some other cause than constitutional timidity. The number of men in each tribe is so small, the difficulty of rearing new members amidst the hardships and dangers of savage life so great, that the life of a citizen is extremely precious, and the preservation of it becomes a capital object in their policy. Had the point of honour been the same amongst the feeble Naga tribes as among the powerful nations of Europe, had they been taught to court fame or victory in contempt of danger and death, they must have been ruined by maxims so ill adapted to their condition. But, wherever their communities are more populous, so that they can act with considerable force, and can sustain the loss of several of their members without being sensibly weakened, the military operations of the Nagas more resemble those of other nations. They openly defy their enemies to the combat, engage in regular battles, and maintain the conflict with that desperate ferocity which is natural to men who, having no idea of war but that of extermination, never give or take quarter.

The universal weapon of the Nagas is a javelin, which is usually adorned with coloured hair, and ornamented with strips of rattan of various colours. The Loohoopas make use of a long spear, and some of the eastern Nagas handle the tomahawk. The total disuse of the bow[1] among the Naga tribes seems a very singular

[1] The bow is not entirely unknown to the Naga tribes, though its use as a weapon is not common, possibly because it requires to be operated by both hands, whereas the Naga warrior needs one of his hands to carry his shield. 'While the cross-bow,' says Hutton, 'is the weapon of the Singphos, and has been adopted from them apparently by the Naga tribes of the north-east, it is not in general use among the Naga tribes. The simple bow is also not the natural weapon of a Naga. While the Kukis, before they acquired guns, relied, like the Khasis, principally on the bow, the Naga rarely uses it. The weapon was known to the Semas and is still employed by children as a toy, and the Angamis have learnt the use of the pellet-bow, possibly from the Kukis, and use it for killing small birds, but as a serious weapon the bow is not used by either tribe; and though the Semas believe that their ancestors used it, the Angamis appear never to have done so, a fact which is interesting in view of the apparent absence or scarcity of the bow in Borneo, Sumatra and the Celebes.'—Hutton's Introduction to J. P. Mills' *The Lhota Nagas* (1922), p. xxvii.

circumstance, especially as the weapon is common to all the surrounding hill tribes, and the advantage given them by the use of it is acknowledged by the Nagas themselves. The steadfast retention of their own weapons of offence may be considered as one strong mark of nationality, and an indication of a common origin; in it may also be traced the continuance of a long established custom, which could scarcely be preserved amongst tribes now so diverse, and that too, contrary to all the dictates of experience, were it not possessed of some sanctity, or consecrated in their recollection as the weapon of their forefathers. Their shield consists of a long mat, lined inside with leather or thin boards.

In general, neither men nor women make use of any superabundance of dress. To some of the tribes in the interior ranges, nature has not even suggested any idea of impropriety in being altogether uncovered, whilst those tribes that see the necessity of it, are satisfied with a very slight covering, and in some cases scarcely compatible with decency. The cloths in use by the Nagas are made of cotton, usually woven in small breadths by the women, and dyed with various colours. The women wear a short frock, generally dyed blue, and have their necks and arms ornamented with beads and brass rings.

The war dress of the Nagas consists in a number of odd contrivances, to give themselves a fierce appearance. They bind up their legs with brogues of parti-coloured rattans, and adorn their heads and necks with bands of the same. On their heads they wear bunches of feathers intermingled with plates of brass, and the horns and teeth of wild animals; and as though their appearance were not sufficiently fantastic, they affix a bunch of hair to supply the deficiency of a tail.

2

THE UNGLEE-CUT

(John Owen, *Notes on the Naga Tribes, in communication with Assam*, 1844, pp. 10 f.)

WHAT strikes the stranger most on entering a Chief's residence is the collection of skulls, both human and of the field, slung around the walls inside. Here repose heads of Chieftains slain in battle, or perhaps coaxingly seduced—from some wrong, real or imaginary—with a view to settlement, and too often treacherously murdered. The following is an instance.

Unglee-Cut—so called by the Assamees from having had one of his fingers removed for committing some error, while premier to the Chieftain, or Bur Khoonbow—hearing that Bangoneea, one of Dant Seegah's sons, was proceeding on an excursion to the Abor ranges, sent to him with a plentiful promise of presents, desiring the messenger to express his deep sorrow that their quarrels should have remained so long unadjusted, merely on account of a few villages, and requested an interview on a certain hill, to which place he would dispatch empowered parties to meet and settle all differences. On Bangoneea's approach to the appointed place, he was surrounded and treacherously murdered, with a number of his followers, by people who had lain in ambush for them.

Happily such records of crime are now less numerous, corrected by the interference of our Government, which has promised protection, on the understanding that all causes of grievance be referred to its officers.

There is an extraordinary value attached to iron by these hardy mountaineers, and they appear with manly pride to think the article to have been discovered, and brought into the shape of weapons, only for warriors.

Their instruments of war are the battle-axe, of which there are three kinds; the handles, two feet in length, covered with a jet black varnish, hold the different-shaped blades. The spear, which is of an usual size, is ornamented with goat's hair, dyed in Munjeeth, and further embellished with narrow strips of rattan of various hues. The shield, three and a half feet long and two feet broad, of a triangular shape, and lined with mats, is impenetrable to the spear and battle-axe, but far from being ball-proof.

It is a curious fact that they do not, like all their neighbours, use the bow and arrow; this distinguishes them as being of an entirely different race from all the others, and assists in tracing them from Tartary or China, rather than from Bootan;—for, this fatal instrument, when poisoned with Be, a Mishmee herb, deals in the hands of a Singphoe active death around. Such a value do the Nagas attach to their *daws* and spears, that one would almost imagine them to have been consecrated by some great unknown. The battle-axe is his companion whether asleep or awake, in sanguinary conflict, in his agricultural pursuits, and in the domestic exercise of making a basket, or shaping out a wooden ornament.

In expectation of an attack they collect strong slips of bamboos which they cut into lengths of eight and ten inches, and finely point either end, one of which is impregnated with the fatal Be, while the other is inserted in the ground amongst the grass, near the approach to the village, where it is imperceptible to the eager invader. Along the passes they are likewise planted, and as the cautious Naga crouches to the place of attack in the depth of night, one by one falls to the ground and meets instantaneous death, with little if any suffering. This stratagem is invariably resorted to.

The more timid, and inhabitants of less populated villages, in anticipation of danger, to prevent the enemy's approach, knock down all the trees on each side of the pathway, leading from the main one to the village—so as effectually to block up all chance of ingress; and so cunningly is it executed, that in many cases, although the enemy may be well acquainted with the neighbourhood, they become so perplexed by the delay, as to find the day dawn, when they fly to the forests, and often superstitiously fear to renew the attack.

3

A SINGULAR MARRIAGE PRESENT

(E. T. Dalton, *Descriptive Ethnology of Bengal*, 1872, pp. 39 ff.)

THE Nagas east of the Doyang river are divided into great clans under hereditary Chiefs, who appear to exercise great influence over their people. They live in large villages, some of not less than 300 houses. The villages occupy commanding and secure positions on the peaks or ridges of hills, the spurs or approaches to which are fortified, and the steep places made as inaccessible as possible.

The houses of the Chiefs are of great size; that of the Sangnoi Chief was found to be 250 to 300 feet in length, a well-constructed building occupying the centre and highest position in the village as the manor house. The houses of the common people are very much smaller, but still considerable and substantial buildings. I find no written description of any of these houses, and so many years have elapsed since I saw one, that I cannot altogether trust to my memory.

In front of the Chief's house, as well as inside it, are numerous trophies of the chase and memorials of feasts, and in a separate house, dedicated to the collection, memorials of ferocity and vengeance—human skulls arranged in shelves like books, the records of recent achievements, and baskets full of fragments of skulls, the memorials of the bloody deeds of their forefathers.

On our assuming the government of Upper Assam, attention was soon directed to the cold-blooded murders committed by the Nagas on British subjects, and several expeditions to their hills were undertaken with the view of putting a stop to the practice. We thus became acquainted with various tribes of Abor Nagas as the Mithun, Tablong, Changnoi, Mulong, and Joboka. The Namsangyas, Bordwarias and Paidwarias, Soto, and others, had been previously in the habit of peaceful intercourse with the people of the plains.

It was the custom of these clans to allow matrimony to those only who made themselves as hideous as possible by having the faces elaborately tattooed. The process of disfiguration is carried to such a length, that it has given them an unnatural darkness of complexion and that fearful look which results when a white man blackens his face.

To this rite of disfiguration they are not admitted till they have taken a human scalp or a skull, or shared in some expedition in which scalps or skulls were taken. It is by no means essential that the skulls or scalps should be trophies of honourable warfare, or that they should even be taken from the bodies of declared enemies. A skull may be acquired by the blackest treachery, but so long as the victim was not a member of the clan, it is accepted as a chivalrous offering of a true knight to his lady.

The various tribes were gradually induced to enter into engagements to give up the horrible custom; but how, in refraining from it, they satisfied the cravings of the young women for this singular marriage present I know not.

The communications between friendly villages in the interior of the Naga Hills are admirably kept up. The paths are of course steep and difficult, but considerable engineering skill is sometimes shown in zig-zagging and bridging them. Much of the cultivation in the villages is of a permanent character, terraced and irrigated, but the glorious forests are very wantonly destroyed for the dry crops. They appear to have no superstitious dread of the sylvan deities like the Abors to restrain them. The trees are not cut down, but they are tortured by the ringing process till they are leafless and dry, then set fire to, and the cleared ground, scraped and sown, yields sufficient crops for a year or two.

The approaches to the village are often carefully planted with mango and jack trees and bamboos, and under the shade of these groves are miniature houses which contain or cover the bones of their dead. At least it was the custom of the Nagas of the interior between the Deko and Dihing rivers, thus finally to dispose of them.

4

A REVIEW OR SHAM FIGHT

(E. T. Dalton, *Descriptive Ethnology of Bengal*, 1872, pp. 41 f.)

THE Naga war dances commence with a review or sham fight. I witnessed one at Sangnoi, in which vast numbers were engaged. The warriors are armed with a spear used as a javelin, a battle-axe or *dao*, and a shield of buffalo hide or of bamboo work covered with tiger or other skin, large enough to cover the whole person.

They advance in extended order, making admirable light infantry practice, for nothing can be seen but the black shields creeping along the ground. They are thus impervious to arrows, but their cover is no protection against a bullet. When sufficiently near to their imaginary enemy, they spring up and fling the spear; this is supposed to take effect; a tuft of grass represents the head of the dead foe; they seize it with the left hand, cut it out with the battle-axe, and retreat with the clod hanging by the grass over their shoulder as the skull or scalp. A sort of triumphant song and dance in which the women join follows this.

5

THE FEATURE OF SURPRISE

(S. E. Peal, 'Notes on a visit to the Tribes inhabiting the Hills south of Sibsagar', *J.A.S.B.*, 1872, Vol. XLI, pp. 25 ff.)

THE raids and isolated murders for which this large tract of country is so celebrated, have one feature in common, viz., surprise. Cover is so universal, and favourable to the attack, that advantage is invariably taken of it until the last moment. As a rule, when a whole tribe is at war, the cause is a general one. One Rajah or tribe has been grossly insulted by another. In such cases a *chang* may be surprised and burnt by a combination of several villages. In other cases a single village of one tribe is at war with another village of a different tribe, without involving the other villages in hostilities. Bor Muton may be at war with Unu, and not involve Kuluns or Longhong. Or again, what is a common form, the young and untattooed men of three or four villages of say two distinct tribes may combine, and, headed by a few older men, quietly traverse the jungles to a more distant tribe and village, and suddenly attack the people in their cultivation, the object being simply heads.

Returning to the Banparas, I may say that with regard to weapons, they use, like most Nagas, the *jattie* or spear, and the *dhao*. They also use the cross-bow. I see that Robinson lays great stress on their not having bows and arrows; he considers its total disuse a very singular circumstance, and draws rather weighty conclusions from it. It is not, I hear, of recent date. In the use of the *jattie* they seem clumsy and bad shots; I have tried batches of several tribes at a mark for prizes, but found them unable to reach eighty yards. Nor could they touch a sack of straw for half an hour at sixty yards (where I volunteered to go and be shot at), but at forty yards one did succeed.

Captain Norton says in his book on *Projectiles*, that he could once throw a spear a hundred and seventy yards, and saw the wife of an Australian Chief throw one a hundred and twenty yards; hence the Nagas do not seem very formidable on this score. They use their *jatties* for close work, usually from ambush, and never attack in the open.

The *dhao* is used as a hatchet or mace, and held by both hands. One blow is usually enough, if fairly given in a fight, as they can cut with tremendous force. The jungle is so thick and common, that their warfare is wholly by ambush and surprise, and this gives the *dhao* great advantages.

The bow is chiefly used for game and pigs.

They have a shield, or *phor*, made of buffalo or boar skin, and often ornamented by goat's hair dyed scarlet, or by cowries. It figures in their war dances, but I suspect is not much used elsewhere, unless in a premeditated onslaught.

Like most savages, the Naga seems to aim at making himself look as hideous as possible, and their decorations at times of festivity have solely that object. Their head-gear seems generally to have some bunches of hair fastened to long light stems so as to jerk about while moving. It is the hair of the man or woman who has been killed; and in all cases, I think, is human hair, if not of an enemy. But there seems no one particular head-gear which all adopt; on the contrary, there is infinite variety; and one who can dress or look more hideous than his neighbour, is at perfect liberty to do so.

The Chiefs often wear a long dark blue coat like a dressing-gown not tied, that contrasts strongly with their usually nude condition. Assamese cloths are also bought, and worn by the Nagas who can afford the luxury, during the cold season, but those who cannot, wear the little scrap commonly seen at all times and about the size of foolscap. Women wear an equally scanty morsel, which in some tribes, I hear, is even dispensed with. Pewter, or red cane bracelets or armlets are considered of far greater value and moment. As far as we could see, the women wear no head-gear at all, and about half have the hair cropped short.

The bunches of hair and feathers on the *topis* are all usually mounted on thin slips of buffalo horn exactly like whale bones.

Of trade there is little or none. With the exception of the salt mines or springs eastward, and some *pan* and *kachchus* brought in exchange for rice, there is no such thing as trade. The tribes are too poor to be able to trade, and the constant state of warfare renders commerce impossible. On concluding a peace, some *dhaos* and Abor cloths change hands, or a *mitton*; but as a rule, the border tribes act as a most effectual barrier to all attempt at commercial transactions with those beyond.

It may be worth noting that the border tribes have now lost the art of weaving, or very nearly so, as the little scraps of cloth they require are procured in Assam; while the Abors are able to weave very pretty, though coarse, pieces of parti-coloured cloth, as they cannot trade with Assam.

6

THE NINU TRAGEDY[1]

(Report by W. F. Badgley, in *General Report on the Topographical Surveys of India, 1874–5*, 1876, pp. 51 ff.)

I HAVE the honour to inform you that on Monday, the 1st February 1875, we arrived at Ninu (an Abor[2] village four marches from the plains). I was detained as usual by survey work on the road, and did not pass through the village till some time after Lieutenant

[1] This extract and the next describe the tragedy which befell Holcombe's survey party and the measures which were taken to avenge it. The story is summarized by Shakespear in his *History of the Assam Rifles*, pp. 112 f. and 143. Captain Butler, with the engineer Woodthorpe, author of the succeeding passage, and a party of surveyors and a strong escort, began work in the Naga Hills working eastward through the Lhota and Ao country. They met with hostility at Wokka, but strong action quickly changed the situation until in March 1875 the party was summoned to what is now the Tirap Frontier Division to assist in punishing a crime of grave importance.

For while Butler and Woodthorpe had been moving east through the Naga Hills, another survey party led by Captain Badgley and Lieutenant Holcombe (who was then Assistant Commissioner of Sibsagar) was working west in order to define the boundaries of administration between Sibsagar and the Naga Hills. On their arrival at Ninu, however, the tragedy described above occurred. Almost at once a military expedition set out to avenge the massacre: it was commanded by Brigadier Nuthall who came with Butler from the Naga Hills with a strong force. Senua was taken and destroyed, and Ninu, Nisa and Lonkai were also burnt. Shakespear considers that 'nothing like adequate punishment for such gross treachery was inflicted', that the expedition was futile, and that 'it left the hills far too quickly to have made any real impression on the tribe'. Indeed before the year was out another expedition had to be sent to destroy Ninu, which had been rebuilt, yet again. Butler and Woodthorpe continued their survey operations, but in December of the same year Butler was ambushed and killed in a Lhota village.

[2] At this time the words 'Abor', 'Dafla' and 'Naga' were used indiscriminately. Ninu is a Wancho village in what is now the Tirap Frontier Division.

Holcombe and the rest of the camp. The people seemed sulky, but Lieutenant Holcombe said they were frightened, and did not come out of their houses at all when he came through. In the evening some of the headmen brought a small present of rice, fowls, and roots. They were told not to be afraid, to bring more in the morning, and that the whole village was to come and see us. About sunrise next morning there were a number of Nagas in camp. Sitting in my tent I heard one of the headmen say to Lieutenant Holcombe: 'The Raja (village headman) is there, but is afraid of the gun.' Lieutenant Holcombe took the rifle from the sentry and gave it to the Naga, who then began to laugh and dance with the gun on his left shoulder, flashing his *dao* in his right hand. Lieutenant Holcombe then turned apparently to draw the sentry's bayonet, when one of the young Nagas felled him with a blow from behind on the side of the head. There was a yell raised all through the camp. I sprang up to draw my pistol hanging to the back pole of the tent, as several of them rushed in. Firing into them, I made my way out behind (my tent providentially being made to open at both ends), and was followed by two of them, whose blows I avoided as well as I could, firing meanwhile, when at the moment I fired the fourth shot I tripped over a stump and fell. When I got on my feet again the men had disappeared, and a wail was rising from the camp instead of the cries and shouts of a moment before. Running to where Lieutenant Holcombe lay, I found him with two cross cuts on the right side of the head exposing the brain, the sentry near him with his head hanging by a strip of skin. I ran on to the Sepoys' lines, where I found a few men firing at the retreating Nagas, and getting a rifle did what I could in revenge, which I think nothing should satisfy for the work of that one minute of treachery, which cost us the lives of eighty men, and such a fine and kind-hearted young officer, than the extermination of the whole tribe of those who were engaged in it. I did not know till it was all over that I had not escaped scot-free, so little do sharp cuts pain at first, but I found that I had a cut on each arm and each leg, the worst on the inside of the right thigh which I expect will keep me quiet for some time to come.

My escape I can only suppose to have been through having killed the leading man attacking me with my last pistol-shot, when his second, seeing me fall and thinking I was done for, carried him off according to Naga custom. I encouraged my men; the camp was searched for wounded, arms and ammunitions; each person was told to take a little rice with him; the unwounded coolies were told off to carry the wounded and such things as it was important to save, and I called on the men to advance with me against the village. But they had been too much shaken and refused, and entreated me to lead them in the opposite direction. The Havildar, a noisy Hindustani, would do nothing to assist me in controlling them, and as whatever was to be done must be done quickly, I was obliged, which I shall always regret, to choose to retire, though now on consideration I think that that was the wisest course.

We seemed a mere handful, overladen with spare ammunition and encumbered with wounded and coolies, and the arguments against attacking the place, that more than half the guns had been taken, that we were nearly all wounded, and that the village would have been specially prepared for defence, were not to be answered. There was a spur to the west leading down to the Disang, above where we crossed it on our march from Sanua to Ninu, which was for the most part cleared for cultivation, and I saw my way to getting by a pretty open route up to and past Sanua. The Nagas followed and surrounded us, but we killed some and drove them off, and dispersed a last party who were making a rush at us, when we reached the wide bed of the Disang, after which we saw no more of them, which I think proves my suspicion, that an ambush was prepared for us on the direct path, to be correct.

The march along the winding stony river was most slow and toilsome, and we did not get to the Sanua spur till nightfall. Two of the wounded had died on the way. We cut our path for some way through the jungle to where the spur was clear, and after following the cultivation path some way, turned to the left to pass under Sanua: all this took up much time. The jungle was thick, and the side of the hill very steep and of loose slippery shale, and when the morning star rose, I saw that it would be impossible to pass unobserved, so gave the party an hour's sleep. At dawn we took up a good position near the village, and were soon seen from all sides. The Sanua men swarmed down, but I warned them, through a Naga with me, not to come near, and they gave way as we went on. They tried to persuade me to pass through the village, even going through the pantomime of exhorting their headmen to induce me to do so. Passing round the village we found at our old camp a Khalasi and three coolies of the party who had brought up a post. Here I had intended to have halted and waited for relief, sending off the wounded, but fortunately one of the three coolies was strong enough to carry me, which was most fortunate, as my wounds had become most painful and stiff, and had given me fever and a swelling in the groin, so that I could not have walked further. So after resting from eight to two, we marched and encamped near Bor-Bansang. On the 4th we passed through Bor-Bansang and Bor-Mutan (where we got food for the first time); continuing through the night we reached Borwasali on the afternoon of the 5th, and arrived at Jaipur next day.

7

A PUNITIVE EXPEDITION IN 1875

(Narrative Report of R. G. Woodthorpe, Naga Hills Expeditionary Survey, in *General Report on the Topographical Surveys of India, 1874–5*, 1876, pp. 58 ff.)

WE halted at Assiriugia[1] on the 7th of February (1875) to enable me to visit the villages of Chang-chang and Lakhu, and complete the survey of that range towards Japu. We marched on to Kampunga on the 8th; the day was very foggy, and we did very little work. Our next march was to Deka Haimong, and as we were running short of supplies, two villages we had lately visited having been unable to give as much rice as we required, Captain Butler determined not to remain at Kampungia, but to go on to Deka Haimong, whence he could send down to Amguri tea garden for rice to fill up all our spare bags, a proceeding all the more necessary, as you had told us that in the country we were about to visit, no rice was grown, the Nagas there subsisting principally on *kutchus* (a species of yam).

[1] In the earlier part of his narrative, Woodthorpe describes the adventures of his party at Wokka and other places in the Naga Hills, where they had been on tour since 31st November 1874.

I found that three young planters from Amguri had just arrived to spend a day in camp with us; we were very pleased to see them, and not less so, as they brought up a large supply of beer, potatoes, cabbages, and other vegetables for us, all of which were absolute luxuries to us, and a pleasing change on the monotony of *kutchus*, the only kind of vegetable we can rely on getting in these hills. We should have been a very happy party had they not also brought up the news of the sad disaster to the other survey party, of which only vague accounts had then reached Amguri, the only thing certain being that poor Holcombe was killed. No one knew where the attack had been made, nor what had become of you. On the 11th I visited the mark which Mr McCay had put up, and in the afternoon went to Baru Haimong. On the 12th, Captain Butler, having arranged the day before for daks from Amguri, started for Sibsagar to find out further particulars of the massacre and to offer the services of our party if required to assist your party. He returned again on the 13th, but the same evening's dak brought letters from the Chief Commissioner, the contents of which made Captain Butler anxious to see him if possible, and on the 14th he again started for Sibsagar, remaining there till the 17th. Mr McCay and myself had taken all our observations and finished all the plane-tabling we could get in the neighbourhood by that date. Captain Butler brought with him instructions to close our survey work and join the punitive expedition about to proceed against the Eastern Nagas.

In the evening our coolies celebrated the order to march by a grand dance before our camp-fire. The Khasias first set the example; two or three of the youngest personated females, arranging their clothes in admirable imitation of the Khasia women's dress, and demurely casting down their eyes began the dance *a la femme*. The motion is very slow, the body and arms being kept perfectly steady, and feet seeming to ripple about; a dozen men danced round these ladies with a much more energetic movement of arms and legs, waving cloths in the air and at intervals bursting into a few wild snatches of song. While this was going on we heard the notes of a small drum accompanied by low deep singing, rather chanting, gradually approaching, and I recognized these sounds as the prelude to a Kuki dance, the Lushais having once favoured us with an entertainment. The Kukis to the number of about fifteen came slowly, but irresistibly onwards, swamping the unfortunate Khasias, who from performers suddenly found themselves deposed to spectators. Only three Kukis engaged in the dance, all the rest standing round, beating the drums (which they had borrowed from the villagers with whom our coolies had become extremely friendly) and keeping up a continuous and slightly monotonous but singularly impressive chant the whole time. The performers were supposed to be two women and one man; the latter danced face to face with one of the women, while the other kept close behind him, following his every movement apparently with the object of not being seen by him. Whether she was supposed to be his wife jealously watching his flirtations with the other danseuse, or his mother interested in the success of her son's courtship, I did not discover. After some time the music and dancing became quicker, and at length amid shouts which were interpreted to mean 'let them be united' the performance came to a close. The night was very fine with a bright moon, and the scene was a most picturesque one, the moonlight and fire-light struggling together on the crowd of figures, representations of many tribes and races in the foreground, the quiet village with its tall *morangs* standing up above them sharply defined against the clear sky. The Kukis drummed themselves back again to their huts just within the stockade, and soon all was still, save when at intervals during the night the village watchers sounded the big drum. They say this is beaten occasionally in case any enemy is approaching to attack the village. On hearing the drum the foe remarks: 'They are on the alert there, it's no use going on any further to-night,' and returns to his own village.

On the 18th February we marched out of Deka Haimong to Naogaon, and the next day arrived at Kanching and visited your mark there in the afternoon, getting a few observations. The next morning, having explored the range west from Kanching for about four miles, I returned and descended to Gelekie tea garden; here I met Mr McCay, who had been to take an angle at the Kanching H. S., which we had not been able to observe the night before, and after being hospitably entertained by the gentleman in charge of the gardens, we went on together to Nazera where we found Captain Butler. The next day we continued our march and arrived at Buruarchati on the 24th February. The kind assistance of all the planters along our route, who each and all helped us in many possible ways, alone enabled our coolies to accomplish the long and trying marches in so short a time, the road in many places being ankle-deep in mud.

Arrived at Buruarchati we found that the troops would not be there before the 1st March. Major Tulloch with a detachment of the 44th Regiment had been there some time, and huts and lines had been built in a large open rice-field which even then was sloppy in many places and moist in all. I received letters from you, telling me that you had obtained permission for Mr Chennell to accompany the troops, and that he would join me when the troops marched in, bringing with him the plane-tables, &c., necessary to carry on the survey of the Eastern Naga Hills. Captain Butler went into Dibrugarh on the 25th and returned on the 28th, and hearing from him that he had not seen Mr Chennell with the troops, I walked into Jaipur, at which place the latter were to arrive that day to find out where he was and make arrangements for his following me into the hills. Captain Butler was going on to Bor-Mutan ahead of the troops, and I was anxious to join him there as soon as possible, as there was much to be done in that immediate neighbourhood. Arrived at Jaipur I found, to my relief, that Mr Chennell had overtaken the troops and was there. The Chief Commissioner's orders were that the survey party could go on only if our coolies were not required by the military, in which case we were to remain in the plains, making over our Khasias to the troops. At first permission to go into the hills had only been accorded in any case to Mr Chennell and myself, but there was nothing for Mr McCay to do elsewhere, as all survey work had been stopped, and I could not obtain permission for him even to survey the small gap near Samaguting. While at Jaipur I had an opportunity of talking all these matters over with Colonel Nuttall, whom I found in command, and I was very glad to hear that I should be able to keep as many coolies as I required for myself, Mr Chennell and Mr McCay, for whom I also obtained permission to accompany us, and I gave him a board on the quarter-inch scale, as we did not know how far we might go in after the offending tribes, and it was just possible that we might be able to ascend some of the peaks of the Patkai.

I returned to Buruarchati on the 1st, and on the 2nd we marched to Bor-Mutan, where Colonel Nuttall and Major Heathcote,

Assistant Quarter-Master General, arrived the same day; the troops and Cooly Corps followed in various detachments, but unavoidable delays occurred in getting up the necessary amount of supplies, and we remained at Bor-Mutan till the 13th March 1875....

On the 13th March, a very wet and cold day, we marched to Bor-Bansang. Huts had been built for us by the villagers who evinced great friendliness, and on the following morning a large number assembled to see us start. It was very doubtful whether we should be opposed or not at Senua, which was to be our halting place that night, but the Bansang Chief went through an expressive pantomime, intimating that the Senua men would shoot us with guns, bows and arrows, that they would spear us and cut off our heads, but that he had no fear for our ultimate success, and saw us depart with a farewell flourish of his arms, which, being interpreted, meant 'go in and win'. We marched on and on through open fields and jungly ravines without seeing anything of our foe and passed the old survey camp, several huts in which were still standing, and on the hill to the left the mark put up by you was to our astonishment still intact. About midday we arrived within hail of the village, and came suddenly upon a party of Nagas, who cried, 'Is it peace?' to which the reply was a demand for the Chief of Senua to appear before Colonel Nuttall. This they promised he should do, and we halted. After some time, Sombang, the Vangam or Chief, appeared and came down to where we were. He was questioned about the massacre, and admitted that five men of Senua had been concerned, but contrary to his orders, in the tragedy at Ninu, and had brought back four guns, but no heads. He added that he had prevented a party of coolies with *russad* and daks for the survey from going on to Ninu on the morning of the 2nd February, and had thus saved them from destruction. Colonel Nuttall and Captain Butler had from previous evidence decided that Senua had not as a village been concerned in the massacre, and that if we were not opposed here, the surrender of the five men and the four guns would be sufficient punishment. These terms were explained to the Chief, who promised to comply with them, and sent back two men who had come down with him to the village, he himself being detained. Senua is situated on a very strong and commanding position, the ground falling precipitously three or four hundred feet on three sides. On the north and west, the ground below this fall is gently undulating, and here we were halted, and we could see that the approaches to the village had been strongly stockaded, and behind each defence large numbers of fully armed men were collected and especially on what might be called the citadel, where the Chief's large house stood, on the highest part of the village, a fine plateau of rock capable of a very strong defence, being almost inaccessible on three sides and shelving away gradually to the fields on the fourth. We waited nearly for about an hour and a half, during which time the Chief shouted pathetic appeals to his men to do what he had promised and procure his release, but without avail, and so we received the order to advance on the village. Colonel Nuttall with the 44th and Naga Police advancing by the north, and Colonel Sherriff with the 42nd making a detour to the west, to take the village in flank in case of opposition. The former route was a very difficult one, two strong stockades having to be broken through and two nasty *panjied* ditches to be crossed, but at length we reached the village, the Nagas falling back to the high plateau before mentioned. Further parley ensued without any better result, and we finally took possession of the plateau, the villagers retreating to the jungles; Colonel Sherriff had got round quickly by a comparatively easy path and joined us on the plateau, many of the houses on which had a deserted appearance; probably the owners who had built temporary huts in the jungles, not knowing how things might go with their villages, had left them at the first intimation of the preparations at Buruarchati. Camp was formed at once, some of the houses being told off for the sepoys and coolies, and others on the slope pulled down to prevent surprise from that side. Under the big tree in the centre of our camp we found six heads in a row of small baskets set upon bamboos. Adal Sing, your chuprassi, told us they were there when you passed through Senua, and a closer examination revealing tattooed faces showed that they were Naga heads. We got a little work done this afternoon from a small hill near Senua, whence we could see all the implicated villages.

We halted at Senua on the 15th; it was showery and foggy all day. During the morning three guns were sent in by the villagers, and a man coming in with food for the Chief was recognized as one of the offenders and secured, and later on the Borduarias and Namsangias (many of whom were accompanying us as guides, &c.)

captured Nokdon, or leader in the attack of the 2nd February, and another. Adal Sing on that day had escaped a blow aimed at his head in a most wonderful manner, the *dao* slung off only a small patch of skin and with it the sacred tuft. When Nokdon was brought in, Adal Singh went up to him, showed him the scar on his head, then turning round shook his fist in Nokdon's face, and by an unmistakable piece of pantomime expressed to Nokdon his hope that he would be hanged, then he returned with a satisfied air to his breakfast. Nokdon pointed out Lieutenant Holcombe's double-barrelled gun concealed in some grass hard by. The Senua Chief was granted his liberty during the day, with the understanding that he was to bring in the other men on our return to Senua, which place was to be held during our absence by Lieutenant Abbott with eighty men of the 42nd.

The 16th February dawned dark and wet, and as light increased there seemed little chance of any break in the steady downpour for several hours at least. About 8 o'clock the troops marched out of the village to the Dili River, which we reached about 11 a.m. It was very much swollen, and the turbid waters were rushing angrily past the low, stony tongue on which we assembled, gazing despairingly at the torrent through which it was impossible to wade. Some rafts were moored on the other side, apparently having been used by Nagas to cross on in the early morning, and one of the head-constables volunteered to swim across and bring them back. He got over safely, but failed to steer the raft back through the fierce current, and had to abandon it and save himself by swimming. He was joined by several more volunteers, and other attempts were made unsuccessfully to get the rafts back. They tried next to fell a tree, which if it had fallen across the stream would have given us some foundation for a temporary causeway; but the task was too much for them with their small numbers and having only one hatchet with them. After they had worked for several hours, at the end of which the rain was coming down more pitilessly than ever, and the river having risen two feet since our arrival, Colonel Nuttall decided to return to Senua. The order was given to the six men on the other bank to return, and they got on to the remaining raft and prepared to obey. The raft came down with tremendous velocity, and as the men neared us, who were anxiously watching them, they threw themselves off and struck out for the shore, which they all reached, except one poor fellow, who lost his head or was disabled by striking something, for he turned back as if to regain the raft, and was swept away beyond chance of help, notwithstanding all our endeavours to save him.

On the 17th the sun at length came out, and a large working-party was sent down to try and construct some sort of bridge across the stream. Sending Messrs Chennell and McCay up to the Senua mark to observe and do what plane-tabling they could from there, I went down to the river with Lieutenant Macgregor, 44th, in charge of the working-parties, to assist him in making the bridge. We found that the river had fallen considerably, and about two hundred yards above the point where we had attempted to cross the day before were the remains of an old fishing weir: three large portions of it, one at either bank and one near the middle, still existed, and having stood the rush of the day before, Korom Sing, the head-constable, said if I would leave it to him and the other constables (all of whom are by nature and habit very clever at this sort of work), he thought he could do it. Working-parties were at once told off to get the necessary materials, and the constables, and sometimes Nagas, set to work. The *modus operandi* was as follows. A very short distance in front of the pier, formed by the standing portion of the weir, a strong stake was driven to which two stout bamboos were lashed, the inner ends being firmly secured to the weir, the bamboos being run out horizontally and about two feet apart one above the other. These afforded supports to a man while driving another stake in advance of the first, the bamboos being lashed to this stake, and so on, each stake being strengthened by other men working behind. A similar process was carried on about six feet higher up the river, and when these parallel lines were sufficiently advanced, they were connected by cross-pieces, and a rough roadway constructed and about 4 p.m. we had got a slight framework across to the centre piece of the weir. At 4½, the working-parties were marched up again to Senua, a long and trying ascent; a small guard was left to protect the bridge during the night. A heavy storm came on at 9 p.m., and made us tremble for the work, but fortunately it did not last very long.

On the 18th March, a beautifully fine day, all the troops were once more marched down to the river, and on a flat-open bit of ground close to the bridge camp was formed, and as the river was still unfordable, working-parties were at once detailed to continue the bridge and strengthen that portion already made, and to collect materials, &c. Soon after our arrival the Nagas opened fire on us from the opposite side, fortunately without damage to us, and being promptly replied to were soon silenced, and work proceeded. Everyone worked well, being anxious to reach the opposite bank, whence Ninu was distant only a three hours' march, and by evening the bridge was *un fait accompli*, and a picket was posted on the opposite bank, and early next morning the march on Ninu commenced. A small stream rising close to Ninu flowed into the Dili, just opposite our camp, dividing two long spurs, which forked at the village, a path running along the ridge of each. It had been decided that a column should advance by each of these spurs, taking care to arrive at the village together. The coolies followed under a strong escort, in order to leave this attacking force free. Colonel Nuttall with the 44th under Colonel Cory, and Captain Butler with his police took the eastern route; Colonel Sheriff with the 42nd taking the western route.

As we marched along under burning sun, we saw large numbers of Nagas, in full war-dress, coming down through the fields on our left from Lonkai. We turned a corner, and found ourselves only half a mile from Ninu, which the long grass had hitherto hidden from our sight. As we continued on our way, a column of smoke rose slowly from some houses in front of us; at first we thought that the enemy intended burning their own village, and not making any stand, but seeing that these houses were a few detached from the main village, which would have afforded shelter to our skirmishers covering the attacking party, on the very strong stockade which surrounded the village itself, we gave them credit for their military skill, and hoped they intended to make a good defence, which hope was strengthened by their calling out 'come on; we are quite ready for you', and at once opening fire on us. We had caught glimpses of the 42nd approaching up the other spur; they arrived almost as soon as we did, and were received on their side by a body of Nagas stationed outside the stockade with a volley. When we, on our side, were close up to the stockade the firing ceased, and again an ominous cloud of smoke, followed at once by flames, rose again, this time within the stockade, which the Nagas had now abandoned. Had they stood up a little more boldly and fired more carefully, we must have suffered severely, as our advance was necessarily made over open ground, up very steep approaches, very thickly planted with *panjies*. We clambered over the stockade without delay, but the Nagas were quicker, and before half-a-dozen of us were over, the greater portion of the village was in flames, the Nagas dispersing in every direction. After the fierce heat of the sun, the change to the fiercer heat of the burning houses closely built was not a pleasant one, and we ran through the village as rapidly as possible, our pace being accelerated every now and then as some large house subsided suddenly, threatening to involve us in its fall and covering us with a shower of fire-brands, while the hot, pungent smoke blinded us. At last we were once more clear of the village, and could see the Nagas rapidly retreating along all the slopes in the direction of Nisa, a village four miles distant from Ninu.

The scenery was magnificent; a high, darkly-wooded range behind Ninu descends abruptly for about 1,500 feet, when it suddenly changes its precipices for beautiful open, undulating country, well watered by a succession of clear, babbling streams, at the cool waters of which, in the deep shade of clumps of trees, dotted along their banks, magnificent *methna* quench their thirst; across the Dili, into which these streams all flow, rise other lofty hills wooded along the ridges, but cultivated below on the more gentle slopes, over which the cloud-shadows are lazily moving, and on which numerous villages glitter brightly. To our left the high peaks of the Patkai range lose their outline in the hot and hazy atmosphere; it is a beautiful country and today basking in the still sunlight all is so calm and peaceful before us, it would seem almost impossible that treachery and murder could find a place here; but the black cloud already darkening the sky and changing the blue of the air to a murky brown, the roar of the flames and crashing of timbers behind us, and the thought of the scene of the massacre, which is still before us, remind us of the eternal truth that even in earth's fairest spots the fiercest passions of man may make their home.

Half a mile from the village, we came upon the dreadful spot where the bodies, now little more than skeletons, of our poor friend and his ill-fated companions were still lying in every direction, and our imaginations pictured the fearful incidents of that February morning. Here I joined Major Heathcote and Captain Butler, and with about sixty sepoys we at once followed up the retreating

Nagas to Nisa, which they also fired, escaping into the deep ravines beyond, whither pursuit was useless. Colonels Nuttall and Cory with the 44th, Lieutenant Macgregor, Messrs Chennell and McCay, also came on to Nisa, the rest of the troops under Colonel Sheriff remaining at Ninu. It was fortunate for us that a few houses had escaped the flames in Nisa, as most severe hailstorms raged during the night, against which waterproof sheets would have been as great a protection as brown paper. In the morning all the gutters and ditches in and about the village were full of large hailstones, and when we climbed to the hill-tops in the afternoon, we found them still covered to the depth of several inches, and some of the ravines were filled to a depth of two feet in many places. Small detached parties were out all that afternoon, from Nisa, scouring the jungles all round, climbing up and down in the dense forest which clothed the precipitous faces of the hills, and coming suddenly in the most unexpected places on Naga encampments, sometimes even catching the men engaged in cooking operations. The closeness of the trees and undergrowth saved them from any great loss, though occasionally a quick-eyed sepoy would bowl one over. In some of the huts we found little dogs sleeping calmly before the fires, and in the paths were bamboos of water hastily put down by those who had been carrying them. In one encampment the Nagas had not time to carry off an old woman, but left her in a hollow tree. From all which it will appear that the Nagas imagined themselves perfectly safe in these retreats to which they had removed their property, and never expected us there. While we were thus engaged at Nisa, Colonel Sheriff marched against and burnt Lonkai.

On the 21st the Nisa column started for Kamhua. We had a very long and steep descent to the river, and another long pull-up to Kamhua under a very hot sun. We arrived at the first village about 11; the Nagas as usual, made a very faint show of resistance and we soon entered and burnt it. In the big tree we found a head recognized by the Khasias as one of their race. We proceeded on to the second village and burnt that also without opposition. These villages are well placed on a long spur from the Patkai, and from several knolls and fields I was able to fill in a good deal. We got back soon after dusk to Nisa. The Doctor while at Ninu had been busy examining and classifying the heads, seventy-one in number, which were found in a long basket in the sacred grove in that village, and he came to the conclusion that all of them had been taken after the massacre from our unfortunate people. These heads and all the bones found on the site of the camp were collected and burnt and the ashes buried. On the 24th, I accompanied Captain Butler to Voka, a village close to Patkai, and I managed to complete our work up to that range in this direction. The Voka men received us in a very friendly manner indeed. On the 26th we all left Nisa and joined the others at Ninu. By this time Malmoi had also been burned, Kamhua, Lonkai, &c., revisited, and all the jungles thoroughly scoured, and much of the stolen property recovered. In holes, in trees and such hiding places, we found gongs, sepoys' cooking-pots, waterproof sheets, medals, and even rupees and halves of currency notes, so thorough was the search. The guns were evidently objects of their most jealous care, for we never found one, though we came across small packets of ammunition once or twice. A large number of women and children were captured from time to time, but of course they were released, and though on the first occasion they expected instant death, one, a Nisa woman, requesting that she might be cut up on the site of her own house which she pointed out, yet the news that we respected women and children (though they probably looked on us as fools for doing so) soon spread in the jungles, and I believe the women came to regard a capture as a pleasing little excitement, affording them an opportunity of seeing what manner of men their captors were.

We remained at Ninu till the 31st, and while there I one day visited Khanu and squared up all my work there, the day being exceptionally fine. While we were at Ninu, several guns, including Captain Badgley's double-barrelled rifle and some sepoys' property, were sent in from time to time; the Nagas, bringing them to an open spot on the road through some cultivation which was visible from the camp, deposited them there, retreating precipitately as our men went forward to take possession. On the 31st March we all returned to Senua, and on the 1st April, Niaonu was attacked and burnt, and on the 2nd Mr Chennell and I visited Niaosa about four miles beyond Niaonu and finished our work in that direction. We saw a large number of fully armed Nagas on a spur leading down from the village. We shouted to them that ours was a friendly visit —to which they replied—'If you are friends do not come near us or our village, but go back at once.' We told them that we must go to the village, but that no harm should be done to it or them. They expressed their satisfaction at this, but kept at a respectful distance the whole time. On the 3rd Messrs Chennell, McCay and I marched into Bor-Mutan, the troops, halting one night at the Bor-Bansang, went into Bor-Mutan on the 4th, and on the 7th the last detachment marched out of that camp. Captain Butler and my party halted at Halwagaon at the foot of the hills that night, going on to Boruarchati the next day and leaving that place again on the 8th, and marching daily arrived at Dibrugarh on the 11th. Owing to the continuous and heavy rain which had fallen since the beginning of March, the roads between Boruarchati and Dibrugarh were in a dreadful state, being ankle-deep in mud in the better parts, and in many nearly knee-deep. The coolies consequently had a hard time of it, and many falls resulted, the men and their loads undistinguishable from each other, coming into camp walking mud heaps.

Chapter IV

TRAVELS IN THE PATKAI HILLS

1

A VISIT TO THE BANPARA RAJA[1]

(S. E. Peal, 'Notes on a visit to the Tribes inhabiting the Hills south of Sibsagar', *J.A.S.B.*, 1872, Vol. XLI, pp. 15 ff.)

THE path, at first very steep and up a ferny cleft, soon became more level, and passed round the shoulders and along the ridges of a series of small hills tolerably level in the main, and at a sufficient height to give us a good view of our surroundings. A part of the road had just been cleared for us, or the jungle and grass had been thrown aside, for which we were much obliged to them as the grass was literally dripping with dew. As in Assam, the morning dew here is like a shower, and, on pausing for a moment, it sounded quite loud falling from the trees and jungle.

At about half way to Banpara, we came to a kind of abbatis, at a point that could be easily defended, i.e., a narrow ridge with a precipice on each side, and not more than four or five yards across. The obstruction was commanded by a rise in the ground beyond, on which there was good cover, while there was none on the near side. The fortification could not be seen even from a distance, and was no doubt the best point of defence on the route. There was, however, another point further on where the road for a short distance was cut on the face of a precipice, and only a few inches wide. Here a few determined men could hold any number in check for some time, the precipice being so steep that I plucked a leaf off a tree-top that was fully eighty feet high. We soon after came to the region of Dollu and Wattu bamboos, of which there were immense numbers, and here saw cattle tracks, both cows and buffaloes, and were told they came by the same route as we did, which we could hardly credit.

They here asked our permission to fire a salute, no doubt to warn the Rajah's people of our proximity. We soon after reached the

[1] A summary account of this visit, by Dr Stoliczka, was published three years earlier in the *Proceedings of the Asiatic Society of Bengal*, 1869, pp. 76 ff. The author's name was incorrectly given as A. C. Peal.

first point in the village, finding it a counterpart of Longhong, extremely irregular and broken up, the houses all thatched with *tocoo* leaves, and the centre posts projecting. The jack trees were both large and numerous; we also saw a Naga poison tree, the leaves of which are used to intoxicate fish, an endogen and not unlike an aloe on a long stem. They at once conducted us to the Rajah's house, the largest by far in the *chang*, and also the highest. It was a repetition of all the other houses. We had to climb up a notched tree stem to reach the bamboo floor, and found ourselves at once in the royal presence.

The Rajah seemed a shrewd man, about forty to forty-five years old, tall and, of course, tattooed. He was seated on a sort of huge stool about eight feet by four or five, over which there was a coloured rug of either Indian or English manufacture, certainly not Naga. We were pointed out to a similar sort of bench opposite, at about eight or ten feet distance, where we sat down, glad to get a rest after our toil and to look around us a little. The heir-apparent sat on a smaller throne to the Rajah's right and at some fifteen or twenty feet, a strapping fine young fellow. He had an heir-apparent manner about him which was to some extent very telling, and was decorated *à la Naga*; for with exception of a black cloth flung round him while he sat, he had but a bead and cowrie costume, and was tattooed also of course. The royal brothers of the Rajah were all *en suite*, and sat about Royalty on little three-legged stools, the whole of them with faces of such intense gravity shaded off by a futile attempt at indifference, that they looked supremely ludicrous. Of the brothers we found there were six; we had only heard of two. On the outskirts of this upper ten, sat and stood the sons and nephews, &c., some of them very smart young fellows, and decorated in the most fantastic style, and very few tattooed. In the distance sat the outsiders, and not a few. Most of the Khunsais, Hundekais, and Sowdongs, who could do so, came to see us.

We were now treated to unlimited discourse, several speaking at once, sometimes in Assamese which we could understand, and often in Naga which we could not—chiefly as to how the Rajah had heard of us, and wished to look on us as 'brothers', that I had been some three or four years so near and had never visited him before. The Rajah spoke of the difficulty which his people often had in getting grain, and that they then relied to a great extent on several villages in the plains. We in fact heard that in the Rajah's house alone was there any considerable quantity of grain from last year's crop. Some little stress was laid on our passing 'their *duars*', and we could plainly see that they had but vague ideas regarding their position. We were invited to behold the power and grandeur of the Rajah of Banpara, whose sway extended over several mountains and four villages, i.e., Banpara, Longhong, Unu, and Nokrang, while neighbouring Royalty often was confined to one, and whose warriors were literally countless, at least by Naga numerals.

We were then asked to perform a few miracles, in a general way, with which we immediately complied, firing our revolvers into a large tree stem close by. My friend led off steadily, and when I began he reloaded and kept it up and put five more from my revolving carbine. This was a good beginning, and there was a great deal of wind expended over it in 'wha-wahing', it was considered awful. He then drew fire from heaven, or rather the sun, through a lens of the binoculars. And no amount of persuasion would induce a Naga to hold his hand under the focus. Matches were inquired after, and seemed to yield endless jabbering when struck. I happened to strike one on my waistbelt, having nothing hard enough near, and I afterwards heard that they thought I lit it by simply touching my skin, and that my *deota* must be a 'knowing devil'. A magnet attracting or repelling a needle, even from underneath the paper it lay on, was medicine, and seemed to astonish less than I had expected.

An inspection of the house was then suggested, and it seems the correct thing to sit in audience for a time at one end and then walk through to the other, letting off a few polite ejaculations en route.

The house must have been 200 feet by 50 at least, though perhaps in the centre not over 30 feet high, from the floor. Like most of them, it was built two-thirds on the rock, and one third continued out level by a *chang*, where the ground fell considerably, and was supported on posts. This last is the audience end, and had in this case no gable wall, the roofing being semicircular, so as to keep out wet. For the first fifty or sixty feet where the floor rested on posts, it was like a huge barn inside, and had no partitions, the large jack posts showing well in three rows, one down the centre, and on each side at about fifteen feet. Some of the *marolis*, or horizontal beams (wall plates of the builder) were enormous, fully a foot or a foot and a half thick at the butt end, and some fifty to sixty feet long. How they were ever raised to their places, let alone up such a hill, was a mystery to us, though we were told that men lifted them on their shoulders. On the right-hand wall were hung bones and skulls of pig, deer, *mitton*, buffalo, &c. About fifty or sixty lower jaws of the boar made a fine display all hung in a row, some huge tusks among them—evidently all hung as trophies of 'feasting'.

The central portion of the house through which we next passed appeared to have a series of cattle-pens on each side of a central passage; the floor being rock, it was dark as pitch, and by no means fresh. From the tittering and whispering we heard as we passed or stumbled through, we concluded it was the realm of bliss, and after a hundred feet of it we came out into another large room or hall, dedicated to *dhan* husking and pounding, the huge *ural*, cut out of a solid tree, being placed lengthwise and having places for about forty people to pound at once; the floor was also covered with husks. Here also we saw a small bamboo quad, for refractory youth.

On returning to the audience end, we were told that the Rajah was ready to receive his presents, 'as most of the Khunsais and Hundekais had gone'. So we made our men produce what we had brought, having been previously told by our own people that we must expect them to be dissatisfied, but not to mind it. We had a large purple cloth with broad silver lace for the Rajah, a scarlet shirt, clasp knives, a red blanket, and Rs 20 in cash. The others came in for similar things of less value, but which were reduced by there being six brothers instead of two as we had expected.

No end of palaver followed, and as we had been warned, they wanted more. The Rajah, it seems, had set his heart on a gun. This we assured him was very strictly prohibited, and that we of course dare not give one, and this I had often told them, but no attention was paid to our remark: the way they urged it showed how little they understand us. One of the oldest Sowdongs who has seen three Rajahs, a man I know well, and who understands me better than most Nagas do, got up and made a long speech in Assamese, reiterating all the arguments, and eventually proposing seriously that I should write direct to the 'Maharani', and explain clearly that it was for the Rajah of Banpara, and she would at once accede to the proposition. This was hailed by all as a *coup de grace* for us, and the general buzz as he sat down clearly proved he had brought down the house. To this we had to answer, that if guns were granted to one Rajah, all would claim them, and some were, as he knew, very insignificant, and that we knew no exception would be allowed. A revolver was next tried for, but we said that they were very complicated, often going off when least expected, and killing those dearest, as well as nearest. I was then offered a slave, if I would yield the gun question, and I understood, a slave for life; but this we had to shake our heads over, and look serious.

The palaver continuing, we retired to where a part of the hall had been partitioned off for us by mat walls; under cover of a remark we heard, that if there was much talk, a sahib's head ached. We now enjoyed a little peace, a biscuit, and a cigar, in more privacy. A deputation soon after came in to urge the gun case, but we ordered them out, in a mixed dialect, saying that sahibs were not in the habit of paying taxes this way, and if they only wanted our presents, we should return at once. This had the desired effect. A procession now came up the house, headed by a Khunsai and the Rajah's brother, the former beating a little gong, which was laid before us as a present from his Royal Highness, together with a couple of young goats; but we had been so worried, that we told our people privately, if possible, to forget them when coming away.

A visit to the houses of the chief brothers was next suggested and we started off on a tour. They were all much alike, though smaller than the first: an audience end, open and with trophies of the chase and poison, then a series of the cattle-pens as before mentioned, on each side of a dark passage, and a room at the other end for *dhan* husking with its *ural*. The floor in all rose as we went on, the first portion being a *chang* raised on posts, and matted. We saw here some Abor women or girls, wives of the owners, one of whom, we were told, had cost five buffaloes, and was the daughter of an Abor Rajah. They seemed far more sprightly and intelligent and good looking than Naganis, and could, we thought, understand us far better too; whether they were exceptional cases, I cannot say. They wore the hair in a long queue, tied up with beads and wire, and in many cases it was long, not cropped at all, as is common among Naganis. Costume as usual was at a discount, and as is often said, 'a pocket handkerchief would make four suits'; yet with all this, I doubt if we could beat them in either real modesty or morals, and this applies to Naganis too.

The Morrang (dead-house), or place where the skulls taken in their wars are put, was next visited. It also contained the great drum cut out of a tree stem and hollowed like a boat. I had reason to think that they might have scruples to take us in, and as I had often tried to get a skull, I did not show my interest in it outwardly. Roughly estimated, there were about 350 skulls. About half of them hung up by a string through a hole in the crown, and in the open gable end, the other half lying in a heap on the ground. No lower jaws to be seen, nor hands and feet, as I had expected. The latter are always cut off with the head when a man is killed, and confer another kind of *ak* or decoration. None seemed fractured by a *dao*, and a large number were of young people, or children, being small and smooth.

We were conscious of being face to face with the great cause of this tribal isolation, constant warfare, evidently a custom of great antiquity. As long as social position depends on tattooing, as here, and can only be got by bringing in the head of an enemy, so long shall we have these wars and consequent isolation of clans. The man who brings in a head is no longer called a boy or woman, and can assist in councils of state, so-called. And he seldom goes out on a raid again, I hear. The head he brings is handed to the Rajah, who confers the *ak*, or right of decoration by tattoo, at which there are great feastings, and pigs, cows, or even buffaloes are killed, and no end of *moad* or fermented rice-water is drunk. Those who are not tattooed, when old enough, make a party and lie in wait for stragglers, men, women, or children, anybody in fact with a head on him; and as cover is plentiful, they can get on the enemy's land and lie in ambush alongside his paths, never breaking cover unless certain of success and getting clear off. All those who get heads, get the *ak* on the face; those who get hands and feet, get marks accordingly, for the former on the arms, for the latter on the legs. No two tribes, however, have the marks alike, and some even do not tattoo the face.

The worst of this kind of warfare is that women and children are as often killed as men, without any compunction. I had a smart little fellow here at work for a long time, named 'Allee' (four), and once asked him how he got his *ak*. He said he went out and lay in wait a long time near a spring, and at last a woman came for water, and he crept up behind her, and chopped her on the head, and then cut it off, and got off himself as quickly and quietly as he could. It was utterly incomprehensible to him how such a thing could be unmanly. I found it waste of time and breath trying to convince him.

Besides the skulls, the Morrang also contains the big drum, which is nothing more than a dug-out. It is beaten by short heavy sticks, and can be heard a great distance. The drum from the Muton Chang can be heard here, at least six or seven miles in a direct line. Some are made of a hollow tree with the inside gradually burned out, and open at the ends, some 20 feet long by 3 to 4 feet in diameter.

From here we went back to the Rajah's house, and heard an alarm of fire, which from the general excitement, seems to be rather dreaded. On the *chang* we had a good wash, water being poured out of bamboos. It is here also rather scarce, and I dare say they considered it woeful waste to use it for such a purpose.

Our dinner was now ready, and as it was getting dusk, we went into our apartment, not, however, to dine in private, as we had hoped. Our mat wall contained too many loopholes to be resisted by feminine curiosity, and an audience of thirty or forty had to be submitted to, whose exclamations at every new phase in our proceedings gave us proof of our being among many people who had never before seen a white face. I have no doubt that the *modus operandi* was to them mysterious in the extreme; our candles, tumblers, knives, forks, and spoons, were as good as news in a foreign tongue.

It being now dark, we made preparations to let off a couple of rockets, which I had brought, as a final exhibition. A good site was selected where they could fly over an uninhabited precipice, and yet be seen by the whole village. A bamboo tube guide was soon placed and the fuse lit, after placing the Rajah's party where it could be well seen. The fuse, however, went out and had to be re-lit, when the rocket flew off beautifully, just in the direction I had wished. A gun had been fired to warn the pykes to be on the look-out, and we heard a hum of exclamations at once. After about five minutes, I fired the other and it flew, if anything, higher than the first, and burst well, the stars coming out well too; a piece of the case kept burning just long enough to let them see their value.

It was evident they were in mortal dread, as they told us that they were all very sleepy. I afterwards heard that the rockets were looked on as two devils, which I do not wonder at. As a 'peace-offering' they were very valuable, I have no doubt. Our audience had to be turned away at last, as they showed signs of staying by us all night, and we went to sleep. We were disturbed about two or three hours after by a torch being thrust in, and found we were being 'interviewed' by some fresh arrivals from another *chang*. To this we responded in Anglo-Saxon and Assamese adjectives, and had them bundled out, and got peace at last.

2

A TOUR DIARY OF 1879

(S. E. Peal, 'Report on a visit to the Nongyang Lake, on the Burmese Frontier, February 1879', *J.A.S.B.*, 1881, Vol. L, pp. 1 ff.)

LAST year, I prepared a short note on the old Burmese route over Patkai, via Nongyang, viewed as the most feasible and direct route from India to China, and, having a month's leave in the cold season, I determined to proceed, if possible, to the pass over the Patkai leading to Upper Burmah, report on the same, take altitudes, &c., and explore the Nongyang lake, in the valley of the same name beyond, on the Burmese side of the water-parting.

Permission to travel east and to cross the frontier was kindly given to me by the Chief Commissioner of Assam, in time to enable me to start from Jaipur, on the Dihing river, by the end of January 1879.

Hitherto, on this line of route considerable delay and inconvenience have always been caused to travellers from the want of a sufficient number of trustworthy load-carriers; parties have been detained eight and ten days while the necessary men were collected, and en route exorbitant demands have often been made. At times, as in the cases of Major Sladen's, and Mr Cooper's parties, it completely frustrates all attempts at progress. I therefore secured enough men whom I could rely on as porters before starting. The party consisted of seven picked Bengali coolies, an Assamese orderly and his mate in charge of my arms and instruments, &c., a cook used to camping, a Khampti boatman and his Duania mate, and, subsequently a Singphu guide,—as small a party as possible.

Among us all we could manage to speak English, Hindustani, Bengali, Sonthani, Assamese, Khampti or Shan, Singphu, and Naga.

The lingua franca of the party was Assamese, though as we went east Singphu and then Naga of the Namrup was chiefly spoken to outsiders.

Three Alpine tents, 7 ft. × 7 ft., weighing about 8 lb. each, poles included, enabled us at any moment to camp comfortably and very quickly; at the same time, when rolled up they served as padded poles on which to tie baggage. Six small and extremely light boxes, measuring 10 in. × 12 in. × 18 in. and provided with locks and hinges, served to carry stores, presents and sundries securely, a great object being to avoid bulky and heavy or open packages. As it was desirable to explore the Namtsik river and Nongyang lake, a small dug-out (Rob Roy) was also taken slung on a bamboo between two men, with bedding stowed inside. A Snider carbine, a double-barrelled central-fire No. 12 shot-gun, a revolver, and a Deringer were the arms.

Our first day's march was east to Jaipur, at the junction of the Dhodur Ali with the Dihing river, formerly a place of considerable importance, and likely to become so again. Large steamers can reach it from the Brahmaputra in the rains, and small ones during about eight months of the year. Coal, petroleum, and timber are also to be found in large quantities not far off. It is also the point at which a route from Burmah would practically emerge. Government has wisely reserved large tracts of forest upstream, and already some teak has been planted.

The first care on arrival was to secure a good boat for the heavy stores to go by water up the Dihing, and, this done, an application in person to old Turkong, of the Phakial or Khampti village, secured me a good boatman named Mung, a Khampti who has piloted many up and down this river, who knows all the people, villages, and folk-lore of these parts, and is withal intelligent and communicative. By noon all supplies of rice, tobacco, salt, opium, cloths, &c., were stowed, and six of the men started lightly laden, by land, the rest of us in the large canoe.

Soon after leaving the station of Jaipur we passed up some very beautiful reaches of the river, where the water, deep and still, slowly winds among wooded hills (the gorge in fact), with huge bedded sandstone rocks along the flanks covered by ferns, bamboos, wild plantains, canes, and other products of a subtropical jungle. Towering above all, here and there, rose the great bare branches of dead rubber-trees, once so plentiful and now so rare, a silent protest against reckless tapping.

Some of the reaches are nearly a mile long, water 30 and 40 feet deep, though here and there becoming more shallow and rapid.

At one spot a picturesque pile of rocks, capped by forest trees, divides the stream equally, and is called Hita Tatol, from Sita's *tat-hat*, the weaving-hall in which Sita was found by Ram.

Here and there we passed camps of people who were cutting bamboos to raft down to Jaipur for building, also native boats of the usual small dug-out pattern. Having the Rob Roy, I was enabled to paddle ahead or stay behind sketching, and at one place made a small careful memo of a huge dead rubber-tree that had fallen over into the river,—the trunk and branches resembled a huge dragon.

As rain appeared to be coming on, we camped early at a large high sand-bank, near a rapid called Digoli Gagori. In a very short time we were all comfortably housed, fires blazing under the cooking-pots, and a pile of dry logs got in ready for the night-fire. Our three tents and the boatmen's bivouac were generally so placed as to form a cross, the openings facing a log-fire in the centre that was at once light and heat for all. The assembling round this camp-fire every evening after dinner was generally looked forward to all day. Here we met strangers, heard the local news or stories, the inexhaustible Mung generally giving us the traditions, often illustrated by very creditable maps in the sand. Villagers, if near, always joined our circle, enabling me to collect a large amount of information, or explain the objects of my trip, which is an item of some moment in cases of this nature.

The monotonous rush of the rapid at last was the only sound heard. The night turned out cold and foggy. Once the echoing bark of the little hog-deer roused me, and I put the logs together that had burnt apart. In the early morning the dew-fall was sufficiently heavy to be audible several hundred yards off, the moisture condensed on the higher foliage falling like a steady slow shower on the dried leaves on the ground. Ere starting at 9 a.m. I made all the people cook and eat their breakfasts. At 10 a.m. we passed the mouth of the Namsang river on our right (but the left bank of the river). It rises among the hills of the Namsang Nagas, and near its mouth is a small tea-garden.

More or less scattered up and down the river Dihing, there are names and traditions that unmistakably indicate this as the old Ahom route to and from Burmah,—a highway of the past. The earlier portions of the *History of the Kings of Assam*, detailing the Ahom invasions, clearly enough point to the Dihing river as the line of entry, and Nongyang as the part of the Patkai where they crossed, the name Patkai having originated there.

As we went up the river, the hills on either flank gradually subsided, and gave place to level land, covered with mixed forest, the waterway became shallow and wider, several Duania villages were passed, built more or less after the Singphu pattern, i.e., long sheds of bamboo, the floor raised on small posts. These people are the descendants of Assamese carried off by Singphus some 80 or 100 years ago, and reduced to slavery. Many escaped from Hukong during and after the Burmese wars, and are now located about the Dihing river, speaking both Assamese and Singphu,—dressing like the former, but having the gross superstitions of the latter.

During the day the Namsang Purbot, or hill, was a conspicuous feature in the landscape, generally forming a fine background to the views on the river. Its outline is good, and the colour at times dark green to blue, or even purple, is seen reflected beautifully in the long still reaches of water, with, at times, a wooded island in mid-stream, and a foreground of sand piled in picturesque confusion.

We were in no great hurry, so camped at the Juglo Duania village, the ten or twelve houses of which were placed end on, at a few yards back from the edge of the bank of yellow clay 30 feet high.

Selecting a clean stretch of sand by the water, under the cliff, we soon pitched our tents, and were visited by the headman, who brought the usual little present of fowls, eggs, and some rice. The Rob Roy caused some amusement, and one of the young men paddled it about very creditably, considering it was rather crank, and the stream strong. As usual, great interest was taken in my journey, and routes discussed after dinner. My kerosine wall-lamp, revolver, and guns were duly wondered at, and a tiger happening to announce himself by a loud whistle on the opposite bank, I was enabled to gratify them by a shot from the Snider to frighten it away, the echo rolling through the forest on each side for a long way, and sounding unusually loud and prolonged in the still night. At 9 p.m., the thermometer stood at 65°, and we had a fine night.

In the morning there was a heavy fog, with the usual light west-by-south-west wind, threatening rain; temperature of the Dihing water 68° and air 63°. After all had cooked and eaten we started up-stream between two islands, the river bed becoming wider up to 400 yards. Extensive shallows over sandy bottom often rendered it difficult to keep to the passage, a line of deeper water frequently ending in a wide shallow that compelled all hands to get out, and by sheer force push and drag the canoe to the nearest channel.

Near Poai Muk there were large islands of dry sand in mid-stream, which are evidently well covered in the rains, thus indicating the large body of water that must then be needed to fill the river bed.

It was about here that some forty years ago a small cannon fell into the river during an expedition, and which is now commonly reported to go off with a loud bang under water once every three years.

About 11 a.m. we reached Makum, a village on the right bank, now celebrated for its fort, situated on a clay bluff overhanging the river. A native officer and 20 police are in charge. The plan of the building is a Maltese cross, walls 4 feet thick and 50 feet high, loop-holed in three stories. It was erected by the late General David Reid, R.A., who had long experience on this frontier, and to whom we are indebted for most of the little permanent work of this kind in Eastern Assam. The fort is impregnable to savages like the Nagas. While at Makum I saw old Gubor Jemadar, formerly in charge here, but who is now pensioned. He has great influence among the hill tribes about, and by timely tact has on several occasions saved us from political complications with the Nagas.

After hearing the object of my journey, he quite agreed as to its feasibility and safety, giving me also some valuable information regarding the tract I was about to visit, though he had himself never seen it.

At Makum the Dihing is 350 yards wide, and at this season runs shallow over shingle. Not far off there are valuable beds of coal up to 20 and even 30 feet thick; there are also petroleum springs. The river here takes a huge bend, the concavity facing the Naga Hills opposite to the south. On a fine day the view from the fort, across the river and low forest and lower ranges of hills, is very fine, the higher ranges bordering the basin of the Tirap running behind, at Rangatu, 3,500 feet. Beyond these again lie the hills near Yungbhi and Yugli, and the Patkai in the extreme distance at 5,000 and 6,500 feet, rising here and there to 8,000.

Having made the necessary arrangements as to parcels and letters, we started next morning at 11 a.m., reaching Insa, or Bor Phakial, in the afternoon, and camping on the huge sand below the village. The inhabitants are mostly Khamptis, or Shans, a race from the south-east, who are scattered more or less about near here, their headquarters being at Manchi or Bor Khampti, on the Mli Kha branch of the Upper Irawadi. They speak and write Shan, using the Burmese character, and are Buddhists.

They dress in white or dark blue cotton jackets, have, like the Singphus, a sort of kilt of plaid pattern, dark blue, green, and yellow the prevailing mixture, and round the shoulders wear a large thin *chudar*, or wrap, 10 feet by 3 feet, of some bright red and white check pattern, and a white *pugri*, generally worn in a conical form, covers the characteristic knob of hair on the tops of their heads; their cloths are home-made, like their rude pottery; the manufacture of each can be seen going on daily here and there. Amber ear ornaments are common to both sexes, and the men generally have the so-called Khampti *dao* worn in or on a sheath, slung under the left arm by a cane-loop passing over the right shoulder.

The women now wear clothes more or less like the Assamese, though now and then a Shan costume of dark blue can be seen, skirt and jacket, the latter having a close row of silver buttons, the head covered by a dark blue *pugri* laid on in close coils—a remarkable and pretty *tout ensemble*.

In colour these Khamptis are paler than the Assamese, though at times with a yellowish tinge, the hair and eyes black, and faces clean; the moustache, if worn at all, is generally a failure; high cheek-bones, small eyes, and wide flat noses are the rule, giving the well-known Mongolian cast of features. Both sexes are rather short and stout in build.

After dinner, the elders paid me a visit, and, having been there some ten years before, recognized and welcomed me, and made many inquiries after 'Jenkins Saheb', whom they all remembered. As usual, they were greatly taken with the guns and revolver, the fitting and finish being well appreciated by men who are more or less naturally workers in metal.

The ability to raise and lower rapidly the light from the strong kerosine wall-lamp struck them all as something quite new, and they were equally astonished to learn that the water-like oil was simply their dark petroleum purified.

One and all showed considerable interest in my trip, though, as it was through the Singphu country, no one would join me. I found that Khamptis do not often travel east or south in small parties. At the same time, though none of them had, as far as I could learn, been to Nongyang, some of the old men gave me information regarding those parts that was more correct than that which I obtained from those who should have known far better. This I partly attribute to most Shans being able to read and write, and their being possessed of manuscripts handed down for many generations. As a finale to a pleasant evening, I amused the big and little boys by burning a piece of magnesium tape.

Next morning, while the men were cooking, I was shown all over the village, and the Chang, or sacred house, containing their books, pictures, images, offerings, gongs, &c., and into which I believe no females are allowed. It is a building raised some 7 feet on wooden posts, measures some 35 feet by 50 feet, and with six of the central posts continued up to carry a second central raised roof; the caps of these six columns were carved, and under this raised portion was the shrine with some different sized images of Buddha. At one end hung a large cotton *pardha*, with horizontal rows of very well painted figures, about eight inches high, illustrating their idea of the earth and its inhabitants; near the lower edge there was one group inverted and said to represent the people who lived below us, with their feet upwards! The whole picture was in fair preservation, but from all I could learn, not very old, and executed by a Shan from Burmah, who travelled on to Bor Khampti.

The houses of the people in the village were ranged more or less in lines, and, though long, were parallel, leaving room enough for a road in between each. They were invariably raised platforms with the Jengo roof coming well down over the sides, and arched and rounded end in front, beyond which the platform always projected, so as to enable the people to put things out in the sun and yet be safe from the inevitable pit; it also serves as a sort of semi-public reception place. It seems also a feature of all Naga houses, though not seen among Singphus.

These houses run from 20 feet wide to 100 feet long, contain one family, and, unless large, are often built or re-built in a remarkably short time. While at Bor Phakial the Gaonbura's house was being re-built, and he told me that it would be done in two days by the able-bodied men and lads of the entire community, who during the erection are fed at the owner's expense,—a custom which prevails more or less all over Eastern Bengal, Assam, and the hills adjacent.

Passing up the Dihing now again after an absence of several years, I was struck with several changes. The Bapu, or Khampti yellow-robed priest of Bor Phakial used to teach all the lads to read and write. He had now gone to Burmah, might not return, and the boys could not all read. Again, Nagas are now seen in numbers, and have boats, villages, and lands on the Dihing, where there were formerly none. These people and the Duanias, indeed, seem to be getting more mixed up as time goes on. Kaiyas, or Marwari merchants, or their agents, are now seen at every place of importance, they exchange opium, brass-ware, and clothes for ivory, rubber, and such like. Indirectly, they have been the cause of the extermination of the rubber-trees over large tracts; the ready sale for ivory has also added to the natural tendency among the Nagas to hunt and kill elephants for the sake of their flesh. Not long ago eight elephants that crossed the Patkai were so carefully watched and hunted that only one escaped.

There is now a great want of blacksmiths up the Dihing and *daos* cost double what they did in 1870, which is generally attributed to Government purchasing too indiscriminately. At Bor Phakial, ere I left, some twelve Singphus from Hukong came in en route home from Assam, having sold all their amber. Happening to ask if they knew certain villages, Mbon and Nmphin, I found they were from the first one I named, and I at once had pressing invitations to go and see them on my return, they offering to guarantee my safety. The advantages of our rule to Assam was here, as on some other occasions, dilated upon; security to life and property here contrasting favourably with the insecurity there, where there was no paramount authority.

After breakfast the whole village lined the bank to see me off in the Rob Roy, which seemed to amuse old and young, boys and girls alike.

Passing Bhaigirot, we were joined by a Singphu and his wife and family in a small dug-out, the woman and an infant in the centre under a little bit of curved roof, the man paddling as he steered, while a boy of ten, and a girl of twelve poled at the bows, keeping pace with us easily and crossing shallows we dared not venture near. By 4 o'clock we reached the Tirapmuk, whereat is situated the village and residence of Kherim Gam, the young Chief of the nearest Singphus, whom I knew well, but who was now up at the Namtsik elephant stockade.

The Tirap river falls in on the left bank of the Dihing, after a long course, draining a huge valley along the northern flank of the Patkai, which is densely populated by the Nagas.

A route from this point enters the hills, passing Wadoi, Hongtam, Rangnem, and Yungbhi, crossing the Patkai at 5,000 feet elevation, and afterwards other ridges of similar height, including the Gedak Bum, to emerge at Namyang village in Upper Hukong. It is a long and tedious route, crossing great elevations, and was taken by Griffiths in 1837, there being no carriage via Nongyang. From the Tirap to Namyang takes twelve days generally. In the morning I visited the Gam's houses, a collection of dilapidated sheds, having raised floors, beneath which the pigs luxuriated in unlimited mud. The Gam's mother complained to me, through an interpreter, that the Nats, or evil spirits, tormented her with pains, so I gave her a small present of opium and departed.

As a race, the Singphus are more rude and headstrong than the Khamptis, and would make remarkably good soldiers, like most of these hillmen; the pity is they are not utilized.

Kherim, Gam's brother, paid me a visit as I left in the morning, and said he knew the Gam would be sorry that he had missed me.

En route we had some fine views of the hills to the south and of snowy peaks to the eastward; the river bed was still very wide, shallow, and full of snags above Tirap; how some of the little canoes that shot past down-stream filled with Singphus escaped a capsize was a wonder.

At Ntem we came to the first rapid since leaving Namsang, and a little above it camped on a wide sand, whence a Singphu, a Duania, and a Naga village were visible at once, all quite small and unfortified, showing the security of these parts. Here, again, a tiger came out at night, and prowled about a good deal, as we saw by his tracks in the morning.

By 9 a.m. we were off, after breakfast and a visit to the Duania village, and landed at Saiko at noon, finding the village of six houses nearly deserted. I here saw some very pretty silk ornaments being woven for a bag, but the price, (Rs 10 for 2 square feet) was more than I cared to pay; the loom was a rude little contrivance 2 ft. by 2 ft. by 2 ft., made of some sticks and bamboos.

I here also measured a peculiar kind of bamboo, 22 inches in girth, with close joints, and from 70 to 80 feet high. I hear they are not known wild, and the internodes are made into mugs, jugs, boxes, and such like. The stem is of bluish white colour.

Later in the day we reached the Kherim Pani, or old bed of the Dihing, now more or less silted up. There are two other passages through which the Dihing comes in the rains, i.e. the Mganto and Kasan; from this upwards, the river is called the Namrup.

Selecting a dry sandbank, where there was plenty of fuel, we pitched our camp and made all extra taut and snug, expecting a storm at night, which duly visited us; the thin waterproof sheets, however, kept everything dry, notwithstanding a strong gust or two. At dawn we were all astir. While some of the people cooked, I went with the others to Bisa, about a mile up the Dherim Pani, a place celebrated as the headquarters of the Singphus of our side of the Patkai, and the residence of the late head Gam, Banka. There was little to distinguish it from other Singphu villages,—the same long shed-like house, traces everywhere about of the depth of the mud in the rains, pigs and children. Very few men were to be found, as most of them were out hunting for rubber.

In exchange for some opium, I secured 300 lb. of clean rice, a few fowls and eggs, also a few chillies. Chautong, son of the late Chief, a smart lad of ten or eleven, was pointed out to me, and Chauing, his nephew, a lad of seventeen or eighteen, was a very fair sample of a Singphu, tall, quiet, and obliging. His father, Latua, about sixteen years ago having determined to raid some villages in Hukong, on the Upper Dinoi, departed with his men, saying that, if successful, he would return. As he was not successful, he has not done so to the present time, though he has been frequently asked to come back.

On the way to the boat and camp we found the funeral pyre and monument of the late Chief, a small square enclosure, railed 6 ft. by 6 ft., with pillars at the corners, and long bamboos with strips of cloth dependent, a highly ornamental post in the centre with a kind of carved gilt cap or mitre, split bamboos also at the corners to hold offerings, and a long rich red silk Burmese cloth hung on a bamboo some way off, strips of red and white cloth hung all about on sticks and waved with a curious effect, the jungle forming a background.

On reaching the canoe I gave Chauing a dozen rounds of Snider ammunition to shoot a tiger which was killing their cattle, and started on up the Namrup, finding that the rapids at once became more frequent and difficult. At places we had to clear out a track or passage by rolling the boulders aside ere we could drag the canoe up, a work that we became pretty expert at, and these same passages were again very useful on our return.

At the Singphu village of Sambiang, or Gogo, we landed and secured a guide named Lah, who was known to Mung, our boatman, and was reputed to have influence among the Tkak Nagas. He owned a gun that he desired to fire off 'for luck' ere starting, so sitting on shingle he pulled the trigger several times in vain, as the hammer stuck at half-cock. I advised a hard jerk and turned to go to the canoe. Hearing a fearful bang, I returned and saw the guide's feet and gun pointing skywards through the smoke. He assured me, though in a nervous way, that it was all right, and usually did that when he put in six fingers of powder and two balls!

From hence to Tkak we had three other Singphus travelling with us, and at starting most of us walked over the shingle, gravel, and sand near the river to lighten the boat. I noticed these men at one place busy catching some insects, and found that they were bugs an inch long which lay under the stones, and which had an unmistakable odour. On inquiry, one of them said they were going to eat them as they were a capital substitute for chillies, and asked me to give them a fair trial!

By 4 o'clock we found a good camping-ground near the Nmbai Muk, on the wide dry sands of an *era hute*, open on each side and with high forest behind and in front. Fires were soon blazing, everyone felt comfortable, and dinner was over by sunset. Gradually the moon rose over the tree-tops and lit up the entire scene. While I enjoyed a cigar, the Bengalis did justice to their *tamaku*, Mung and the Singphus lit up their little brass bowl pipes, and we enjoyed the long evening. There seemed few birds or beasts about, the ripple of the rapid not far off yielded the only sound. Then we discussed Nongyang and the routes: none except Lah had been there. Queer stories abounded, such as that the island in the lake floated about and shifted its position with a change of wind. I heard also that the valley had once been densely peopled with Khamongs or Kamjangs, Aitonias, and Turong Turai, who had all left in consequence of raids by the Singphus.

Some of these same Aitonias being now near Golaghat, and the Kamjangs gone to the east, the valley is now-a-days utterly destitute of people. Mung drew some creditable maps on the sand, and seemed to thoroughly understand the relative positions of the various countries, routes, passes, rivers and mountains, with their inhabitants. From all he could learn, the Singphu track via Sitkha was difficult mainly on account of the want of supplies en route, and at best not so easy as that over Patkai. All agreed that the line over Dopha Bum to Manchi from the Upper Dihing was reported both long and difficult, and people very seldom traversed it. After a while, the moon sank, leaving the line of forest opposite strongly marked against the sky. One by one we went to sleep, and all was quiet.

About 6 a.m. we were all astir, boxes packed, camp-chair folded and stowed, tents rolled up, and for once we pushed on before breakfast. A cup of hot coffee and milk with a biscuit was my *chota hazri*. This same prepared coffee and milk is a most useful item, and can be made almost in a moment when milk cannot be procured en route. Here and there we occasionally saw some fine mahsir, 20- and 30-pounders, and I regretted not having tackle.

Fine views of the snow-capped hills to the east were seen ere the mists rose, and Dopha Bum looked beautiful in the early light, the shadows sharp and blue, while the snow was of that peculiar creamy white, so difficult to get out of any colour-box, the sky colour behind all being a clean pale grey. A good telescope, to one travelling eastward is a necessity; without it he misses half the 'sights' of these parts.

About 11 a.m. we passed the Mganto Muk, one of the three old channels of the Dihing, and saw there some huts of elephant-catchers and rubber-cutters. After passing it, we again found the Namrup perceptibly smaller, several long shallows so bad indeed that the men had all to carry their loads ahead and return to drag the canoe over. My Rob Roy, drawing only two inches of course, experienced no such difficulty. Later in the day we passed the entrance to the Nmbai, or Lumbai as some call it, for at times they seem careless which it is. This is not really a river, but a loop from the Namrup which leaves it here and rejoins the main stream above Kherim Pani.

Still later we passed the third channel of the Dihing called the Kasan of the same (right) bank, reaching Namtsik before sunset, and camping on a sand below the huts of the elephant-catchers employed by Mr Vanquelin. He was encamped close by, and paid me a visit, giving some information in reference to routes, and kindly lent me a smaller boat to assist me in getting up the river Namtsik. I was here induced to take the Namtsik and Tkak route via Sonkap, instead of the one straight on via the Namrup, or, as it is here called, Namhuk, the route by which Mr H. L. Jenkins and my brother travelled in 1869.

Next morning we re-arranged the baggage, leaving some needless items till our return, and taking only loads which the men could easily carry in the hills. At first the Namtsik was a succession of deep clear pools, among wooded hills, with rapids at every bend. The timber was remarkably fine, the best I had ever seen. Huge *nahars* (*Mesua ferra*), *mekahi* and *gondserai*, rising here and there to immense heights, certainly 100 feet to the first branch, being 10 and 12 feet, or even 16, in circumference at the base. Large tree-ferns and wild plantains rose above on either side, and creepers hung in profusion everywhere, long lines often hanging down into the water; as a rule everything was beautifully reflected in the still clear water. Eventually we reached a rapid towards 4 o'clock, where an immense rubber-tree overhung a deep pool, but a ledge of shingle intervening, on which there were remains of some huts made by the ubiquitous rubber-cutters; these we speedily demolished, and after levelling the ground, pitched our tents in a line. Somehow this evening in consequence of the gloom, the weird look of the whole place, queer hootings, and a slight drizzle, the party all seemed inclined to the superstitious, and I had to compel them to cook and eat. After they had done so, I issued a small tot of grog to all who would take it, which served to rouse them up. During the night it rained, but, as before, our waterproofs kept us dry.

About 9 a.m. next morning, after all had eaten, we started on, passed some long rapids and shallows, where I had even to get out and tow my Rob Roy. At one place I was ahead looking for deer, and enjoying the beauties of the gorge. Some of the tree-ferns I estimated at 30 feet high. Dead rubber-trees were also seen here and there, the dead arms standing out conspicuously against the clear blue sky overhead or fallen over bodily into the river bed.

Suddenly, on turning a corner, I came on some Naga men and women who were out for *jhuming*; they were all nearly naked, the men wearing a narrow strip of cloth and the women a series of fine cane strips, so girdled as to look like a miniature crinoline that hung down about a foot below the waist, and to which a narrow strip of dirty cloth was fastened horizontally. The women also wore nose-studs (which covered the nostrils) made of pewter, and the size of four- or eight-anna pieces. A profusion of glass beads, as usual, made up for the scantiness of the costume in other ways, and brass wire rings were worn through the upper part of the ear, from which the red and green skins of a small bird depended. Brass wire bracelets, a bead coronet, large red cane loops in the hair, two bone skewers, and shin-rings seemed to complete the outfit. Two lads of sixteen or seventeen were quite nude.

None of them could speak a word of Assamese, and seeing me alone they were considerably astonished, especially as but one or two of them had ever seen a white person before (when the surveyors were there). Though taken aback, they evinced no distrust, and by signs I called the lads to haul my canoe up the top rapid; soon after my followers came up, and my guide could talk to the lads. They were from a village up on the northern flank of the Patkai. The dress and general appearance of these Nagas was almost precisely the same as of those found up the Tirap valley, twenty miles west.

As we ascended the Namtsik it maintained its picturesque look, a succession of deep still pools, often overhung by rock and trees, shallows and rapids here and there blocked by fallen trees, at times long ledges of dark slippery rock with narrow channels, through which the river rushed, making it difficult to get the canoes over.

In places the gorge was almost in twilight, in consequence of the masses of foliage all around and above, where it was not always possible to see much sky. The large whitish trunks of immense trees (*hulong* and *mekai* more especially) here and there rose very conspicuously against the darker background; there were also many large trees that seemed new to us. *Huluks*, or *hylobates*, the black gibbon, were very common, and made the forest echo with their hallooings. The great hornbill, too, was seen in flocks of twenty and thirty at a time, and could easily be heard, as their wings seemed to rasp the air, from a quarter to half a mile off. Otters were common, and made off with a great fuss; no doubt, from the signs we saw, they have a nice time of it.

At one place we came to a huge *mekai* stem hanging or projecting out in the air from the jungle on the left hand; after passing under I got out of the canoe and scrambled up on it; the stem was fully four feet thick, and projected about thirty. On walking back on it and dividing the jungle with my knife, I found it was poised on its centre on an island, and that an equally large portion overhung the other branch of the stream,—it had evidently been carried along and lodged there during some big flood.

Towards the afternoon we began to get glimpses of dark green and blue forest-covered hills not far off to the south, the group of Sonkap Bum on which there were several Naga villages. The highest peak of the ridge is about 3,000 feet, and as it stands well out north of the main range of Patkai, it affords some magnificent views.

At 5 p.m. we arrived at the mouth of a small dark gully, which the guide said was the route to the Tkak Naga villages. Here we camped, and in the early morning arranged all the loads carefully. Three men were then left in charge of the boats, while the rest of us went up to the village.

For some way the path led up the rough and slippery stream bed, subsequently over a level spur, through clearings, where we had to scramble from log to log and walk along large and small tree-stems at all angles of inclination, the ground being as a rule completely hidden under a thick mass of creepers, foliage, and smaller lopped branches, all drying so as to be ready for being set fire to about March.

How the leading men kept the path under such circumstances was wonderful, for no trace of a track of any sort was visible. In some forest beyond we met a Tkak Naga and his young wife, who were rather taken aback on seeing our party. A palaver ensued as to which of the two villages we should go to, and during it we suddenly saw a long string of Nagas advance in single file, and, the path being very narrow and in dense undergrowth, they had to pass us closely. As they went by many spoke to our guide, and some stopped and gave him some tobacco, asking who we were and where we were going, many had flint guns, and all carried the Khampti *dao*. Generally, they passed me hurriedly and seemed more comfortable when they had got by, then turned round, and stared. Those who had loads carried them in a conical basket (the Naga *hura*) by a strap over the forehead; more than half had spears, and all wore the little cane crinoline and small strip of cloth passed between the legs which forces the testes into the abdomen, a usual custom among these Nagas (East). They were not tattooed, and hence looked much paler in the face than do the tribes who live further west. I found they had all been summoned by a Singphu Chief to assist in building him a new house.

After passing through another *jhum* we reached Tkak, a village consisting of ten houses on a spur facing the Nambong valley, where the guide made arrangements for us to stay in the outer end of the headman's house. After an hour's rest, the carriers went back to the boats for the other things, and the whole party came up. While they were away I had breakfast. It was no easy matter communicating with these folks, as the only language they knew besides their own was a little Singphu. Lah, the guide, and Mung, the boatman, however, were generally somewhere at hand to interpret.

The village was evidently not more than five or six years old, as I saw the stumps of the forest trees everywhere about, and often the stems as large logs. The houses were not arranged on any plan, but just built where the owner had a fancy, on a fragment of level eked out by posts, not over 30 or 40 yards apart: no two houses consequently were on the same level or faced the same way. They were more or less on the same pattern as are all the houses of the hill tribes in or about Assam except hose of the Garos and Khasias, i.e. a long bamboo shed, with floor raised on posts some 4 or 5 feet.

It is singular how this custom survives even among people who have left the hills and been resident in the plains for some 500 or

600 years, as for example the Deodhaings, who came in as Ahoms in 1228, and are now seen occupying a few scattered villages not far from the Disang river, in the Sibsagar district. The Aitonias and the Miris also afford other examples. The custom in all cases seems due to the necessity of keeping the floor out of the reach of pigs and goats.

It may be called the 'Pile platform' system, and to some extent marks a race distinction between Aryans and non-Aryans. It is probably the same system which occurs throughout the Malay peninsula, and has latterly been traced in the Swiss lake-dwellings, and present Swiss chalet.

Among the Nagas, where houses have been built on a declivity, I have seen one end of the house only a foot or so raised from the ground, while the other end, supported on bamboos 30 feet long, overhung a fearful gully,—the little platform at the extremity, on which the people sit out and sun themselves and their children, having no rail or protection of any kind.

The people seemed very quiet and civil, but were more or less curious to see our things. While they were examining them we heard a loud wail raised in a house not far off, that made all mute, soon after another, and they all went there in a hurry, gradually joining in the chorus. It turned out most unluckily that the old headman, who had been very ill for some time, took it into his head to die just after our arrival. It made my guide and Mung and the three other Singphus look serious for a while. Guns began to go off, too close to sound pleasant, and were pointed about promiscuously; I began to think matters were getting serious, as the son, a grown man, rushed about demented, yelling and slashing and cutting everything within reach of his *dao*,—floor, walls, baskets, all got a fair share of his fury, an unlucky cock that ran past lost his head, and dogs kept aloof.

Guessing that a good deal of the rumpus was 'a form of sorrow' in these parts, I kept our party as unobtrusive as possible, and in about half an hour the bereaved son came to me, quiet, but crying, and asked for some caps, as they had a nipple-gun which they desired to use in the row. On giving him a few, I remarked that had I known the old gentleman was so nearly dead, I should have gone to the upper village, but he explained that his death had been daily expected for some time, and I must not be put out at the noise and fuss, which

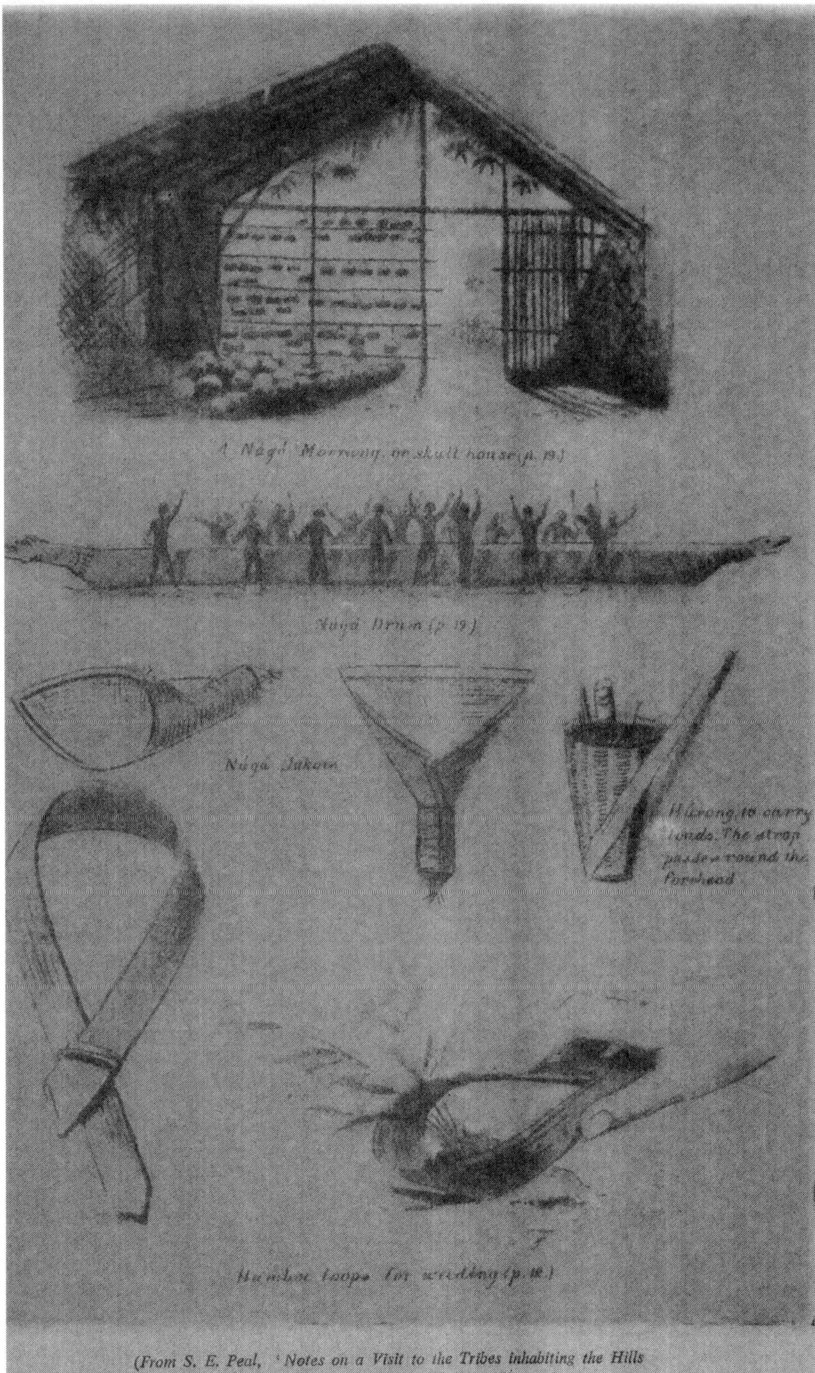

(From S. E. Peal, '*Notes on a Visit to the Tribes inhabiting the Hills south of Sibsagar*', J. A. S. B., 1872)

1. A Naga *morung* and implements

(*From E. T. Dalton,* Descriptive Ethnology of Bengal, 1872)

2. A Chief of the eastern or upper Naga group

(*From E. T. Dalton,* Descriptive Ethnology of Bengal, 1872)

3. A Bor Abor girl, described by Dalton as 'belonging probably to some village near the great Dihong river'

(*From E. T. Dalton*, Descriptive Ethnology of Bengal, 1872)

4. A group of Digaru Mishmis

(*From E. T. Dalton*, Descriptive Ethnology of Bengal, 1872)

5. Chulikata or Idu Mishmi Chief in full dress

(*From E. T. Dalton*, Descriptive Ethnology of Bengal, 1872)

6. Described by Dalton as an 'admirable and thoroughly typical representation of a Tian (Taraon or Digaru) Mishmi girl'

was their custom. He turned out afterwards to be a very decent and intelligent fellow, and rendered me good assistance.

The row still going on, I took my notebook and strolled out by the path towards Patkai. A fine view which I had of the Namtsik valley shewed it to be wide, and filled with low rolling hills and undulating land, and not nearly so steep or high as I had anticipated from the shading on the Government maps, which extend as far as this village.

Patkai here at least presented a high and tolerably level ridge to the south at 3,000 feet up to 6,939 feet at the Maium peak; all seemed deep blue, instead of green, forest-covered to the top, and at some five or ten miles off, the Nambong river below, dividing it from Sonkap, and receiving the drainage from both sides, to flow east and join the Namrup. The six or seven large spurs from Patkai are all included in the prospect.

Early in the evening the men arrived with the remainder of the loads, and I pitched the tent in the usual form on a clear little flat just at the outer edge of the village. After dinner we had a large audience as usual of Nagas, men and women, the latter being in the outer circle. The object of my visit (i.e. to see Nongyang lake) was explained, and routes in various directions discussed. There was but one to the lake from hence, i.e. via the Nambong to Nunki, a stream between two of the large spurs, then across Patkai by the regular and only pass. They made many inquiries regarding 'rubber', and I was able to show it to them in various forms, as waterproof sheet, coat, air-pillow, elastic rings, &c. It was little wonder that they were interested, inasmuch as till about a year ago any enterprising Naga could earn 2 to 4 rupees a day by its collection, and both the inhabited and uninhabited tracts on each side of Patkai had been explored.

Here, as before, remarks were freely made in favour of our Raj, which was favourably contrasted with the state of insecurity known to exist in Upper Burmah, and here also before our arrival in Assam. They spoke of the visit of the survey party some years before, to which they made no objection. A good many of them had been as far as Bisa or Makum and Tirap, but few to Jaipur, and very few indeed to Dibrugarh. They seem to work pretty hard, the men and boys in clearing the forest (*jhuming*) and house building, while the women plant and weed the crops, reap, look after the family, cook, &c., though the carrying of water in the bamboo tubes, often for considerable distances from some gully below, is no joke. They also bring in immense loads of firewood from the clearings, but as a rule the women and girls are remarkably sturdy, and think very little of carrying 150 or 200 pounds on their shoulders and backs, slung by bands across the forehead.

Like most Nagas, they have no special agricultural implements, but use the everhandy *dao*, which is also a weapon. Spears were pretty common. They were iron-headed and of the elementary form common all over the world, the other or butt-end often having an iron spike to help in climbing; the young men also seemed fairly expert with the cross-bow.

Old flint muskets of English make, were not uncommon, the powder being made on the spot by the Nagas, nitre collected from the sites of old cow-houses; where the sulphur came from I could not ascertain. The charcoal was made of the wood of citron-trees, *jaura tenga* of the Assamese. This powder is not granulated or very strong, so large charges are necessary.

At 9 a.m. the boiling-point thermometer showed 209°·60, the temperature of the air being 64°F.

After a fine cool clear moonlight night we were up at dawn, and our party had an early breakfast; the loads were carefully arranged, and I prevailed on five Nagas to carry extra rice for us.

Leaving the village at 11 a.m., we at once passed through the last year's *jhum* towards the south-east, and down a long spur, towards a tract of low wooded hills, on one of which we passed the last Naga village in this direction, a small one of some five or six houses. There are no Nagas east of the Dihing and Namrup. Thence through their *jhum* partly felled, and on down to the bed of a stream, along which we travelled a little way, coming out on the Nambong, a small river that carries the northern-drainage of the Patkai east to fall into the Namrup and Namphuk. There was not much water in it, though here and there we saw pools; the bed was rock, boulders, gravel, and sand alternately. How they kept to the path it was not easy to see, for we often cut off bends by suddenly parting the jungle and finding a rude track below,—at times even this was not to be seen, as it was over boulders and rock. Still, the faculty of keeping or finding the track is part of the savage nature all over the world, and when studied and understood is not at all wonderful.

On opening their eyes anywhere in the jungles, these savages can read the surroundings like a book; it is their book in fact, though sealed up, or the signs invisible, to the civilized intelligence.

Near the mouth of the Nuki, which drains a valley between two of the large spurs of Patkai, we camped at a clear spot, where there was also plenty of firewood and wild plantains for the guide, Mung, and the Nagas to make a hut of.

Bedded rock, laminated shale, was passed frequently inclined at 60° or 70° dipping south.

At dusk, when cooking, the stones under the fires, or supporting the various pots, frequently exploded, so that the operation became rather exciting, and it was agreed by the Bengalis that the Nambong Deo, or spirit, had objections to it; however, it was all over ere long, as we were hungry, and, on the moon coming out, we spent a very pleasant evening. Stories and jokes abounded; now and then a general howl was raised to warn off a tiger that prowled about, though none seemed much afraid of him (his tracks were fresh and plain on patches of sand not far off in the morning). At 9 p.m. the thermometer stood at 60° F.

After breakfast, at 9 a.m., we again started on and soon struck the Nunki, up and beside which we travelled for some hours, and which in places is anything but easy walking, and, though bare-legged, I found shoes were necessary. Here and there a man had an ugly fall, and it was well the things were well packed, as the loads had rough usage. Gradually it began to rain, which was a damper in every sense, as where we went on the banks leeches abounded, and in the river bed the rocks and boulders and the smaller shingle became very slippery. A small lean-to shelter or old hut marked where the path left the Nunki bed to ascend the spur, and here I made the men halt. The Nagas and Singphus and Mung at once pulled out pipes, so I made my fellows all take a little rum 'medicinally'. We then started on and found the first 1,000 or 1,500 feet pretty steep, the path being unmistakably visible both by the track below and the blazes on the tree stems of all ages, from one to ten years; a peculiar feature of the path was that it very seldom varied from a dead level for perhaps two miles or so, and never descended anywhere as much as 30 feet, and was in the main fairly straight. Vegetation began to vary a little, not only trees, but plants and herbs of new kinds were seen, and after about a couple of hours' pretty easy walking the track got steeper and steeper, where the long spur joined the main range. At last the climbing became no joke, to the men who had wetted loads especially, and we had frequently to rest; half an hour or so of this work brought us through some *kako* bamboo to the crest of the ridge, which was quite narrow and densely wooded, the views either way being simply of clouds and mists.

At about fifty yards from the path we camped on a small level, and the rain left off in time for the people to hang out and dry their clothes, blankets, &c. The only thing now needed was what we had too much of already, i.e. water.

Some of the Nagas, however, went away to the bamboos, getting about a gallon from the joints, which sufficed for cooking my dinner and brewing tea for all the party.

I repeatedly told them there was a spring of good water some 400 yards down the path on the east side, in a gully off the same, but both Lah and the Nagas denied it, and said it was useless to go. Subsequently, when at Bor Phakial, I heard that it was true that there was water there. At 9 p.m. water boiled at 205°·75, air being 57°F. Considering our wetting and fasting, the people were all in very good spirits, and we were anxious to see through the veil of mist to the south,—but no such luck, the night proved foggy too. In the early morning I put my orderly to watch for the view at a part of the crest where there was a patch of grass some two acres in extent. At about 8 a.m. he reported by shouting to me that the clouds were clearing and mountains showing beyond. I at once went up with my prismatic compass, and now and then the driving white mists or clouds that swept up showed signs of parting. Suddenly below us, and some way out among the clouds, we saw a patch of bright yellow, and another to west, of blue, both for the moment a mystery. It turned out the yellow was dead grass on the plain in sunlight, and the blue was the lake.

In a little time it had so far cleared that I secured bearings of the most conspicuous features, including the peak of Maium, to the south-west, which is just 7,000 feet high. While I made a hasty outline sketch, the men struck the camp, and by 9 a.m. we were off down the path that leads to the Nongyang ford and from thence via the Digum Bum and Loglai Kha, to Namyang villages in Hukong.

After a short time, having first consulted with the Nagas, we left the path and struck south through the jungle, down across deep *khuds* and over little hills, where the load-carriers had a job to get along, especially those in charge of the canoe, the incline in many places being 50° and 60° from the horizontal. But Nagas are at home in the jungles, and soon piloted all of us down to the level, which we reached far sooner than we expected, but found it so soft and swampy that it was too dangerous to go on, and we had to return to the flanks of the smaller hills trending towards the lake. After about an hour's walk we came to where the bottom was more firm and sandy, and we crossed to the low wooded hills that run along the northern edge of the lake, passing among which we suddenly emerged on it and had a splendid view. Giving directions to pitch the camp on the hill-side facing the lake, where there are some large *hingori* tree, we crossed a patch of reeds and stood on the actual margin.

The Nagas, Singphus, and Khamptis at once began some sort of *puja*, each after his own fashion muttering away, bowing, and touching his forehead with some of the water. I then had the canoe launched, but they all begged me so hard not to take the gun, that I left it, and the wild-fowl which I saw out on the lake's opposite shore got off. One and all said we should be sure to have heavy rain if I fired, or a bad storm, as the Deo of the lake would be certain to be offended. So I turned the Rob Roy's bow out, and felt the peculiar pleasure of being the first who had paddled on that sheet of water, certainly the first who had done so in a Rob Roy. As I went out I saw the margins were low all around, and no forest near, except where I had started from.

The basin of hills, beautifully reflected in the smooth water, swept right round in a green-blue curve, the valley of Nongyang extending south some six or eight miles as a dead flat covered with grass and scrub. The whole bottom of the valley was flat, except where three small tree-covered hills stood like islands in the sea of grass east of the lake. The banks were so low and flat all around that I could see a considerable way inland from the canoe. Turning westwards, I began the circuit of the lake at some 100 yards from shore, and soon found little bays and headlands, though no sign of out or inlet. When half round, I looked across and saw the smoke of the camp fires rising blue against the foliage. The water-fowl had apparently crossed over there. Towards the south-east corner I passed up a channel, separating banks barely a foot high, covered by a small sedge, and found I was rounding the island, a very low flat patch of an acre or two in extent, with some very scrubby trees on it.

The water was here so shallow, being often barely two inches deep, that had not the silt been soft I must have stuck. This silt, however, was so soft and light that the paddle, held upright in it, sank in two and a half to three feet from its own weight. Of course I got out of such a dangerous corner as quickly and quietly as possible,—an upset there meant certain death.

I was surprised to see neither stones, sand, nor clay, all was silt and peat, except a little and where I had started; the outlet was from the south-east corner not far from the island. After about an hour's paddle I returned for breakfast, made all snug, took some observations and memo sketches, and in the evening went out again, going nearly round, and finding several inlets. The number of wild-fowl must be considerable, as the edge of the lake was almost everywhere denuded of sedge or vegetation for a couple of feet in, and had plenty of feathers trampled in. At one place I saw marks made in the bank by the two tusks of a large elephant at water-level, evidently one which had got in and could not easily get out, of which there were other signs beyond. Report says there are large numbers of tusks in the silt everywhere. Other tracks were very common, though no game was visible, but no deer, buffalo, nor indeed any large game tracks except those of elephants.

In the evening we had some strong puffs of wind, and we made all taut for the night, after dinner settling with the men who were to take turns at watching. The Nagas also drew creepers and some dead branches and leaves about us outside, so that anything approaching would at once be heard, then we turned in and slept soundly.

In the morning I started the five Nagas to their homes, they were not wanted and wished to be off, and then prepared to sketch the lake and hills and get bearings. This occupied me all day, and we prepared to start next morning for the Nongyang ford, where I desired to search for the inscriptions in Ahom cut some 500 years ago near the ford, where the road crosses. The men, however, whom I had sent ahead to find a path, returned in a great mess, and declared it utterly impossible to cross the valley, as the peat, or *pitoni*, was too soft and deep to bear their weight. This was most unfortunate, and a second attempt, backed by a good prize if successful, failed equally, so there was nothing for it but to return to Patkai at any rate. I then determined to lash my canoe in the large arms of a big *hingori* tree, and did it so as to prevent its being blown, or shaken down, resting it bottom-up on three boughs; being of a very lasting timber, it may remain safely for some years to come, unless elephants can reach it, which I doubt, or the Nagas hear of it from Lah.

We, therefore, instead of crossing for the Nongyang ford, started back by the road we had come, and found the return to the pass comparatively easy; it took but two hours or two and a half. There being no water on the crest, I had made the men cook and carry extra rations and water in my kettle. . . . Apparently, the crest of the Patkai at the pass is about 3,500 feet above mean sea-level, probably 3,000 above the bed of the Nambong on the Assam side, while the Nongyang lake and valley stand at about 2,200 feet, showing, say, nearly 1,300 feet difference in the levels. The valley of Assam, in fact, being much the lowest, and the Nongyang lake lying about on a level with the Sonkap villages.

From the pass, looking southwards, the valley extends as an irregular triangle for some eight or ten miles north and south, by three or four in width, the lake being near the Patkai end where broadest, and being itself, say, three-fourths by half a mile. Apparently the lake once filled the entire valley, the junction of the level with the hills all around being a well marked line; the surface also mainly consists of grass and scrub jungle, and showing very few trees, is apparently all swamp. The three small conical and wooded hills east of the lake, and at, say, one-fourth to half a mile distant from it, look precisely like islands; the exit from the lake passes close to them.

Later in the day I attempted to get along the crest eastwards, but it was an interminable succession of gullies or saddles and ridges, which would need a whole day to explore, and the dense forest precluded a view in any direction. At a mile east a peak rises which dominates all around and beyond. While we were camped on the summit a party of Singphus crossed from Assam en route to Hukong for buffaloes. Starting from the Nambong that morning about 9 a.m., they intended making the Nongyang ford ere dusk, thus crossing from water to water in one march. Three or four of them had guns.

Early on the 14th we struck the tents, and started back down the northern slope, seeing the tracks of cattle which had crossed since we did. In about three hours we reached the Nunki, where we had breakfast. I here caught some orange-coloured butterflies which seemed new to me, and measured a *mekai* sapling which was 10 inches diameter at foot and 5 inches diameter at the first branch, 60 feet from the ground.

It was a lovely morning, and, excepting for one or two bad falls, we got down to our old camp easily and quickly, finding three Tkak Nagas there. At dusk we heard a barking-deer not far off; a Naga took his gun and quietly disappeared, a loud report soon after told us he had succeeded, though, being dark, he could not trace it; by dawn, however, he was out and returned with it on his shoulders. I gave him some beads for a leg. These men knew the country pretty well, and had cut rubber on the Upper Loglai. They said large numbers of Nagas from our side go east on the side of Burmah, taking food for twenty days, and in parties of thirty and forty or more. It is a large tract of country, and totally uninhabited.

After breakfast, about 9 a.m., we all started on together up the Nambong, thence over the undulating forest land and low hills, *jhums*, &c. One of the Nagas we dropped at the first Tkak Naga village, and soon reached the one we had camped in at night, where we rested an hour and waited for the guide, who had loitered behind. In the *jhum* close by I observed each person's little storehouse of yams, chillies, pumpkins, &c. quite open and exposed, often without doors, yet I was told on all sides that the contents were quite safe. So close to the path were the things, and so very tempting, that I had to collect and warn my people against innocently supposing they might stoop and take what they saw, or there might have been no small row. While resting in the Tkak village, a Naga woman came and presented me with a large basket of *moad* or rice-beer, which, after tasting, I passed round; it was not so good as that of the Nagas living west near me. Like the Singphus, these people make very neat wicker-work baskets, and line or plaster them with rubber-juice, so as to be not only water but spirit-proof. They also make pretty bamboo mugs, with two handles in loops, some of them absurdly like Dr Schliemann's early Greek pottery.

When the guide joined, we went on and climbed another 500 or 600 feet to the Upper Sonkap village of some ten or twelve houses. Several women and big girls at once, and without a word from us, brought out and handed over bundles of firewood for nothing. It was done so quietly that I take it to be a regular custom, and one form of welcome. Water, however, was at a premium. Some for present purposes was given us in huge bamboo vessels, but I had to get the Naga boys and girls to bring more at a pice per tube. Even then, there was a short allowance, till the spring filled, or they found a lower one next day. I went to see it, and how they managed to get down and up in the dark surprised me. The want of water has a perceptible effect on the complexions of these people,—the older women seem especially partial to charcoal dust and ashes.

We pitched our tents in a row, on a clean piece of ground offered us among the houses, and after dinner a most motley crowd of people came round our fire, to whom I had more or less to show myself, my clothes, guns, lamps, &c.

The imperceptible effect of custom was curiously seen in many very trivial things here, as elsewhere: for instance, though more or less all prepared for wonderful guns, I found that whenever I opened the D.B.B.-L. suddenly and the barrels dropped, there was an instantaneous 'Awa! he's broken it', the idea of a joint at the breech being the last to occur naturally. At last we got to sleep, after telling them all I would remain over the next day, perhaps two, and there was plenty of time to see everything.

Early next morning I was up, but the range of Patkai all along was invisible. In the dark, however, I must mention the Nagas were up and the women and girls at work and going for water. The muffled tread of many feet and tinkling of the many shin-rings awoke me, and they came back in the dark; meantime, the dull 'bump, bump' of the rice-husking went on in every house till dawn.

I took a turn to the upper few houses of the village, some 300 yards east, while my man was getting *chota hazri* (little breakfast) for me, and on my return in half an hour, failing to make a sketch east on account of the mist, I found a lot of the women and girls squatted about weaving, and 'got up regardless', in beads, red cane, and such-like in lieu of costume, the *tout ensemble* when some of them stood up was certainly most remarkable. The long and in some cases profuse straight black hair was secured on the poll of the head by two large (engraved) bone hair-pins, from the projecting ends of which, behind, beads depended; round the head or over the hair some twenty rings of scarlet cane were fastened, and over the forehead a bead coronet. A large brass ring hung from the upper edge of each ear, a bright green bird's skin dangling below to the shoulder; the peculiar nose-studs, or nostril-plugs, completed the head. A profusion of large or small bead necklaces hung from the neck, some close, others long and reaching to the waist. Pewter armlets, bright and dull, on the arms, and wristlets of brass of various sorts, from plain wire to a curious piece of casting, were on the arms, now and then red goat's hair being attached in a fringe or bunch. Round the waist was the curious series of cane rings, some fifty or sixty, more or less attached to each other, or long strip coiled round and round, but generally worn as a little crinoline, very much too short, and which was helped out by a strip of native-wove cloth, going all round, but ends not joined,—the whole contrivance barely decent. Red cane bands were often worn round the leg below the knee, as is the custom with the men, and then the remarkable pewter shin-rings, four or five on each leg placed on edge in front and tied round the leg in some way that prevented them all from slipping down. In walking or running these made a pretty loud tinkling as they touched each other.

Today the belles of the village came out strong, they seemed for once to have washed themselves and donned all the finery available. As I went about with an interpreter, looking at the weaving and little sticks used as a loom, and asking all sorts of questions, they seemed as much amused as we were, and when laughing, the whole costume seemed to join in, the nose-studs in particular. I could hardly help every now and then thinking what a sum one would realize as a model at the Academy life-class, especially some of them who were remarkably well made and not bad-looking. The children, as a rule, were not at all prepossessing, and had heads and faces round and uninteresting as a turnip, the nose a little round knob, and little eyeholes as in a mask, utterly destitute of modelling. The men's costume was limited to the cane crinoline and a jacket without arms, occasionally a necklace and *topi* with hair or feathers; but they do not dress themselves as gaudily as the women, or as the Naga men further to the west.

The looms I saw were simply two little upright sticks of any sort driven into the ground, and one loosely tied across the offside, to which the woof was wound, another similar one being in front and looped to a band, against which the weaver leaned back to pull it tight. A huge flat paper-knife seemed to complete the arrangement; being some four inches wide, it when placed on edge, opened out the strings enough to allow a little ball of thread to pass through; letting the said paper-knife lie flat seemed to open the strands the other way, and the little ball was rolled back again: with this they wove cloths with a simple pattern, which were from a foot to eighteen inches wide. Several were weaving men's cloths of the strong *bonrhea*, 5 feet long by 3 inches wide, and with ornamental ends.

After an early breakfast at 9 o'clock I started with several men for the summit of the hill, and after a steep climb reached it and found it had been *jhumed* about two years before, so we set to work and in an hour cleared off a good deal, enough to enable me to see round and get bearings. The view was a fine one, bounded on the north by the Mishmi Hills, north-east by Dupha Bum 15,000 feet, well snowed down to 2,000 feet or so from the summit; east the Phungan Bum, 11,000 feet, was well seen, but had no snow on it, the distance about 53 miles; thence round towards the south I saw the eastern prolongation of Patkai, with the depressions in the range where the old Burmese route crossed, at probably, 1,500 or at the least 1,000 feet lower elevation than the present pass of 3,500 feet. Over and beyond this marked depression could be seen a rather high group of hills,—a feature visible here alone, as elsewhere the range of Patkai hid them from view.

The hills seen beyond were expressively called the Loglai Patkai by the Naga headman, who caught me making an outline and taking bearings. They may be the group that lie between the Loglai and Turong rivers. From this point west, the entire line of the Patkai crest was visible, but slightly undulating till near Maium, where there seemed to be several depressions, before the rise to the 6,939 feet of that peak. The seven large spurs, running north and more or less at right angles, were very distinctly seen with their intervening valleys, all, like the main range, densely wooded, the Nambong draining all that was lying in this direction. Some of the more western spurs of Patkai were sufficiently high, and form the sky-line, as Longvoi Pipoi, and Nongya Sapon, projecting into the

Namtsik valley, which lay west, and seemed filled with low rolling hills, one behind the other, for a long way. Towards the north-west at some miles off, and seen more or less on end, were the ranges dividing the Namtsik from the Tirap basins; some peaks, as Mungphra, Kongtam, Rangatu, and Yungbhi, were from 2,500 to 4,000 feet high; further west again about Makum, the hills gradually sank to the level of the plains, in a sea of forest. I observed that the mists in the early part of the morning, or before noon, poured for hours over the lowest part of Patkai above indicated, like milk from a jug, and the phenomenon was repeated daily during our stay, thus marking it unmistakably as the lowest part of the range. East of this part (which seemed the Upper Namrup on our side and Loglai on the other) the range rose again, though not to any great height. Between Patkai and Dupha Bum, beyond Dihing, rose a fine group of hills called by these people Miao Bum, and between Miao and Sonkap, on which we stood, were the small hills called Nan-nan and Tantuk, between which Pemberton says the old route lay and the Namrup flowed, under the name of the Namhuk or Namhok, and near the village of Namphuk; the alternative route to the Nunki, via Nambongmuk, passed hence also; it was taken by Mr H. L. Jenkins and my brother some years ago, in 1869.

Towards the afternoon we descended through a clearing, where we saw boys lopping the tree branches that overhung a gully, seemingly a very perilous job and needing some nerve, as the branches fell quite 500 feet. In the evening, an old Naga gave many particulars about the Nonyang lake and valley, and the previous inhabitants, routes to Burmah, &c. He gave the length of the valley as one day's journey, and said he lived with other Nagas once on the hills overlooking the western end of the lake, where there are now no villages. The original inhabitants were, he said, Kamjangs, Aitonias, and Turong Turai, confirming what I had heard before, and the Nagas inhabited the hill ranges around on the west.

At night we had again a large audience, the men and boys seated round the camp-fire, the women and girls in a circle standing outside. I was asked all sorts of questions about my country and people, the Queen, railways, and steamers, on which Mung had been dilating more or less.

Next morning after *chota hazri*, I started eastwards with my orderly and a couple of Nagas, and got into a *jhum* on the eastern flank of our hill, from whence I obtained a fine view. At noon we returned and had breakfast and after a rest, I made an outline sketch of the Namtsik valley, and then saw a fine sunset. I also fired a few rounds from my revolver at a mark, to the delight of the young men, who cut out all the bullets at once from the old stump. Some eight or nine Kessa Nagas came to the village from the other side of Patkai, and were pointed out to me. They were, I could see, in various ways somewhat different to the Nagas I was among. Paler in colour, more ugly and sinister in looks, destitute of arms or of ornament, and each wore a large wrap of *bonrhea* cloth. They also did not tattoo. It was difficult to communicate with them, as only one or two knew a few words of Singphu, and their 'Naga' was also very different. The Sonkap headman and others told me they belonged to a tribe who sacrificed human beings, and, as this was news to me, I took some pains to get it confirmed by them. The Nagas replied by explaining that it was done as an old custom, to secure good crops when there was likelihood of failure, and not through wantonness, and that they explained this to the victims, men and women, captured or bought, who were tied to a stake, and killed, as far as I understood, by a cut across the abdomen transversely in some way. It would be very desirable to verify this on the spot, and, if it proved true, endeavour to suppress the practice of such a custom at our doors.

The entire Naga question must be taken up sooner or later and properly settled, or it will be a source of constant trouble to us. We have had very fair success with the Aryan populations of India, but seem to fail signally among non-Aryans. Dr Hunter's remarks regarding such races are worthy of the most careful attention. They seem to need a combination of the autocratic and patriarchal, —an essentially personal as distinguished from a Departmental Government, with its cloud of Babus, a race mortally detested by the Nagas and such-like tribes (and with reason). This indispensable element of personal regard our Government seems to systematically ignore, the most potent tie which can connect us with these people is frequently and recklessly severed, with results that act disastrously on them. Yet, instead of blaming ourselves, who should know better, we blame the savage, and wonder at the result. In time no doubt these people might be educated and understand us and our institutions, but in the meanwhile they need an intelligent

Chief over them, rather than a department, and one not changed for every little frivolous pretext, but one who will elect to live and die among them and work for them. From being a set of treacherous and turbulent races, they would become a prolific source from which our Indian army could recruit most valuable and trustworthy material. They are particularly susceptible to personal kindness. It is to be lamented that with the opportunity and power to govern them successfully, there should be deliberate blundering through thoughtlessness. Such men as Captain John Butler are needed; they are few and far between perhaps, but are still to be found with a little trouble.

But to return to these Kutcha Nagas; what they were like in their house I can't say, but here they wore a sinister truculent look, and there was more difference between them each individually than is usual, though the colour was somewhat uniform; they wore the hair cropped to a horizontal line across the forehead, as is so common among all Nagas. They spoke very little, and in undertones, to each other, their numerals, like those of all the races in Eastern Assam, being on the same basis, with minor variations.

At last we got to sleep, and after a pleasant night were up at dawn. I asked the Naga headman to assist me in procuring some curios, personal ornaments, costumes, &c., but it proved to be no easy matter. They might give away, but how could they sell such things? Of course, if given, a present was expected in return of, say, at least double value.

At first they quite failed to see why I wanted their costumes and ornaments, unless for some unstated purpose, not a good one,—to perform magic with, perhaps; but gradually I got them to see it as a harmless and laughable peculiarity of mine, and I secured a few of the things, though at exorbitant rates. I got them to see it best and easiest by selecting a girl well got up, and saying I would like to take the 'lot' as it stood, bar the girl. Naga-like, they could not resist the temptation to palm off bad things for good. Eventually, we got what we wanted, had breakfast, and, while packing, I showed them all another village through the telescope. Their astonishment was considerable, and, as usual, they thought the village had been brought near by magic.

Ere midday we were off down for the Namtsik, where, meeting a young Naga I secured some samples of his gunpowder in exchange for some bullets, on which he set a high value. The powder was kept in dry bamboo tubes, with a stopper and bit of cloth. I also made him sell me his jacket and crinoline, or at least three-fourths of it, for he said if he went up home without it, he would be a laughing-stock to all the girls, even though he had his cloth on. Our men soon appeared emerging from the gully, and we shipped everything and got off, the dropping down stream being very pleasant work, and the rapids giving very little trouble. At one place, a long deep pool shaded by overhanging rocks and trees, we found a party of Nagas fishing; their mode was to stake the shallows above and below, and set a series of traps, then to hoe or dig in by stakes or *daos* a lot of the bright red fine clay of the bank at that place, which renders the water like pink cream, whereupon the fish in the pool clear out, and in so doing all get caught. They go about, too, on bamboo rafts, and beat the water to scare the fish; generally each person gets two or three big fish to take home. We shot along pretty quickly, and at last camped on a bed of shingle at the river-side, where there was plenty of grass to sleep on, and firewood. Here the *dam-dums*, or *moans*, small flies on silent wings tormented us. Their bites or stings itch the next day and often cause bad sores.

Next morning we got off early, and shot some rapids in a way that made us all hold our breath. The river had risen somewhat. At one place we came to a huge rock that rose out of the Namtsik, in a deep pool, and it had four large sculptured circles on it in contact, each about a foot in diameter, and containing an eight-petalled rose,—whether a Hindu or Buddhist emblem I cannot say. It is, however, well known to the people about, who declare it a work of the Ahom Rajas many years ago; a part of two circles which is missing is said to have been struck off by lightning.

By 4 p.m. we reached the mouth of the Namtsik and the elephant-stockade; having taken in our remaining stores we pushed on to the Nmbai-muk the same evening. I had seen the young Singphu Chief, Kherim Gam, at Namtsik, and he agreed to meet me at Tirap.

Next day we pushed on, passed the Kasam, Mganto and Kherim Pani, into the Dihing river, landed at Gogo and saw some peculiar men, said to be Eastern Singphus, from far up the Dihing; the headman wore a peculiar Chinese-looking cap, jacket, &c., and had a most celestial look about him, he proved kindly and intelligent, and made some shrewd remarks. I also saw here a huge pair of *jangphais* or amber ear-plugs, worn by a very old but remarkably good-looking woman. She would not part with them, though I offered a large sum, their full market value in Assam.

Again we started on and shot some very bad rapids in a way that astonished all on board; in some places we went for fully 300 yards at about ten to twelve miles an hour flying over the boulders only just below us, and which seemed to pass like bands of colour,—to have caught in one would either have split the canoe in two, or sent us and it rolling pell-mell into the deep water below.

Mung, however, seemed to know his work, and only once showed a little weakness, when in shooting down a rapid with a bend in it, and that seemed to end in a huge pile of snags and branches; the leading paddlers jumped overboard, and I had just time to jump forward and give six or seven hard side-strokes with my large-bladed Rob Roy paddle, which served to convert a frightful upset into a hard bump. We reached the bend above Tirapmuk about 3 p.m., and most of us got out and walked across the chord of the arc on the sand and grass; five or six of the men, who had gone on foot and carried light loads, here joined us, and we got to Tirap itself about 4 p.m., camping where we did before, on the sands, just above where the rivers joined in the fork, and opposite the end of Kherim Gam's village. They soon had the tents up, firewood in, and were hard at it cooking, when my dak by two men turned up; it had been waiting a week. They also brought a few acceptable stores. Kherim arrived at night, and in the morning came over and we had a long talk together on many matters. He seemed much pleased to see me, and asked after Jenkin Saheb and my brother with whom he had gone to Hukong in 1868–9. He particularly wanted me to promise to repeat my visit next cold season, and offered to go anywhere with me I liked,—especially Hukong, where he was well known, and has two sisters married to Chiefs. One of these two, over on a visit to Assam, came as soon as Kherim was gone and interviewed me. She is married to Dubong Gam, on the Turong, and asked me to visit them, guaranteeing my safety. She was a smart, intelligent little woman, and it was now twenty years since she had been home to Assam. She had her four children with her. Through an interpreter we had a long conversation. She seemed thoroughly to understand the relative positions of the Singphus on our side and hers, and declared the keeping of slaves not so bad after all, and in some cases necessary; at the same time, they all admired the peace and security to life and property seen on our side. As usual, she came with a small present,—fowls, rice, milk, &c.,—and in return I gave her an assortment of strong needles, some threads, tapes, and handkerchiefs for the children. She was soon to return to Hukong, and several of their slaves had come to take her and the children back, a ten days' journey via the Naga villages and Namyong. As far as I could see, the system of slavery in force in Hukong is not the curse John Bull so often supposes it to be, and seems particularly well adapted to the state of society prevalent there. The slaves, often either Assamese or their mixed descendants, are treated more or less as part of the family, a proof of their happiness being that they do not run away and join our side when possible. Leaving the Tirap, we went down to the small Khampti village of Manmo, where I saw and sketched a pretty little Buddhist chang and schoolhouse with very fair carving about it. For some reason, the Bapu, like the one at Bor Pakhial, has gone to Burmah, and they did not know whether he would return. It seems a great pity if Buddhism is doomed to die out here among these people; theoretically and practically it seems infinitely better than what they are getting in lieu of it, i.e. a mixture of the dregs of several superstitions.

We reached Bor Pakhial about 3 p.m. and camped this time up on the bank near the houses and some bamboos, and soon had a collection to learn of our success. A little before sunset I fixed up the telescope pretty firmly, and showed them several canoes full of people in the distance; there was great excitement over it, for, though very far off, the boys kept calling out the names of the girls and women in the boats, and were able to recognize them. As they came nearer it was a pretty sight, and they made the boats travel, as most of them had oars and were paddling. As the canoes were too small to sit down in, all were standing in a row, five or six in each long and narrow dug-out; then they all ran up to see us. Several old men reiterated the story about the people who had originally inhabited the valley of Nongyang, and who were driven out by the Singphus. They also indicated the difficulties of a route east via Manchi or Bor Khampti, up the Dihing, or the Sitkha; of this latter route, they could only speak by repute.

Taking the configuration of the whole country and the ranges around, in regard to the countries beyond, it seems that the only feasible in or outlet is via the Namrup basin and Nongyang or Loglai; eastwards the Patkai not only rises, but the approaches from either side become more and more difficult and traverse an uninhabited country. Westwards, again, though inhabited by Nagas, the hills are also more difficult, and the actual water-parting at a much higher elevation, the tract of mountainous country on either side becoming much wider.

The discovery of the actual route where it crossed the Patkai in olden times is not now very difficult, its locality is known, and exploration on the spot is all that is necessary.

It is not unlikely that in ascending some one of the several gaps in the lower part of the range east of the present pass, and not more than two or three miles distant, the path may be found to debouch almost at once on the level, or but little above it, rendering a route anything but difficult to open there.

Certainly, the elevation cannot be over 600 or 800 feet above the tributary of Loglai first met, that river itself probably running at about 1,000 feet below the crest. Nongyang is but 1,200 feet below a much higher portion. There are reasons for presuming that this old route was in use as the 'Doi bat' in A.D. 592 by the earliest Shans from Mogong.

Chapter V

EXPLORATIONS ON THE SUBANSIRI

1

A NOBLE AND RAPID RIVER

(R. Wilcox, 'Memoir of a Survey of Assam and the neighbouring Countries, executed in 1825–6–7–8', *Asiatic Researches*, 1832, Vol. XVII)

AFTER some deliberation as to the route I should attempt, Mr Scott recommended that I should try the Subansiri before proceeding further eastward, and I started with a liberal supply of red cloth, beads, and such other articles as were likely to please the mountaineers. Having arrived at its mouth on the 28th November, I commenced my survey on the following day. I was disappointed to find my further progress impeded on the sixth day by rapids, occasioned by the accumulation of round stones brought down from the hills, where, from its mouth, I had got but twenty-two miles latitude to the north.

Some of the Chiefs of an Abor tribe had arrived at this time to make their annual collections from the district north of the Buri Lohit. They claim the whole of those plains as their domain; but whether this claim is the origin of their exactions, or whether the imbecile[1] government of Assam had allowed it to grow into a confirmed custom, an evil which they could not counteract, does not appear. However, from the Bhuruli to the banks of the Dihong, the whole of the hill tribes pretended to similar rights, and have never been interfered with when at the accustomed season they have descended from their strongholds and peaceably taken their dues from each separate dwelling.

I had an interview with Taling Gam, the most powerful of these Abor Miris, and my presents of rum and cloth wrought so well

[1] 'The maintenance of peace and tranquillity . . . constitute the common objective of every Government. But the Ahom rulers of Assam were confronted with the additional responsibility of protecting the subjects from the inroads of the tribes inhabiting the hills on the immediate borders, almost all of whom were of a most rapacious nature and anxious for opportunities of plunder which might be offered by the slackness or imbecility of the government.'—S. K. Bhuyan, *Anglo-Assamese Relations* (1949), p. 32.

with him, that I entertained hopes of starting for his village in his company, and had arranged to move off in canoes, to have the advantage of water conveyance for my provisions [over] the remaining navigable portion of the river, which is said to be but three days.

My inquiries had not elicited any information to warrant the expectation of a successful result from this trip, as it appeared that the few articles of Thibetan manufacture found amongst this people were acquired by traffic with tribes more to the eastward. They would not acknowledge any acquaintance with the countries to the north, but described them as an uninhabited wild tract of hill and jungle. To their north-west, however, they place the Onka Miris, whose country, they say, is a level tableland, and they are of opinion that these come in contact with the Bhotiyas. I thought that by gaining a footing in the first villages in the hills, I might either induce the people to throw off this reserve, if my suspicions of their concealing their knowledge were correct, or perhaps advance sufficiently far towards the north to make more effectual inquiries. I was disappointed through the interference of the Assamese of the Sonari villages, who anticipated some unknown evil from our communication with their hill neighbours, and this friendly Chieftain positively refused to accompany me, or to let any of his people guide me, till he should have returned and consulted his people.

Of the Subansiri, they could only tell me that it is divided above into three branches. It is called by them Kamla, and the principal branch rises in the north or north-west. Snow, which I had seen lying on the mountain in a northerly direction, they told me was fifteen days' journey from their villages, and added that in the north-east they could perceive it hanging on the mountains in great quantity throughout the year. The Miris bring down to exchange with the lowlanders ginger, pepper, *manjit* (madder), and wax. The Abors of Sueng Meng and Dohar Doowars, more eastward, have also copper vessels, straight swords, and elephants' teeth.

The Subansiri river is scarcely inferior to the Ganges at Allahabad in December. I found the discharge at its mouth 16,000 cubic feet per second, and up to the hills its tributary streams are few and of little consequence. I think there is no doubt of its being the Omchu of Du Halde and Rennell. Its low banks are covered with tree jungle, and are subject to inundation; there are very few villages visible from the river, but inland, on both sides, the country is better cultivated and more populous than other parts of Upper Assam, with the exception of Jurhath and Char Dwar.

It had been agreed with Mr Scott that in the event of my meeting with no success here, I should go on to the Dihong and Dibong; and if Captain Bedford had not already explored those rivers as far as practicable, that I should make my attempt there.

My own belief, founded on the reports of the Miris, now on the Subansiri, who had emigrated from the banks of those rivers, was that neither would be found navigable, and I was prepared to move overland wherever I could find admittance. The Miris did not pretend to any certain knowledge of the origin of the Dihong, and they seemed to think the notions current amongst their tribe and the Assamese as little worthy of my attention. They informed me that a tradition prevails with the Abors of the Subansiri that their hunters once, travelling in quest of game, went much further towards the north than usual, and that they arrived at the banks of a noble and rapid river separating their wild hills from cultivated spreading plains, whence the lowing of oxen was distinctly audible. Another singular account they mentioned of the Dihong Abors, that the Dihong is an anastomosing branch of a river of great magnitude, called Sri Lohit, which also throws off the Brahmaputra and passes into unknown regions to the eastward. The Abors are supposed to see this Sri Lohit, and on the opposite bank numbers of people of a strange tribe are perceived coming down to the Ghat to bathe, but it is too rapid and too broad to be crossed. Another tale is that the Sonaris, not finding the sand equally productive as usual in their old washing haunts, continued their way in a small canoe up the river, renewing their search for gold continually, but in vain, but that they suddenly arrived in a populous country, the manners and appearance of the inhabitants of which were strange to them; that on mentioning what had brought them so far from their houses, they were instantly rewarded for their toil by a large gift of the precious ore, and sent back delighted.

2

AN EXCURSION UP THE SUBANSIRI

('Report by Lt. E. J. T. Dalton[1], Junior Assistant Commissioner of Assam, of his visit to the Hills in the neighbourhood of the Soobanshiri River', *J.A.S.B.*, 1845, Vol. XIV, N.S., Part I, pp. 250 ff.)

i

Pathalipam Mouzah, January 6th, 1845.—Reached this yesterday evening from Luckimpore station, preparatory to setting out on a short excursion up the Soobanshiri as far as I can go in canoes, and thence to the nearest Meri villages by land. My object being to pay Tema Hazaree a friendly visit, and to ascertain if it be practicable to make a more extended tour through the country of the Hill Meris and Abors next cold season.

This day will be consumed in making the necessary arrangements —tomorrow I hope to start.

January 7th.—On the Soobanshiri. With quite a fleet of canoes, I started from the Pathalipam Ghaut at 11 a.m., and considering the difficulty of procuring boats and the number of people to be provided for, there was less trouble, confusion and delay than might have been anticipated.

Including my own boat there are eleven canoes, thirty-two boatmen, and with servants, Tecklas, Katokees and Meri Bhoteas, a guard of five sepoys; not less than seventy individuals, all packed as tight as herrings in a barrel. The canoes are moved by gold-washers who, from constant practice in their gold-washing expeditions, are masters of the art of managing boats in the difficult rapids of this river. Indeed I am told that no other men could venture to work up in canoes to Siploo Ghaüt, whence we are to proceed by land. The canoes are very small, and, except a light mat over my boat, no *choppers* allowed.

Amongst these gold-washers are the Pawwas men, whose business it is to convey the Hill Meris and their families who annually visit

[1] In his earlier work Dalton gave himself the initials 'E.J.T.', but by 1872, when he published his *Descriptive Ethnology of Bengal,* he had dropped the 'J' and was simply 'E. T. Dalton', the style by which he is generally known.

the plains by this route from Siploo Ghaut to a Ghaut about six miles above Pathalipam. These men, six in number, being most expert of all, act as our steersmen.

They use paddles of *Hingoree*, short and stiff in comparison with the long elastic *Bhola* paddles of the Suddiah and Debroo Thooms. They work the boat however exceedingly well; and no doubt in the pattern and material of their paddles, they have adopted what experience has taught them to be most serviceable for the rapids of this river. In the shallows I see they chiefly work with the *luggee* poles. There is a rapid, but a slight one, immediately above Pathalipam; and from this to the Hills the river is divided by wooded islands into numerous channels: two of these islands are partly occupied by Chuttiah Meris, and they are moreover a fruitful source of quarrelling among the gold-washers. On one of them, called 'Indoor' Majali, they brought to our canoes, and commenced making preparations for halting there. I protested against this, as it was not 4 o'clock; but they asserted very positively, that there was no ground on ahead fit for encamping on that we could possibly reach that night, and as I liked the appearance of the place, a fine shelving beach of sand and gravel, I gave my consent.

They waited till my cook had arranged his temporary kitchen and the dinner was in course of preparation, and then their object of halting on this island was made manifest. A number of gold-washers from the Bor Dolonee Mouzah, on the left bank of the river, were washing a little above the halting place. The Pathalipam gold-washers considered the ground theirs, and wished me to serve the intruders with a summary ejectment. The left bank people as stoutly asserted that they were on their own ground, and it was by no means an easy dispute to decide. It depended on which of the channels is the main channel of the river, but the river takes to them all in turn about.

January 8th.—Started after all had breakfasted at 8 a.m. The back ranges of the mountains are disappearing one after the other behind the upstart lower hills. The rapids numerous, but not difficult.

The Sonaris have boat songs, or professional melodies of their own: when wading and hauling the canoes up the rapids they sing a sort of 'cheerly boys', the chorus of which is 'Yoho Ram', and which heard above the roar of the waters has a good effect.

In hollowing out these canoes the carpenters make in them holes of about an inch square to ascertain the thickness as they proceed. These holes are afterwards plugged. In my boat being driven in from above they protruded below, and two of them were at the same moment unshipped as we bumped on the stone of a rapid. The boat commenced rapidly filling, but we got her on shore and the baggage all removed, before any serious damage was done. I mention this as a warning to others. One minute's delay and the boat would have sunk; we were fortunately near shore, had surmounted the rapid, and the crews of the other boats all at hand in a moment to assist.

Digression up the bed of a small stream called the Doolooni, to see the Raj Ghur. This Doolooni was one of the gold streams; but last year its bed of shingle was covered with fine sand which the gold-washers can make nothing of, and they have abandoned it. It forms also one of the passes by which the Turbotiah Meris descend, the Dirjoo flowing through Sugal-doobey, which forms the other starting from near the same point in the hills. The Raj Ghur we found about a mile from its mouth. I have seen this Ghur at Goomeri, where it crosses the Booree river, and there it still bears the appearance of having been constructed as a rampart against the inroads of the hill people; but here it has more the appearance of an old road. It is however a stupendous work, and great is the pity that it is too far north of our population to be used as a line of communications. Previous to the Moran or Muttock wars, the villages of Luckimpore are said to have extended up to this Raj Ghur, and there is every appearance even now of such having been at some period the case. At the mouth of the Doolooni the Soobanshiri expands with a fine broad, deep and smooth basin, which it enters by three channels formed by two islands, where the stream again meets; above them it emerges from the hills, and here we halt for the night; our encamping ground is in the dry bed of the Bergoga.

January 9th.—Our last night's bivouac was not a comfortable one. A stiff breeze blowing down the bed of the Bergoga, was met by another coming down the valley of the Soobanshiri, and they enjoyed themselves together at our expense, blowing the sand into the people's dinners, and the smoke into our eyes, and knocking the canoes against the stones. But we are now fairly amongst the hills, and truly the scenery is sublime. Beneath these hills, the great river winds in graceful serpentines. The bases forming the cliffs are rocky and precipitous to a considerable height, along which foliage of various hues and a most vernal and velvety appearance waves in the breeze. The stream is about 250 yards in breadth, but of a depth (sounded several places on returning and found between sixty and seventy feet in depth throughout this glen) unfathomable by any means we have at hand. There the rock of storms (the Botahkhowa hill) stands boldlv out from the mass on a bed of huge boulders screening the mouth of a deep, dark, narrow dell, the winding of which I explored for a little way—a way, where the sun's rays never penetrate; sometimes huge Bon-trees springing from the rocks above stretch their sinewy limbs over the deep waters, which reflect them; and the fibres that descend from them, finding no earth below in which to fix themselves, swing in the breeze.

As we advance the river becomes still narrower, but not less deep or smooth. Gockain Potana, a rock not less than 800 feet in height, rises perpendicularly from the stream. The face is almost smooth to the top which is clad with trees; on the opposite side a similar cliff, but not so high: on the summit of the former a god killed a deer; and, walking (clever fellow) down the face of the smooth rock with his quarry over the shoulder, he ascended with it the opposing cliff, *unde nomen*. From above, the rock called the Gockain Potana looks like a huge church-steeple rising from the stream. We stopped for some time at a place called Pabo Ghaut to collect cane to be used in towing the canoes up the rapids on ahead. The Ghaut is so called from its having been some fifty years ago the watering place of a tribe of Meris called Pabon. One of the young men of this tribe stole from her village a young virgin of Tema's tribe, then under the management of his father Temees. For this offence the insulted Temeeans waged a war of extermination against the Pabo tribe. The villages of the latter were attacked by night when the inhabitants slept, and men, women and children were promiscuously slaughtered or carried away, and sold into hopeless captivity amongst the Abors. The tribe, consisting of two large villages, was utterly extinguished. Not far from this we halted for the night, on the right base of the river, at the mouth of a beautiful stream called the Gaien Panee, issuing from a dark glen and dashing down the rocks into the well-bound channel through which the Soobanshiri noiselessly flows. Notwithstanding the absence of large timber which appears to grow only near and on the summits of these precipitous hills, the verdure of this valley is very beautiful: the rocks themselves are frequently covered with moss and ferns of the brightest emerald green; whilst springing from the soil above them bamboos of a peculiarly light and feathery appearance, the shafts not thicker than the most delicate trout rod, curve and wave in the slightest breeze. The pine-apple tree, the drooping leaves of which are found upwards of sixteen cubits in length; the Toka palm, varieties of cane and the mountain plantain, are all characteristic of this scenery, and blend together in luxuriant mass.

January 10*th*.—Early this morning we emerged from this great glen, and found the first of the great rapids at its mouth. The canoes were safely pulled up with the long cane ropes we had provided; above this rapid the stream widens, the valley expands, and more distant mountains appear in sight. Huge blocks of rock obstructing the river in its descent render the navigation more and more difficult. We were obliged to lighten our boats, and for some distance the baggage was all conveyed by land, whilst the canoes were dragged through fields of hissing foam, or over rocks nearly dry; after surmounting several such rapids we reached Siploo Mookh whence we are to proceed by land.

ii

Luckimpore, February 11*th*, 1845

My Dear Major,[1]—This being a holiday, I shall devote it to giving you some further account of my late excursion.

I wrote you a few lines from Siploo Mookh, detailing briefly my proceedings up to the date of my letter. On the 15th January all the headmen of Tema's tribe made their appearance, together with the ladies of Tema's family, who came expressly to welcome me—his two wives and daughter. I held an assembly, and particularly

[1] This is Major (later General) Jenkins, to whom the previous extract was also addressed. As a young Captain, Jenkins had in 1832 forced his way through the hills from Manipur into the Assam valley and had had to fight with the Nagas the entire journey. In 1834, he became Commissioner and Agent to the Governor-General for the North-East Frontier of Bengal. He was one of several claimants to the honour of having discovered tea in Assam, and was given a gold medal for it.

explained to the Chiefs that if they had the smallest objection to my proceeding further I was ready to return; but they all assured me that such a proceeding would cause them great pain. They would be delighted to shew me all the lions of their country; but only begged, that as the small-pox was raging in the Pathalipam village, I would leave behind me all the Pathalipam men. This I readily consented to do, provided they procured me a sufficiency of Meri coolies. Affairs having been so far amicably arranged, a distribution of salt and rum concluded the conference; and the Gaums in high good humour disported themselves before me, shewing their agility in racing over the rocks, and their prowess in throwing stones across the river: meantime I gave the ladies who had come to greet me some gay coloured cotton cloths; and here, alas, was cause for jealousy. The other Gaums would know why Tema's family alone should be thus favoured; but I told them that when their wives and daughters came to greet me (as Tema's had done) and were neglected, they might take umbrage at my partiality, but not now; and with this they appeared satisfied.

Late at night Tema and one of the Torbottiah Gaums again visited me. They said a sufficient number of coolies would by morning be collected, but they expected to be paid for the trip; considering the friendly nature of my visit, and the honour thus done them, they (the Gaums) were ashamed to ask me to pay the people for conveying the baggage, but they had no power to give men without such payment being made; and they therefore wished, if agreeable to me, to be allowed to defray the coolie expenses between them. Of course I declined this offer, though I was not a little pleased at its having been made, evincing as it did a genuine good feeling towards me. The rate was to be one seer of salt, or four annas, for the trip for each coolie, which the Gaums assured me was what they paid when, in bringing, as they yearly do, various commodities from the plains, they are necessitated to avail themselves of extra hands. Those who call themselves Gaums have no authority in their hills, but that of the rich over the poor. After the above noticed trait of liberality on Tema's part, and of the independence of the Hill Meris in general, I was not a little amused next morning when the Meri coolies, male and female, were receiving beforehand their seer of salt, to observe amongst the applicants for a load and a *douceur*, Tema's second wife and his eldest daughter, both fine young women; but the latter much disfigured by small-pox. The loads were light, not more than twenty seers; but boys and girls, men and women, were all paid the same. Considering all these arrangements had to be made, and that the greater part of the coolies had only arrived in the morning, I thought myself lucky by getting off by 10-30 a.m. For the first two miles we proceeded along the left bank of the Siploo flowing from N.W., then turning north ascended a very steep hill; sometimes almost creeping under jungle so dense, that nothing could be seen beyond what was a few yards to our right and left; the path was less difficult than I had been led to suppose it, but it sometimes zigzagged up or wound round precipices in an awkward manner for nervous people. Tema was my constant companion, always prepared to give me a friendly hand if necessary. He seemed at first to be under great anxiety on my account; but finding me more active than he expected, he appeared more at ease.

Of the various timber trees and underwood, you know I am incapable of giving any account; the most remarkable of the former were Seea trees, a seed of which you returned me split open; the wood is hard, close-grained, and finely coloured as the Nahore; the Assamese call it the Seea Nahore, and the fruit contains a poison with which the Meris kill fish. Great varieties of bamboos and cane. The Meris thatch their houses with the leaves of a species of the latter called Tor, the pine-apple tree, and the fern.

We passed several squirrel traps of an ingenious and simple construction. On an overhanging branch a seed (chestnut) of which the squirrels are fond is placed, and bound to the branch by a double band of cane; the squirrel cannot get at the seed without putting his head through a noose of the cane, and on his disengaging the bait the stone drops and tightens the noose round the squirrel's neck: they eat the flesh of this animal as a great delicacy. As we ascended this hill, the hill people frequently gave us lowlanders a warning to be careful not to loosen a stone from its bed. This was very necessary, people are apt to kick away stones on a hill that are easily dislodged; and had this been done on the present occasion, they must have fallen on or bounded near those coming up the winding path below us. Having descended a valley in which there was water, we commenced the ascent of another and loftier mountain called Teepooka. On this hill there are magnificent

Nalok trees of enormous dimensions; descending again we came to a rocky stream called the Tiks, up the bed of which our path now lay, and this was to me the most difficult part of the road. The current was strong, and the rocks slippery as glass. It was difficult for me to maintain my footing, and as I proceeded along slowly and cautiously, the Meri girls with their loads came up and laughingly passed me, bounding with astonishing activity and sure-footedness from rock to rock.[1]

This stream takes its rise in the Moyur mountain, over which our path now lay; and learning that we should not see water again till evening I halted for stragglers, and when all had come up it was too late to think of attempting to proceed further. Crossing the stream accordingly, we formed our bivouac for the night. Tema endeavoured to persuade his people to assist in clearing a space for me, and to cut and bring wood and materials for a temporary hut; they treated his orders with the utmost contempt: upon my applying to them in a more persuasive strain, they bargained that I should shew them some fun with my guns, and in this way I got them to do all I wanted.

We started next morning at 8 a.m., and commenced a toilsome ascent of the Moyur mountain, the summit of which we did not reach till 11 o'clock; the ascent was very severe in many places, the natural ladders afforded by the roots of the trees alone rendered it practicable; near the summit it was less precipitous, and here were the timber trees and Seeas, wild mangoes, chestnuts and oaks, the seeds of all which I have sent you; but unfortunately the acorns were all dead. From the top of the Moyur no view was obtained. Descending, occasional openings gave us glimpses of new mountains, for we were now on the north side of the great range seen from Luckimpore, but no extended view; the path less difficult, but occasionally presenting but a mere ledge over a precipice, and

[1] Much of this letter, somewhat rewritten, was used by Dalton for his account of the Hill Miris in his *Descriptive Ethnology of Bengal,* published over a quarter of a century later. The changes are towards greater liveliness and precision. Thus the above sentence becomes in 1872: 'Two long marches over a most difficult road, impracticable for any quadruped except a goat, and infeasible by a biped who had not the free use of his hands as well as his feet, brought us to the settlement. My baggage was nearly all carried on the heads of sturdy-limbed hill lasses who merrily bounded like roes from one slippery rock to another, laughing at my slow progress.'—E. T. Dalton, *Descriptive Ethnology of Bengal,* p. 31.

dangerously slippery from decayed leaves. We descended about one-third of the distance we had ascended, and then crossed over several smaller hills, the northern outworks of the Moyur. In one place a large tree had fallen across a chasm deep and dark, and was used as a bridge. It was slippery as glass, and even the Meris passed over very slowly and cautiously; I did not like it much, but Tema gave me a hand, and I got safe across.

We now came to hills that had been cleared for cultivation, and other symptoms of a near approach to human habitations; not that the road was better, it continued just as before, but here Myttons had been grazing, and they do not stray far from their villages. Several times we passed what appeared to be a well cleared path, but I was told that they led to where spring bows had been set to kill wild animals, and the clearance was made to warn human beings not to go that way. Depending much upon such stratagems for a supply of animal food, they have various ingenious methods of taking or killing wild beasts. A deer trap is constructed by running a light palisading between two precipices or other obstacles, in the centre of which the trap is placed. It appears to offer an exit to the unwary animal, whose course has been obstructed by the palisading and through it he attempts to rush, when the top, composed of logs of wood bound together, drops on and crushes him.[1]

Bina Meri's village was now before us, and drawn up on the side of the road a deputation of the Sonrok Meris (the Bor Dolonee Meris) awaited my approach. These Sonroks I had hitherto regarded as not near so well affected to us as the Temas and the Torbottiah tribes, and I had been informed by Tema that they were very irate with him for having encouraged this excursion of mine. I was by no means anxious to meet them, and had not invited them to an interview: but here they were, and I could not decline it; so putting a bold face on the matter, I took a seat under a tree and gave them an audience. After having explained my object in visiting these hills, and thanked them for their civility in coming to meet me, very much to my surprise, instead of any objections being raised,

[1] Dalton shortens and enlivens this for the *Descriptive Ethnology*: 'They have various methods for entrapping animals of all kinds, from an elephant to a mouse, and all is fish that comes to their net. The flesh of a tiger is prized as food for men; it gives them strength and courage. It is not suited for women; it would make them too strong-minded.'—ibid., p. 33.

(*From E. T. Dalton*, Descriptive Ethnology of Bengal, 1872)

7. A young married Khampti woman

(*From E. T. Dalton*, Descriptive Ethnology of Bengal, 1872)

8. A Gallong, called by Dalton in the manner of his day, 'a Dhoba Abor'

(*From J. Butler*, A Sketch of Assam, 1847)

9. Akas in 1847, from a sketch by J. Butler

(*From J. Butler*, A Sketch of Assam, 1847)

10. A Dafla and a Dafla Chief's widow, from a sketch by J. Butler

(From E. T. Dalton, Descriptive Ethnology of Bengal, 1872)

11. An Idu (Chulikata) woman described by Dalton as 'a typical but not favourable specimen'

(From E. T. Dalton, Descriptive Ethnology of Bengal, 1872)

12. An Abor Chief. He is suffering from the very common goitre

they gave me a most cordial and pressing invitation to proceed to their villages too, saying as I had come as a friend to visit Tema, it was not fair that the honour should be conferred on him alone; they too were most anxious to entertain me, and would gladly provide everything necessary. One of their villages, that in which the principal Gaum resides, was an easy march from where we stood. They did all they could to induce me to go, overruling all my objections as stated. I had only supplies for three days,—they would provide everything. At last I said it would be improper for me to go to their village without bringing with me some presents to bestow on their wives and daughters to cause them to remember my visit. That the few things I had brought of this description, had been disposed of, or were bespoke, and were I now to go empty-handed to visit them, they would all say that I had bestowed many marks of favour on Tema's people and to them had given nothing. I therefore could not now go; but if all turned out well, and they behaved themselves properly on their next visit to the plains, they should receive a visit from me at another season intended for them, as my present visit was for Tema. With this they appeared satisfied, and only further begged that I would excuse the old Gaum coming to meet me in another Gaum's village, which would be derogatory to his dignity, and allow him instead to pay his respects at Siploo Mookh, or on the road down. This was so ruled, and thus quietly ended the conference with the ferocious Sonroks.

Bina Gaum's village which we now entered, is situated on one of the low hills under the Moyur mountain; the houses are long, and raised considerably on posts of cleft timber, indiscriminately constructed on the top or side of the hill; but the level of the flooring is tolerably well preserved by varying the height of the supporting posts. It contains only ten dwelling houses; but as each house holds an entire family, including brothers and their wives, and married sons and their children, each may on an average contain about twenty individuals. The situation of the village is very beautiful. The low hills around,—some partly cleared for the purposes of cultivation, some entirely so, and now covered with the straw of the crop last reaped,—appear in fine contrast with the dark tints of the lofty mountains of Moyur and Yaloo, and others more distant that surround it. The inhabitants, men, women and children, far from evincing any signs of fear, crowded about me as I passed through the village. The road from this to Tema's village, which is about two miles distant and north-west of this village, continues over low hills, many of which have been cleared and are now fallow, and after a time will be again taken up. Between the villages barricades are constructed in different places to keep the Myttons from the cultivation when necessary.

We followed the windings of a stream called the Kutoo, and were led by it into a pretty little valley comprising a level space of cleared ground of some extent, watered by the Versing river which winds round the hill on which Tema's village is built, and here we encamped; Tema's village within hail above us to the S.E., the river flowing from the N.W. Here were assembled to me, besides the notables of the three villages of Tema's, or the Pambottiah tribe, all the headmen of the Torbottiah *duwar*. They seemed to wonder much at my visit. What could it portend? and to be in some alarm; but this soon wore off. They describe their country as much better worth seeing than this. The villages are larger, more numerous, and nearer to each other than those of this *duwar*; the nearest a day's march from this, about twelve miles in a direction north by west. The villages are six in number, and within hail of each other, on hills as Tema's and Bina's, and the houses similarly fashioned; their cultivation is more extensive, the crops fewer, and more varied. They have *asso*, *dhan*, and *hali*; but the latter is not planted out. They sow the seed as we sow peas. They kept me talking till dinner time, and then all retired with Tema, who had a grand feast; not less than eighty individuals were entertained by him; all that came to see me were invited, and I am told his house was crammed; nor were we neglected, a fine fat kid and fowls and eggs, yams and sweet potatoes and Indian corn were supplied. Temá asked me if I would drink *mhud*, the spirit they distil; but this I declined, or doubtless a large supply would have been sent.

Next morning I proceeded to the village, and found them all busily engaged in divination as to whether my visit was to bring them good or evil. I was told that the auspices were favourable. A man sat apart from the rest holding in both hands a puny chicken, and invoking all the spirits of the woods by name. Those deities who delighted in the blood of Myttons, and those who rejoiced in the slaughter of pigs; those who were propitiated by the sacrifice of fowls, or those who were content with a vegetable offering, all are on such occasions invoked; and after the *Chout* is terminated, the chicken is cut open and the entrails examined, from which they augur good or evil. Often as this 'auspicium' to my knowledge has failed them, they most pertinaciously adhere to the practice; and undertake no expedition, journey or work, without consulting it. I was sketching, and when the 'auspiciums' were being taken, and when the ceremony was concluded, they sent to me to beg of me to return to my hut to give audience. I desired for peace sake to give it where I sat; but the Torbottiahs who wished to pay their respects in regular form, could not, they said, with propriety do so in Tema's village. However, previous to descending I paid Tema's house a visit, to which he made no objection.

The house is seventy feet long, raised on timbers, some perpendicularly and some diagonally placed in which is laid a platform of bamboos for a flooring. The roof has gable-ends, and is pitched very high; the thatch being composed of the leaves of a species of cane as before mentioned. Under the gables a cross *chopper* covers in an open balcony, one at each end. The interior consists of one long apartment sixty feet by sixteen, from which a passage extending the entire length is partitioned off. In the large apartment down the centre no less than four fires were burning on hearths of earth. On one side were ranged, with some appearance of order, their arms, pouches, travelling apparatus, &c.; another portion of the apartment was decorated with trophies of the chase. In the centre between the fires frames of bamboos suspended from the roof served as tables, on which various domestic utensils were deposited. I had hoped that the passage which was partitioned off from this apartment contained the dormitories of the family, but on examination it was found to be the *mhud* cellar. In it were ranged conical baskets lined with plantain leaves, in which the *mhud* is fermented, and received in vessels placed underneath: in the large apartment the whole family eat, drink and sleep: Tema and his wives in the upper end or first fire, his sons and daughters round the next, other members of the family round the third, and slaves and dependents round the fourth. Fearful of being pillaged by the Abors, they do not venture to display much property in their houses. The greater portion of it lies buried in some remote spot known only to the heads of the family. Besides cattle, ornaments, arms and wearing apparel, it consists of large dishes and cooking vessels of metal, and what are called Dao Guat,[1] such as little bells with various devices and inscriptions, in what I fancy must be the Thibetan character; but I know it not. The Meris do not know where they come from; a few are occasionally obtained in barter with the Abors, but the most of them have been handed down as heirlooms in the family, and they are regarded as the most valuable portion of their property. They are occasionally used as money, and valued at from four annas to twelve rupees each, according to shape, size and ornament. Those with inscriptions inside and out are most highly prized. Those without inscriptions are little valued. These bells are common amongst the Dufflas, who can give no better account as to how they became possessed of them. I am told the Butias sell them and if so you can perhaps tell me something of their origin. The Meris tell the same story if asked where they get their fine blue beads, i.e. that they are heirlooms; very seldom, they say, are they now procurable in barter or exchange, though some few are occasionally procured from the Abors.

It is not impossible that numbers of these bells and beads thus handed down as heirlooms may have been brought with them from the country from which they originally emigrated. Regarding their migrations they have no traditions. They believe, and they are not singular in the belief, that many orders and races of men were created, whom the Creator allotted to dwell where soil and situation were best adapted to the constitution and habits he had given to each; and thus that the Meris were created for, and have ever dwelt in these hills. Their religious ideas are very vague. They believe in a future state, and have an indefinite idea of a spirit who presides in the regions of departed souls, as is shewn in their mode of disposing of their dead. The body is interred fully clothed and equipped with arms, travelling pouch and cap, in a deep grave, and surrounded by strong timbers to prevent the earth from pressing on it. Nor do they omit to supply the departed for his long journey with food, cooking utensils, and ornaments of value, so that he may make a respectable appearance in the other world. They

[1] In 1872, Dalton spells 'these bells' more correctly as 'deogantas' and says that the inscriptions on them are nothing more than repetitions of the shibboleth, *Om Mani Padmi Om*. He compares the superstition regarding them with the veneration of the Garos for the vessels called Diokoras, 'also it is believed of Tibetan manufacture'.

attach great importance to their dead being thus disposed of and buried near the graves of their ancestors. If a man of any influence dies in the plains his body is immediately conveyed to the hills to be so interred, should the disease of which he died not be deemed contagious.[1]

Marriage, although its violation is considered the direst of offences, is with them a mere matter of barter or exchange. Young ladies are in the first instance valued according to the wealth and respectability of their parents. The price is such that few suitors are able to make it up for several years after preliminaries have been arranged, and they pay it accordingly by instalments. It consists, if the damsel be of high family, of two or three Myttons, twenty or thirty pigs, fowls, *mhud*, and sometimes clothes. When the parents are content, or the stipulated amount has been paid, they invite the suitor with his family and friends to come for his bride, and he is entertained that day by the father of the lady. On his return with his wife all the friends and relations accompany him, and the bridegroom or his parents now in their turn have to feast them and his own friends into the bargain for several successive days. There is no further ceremony. The parties are now considered man and wife; and woe be to him that seduces from her lord the wife so wedded. The adulterer is seized and securely bound, detained under most rigorous treatment for a day or two. If he be powerful his friends come to his assistance, and make offers for his ransom which must be considerable to be accepted; but the chances are, he is left to his fate, and if such be the case he is put to death. The woman who has committed the *faux pas* is less severely dealt with. A little wholesome chastisement, and she is again admitted into the family circle.

It must not be omitted that when a marriage is concluded, the bridegroom expects to get fair value with his bride for his pigs,

[1] It will be of interest to quote Dalton's revision of this passage, hardly for the better, in the *Descriptive Ethnology*. 'The religious observances of the Miris are confined to the slaughter of animals in the name of the sylvan spirits, and vaticination by the examination of the entrails of birds when the deities have been invoked after such sacrifices. They profess a belief in a future state, and have an indefinite idea of a god who presides in the region of departed souls; but, as they call this god Jam Raja, I believe it to be the Hindu Yama.' The rest of the paragraph follows our text, except that Dalton says that the departed is given gifts 'according to the position he enjoyed in life, in order that Jam Raja may know whom he has to deal with'.—ibid., p. 34. Jam Raja is not, of course, a Miri deity.

&c. that he has expended on her. If personally, or in default of an adequate trousseau she be found wanting in this respect, there is a dinner, an assemblage of mutual friends, and the parents of the bride are made to disgorge should it be so determined; or should they refuse, their daughter is treated as a slave, and not as a member of the family: notwithstanding this, a widow cannot leave her husband's family and heirs to contract a fresh marriage unless she can find the means of defraying all that was originally paid for her; if she can do this and furnish a feast on the occasion, there seems no objection to her making a second alliance.

The costume of the women is peculiar: a short petticoat extending from the loins to the knees is secured to a broad belt of leather which is ornamented with brass bosses, besides this they wear round their middles an infinite number of rings made of filaments of bamboo embroidered with the fibres of another plant. A band of similar material, from which a bit of cloth is suspended in front, is bound tightly round the breast under the arms. This is their travelling and working dress; but at other times they wrap themselves in a large cloth doubled, brought over the shoulders, and pinned in front like a shawl. They wear round their necks an enormous quantity of beads, mostly of blue, like turquoise but also of agate, cornelians and onyx, and glass beads of all colours. They have bracelets of silver or copper, and anklets of finely plaited cane or bamboo. Their hair is adjusted with neatness, parted in the centre and hanging down their backs in two carefully plaited tails. In their ears they wear most fantastic ornaments of silver, which it would be difficult to describe; a simple spiral screw of this metal winding snake-like round the extended lobe of the ear is not uncommon amongst unmarried girls; but the ear ornaments of the matrons are much more complex. They generally have very sweet countenances, though few could be called handsome. The almond-shaped eye is common, but not universal; mouths generally well formed; and teeth, notwithstanding the free use of tobacco, very fine and white; their complexion what the natives of India would call fair, but they have rosy cheeks and ruddy lips, which is a decided improvement on the Assamese complexion; they are very stoutly built, generally short of stature, but to this there are remarkable exceptions.

The men have fine muscular figures; many of them tall and with good features, but the countenances of some are repulsive. The variety of feature denotes an admixture of races, and no doubt many of them have Assamese blood in their veins, but usually there is the high cheek-bone and almond-shaped eye, lips rather thin and face devoid of hair except a few over each extremity of the mouth forming an apology for a moustache. They gather the hair to the front, where it protrudes out from the forehead in a large knob secured by a bodkin; round the head a band of small brass or copper knobs linked together is tightly bound. In their ears they as well as the women wear a variety of ornaments, but of a distinct kind. The lobe is distended so as to hold a knob an inch in diameter. It is gradually enlarged by the insertion of a roll of the leaf of the pine-apple tree.

The Chiefs wear ornaments of silver, shaped like a wine-glass or egg-cup; young men do not venture to attach so heavy a weight to the slight ligament, and insert a hollow plug of silver instead. The males also wear a profusion of the blue beads before mentioned, and others, all very large. Their costume is simple enough—a band round their hips composed of rings of bamboos, the same as worn by the women but not so numerous; an apron attached thereto before and behind, and a cloth wrapped round their body and pinned so as to resemble a shirt without sleeves; a cap of cane or bamboo work with turned-up peak, which however is worn behind, and over their shoulders as a cloak, which also serves as a pouch or knapsack, they throw a covering made of the black hairy fibres of a plant, which at a little distance resembles a bearskin. Their costume is not complete without placing on their heads and over their caps a piece cut out of tiger or leopard-skin, the tail of which hanging down their backs has a droll appearance! They are all very filthy in their persons, many of them appear never to have had their faces washed since their birth.[1]

As this was not their cultivating season, and the crops had been reaped, it was chiefly from information that I could note anything on the subject. Each village has a certain extent of ground, comprising hills, sides of hills and valleys, which they have been in the

[1] In the *Descriptive Ethnology*, Dalton omits this uncharitable sentence, but complains instead of the smell of drying meat and fish: 'A Miri encampment, while this process is going on, may be sniffed from afar, and the unpleasant odour clings most disagreeably to the people, rendering it desirable to keep to the windward of all you meet.'—ibid., p. 34.

habit of cultivating from time immemorial; but not more than a fifth of this ground is under cultivation each season. They cultivate each patch two successive years, and then suffer it to be fallow for four or five, taking up again the ground that has been longest fallow in lieu. They have a superstition, which deters them from breaking up fresh grounds so long as their *gra* (fallow) is sufficient —a dread of offending the spirits of the woods and forest by unnecessarily cutting down the trees. In Tema's village the chief crops are *bobesa* or *bobsa dhan*, the grain of which is large, pear-shaped; and *goom dhan*, or maize. Many of the villages have *aoosa* and *hali*, resembling that which is grown by the Assamese; but the cultivated tracts appertaining to this village get too little sun for those crops. The *bobsa* and *goom dhan* are sown in the same ground and at the same time, and round the squares which contain these crops they plant yams and other edible roots; they have not got the potato, but it would most likely grow well and be serviceable to them; they sow red pepper, which succeeds admirably. Tobacco is generally grown in patches near the houses. The labour of cultivation and all labour falls chiefly on the women. They have few other implements than their *daos*, which are used to clear, cut and dig with. The men consider it sufficient to occupy themselves in hunting and attending to their various snares and spring-bows for wild animals, and when the season arrives for the trade, in collecting *manjeet*, which is performed by both sexes.

The *manjeet* grows in steep declivities, interlaced and entangled with other shrubs, so that it is not easy speedily to collect a quantity, at least all that I found of it was little; the leaf of the genuine kind is small, narrow and pointed, and slightly suffused with a tinge of the colouring matter. There is a bastard kind also found in great quantities, the leaves of which are very much larger and the plant altogether coarser in appearance; it is called the female *manjeet* by the Meris, and though similar in growth with the other, its flexible shoots contain scarcely any colouring matter. Nevertheless, it is sometimes brought down mixed with the finer. The Meris assured me that this fraud was not theirs, but was practised upon them by the Abors. I recommended them for their own sake to bring down none but the best, and they promised that none other should leave their country. They collect and tie it up in bundles when fresh and flexible, then lay it on frames or hang it up to the eaves of their houses to dry; when it becomes rather brittle, it is fit for exportation.

The Mytton is the only species of horned cattle possessed by the Meris. It is rather a clumsy looking animal in make; but a group of Myttons grazing on the steep rocky declivities they seem to love, would be a noble study for Landseer; some are milk-white, some nearly black, some black and white, and some red and white. To the Meris they are only useful as food. On festive occasions one is killed, and I should think the beef must be excellent; they feed most delicately on young leaves, and keep in excellent condition. The cows would, I have no doubt, give a large supply of milk; but the Meris have not yet found this out. I asked them to procure some for me, but received the usual answer, 'Meris don't know how, not our custom.' The females appear tame, and submit to be tethered; the bulls rove their own masters, but do not wander far from the tethered females, so are in a measure tethered too; just now they all roam where they please, but when the crops are on the ground a mountain or so is fenced round by strong timbers from tree to tree, and into this enclosure they are driven, and remain till the harvest is stored. They have pigs and poultry in plenty and a few goats.

I suppose there are no people on the face of the earth, more utterly ignorant of everything connected with the arts than are the Hill Meris. With the sole exception of the bands and other articles of bamboo, cane and fibres above-mentioned, which the women are everlastingly making, everything they use is imported; were their communications directly with the plains, and indirectly by means of the intervening tribes, with the civilized countries on the other side of the great range cut off, the use of metal and of women's clothes would be lost to them. The Abors can forge themselves *daos*, but the Meris know not the art. The most distant tribes manufacture coarse cotton clothes; but though the Meris are in constant communication with them, as well as with us, they have not the remotest idea of weaving. They cannot journey two or three days from their village, without having to cross a considerable river. If it be not fordable, a rough raft of Kakoo bamboos is hastily constructed for the occasion; but though constantly requiring them, and annually using them, they have never yet attempted to construct a canoe: this the more strange, as the Abors of the Dibong push a considerable trade in canoes cut in the rough. I suppose that until the

Meris discovered the fertile plains of Assam, which they were first led to visit by having killed birds in whose bellies they found rice, and discovered by proceeding in the direction of their flight, they were mere savage hunters; the skins of beasts their only clothing, and the flesh their chief, if not only food.

Could they be stimulated to a more industrious course of life, they might considerably improve their commercial relations with us. The great rivers that enter their country abound in gold grains; the process of washing is simple, and the Meris have had for two centuries constant opportunity of watching it in all its phases.

The last process of separating the gold from the remainder of the sand or scoria, they might leave to the Assamese gold-washers; but the rough washing with the *doorunnee* and bottle gourd might be performed by them, and a considerable quantity of gold introduced. The *doorunnee*, or tray, is very simple and easily made, and the gourds are obtained from the Meris by the gold-washers. This would be a most lucrative trade for them. By a little attention to the *munjeet* also, which they are too lazy to give, its growth might I think be improved and its collections facilitated, simply by the removal of other plants that choke it. I have not much more to say, but I may send you another chapter if you are not tired of me and the Meris. But this letter has grown to such a length, I fear you will be inclined to throw it into the fire without reading it.

I have no doubt that there are sundry errors in this account; but I cannot stop to correct them, for I feel sure if I were to read over what I have written I should hesitate about sending it. I had not intended sending you the journal up the river, it was copied to send home with sketches; but as you seem interested in the scenery of the Soobanshiri, I have ventured to add it.

Yours very sincerely,
E. T. DALTON

3

A LETTER OF 1845

('On the Meris and Abors of Assam', by Lt. E. T. Dalton. In a letter to Major Jenkins, *J.A.S.B.*, 1845, Vol. XIV, N.S., pp. 426 ff.)

MY DEAR MAJOR,—I have this moment received yours of the 8th, for which many thanks. I fully intended sending you a supplemental paper, giving such information as I was able to collect regarding the Abors, their trade with the Meris, and communication with Thibet. The account I sent you was hurriedly written, and is, I know, very incomplete in many material points; but as a mere programme for the more ample narrative we may next year be, I hope, enabled to compile, it may not be necessary to add much to it at present.

The Customs, Language, Religion, &c. There is no very material difference between the Abors and Meris. They are evidently of common origin, and the Duphlas are of the same race. The Meris from their intercourse with the plains are, in some respects, more civilized, but almost all I have said concerning them applies equally to the tribes more remote. They intermarry with them, exchange slaves, and are generally in the habit of constant intercourse. The Meris, many of whom have become rich in cattle and goods, appreciate the value of combining for mutual support, and dwell in villages. The Abors, as they themselves say, are like tigers, two cannot dwell in one den; and I understand their houses are scattered singly or in groups of two and three over the immense extent of mountainous country occupied by them.

The Meris say, that whenever a few families of Abors have united into a society, fierce feuds about women and summary vengeance, or the dread of it, soon breaks up or scatters the community. They therefore prefer building apart, and depending upon their own resources for maintaining themselves in their isolated positions. They are compelled to be more industrious than the Meris, and can fashion themselves *daos* and weave coarse cloth. The iron for the former is, I believe, obtained from the other side, for I have not learnt that they understand the art of working the ore, and that which the Meris import from the plains they purchase ready-made into *daos* for their own use.

The cotton used in the coarse cloths they weave is grown by themselves, very little of it ever finds its way down here; but I saw one load of it this year, and it appeared of excellent quality. Between the Abors and Meris there is a considerable trade. The Meris import from the Abor country *munjeet*, beads, *daos*, *Deo guntas*—the little bells I have described in my former account, and cooking utensils of metal, Myttons, slaves, and I may say wives, their marriages being so entirely a matter of barter. In return for which the Abors take cloths of Assamese manufacture, salt or any articles imported by the Meris from Assam. Of the mode in which their intercourse with Thibet is carried on, I have as yet obtained very little information. I have never yet met with an Abor who had been across, and the Meris I have questioned on the subject assert they had not seen the tribes who are in direct communication; but from those who had seen them they had heard of a fine rich country, inhabited by people who wore fine clothes, dwelt in stone houses, and rode on horses, which was watered by a mighty river. However they manage it, the Abors import from this country everything above enumerated, save the *munjeet*, slaves, and wives that they interchange with the Meris. The large metal dishes thus imported are of superior manufacture, and fetch high prices when brought in here by the Meris. The Meris possess cooking vessels of great size so obtained, which they use at their feasts, but are very jealous of producing before strangers. The *daos* are of superior temper, but of rude finish, and of the workmanship, as I believe, of Thibetan blacksmiths; they are probably made in the rough for the express purpose of barter with these people, as they are made in Luckimpore for the Meris. In addition to the articles I have enumerated, the Abors import salt (from the description given of it, rock salt) from the north, for it appears they have a very scanty supply of it, and gladly take our salt from the Meris when they can get it. I presume it to be an importation: what they export in return I know not, but most likely cotton and *munjeet*. Between the Duphla and Meri countries there is a tribe called 'Auks' and 'Auka Meris'[1] by the Assamese, who never visit the plains, but

[1] Clearly, the Apa Tanis.

yet appear, from all I have been able to glean regarding them, very superior to the tribes of this family we are acquainted with. Surrounded by lofty mountains, the country they inhabit is an extensive valley, represented as being perfectly level, and watered by a branch or perhaps the principal stream of the Soondree, and richly cultivated. They are said to possess fifteen large villages, the cultivation of one adjoining that of the other, so that there is no waste land between. Their chief cultivation and sole staple appears to be rice, to rear which they irrigate the land, and are said to have magnificent crops in return. Their lands are not, I am told, adapted to the cultivation of cotton, but they procure as much of it as they require from the Abors in exchange for rice. In industry and art they are acknowledged by the Meris to be very much their superiors, who however, perhaps for this very reason, look upon the Aukas as their inferiors in the scale of creation. The Auka ladies wear blue or black petticoats, and jackets of white cotton of their own manufacture; their faces are tattooed *unde nomen* Auka, which is given to them by the Assamese. They call themselves 'Tenae'. The males do not rejoice in much drapery; they wear a girdle of cane-work painted red, which hangs down behind in a long bushy tail I am told, and must have a comical effect. Of their religion all I have heard is, that every fourth year there is a kind of religious jubilee devoted to sacrificing and feasting at the different villages by turns; and on these occasions, someone officiates as priest: other particulars in which they differ from the Meris have been related to me. The Meris, however extensive the family and the number of married couples it includes, all occupy one house. The young men of the Tenae tribe when they marry leave their father's house, and set up for themselves. During the Moamorya troubles many of the Assamese of this division are said to have sought and found in the Tenae valley a refuge from the persecutions of that sect; the refugees appear to have been generously treated, and no obstacles were opposed to their return to their own country when the dangers that threatened them were removed; but I have sometimes heard that a few remained of their own free will, who settled in the valley, and are still to be found there.

The Tenae appear to be a very peaceably disposed people, but they occasionally are compelled to take up arms to punish marauding Abors, and they are said to do the business at once effectually and honourably, whilst the Meris and Abors confine their warfare to nocturnal and secret attacks, and, if successful in effecting a surprise, indiscriminately massacre men, women, and children. The Tenae declare hostilities, march openly to attack their enemy, and make war only on men, and their revenge does not extend beyond the simple attainment of their object in taking up arms. If this be true, it places them in a high rank, as a humane people, amongst our Mountain tribes.[1] Tema is my authority for both assertions, humiliating as it should have been to him, and honourable to them; but he made the confession of the Meri mode of waging war without any remorse of conscience.

Assured that a more particular and better authenticated account of a people so sequestered and peculiar would be interesting, I would, if permitted, next cold season make every effort to visit them, in the manner least calculated to excite jealousy or alarm. Their country is most easily accessible from the Duphla Door; but I am not yet well acquainted with this tribe, and am not prepared to say that it would be safe to attempt a passage through their country without a strong guard, which would defeat my object entirely; and having, I think, secured the goodwill of the Meris, I would prefer their route, though said to possess more natural difficulties; ascending the Soobanshiri as before to Siploo Ghaut, I propose, after having paid Tema's country a second visit and explored such of the Sowrock country as lies on this side of the Soobanshiri, to proceed to the Turbotheah villages. The Turbotheah have promised to assist me in every way from Tema's village to their own, and as the Aukas or Tenae are only two good marches from the Turbotheah Meris, I should hope to be able to make amicable arrangements with them and the intervening Abors to permit me to proceed in safety to their valley.

I cannot hold out any very sanguine expectations of being able to penetrate so far as to behold Thibet from the mountain tops, or to gain much knowledge of that country; but without crossing the snowy range there is a vast extent of interesting country to explore.

This time next year I hope to be able to propose an excursion to explore the Duphlas' country. I had an interview yesterday with a

[1] The Tenae may, adds Dalton in 1872, 'claim a hearing as the most humane of belligerents at the next International Congress'.—ibid., p. 35.

considerable number of them, those for whom the salt has been sanctioned; and having concluded the business of the day, I had an amicable talk with them, and, on the question of a visit being started, they made no demur.

E. T. DALTON

Luckimpore, the 23rd March 1845

4

AN OLD GREY-BEARDED MAN

(*Assam Census Report*, 1881)

THE religion of the Hill Miris, who come down to the valley with madder in the cold season, is quite as vague as that of the settlers in the plains; but here the place of Nekiri and Nekiran is taken by the Yapum, a kind of sylvan deity, who suffices for the needs of everyday life, though in critical conjunctures some greater god has to be gained over by the sacrifice of a *mithan*. A Hill Miri told me how he had once, while a boy, actually seen a Yapum. The character of this god is that he lives in trees, and all the beasts of the forest obey him. My informant was throwing stones in a thicket by the edge of a pool, and suddenly became aware that he had hit the Yapum, who was sitting at the foot of a tree in the likeness of an old grey-bearded man. A dangerous illness was the consequence, from which the boy was saved by an offering of a dog and four fowls made by his parents to the offended Yapum, who has subsequently visited him in dreams. The hillmen propitiate also the spirits of the dead, called 'Orom' in their own language (apparently), and 'Mora deo' by them in Assamese.

5

THE HILL MIRIS

(*Preliminary Notes on Miris*,[1] 1897)

THE Miris are bounded on the south-east by the Dirjemo river, which separates them from the Abors inhabiting the low hills north

[1] This, like the *Preliminary Notes on Daphlas*, also printed in 1897, from which an extract is given in the next chapter, may be by G. W. Dun.

of Dibrugarh; on the north-east by a low range of hills forming the southern boundary of the Dihong valley; on the south by the subdivision of North Lakhimpur; on the south-west by the hills to the east of the Ranga river which separate them from the Daphlas.

The Subansiri river divides the Miri hills into about equal proportions east and west, while its principal tributaries from the east and west, viz. the Sidan and the Kamla, divide the hills north and south. The range from which the Sidan flows is the comparatively low one on the south-west of the Dihong. The Kamla flows from the high mountains of the north-west. About the Subansiri we have no accurate information, except we know it to have a long course north and west. The Miris inhabit the low hills overlooking the rivers, but do not appear to build their villages on mountains exceeding 6,000 feet in altitude. Looking due north great snowy mountains shut out the view; but to the north-east low passes give a view over the Abor country and the valley of the Dihong. The Miri hills are more rugged than the neighbouring Daphlas, and the steep ascents and descents make travelling through them a most laborious task.

The Ghyghasi Miris inhabit the country to the west of the Dirjemo and to the north of the Sissi subdivision of North Lakhimpur.

The Ghasi Miris live between Dhol river and the Subansiri.

The Sarak Miris live in the outer range between the Subansiri and the Ranga. It is to be noted that the Ghyghasi and Ghasi Miris may be considered one clan, and they are regarded as such by the other Miris to whom they are known as Abors, Dob Abors, and other names.

The Panibotia and Tarbotia clans live in the hills to the west of the Subansiri. The Tarbotia have their villages on the southern bank of the Kamla river, and consequently do not need to travel by wäter to reach the plains; hence their name. Both the Sarak and Tarbotia clans consider themselves our *ryots*.

The Anka tribe, sometimes called Tenai Miris, possess fifteen villages on a tableland to the north-west of Miriland, beyond the watershed of the Ranga river. These people never visit the plains, and are so different in their manners and customs as to make it doubtful whether they really are Miris. They trade with the Daphlas and supply them with salt.

The Miris' neighbours are the Abors, Daphlas, and Lhokaptra.[1] The Abors and Daphlas are fully described in the report on those tribes. The Lhokaptra, or the people of Lhokhalo, inhabit the country south of the Saupo, and were formerly known as the Tacpoui. The country is most fertile, producing magnificent rice crops. They are believed to be a harmless hard-working people who avoid intercourse with both their neighbours of Thibet and Miriland.

Next to the Ghasi Miris we have the Dobah Abors, living in the hills above the Sissi and Dijmur rivers. They call themselves Dobahs, but are called Galongs by our plains Miris. The Assamese give them the nickname of *Kukur-Khoas,* or dog-eaters. These people come in to Sissi and Dibrugarh, the western villages using the Sissi river as far as Dablang, whence there is a path south-west to the large village of Sissi. They are quite a distinct clan from the Passis, and much resemble in appearance and language their western neighbours, the Ghasi Miris. They have occasionally given a little trouble. This year, 1890, however, there has been a police-station and a strong guard at Kathalguri, about six miles west of Sissi.

This people may be Ghyghasi Miris; no mention of what the people are in the Siden valley.

The Sarak Miris came down, as usual, to Bordoloni, and have been encamped there for some months. They drew their *posa,* Rs 249-7-9, in March. The Gams are friendly as usual. The Tarbotia and Panibotia Miris have drawn their *posa,* Rs 876-6-5, including salt. These tribes do not encamp in the plains like the Saraks. The Gams report that the pillars of the Great Trigonometrical Survey in their country are damaged, and want somebody to go up to repair them. The Miris have a pleasant recollection of the Trigonometrical Survey Party and the money they made by it.

The Ghyghasis are small, square-built, muscular men, with deep-set eyes, square jaws, flat noses, and very large mouths.

The Saraks resemble the Ghyghasis, but are inferior in muscular development.

The Panibotias and Tarbotias are much superior to the Ghyghasis and Saraks, many of them being fine tall men of great muscular power. Their eyes are more obliquely set, and features are not so

[1] The appellation Lhokaptra, 'cut-lip', probably derives from the appearance of the face when marked with a tattoo line down the chin.

rough as the clans to the east, and they have a much more civilized appearance.

The Ankas are a still greater improvement on the clans named, but are much disfigured by tattooing their faces.

The Ghyghasis and Ghasis are very meanly clad, their whole costume consisting of a loin-cloth and a sleeveless flannel coat.

The Ghasis of the Sew river are perfectly naked as to the loins, but wear a sort of woollen mantle. Both these tribes wear their hair cut square.

The Panibotias and Tarbotias dress much the same as Daphlas; they gather their hair to the front of the forehead, and having made a bushy knot of it place a bodkin through it. Round the head they wear a fillet of leather studded with copper knobs. A girdle of cane sustains the loin-cloth. On their shoulders they wear a knapsack of a square form made of cane, and covered by a kind of short cavalry cloak made from palm-tree fibre. They wear a cane helmet resembling the Daphla helmet, but they add a piece of tiger or bear-skin as a cover, with the tail attached.

The Ankas differ little in costume from the Panibotias, but instead of a loin-cloth they wear a kind of kilt made from rhea fibre.

Their arms are long straight *daos*, bows and arrows, and among the tribes north of the Kamla, long spears.

Polygamy is usual, and polyandry is sometimes practised among the Miris. The women are the chief labourers in the fields, and are faithful, industrious and cheerful wives. They have a peculiar manner of burying their dead, for they equip the corpse as if for a journey and it is placed in the grave with a supply of food, cooking utensils, &c. In this custom they resemble the Daphlas.

The Ghasi and kindred clans on the east of the Subansiri are great trackers of game which they follow persistently for days through dense jungle. They only trap fish, and in this custom differ greatly from all the tribes to the west of the Subansiri, who are the greatest trappers of game among the frontier tribes.

Among the Miris of the northern hills, with the exception of the Ankas, there is little or no cultivation, and even the Miris of the hills near us are dependent on the plains for food, for their crops of Indian corn, sweet potatoes and rice are not sufficient for their own consumption. The northern Miris exchange cotton clothes and *mangit* for food, while the southern do a small trade in tobacco. Their staple article of food is dried meat, but their supply of *mithun* and goats is very limited, so they have to trade with the plains for cattle which they obtain in exchange for *mangit*.

They believe in a Supreme Being and in certain good or bad spirits. Hinduism is gradually spreading from the plains, but in a pure form is never likely to make much way, as long as the Miri is compelled by poverty to eat every sort of food from a rat to a tiger; there is a strong resemblance between the Miris and some of the Eastern Nagas with regard to religious observances.

The villages of all the clans are very small, 18 or 20 houses being a large number, the average generally being 8 or 9; but sometimes as many as 40 people live in one house. The Miris who visit the plains are in the habit of boasting about the size of their villages, but it has been found upon investigation that villages said to possess 100 houses generally consist of, at the outside, 5 to 10. The houses are from 60 to 70 feet long, built on changs, and thatched with leaves. There is a framed-off passage down the centre of the house where the fermentation of plantain leaves is carried on. The house is divided into recognized partitions by the triangular tray slung from the roof over the earthen fireplace after the manner of the Mishmi. The nearest villages to the plains near the Subansiri are some twelve miles distant from the foot of the hills, and the paths to them are most difficult. They are all built on the slopes of hills, never on the summit, and are absolutely without defence, as there are no feuds between clans or villages.

The Miris appear to have no settled Government, as each village is so small and so far separated from others, that it appears impossible for them to have one system of laws. They adopt no measures for the defence of their houses and fields or for the safety of the community at large. There is no power of combination between different villages, nor cohesion among clans. They are in fact poor, helpless, barbarous savages, without religion, without arts, and without laws. They have just as much as they can do to keep themselves alive, and they have little power to either help or injure their neighbours. We have always been on the most friendly terms with all the villages, and the *posa* we pay them is more perhaps of a charity than any we pay on the North-East Frontier. At times certain Chiefs of villages have used threatening language to managers of tea-gardens, on account of their right of way being stopped by the planters, but these instances have been rare.

All the Miri clans appear to understand one another, though differing so much in dress and appearance. The Ghyghasi Miris also understand the Abors, and many of them travel to the Dihong. There can be little doubt that the Abors, all the clans of the Miris and the Daphlas are one great tribe, quite different to their neighbours on their east and west, namely, the Bhutias and Mishmis, but bearing a strong resemblance to the Nagas on the south bank of the Brahmaputra.

Chapter VI

THE DAFLAS OF KAMENG AND SUBANSIRI

1

HISTORICAL PRELUDE

(A. Mackenzie, *History*, 1884, pp. 27 ff.)

EASTWARD of the Bhoroli river, and occupying the hills north of Naodwar (the Nine Passes) in Durrung, and Chedwar (the Six Passes) in Luckimpore, as far east as the upper courses of the Sundri, lie the numerous cognate tribes of Duphlas. Of them wrote Mohummed Kazim in the days of Aurungzeb—'The Duflehs are entirely independent of the Assam Raja, and, whenever they find an opportunity, plunder the country contiguous to their mountains.' They are, however, not so much a single tribe as a collection of petty clans independent of each other, and generally incapable of combined action. To show the extent of intertribal subdivision among them, Dalton notes that two hundred and thirty-eight Gams or Chiefs of Duphlas are in receipt of compensation for loss of *posa*, amounting altogether to only Rs 2,543. Their form of Government is oligarchical, there being sometimes thirty or forty Chiefs in a clan. The Duphlas call themselves only 'Bangni', meaning 'men'. The tribes on the border of Durrung are now generally called 'Paschim' or Western Duphlas; and those on the border of North Luckimpore, 'Tagin' Duphlas.

From the beginning of our occupation of Assam the Duphlas gave much trouble to the local officers, and many fruitless efforts were made to induce them to resign the right of collecting *posa* directly from the *ryots*. From an account bearing date the 13th May 1825, it appears that the Duphlas were entitled to receive, from every ten houses, one double cloth, one single cloth, one handkerchief, one *dao*, ten head of horned cattle, and four seers of salt. The *paiks* of the Duphla Bohotea Khel, or that section of the Assamese cultivators which had originally been partially assigned to the Duphlas as responsible for their dues, being subject to this heavy impost paid only Rs 3 instead of Rs 9 per *ghot* to Government, the balance being remitted to enable them to meet their engagements. The different clans of Duphlas did not interfere with each other on the plains. Each knew the villages to which it had to look for *posa.* But they claimed a right to collect from their allotted *paiks* wherever these might migrate, and they demanded full dues whether the *paiks* could pay or not. This exacting spirit made them very difficult to deal with. Such indeed was the dangerous character[1] of this tribe that Government did not for many years see its way to insisting upon commutation of *posa* where the clans objected to it. The Duphlas of Char Dwar in Durrung were the first to come to a settlement. Early in 1835 they had raided, probably under the instigation of the Taghi Raja, and as a punishment had been forbidden to enter the plains to collect their dues. In November following, some few months after the Taghi Raja's successful raid near Baleepara, the Duphlas attacked that place and carried off several British subjects. An expedition, consisting of a small military force, was sent into the hills and rescued the captives, taking at the same time several Duphla prisoners. Of the thirteen Duphla clans north of Char Dwar, eight upon this came in and submitted to Captain Matthie, the officer in charge of Durrung. They agreed to resign the right of collecting direct from the *ryots,* and consented for the future to receive the articles of *posa* from the *malguzar* or revenue officer of the villages according to a revised tariff. Any complaints they might have against the *malguzars* they promised to refer to the Magistrate. They undertook not to aid the enemies of the Government, and to help to arrest offenders. One Chief was to live on the plains near the Magistrate, to be a medium of

[1] The Daflas had the misfortune to earn a thoroughly bad reputation in early times. Thus Shyahbu'ldin Talish declares in his *Fathiyya-i-ibriyya* that, while Assam is 'a wild and dreadful country, abounding in danger', most of the inhabitants of the neighbouring hills accept the Raja's sovereignty and 'obey some of his commands'. 'The Dafla tribe alone does not place its feet in the skirt of obedience, but occasionally encroaches in his kingdom.'—J. Sarkar, 'Assam and the Ahoms in 1660 A.D.', *J.B.O.R.S.* (1915), Vol. I., p. 184. A little later in the same century, when Raja Udayaditya Singha proposed to send a force to punish the Daflas for having carried off a number of Assamese subjects including women and children, his Prime Minister said: 'The Dafla miscreants can be captured only if an elephant can enter into a rat-hole.'—S. K. Bhuyan, *Anglo-Assamese Relations* (1949), p. 32. And in the first decade of the eighteenth century, Francis Hamilton described the Daflas as retaining 'the fierce and warlike spirit of the ancient Assamese; they indulge their appetites in eating unclean food as much as the impure nations of China and Europe, and adhere to their old customs, altogether rejecting the instruction of the sacred order of the Hindus and what is called the purity of its law'.—F. Hamilton, *An Account of Assam,* edited by S. K. Bhuyan (1940), p. 74.

communication and represent their interests. Their *posa* was fixed at one coarse *arkut* sheet, one long cotton handkerchief, two seers of salt, one *dao*, and one goat for every ten houses. The other clans shortly afterwards made similar agreements.

The Duphlas of Naodwar were longer in coming to terms. They did indeed in 1837 consent to receive their dues through the *malguzars*, but they claimed a right to two-thirds of all the revenues paid by the *paiks* of the Duphla Bohotea Khel already mentioned, who were, they insisted, their hereditary slaves. In 1838-9 they became very actively troublesome, and it was at one time thought probable that a military force would have again to be sent into the hills. The collection of *posa* was entirely stopped for a time. Somewhat unexpectedly this measure had the effect of bringing the clans to order.

It appeared from facts that came to light at this time that the nearer Duphlas were practically subordinate to the Abor Duphlas of the higher ranges, and these remote clans, feeling the loss of the regular payments, and perhaps not understanding what the borderers were haggling for, had insisted on submission being made. It was not, however, till 1852 that the *posa* was finally commuted for a money payment, and then only because the Court of Directors at home insisted on this being done, if the local officers could enforce it without causing disturbances.

Up to that time the Duphlas had been a source of frequent anxiety, and military posts along the frontier had been necessary to secure its peace. From 1852, however, the Duphlas, much to the relief of the local officials and somewhat to their surprise, settled quietly down, many of them devoting their attention to agriculture and residing permanently as our subjects on the plains. The payments made to them stood as follows at the time of Mills' inspection of Assam (1853-4):

	Rs	as	p
From Tezpur treasury to Duphlas of Char Dwar and Naodwar	2,494	0	0
From Luckimpore treasury to Duphlas of Char Dwar	1,243	14	5
From Luckimpore treasury to Duphlas of Banskotta	392	1	6

with 24 maunds of salt to the last-named in lieu of certain *hath* or market dues.

The tribe remained quiet and gave no cause of anxiety up to 1870, when parties of Duphlas from the hills committed, on two occasions, outrages on certain Duphla villages lying in Naodwar within the District of Durrung.

In one case their object was said to be to recover an absconding slave. This action on the part of the Hill Duphlas did not indicate any ill-feeling towards British authority, but it was nevertheless deemed necessary to visit them with some mark of displeasure. Accordingly the annual allowances of all supposed to have been implicated in the transactions were withheld, and a reward was offered for the capture of the principal offender. At the same time it was pointed out to the local officers that runaway slaves ought not to be allowed to settle in villages near the frontier where their presence incited to attempts at recapture.

The secret of the other raid was not so easily found out. The facts, as at last discovered, appear to have been these: The Chief of one of our Duphla villages sought as a wife for his son the daughter of a neighbouring Chief. The proposals were accepted, and to close the transaction presents were made in Duphla fashion to the lady's relatives. Probably some wealthier suitor appeared, for very shortly afterwards the intending bridegroom was told that his alliance was not desired. To this he might have become reconciled; but to the insult was superadded material injury—his presents were not returned. He was mulcted not only of his first betrothed, but of the means of procuring a second. He laid his wrongs before the Deputy Commissioner of Durrung, and was by that officer referred 'to the civil court'. The fatuity of thus treating the grievances of a Duphla savage will be evident to most minds, and drew forth eventually strong censure from Government. The Deputy Commissioner should of course have dealt with the case in his political capacity, summoning a Duphla panchayat and dispensing equal justice in a simple way. The injured man failing to get redress in the plains (for to him 'the civil court' was a meaningless phrase), betook himself to the hills. His brethren there took a more practical view of the case, descended one night with swift primitive retribution on the village of the dishonest marriage-mongers, and carried off as hostages all on whom they could lay hands. The mere fact of the raid was at first all that the Government came to know. The allowances of all supposed to be concerned in it were stopped, and a reward was offered for the capture of the ringleader. The Duphlas in the course of a few months settled their private quarrel: the marriage presents were returned, and the hostages restored. But when they had so settled their feud, they were astonished to find that Government, or its local representatives, were still dissatisfied and not disposed to overlook the way in which the affair had been conducted. After waiting a time they threatened that, if the allowances were not restored, they would raid upon the plains. A foolish foray made by the Deputy Commissioner into the hills in search of the proclaimed Chief still further irritated them, and at one time the political prospects were reported so doubtful that fresh stockades were established and the police guards increased. Eventually, however, amicable relations were restored. The Duphlas were not apparently at that time prepared to violate the peace they had so long to their own advantage preserved; and though the ringleader in the raid escaped capture and punishment, the tribe as a whole gave no further trouble. Instructions were issued by Government which, it was hoped, would for the future lessen the chances of the occurrence of such raids.

The Duphlas have not yet been brought to see that they are not at liberty to attack men of their own race living within our territory. The Administration Report of 1872-3 gives the following account of another outrage committed by them in that year, and of the views of Sir G. Campbell upon it:

'The Duphlas along the Durrung and North Luckimpore borders had not for many years past given much trouble, though the report for 1870 described an outrage committed for private reasons by one hill Duphla upon another man of the same tribe living on the plains. Many Duphlas have settled as colonists in our territories, and a few even occasionally work on tea gardens. The tribe of Tagin Duphlas living in the hills on the borders of East Durrung and part of Luckimpore, have, however, this year placed themselves in an attitude of positive hostility to the Government, and perpetrated a raid which, though directed against Duphla colonists in the plains, and not against the Assamese, was far too serious to be overlooked. On the night of the 12th February 1872, the village of Amtolla, two miles north of the Gohpore police-station of Durrung, and seven miles from the foot of the hills, was attacked by a body of two or three hundred hillmen. The village was sacked, two persons—a man and a woman—who resisted being tied up, were murdered, and 44 persons—men, women, and children—with their property, were carried off. The villagers who were taken away were all western Duphlas (not Tagins), while a few settlers belonging to the Tagin Duphlas were left unharmed—a circumstance which tended to confirm the belief, since supported by ample evidence, that the aggressors were chiefly men of the Tagin tribe. The guard at Gohpore made an attempt to follow the raiders, but did not succeed in overtaking them. Orders were, however, sent to reinforce the district police with troops. All the Duphla passes to the east of Durrung and along the Luckimpore frontier were blockaded, and payment of the allowances annually made to the Tagins was stopped. Spies sent into the hills traced the raiders to their homes, and by their reports and the statements of one or two captives who escaped, the position of their villages has now been pretty well ascertained. The cause assigned for the outrage is a curious one. The hillmen had, it seems, been much troubled by an epidemic, which they believed to have been imported from the plains. They called upon the Duphlas of the plains to compensate them for the loss they had sustained in children and adults from the disease; and because the Duphlas of Amtolla declined to meet their wishes, they came down to recoup themselves by seizing them all as slaves. The Tagins refuse to surrender the captives save on ransom paid, and even threaten further raids if the blockade is maintained. The blockade has of course been strictly maintained, and it is believed that this exclusion from all trade with the plains has been felt by the hillmen, though as yet they show no signs of giving in. The Lieutenant-Governor, after personal consultation with the Deputy Commissioner, Colonel Graham, has seen reason to hope that strict maintenance of the blockade during the ensuing cold weather may possibly bring them at last to terms. Precautions will be taken against any further raids; but it may be necessary to adopt more active measures of reprisal. The Duphla hills are not specially difficult of access. Elephant-hunters from Assam have been several days' march within them, going up one way and returning another. The villages where most of the captives are, are but four or five marches off, or at most perhaps seven marches. The tribes have no unity of organization; every village is separate, and if one is hostile, the next may be friendly. They have not fire-arms, and for some years, as above remarked, they have not shown themselves hostile to our Government, but have yearly drawn allowances for loss of their practice of making collections from the Assamese *ryots* of the Dwars or passes, and have done much profitable trade with our bazars and markets. There is reason to hope that a small expeditionary force might bring the contumacious to terms, and that the effect of such a settlement would be lasting. The Lieutenant-Governor has, however, rather shrunk from recommending a regular expedition owing to the chronic difficulty which exists in Assam in getting coolie carriage for troops. He has stated to the Government of India his belief that we ought to have for service on the North-Eastern Frontier a permanent coolie corps to be available for expeditions of this kind, which we must expect occasionally until the frontier difficulties are finally solved and the tribes come to find their interest in peace and trade. Such a corps could always be usefully employed in making roads when not required for hill service. Meantime what His Honour has proposed is that we should place on the Duphla frontier next cold season a sufficient number of troops and police to establish a rigorous blockade, and furnish, if called for, a small expeditionary force. Colonel Graham, the Deputy Commissioner, would be allowed, if he saw a good opportunity, and other means had failed, to make a dash into the hills with this force and with the elephant and local coolie carriage available. He would, while looking out for this and watching the blockade, superintend also the operations of the survey, which should carry eastward along the foot of the hills the line of demarcation successfully settled along the Kamrup frontier, so as to mark distinctly for the future the territory which we claim as ours and within which we shall refuse to permit any outrage or encroachment.

'That the blockade will probably secure the surrender of the captives, we may perhaps be encouraged to hope, from the fact that another Duphla village to the north of Luckimpore, which had carried off in similar fashion last year one or two Duphlas of the plains, has lately restored them, when it found that Government insisted on viewing such conduct as a grave offence. In this instance the local officers had, however, been fortunately able to capture one of the offenders, and held him as hostage till his village sent back the captives.'

The blockade proving ineffectual, a military force was sent into the hills in 1874-5, and the release of the captives followed, no active opposition being offered by the Duphlas. Since that year the Duphla members of the tribe have been duly dealt with as matters of police; but our relations with the Chiefs have been uniformly amicable.[1]

2

THE DAFLAS IN 1851

(W. Robinson, 'Notes on the Dophlas and the peculiarities of their Language', *J.A.S.B.*, 1851, Vol. XX, pp. 126 ff.)

THAT portion of the southern face of the sub-Himalayas, which, extending from 92° 50′ to about 94° north latitude,—and forming the northern boundary of the valley of Assam, from the Kuriapara Duwar, to where the Subonshiri debouches into the plains,—is occupied by a tribe of mountaineers, usually known to the people of the valley under the appellation of the Dophlas. This term,

[1] The subsequent history of the Daflas to the end of the century is comparatively uneventful. In October 1887, a party of Daflas raided the village of a Chief called Tarang very near the Harmati Tea Garden. Fifteen persons were kidnapped and Tarang with his brother and wife were killed. This man had been oppressing the hill people who passed through his village on their way to the markets of the plains and had received an official warning only a month before. Government took no action in what it considered to be a domestic feud.

In February 1899, 'a rather curious incident occurred, which shows how strong is the desire amongst these hill people to keep up their population. In these small communities the balance of power is easily affected by a slight increase in the death-rate, and every person counts. This no doubt had much to do with the development of the law, so common on the frontier, that life should be taken for life in intertribal warfare. On this particular occasion, it appears that Chengmara, the village of a *gam* called Pareng, had been raided by hillmen from the Dikrang. Pareng thereupon descended to the plains, and after enlisting in his service some Daflas from the village of Katoni near the north trunk road, attacked a party of hillmen from the Poma Pani, who happened to be stopping in the neighbourhood. Pareng had no previous quarrel with these people, and seems to have been solely actuated by the desire of increasing the population of his village, but in the course of the affray three men were injured and four were carried off. The police however, were promptly on the spot, the captives were recovered, and Pareng convicted and sentenced to two years' rigorous imprisonment'. — B. C. Allen, *Assam District Gazetteers: Lakhimpur* (1905), p. 73.

whatever may be its origin, is not recognized by the people to whom it is applied, except in their intercourse with the inhabitants of the plains. Bangni, the term in their language to signify a man, is the only designation they give themselves.

During the latter days of the Ahom Suzerainty, when internal dissensions, and the growing imbecility of the government furnished opportunities for the bordering tribes to indulge in acts of rapine and lawless aggression on their lowland neighbours, the Dophlas were not slow in exacting their share of the general spoil. Several attempts were made to check their atrocities; and on one occasion, Raja Gourinath Sing is said to have marched an army into their hills for the express purpose of chastising them; when, as native historians tell us, several thousand Dophlas were taken prisoners and brought down to the plains. The Raja, unwilling that they should pine in indolence, obliged them to dig a canal with the view of draining off the large and unwholesome morasses that still exist in Muhal Kollongpur. But, owing to the bad treatment to which the prisoners were subjected, and the unhealthiness of the season, the greater portion of them are said to have perished, and the task assigned them remained unaccomplished.

Others of their tribe, however, nothing daunted, continued their periodical predations, and annually kidnapped large numbers of men and women, whom they consigned to perpetual slavery. The government, unable to put a stop to these atrocities, was at length compelled tacitly to submit to them, and yield to these marauders the right of imposing a blackmail on all the frontier Muhals. But the exactions of the Dophlas fell so heavily on the inhabitants of these Muhals, especially during the period that Raja Purander Sing held the upper portion of the valley, as to lead to the entire desertion of almost all the villages on the frontier.

On the resumption of the Raja's territories by the British Government, active measures were taken for checking the predatory habits of the Dophlas. It was then ascertained that the Chief inhabiting the higher ranges had alone the prescriptive right to the blackmail. Their intercourse with the plains, however, had long been obstructed by their hostile neighbours of the lower ranges. But the able conduct and perseverance of the British authorities, in reopening communications with them, and engaging them in active co-operation, compelled the allegiant clans of the petty Chiefs on the frontier hills to pay due submission to the paramount authority, and to desist from all further acts of violence on the people of the plains; while the Chiefs who held the prescriptive right to the tribute were glad to enter into an agreement to receive an annual sum from the British Government in lieu of all their demands. The sum so paid since 1836-7 amounts to Co.'s Rs 2,543, which is divided among no less than two hundred and thirty-eight different Chiefs.

Of the mountains, inhabited by the Dophlas, we possess no topographical information of any value. The few Asamese slaves, who from time to time contrive to effect their escape from servitude, affirm that the Dophla villages are large and numerous, that the inhabitants keep large flocks of cattle, and are well supplied with grain. The country is thickly covered with forests, and during the winter months, the fall of snow is said to be very heavy.

The climate, generally speaking, is highly healthful. The temperature is as various as the several elevations of the ever-varied surface; which, though nowhere troubled with excessive heat, is so by excessive moisture, generating a rank vegetation, considerably aided by a deep stratum of luxuriant soil.

The Dophlas are divided into innumerable petty clans, who maintain among themselves an oligarchical form of government, and acknowledge the authority of from two or three, to as many as thirty or forty Chiefs in each clan. The influence exerted by these Chiefs seems to be mild in the extreme. The people appear to have no legal provisions whatever for the well-being and conservation of society—the enlightened end of civilized legislation—and yet exhibit among themselves in an eminent degree, that social order which is the greatest blessing and highest pride of the social state. A sort of tacit commonsense law governs them. . . . The grand principles of virtue and honour, however they may be distorted by arbitrary codes, are the same all the world over; and where these principles are concerned, the right or wrong of any action appears the same to the uncultivated as to the enlightened mind. And it is to this indwelling, this universally diffused perception of what is just or otherwise, that the integrity of these mountaineers in their intercourse with each other is to be attributed.

Their ideas of religion are exceedingly crude. They acknowledge the existence of one Supreme Creator and Ruler of the world, but Him they never worship, and their religious rites consist almost exclusively in the propitiation, by offerings and sacrifices, of the spirits or Genii whom they believe to inhabit their hills. Their worship consists of invocations of protection for the people, and their crops and domestic animals,—and of thanksgivings when recent troubles are passed. Sacrifices are considered more worthy than offerings, and hogs and fowls are the animals most frequently sacrificed. Libations of fermented liquor always accompany their sacrifices, and as every sacrifice gives occasion for a feast, the people on these occasions indulge pretty freely in copious potations. The office of the priesthood is not an indefeasible right vested in any family, nor is the profession at all exclusive. Whoever chooses to qualify himself may become a priest, and may give up the profession whenever he sees fit. Diseases are supposed to arise entirely from preternatural agency, hence the priests are also exorcists. They pretend also to a knowledge of divination, and when called in cases of sickness, or in times of temporal distress, consult auspices of many different kinds, but especially by the breaking of eggs, and the examination of the entrails of young chickens.

Marriages are never entered into before the parties have attained the age of maturity, and the ceremonies performed on such occasions are but little perplexed with forms.

The dead are always buried, and that very soon after decease. The body is borne by friends and relatives in silence to the grave, and with it are deposited the war implements and cooking utensils used by the deceased, after which preparations are made for a funeral banquet.

The physiognomy of the people exhibits, generally and normally, what is commonly known as the Scythic, or what Blumenbach terms the Mongolian, type of the human family. This type, however, is in many cases much softened and modified; and where there has been any intermixture with the Arian inhabitants of the plains, it frequently passes into a near approach to the Caucasian. The usual complexion is that of a pale brown or isabelline hue, though in many cases it approaches to a much darker tint.

The ordinary dress of the Dophlas, consists of a short sleeveless shirt of thick cotton cloth, sometimes of the natural colour, but more frequently striped gaily with blue and red, and always excessively dirty. Over this is thrown a mantle of cotton or woollen cloth fastened about the throat and shoulders by means of pins, made of bamboo. The ears are always ornamented with great knobs generally made of some shell, but sometimes of horn and amber. The hair is always worn long, very neatly plaited and turned into a knot just above the forehead. The women are generally wrapped in a shapeless mantle of striped or plain cotton cloth, with its upper part tucked in tightly over the breast, and enveloping the body from the armpits to the centre of the calves. Another cloth is also thrown over the shoulders, answering the purpose of a cloak, the upper corners of which are tied into a knot sufficiently low to expose the throat which is invariably cased in a profusion of bead necklaces of all varieties of colour. The ears are loaded with huge brass or silver rings, and the ear-lobes so stretched with the weight of great metal knobs that they not unusually reach down to the shoulders. Heavy bracelets of mixed metal are also worn on the wrists. The hair, which among the women is generally very long and black, is gathered into a knot tied just above the nape.

The arms used by the people, consist of a long sword slung by means of a piece of cane across the shoulders, a dagger worn in the girdle, and a bow and arrows.

The arts practised by the Dophlas are few and simple. Agriculture is almost the sole business of the men, and to it is added the construction and furnishing of the dwelling house; the boys look after the domestic animals, and the women, aided by the girls, are employed in all the indoor occupations, of cooking, brewing, spinning and weaving. The agricultural products are rice (the 'summer rice' of the plains), wheat and barley, with a few cucurbitaceous plants, greens, edible roots, red pepper, ginger and cotton. Very little is grown beyond what is necessary for household consumption, and the surplus is bartered either with the people of the plains for agricultural implements, culinary utensils, beads, and ornaments, and cotton cloths, or with their neighbours on the hills, for swords and woollen cloths of Thibetan manufacture. The men haft all the iron implements they purchase abroad.

Manjit forms a considerable article of the trade of the Dophlas; it grows wild in great abundance on their hills and is said to be of very superior quality.

Of learning and letters, the Dophlas are totally devoid. Their language, as well as physical attributes, give strong evidence of their connexion with the affiliated sub-Himalayan races of Thibetan origin, and a comparison of the vocabulary will show a very close alliance with the dialects of the Miris and Abors.

3

INTERESTING AND ROMANTIC

(E. T. Dalton, *Descriptive Ethnology of Bengal*, 1872, pp. 36 ff.)

THE Dophlas affect an oligarchical form of Government, and acknowledge the authority of from two or three to as many as thirty or forty Chiefs in each clan. Their villages are larger than those of the Hill Miris. They are richer in flocks and herds, but they are inferior physically, being I think the shortest in stature of this division of the hill tribes.

They have normally the same Mongolian type of physiognomy, but from their intercourse with the people of the plains and the number of Assamese slaves, which they have by fair means or foul acquired, it is much modified and softened, and I have sometimes seen Dophla girls with pleasing and regular features. Their complexion varies much from olive with a ruddy tinge to dark brown.

I never heard of Dophla priests, but Robinson says they have priests who pretend to a knowledge of divination, and by inspection of chickens' entrails and eggs, declare the nature of the sacrifice that is to be offered by the sufferer and the spirit to whom it is to be offered. The office, however, is not hereditary, and is taken up and laid aside at pleasure, so it resolves itself into this, that every man can, when occasion requires it, become a priest. Their religion consists of invocations to the spirits for protection of themselves, their cattle, and their crops, and sacrifice and thank-offerings of hogs and fowls. They acknowledge, but do not worship, one Supreme Being which, I conceive, means that they have been told of such a being, but know nothing about him.

Marriages and marital rights are the same with Dophlas as with Hill Miris. Those who can afford it are polygamists, but polyandry is far more common amongst the Dophlas than amongst the eastern tribes.[1]

A very pretty Dophla girl once came into the station of Luckimpur, threw herself at my feet and in most poetical language asked me to give her protection. She was the daughter of a Chief and was sought in marriage and promised to a peer of her father who had many other wives. She would not submit to be one of many, and besides she loved and she eloped with her beloved. This was interesting and romantic. She was at the time in a very coarse travelling dress, but assured of protection she took fresh apparel and ornaments from her basket and proceeded to array herself, and very pretty she looked as she combed and plaited her long hair and completed her toilette. In the meantime I had sent for 'the beloved' who had kept in the background, and alas! how the romance was dispelled when a *dual* appeared! She had eloped with two young men!!

The costume of the Dophlas is very similar to that of the Hill Miris, except that I do not think the Dophla women wear the crinoline of cane-work.

I have no particulars as to their mode of burial, but it is probably the same as that of the Hill Miris.

The Dophla country extends from the hill course of the Sundri river to the Bhoroli river, comprising the hills to the north of Chedwar in the Luckimpur and of Naodwar in the Tezpur District. They are in communication with the Tibetans as they possess many articles of Tibetan or Chinese manufacture, but like the Dihong Abors and Hill Miris, they tell wild stories of the savages between them and Tibet. It is said of these savages that they go absolutely naked, and have, or assert that they have, an abhorrence of the *smell* of clothes.

The Dophlas are a trifle more ingenious than the Hill Miris. The women spin and weave and are spared much of the labour of the fields that the Miri women are subjected to; but they are still very backward in the commonest arts. I do not think they have any pottery; and they import from Tibet or Assam nearly all their weapons and implements.

[1] The author of the Census Report for Assam, 1881, however, says that the Daflas repudiate the practice of polyandry 'with horror and declare that it would be visited with death'.

4

PLEASANT-FACED AND ROSY-CHEEKED

(H. J. Harman, 'Narrative Report' in *General Report of the Topographical Surveys of India, 1874–5*, 1875, pp. 85 ff.)

THE low ridge above the right bank of the Paing Jilli forms the boundary between the Daphla and Abor districts; the line crosses the Ranga and runs up a prominent spur to the ridge. The Abor country beyond the low ridge is low, undulating grass slopes, and with little forest as far as the Chengreng chain which is clothed with forest. The Abor country of the right bank shows long, sloping, and wide rounded spurs . . . ending in cliffs above the Ranga; there is only dense forest in the valleys. Several large villages and many large clearings are visible from Takha's village. The Daphla District is in dense forest; all the villages (except Tagum's) are on the sharp spurs with intervening narrow and deep valleys. . . . The Ranga flows through some small stretches of plain in which are the curious *Bogi Jamu* trees; some are of great height; the surface of the trunk is hard, smooth and white with a slight green tinge; they have a very thin bark, which they shed. A pony could travel by the Salanibari route to the Ranga, but would find the paths leading up to and from village to village difficult in places. The villages are well built and of the same type as those in the Dikrang valley; many of the houses are large, and Silli's house in Takha's village is 180 feet in length. Piji's village has 20 houses, Tatta and Su 30; Tapli and Tagun each 50; Tada 60 and Takha 150. There is a vast amount of *jhoomed* land about and below the line of villages, which are all from 3,000 feet to 4,000 feet up, and on Tagum's side of the river are also great expanses of *jhoom*. The Ranga Valley Daphlas all belong to the Bodalia clan, except Tagum and Tatta (again in Su's village) who are of the Nirikolia clan.

These Daphlas are a great contrast to those on the Dikrang; they are light complexioned (Tada's boys are very fair), there are lots of pleasant-faced, rosy-cheeked women of short stature but well built, well dressed (I rarely saw a shabby man); were easily amused, very merry, and manifested extreme curiosity about all my ways and things, but are obstinate as mules and prone to tell lies. I saw nothing of a defensive or warlike nature about, or in the villages, and the men seem to me to be men of peace. Their poisoned arrows (for game) are tipped with a piece of wood shaped like a heart, and just below it on the shaft is a lump of brown stuff studded with little yellow seeds; they get this from the Abors (it is *monkshood* —aconite ?).

Tada had, as a constant attendant, a little Abor boy, who carried bamboo *chungas* of the liquor of the country for the Gam. On inquiry I found that this boy had to do duty for a certain time, and would then claim Tada's daughter in marriage. This liquor is in appearance like milk and water, it is palatable and mild, not unlike small beer, and is brewed from a small dark-brown grain (a millet); the Daphlas drink of it every opportunity. I never saw a Daphla drink water. Tada has four wives and Tagun two; I do not know any other men who have more than one.

The Daphlas have few prejudices as to with whom they eat. I once saw a man toast a water-rat and a mouse on a stick without flaying them; and one day after digging some grubs out of a decayed tree they were promptly devoured, and the men were overjoyed when I came upon some queer things with little black scales like beetles. They profess to hold the monkey and dog in abhorrence as articles of food. Twice a day do they cook their fine hill rice in bamboo *chungas*. Some houses have earthen pots, and Tada has a set of brass vessels. To wash the rice first before boiling they consider is a waste of its strength. Soon after midday they eat a meal of cold rice, a portion of the morning's cooking. They feed themselves, not by putting the rice into their mouths with the fingers, but by collecting it in the palm of the hand and passing the palm of the hand downward across the mouth; many of them have bone spoons, which they occasionally use. All, even little children, are inveterate smokers of the coarse hill tobacco; the black remains in a pipe after it has been smoked is swallowed with great relish.

In the Daphla District there is no salt; the Ouka Miris supply a dirty grey, bitter salt produced somehow by evaporation; the specimens I saw consisted of a cake of mud one-eighth of an inch thick, and on this was deposited one-eighth inch salt; the lower surface of the mud was black with smoke.

The method of gathering rubber is to notch the tree all over at distances of about a foot apart, and as the rubber, which exudes in a thin stream, gets firm, it is detached from the bark by winding it up into a ball; in this form it is sold by weight to the Kaingyas of the plains; the rubber is often cunningly wrapped round a ball of mud. At about 4,000 feet and near Takha's village is a fine rubber tree.

They poison fish by pounding the bark of the *Ramal* tree on the stones where the water is flowing into the selected pool, the outlets of which are banked up; the poison spreads through the pool and acts rapidly, they say. There are many fishing weirs on the Ranga, some ingeniously built; the platform is usually suspended by long canes from the trees above the bank; the fish are caught in long funnel-shaped baskets baited with flesh and placed in the runs; we several times got small fish out of these baskets.

There are quantities of the *Tamin*, the madder plant, in these hills; they told me that the greater quantity is taken to the plains by the Abors. I saw some silk cocoons of large size, like those of the *Monga* silkworm.

The Daphlas do not dance, sing, or whistle; a noticeable peculiarity about the Daphla women is the sing-song way they talk; they speak slowly, the voice rises and falls half a dozen times and is pitched in as many keys during the utterance of a short sentence; the effect is very odd and pretty, and sounds like the tone of humble expostulation. Whenever a discussion took place, the women always had their say and were listened to attentively; every village brought to me its one or two old ladies, and their position in the community was explained by the Gam.

5

PHYSICALLY VERY FINE FELLOWS

(*Assam Census Report*, 1881)

THE origin and meaning of the name Daphla are not known. As pronounced in Lakhimpur, it would be written Domphila. They call themselves Niso or Nising. The Miris they call Bodo and the Abors Tegin, but this last word seems to be merely the name of a tribe common to the Abors and Daphlas. The Daphla name for the natives of the Assam Valley is Haring.

The Daphlas, like the Abors, are recent settlers. Of late years they have been coming down in small communities of five or six families at a time, driven by scarcity of food or by the oppressions of the Abors. Some of these little colonies suffer terribly from sickness, and a Daphla hamlet too often presents a sad array of tenantless and decaying houses. The Daphlas are less laborious cultivators than the Miris. Their villages are not so well stocked, nor so comfortable, nor are the men so tall as the Miris, though the eastern Daphlas are physically very fine fellows. They bring the hair forward, wind it in a ball over the forehead, and stick a skewer of wood or metal through it (a silver arrow in the case of a Chief). A habit of slightly contracting the brows gives them a singularly proud and stern appearance. As one goes westward, however, the race degenerates in physique and in the outward appearances of prosperity, and the westernmost Daphlas are squalid and dirty. Yet they regard themselves as superior to the Miris, with whom they will acknowledge no relationship—a fact which seems to bear out the tradition of Miri vassalage.

Daphla and Miri speak practically the same language, and their deities, Yapum and Orom, are the same. The Yapum are male and female, and exist in indefinite numbers. A white goat or fowl is their appropriate victim. The Daphlas also count the sun among their deities, but their great god, who requires a *mithan* to propitiate him, is called Ui or Wi, of whom no Daphla cares to speak much for fear of incurring his displeasure. His character may be guessed from the Assamese equivalent of his name, Yom or Yama, the god of the infernal regions.[1]

[1] The earlier writers, convinced that the gods of the tribes were devils inhabiting the infernal regions, are rather fond of identifying the Supreme God of any tribe with the Hindu Yama, god of the dead. Dalton also does this. It is however an identification which is singularly wide of the mark, as nearly all the tribes locate their higher deities in the heavens and do not associate them with death.

The Ui or Wi are, among the Abors, Hill Miris and Daflas, simply the unseen spirits.

6

NOTES ON THE DAFLAS

(G. W. Dun, *Preliminary Notes on Daphlas,*[1] 1897)

In other reports reference has been made to the use of the term Abor, as being most confusing and having led to endless mistakes and serious misunderstandings when the hill tribes of the North-East Frontier have been spoken or written about.

The Daphlas are a tribe of the outer hills, inhabit the southern slopes of a spur of the Himalayas which divides the Bhoroli from the Subansiri drainage.

This spur is well defined as far as a peak called Lollupo, but at the point it is split into numerous minor valleys and spurs among which the Daphlas have established their villages. On the west a very distinct ridge coming down from Lollupo separates the Daphlas from the Akas, who inhabit the basin of the Bhoroli. On the east another distinct ridge starting also from Lollupo peak divides the Daphlas from the Miris of the Khru river (an affluent of the Subansiri) and of the Subansiri.

Two principal streams drain the interior of the triangle thus enclosed by these two spurs, viz. the Humderi or Ranga on the east, and the Dikrang. The Dikrang has a small tributary from the west called the Borpani, and further west are the still smaller streams of the Buroi with its tributaries the Poma and the Papum, and still further west the Borgang, a stream of the other slopes.

The general direction of the rivers in the above triangle, known as the Daphla country, is easterly. The valleys lying east and west.

The Daphlas thus appear to be clearly separated from the Akas on the west and the Miris on the east, and also from the tribes of the Khru valley, whom we suppose to be Miris, on the north.

Their boundary on the south is generally considered the Daphla *ghur*, an old road running along the frontier from south-west to north-east, but the kingdom of Brigiong extended into the hills; and when we took over the Government in 1825 it was usual to regard the low outer hills as ours.

[1] The authorship of this document, which was printed for the Intelligence Branch, Q.M.G.'s Department, Simla in 1897, is uncertain, but it has been attributed to Captain G. W. Dun and may well be by him.

No name has yet been assigned to the minor range which divides the Ranga valley from that of the Dikrang, but that on the southern side of the Dikrang is usually known as the Misr Parbat.

The inhabited hills vary in height from 2,000 ft. to 7,000 ft.; a great portion of these hills have been cleared for cultivation by cutting and burning the forest, and in the Ranga valley many of the lateral valleys have been terraced and irrigated, and there is permanent rice cultivation. The northern portion of the Ranga valley is open grass country, and from this part of the valley a low pass gives an entrance into the Khru valley.

Boundaries of the different divisions of the Tribe.—As there is no distinction between the so-called Abors, Pachams, and Tangins, in this report the inhabitants of the range nearest the plains and sometimes known to us as the Pachams and Tangins will be called southern Daphlas, while the inhabitants of the hills beyond the Misr Parbat Range will be designated northern Daphlas or Dikrang valley Daphlas, the clans dwelling more to the east Ranga valley Daphlas. These last are divided from the Dikrang valley by a range of hills.

The Daphlas call themselves Nyising, and assert that they are descended from Nyia, the son of Abotani, whose father was Dhangi, the Sun, by his wife Chinne, the daughter of Chatachi, the Earth.

Nyia had a number of sons, and the children of the latter were the founders of the existing clans.

Names of the Daphla Clans.—The clans of the Daphlas appear to partake of the nature of classes of the population rather than clans; but as these classes are much in the habit of frequenting one village, or a number of villages close together, they have been considered *Khels* or clans. The following are known to us. They all have the final term *olia* meaning clan or class: Bod, Nirik, Tan, Tahb, Taching, Bart, Tao, Bapa, Kalinga, Bal, Tasi, Noling, Sakpha, Phering, Opurtak, Rapo, Pai, Opurta, Namta, Chana, Opur Tabung.

The features of the Daphlas are decidedly Mongolian. Their language is closely allied to the Miri. They tattoo their faces, the reason assigned being that it enables them to be recognized in the next world.

There are numerous exogamous clans.

Religion.—The general name of God is Ai, but there are names for each particular deity.

The chief are Sonoli, the god of heaven; Yapum, the god of trees (frightens people in the forest); Chili, the god of water; Prom, the god of diseases. There are a few beneficent deities, such as Pekhong, the god of breath, and Yechu, the goddess of wealth. *Deondies*, sorcerers, are called in when a person is ill.

Manners and customs.—As the Daphlas are perhaps better off than any of the other hill tribes of the North-East Frontier, they have developed an independence of bearing, which is capable of being taken for rudeness by a stranger. No article of attire nor description of food or drink is safe from them; it is first demanded as a right; and if the request is politely refused and a close watch is not kept on the article in question, it will disappear in a most mysterious way.

They bury their dead and build a small hut over the grave in which they place water and food for five days. They mourn the dead for two days, and the dependants of a Gam who carry the body to the grave are given a two months' holiday from work.

They isolate cases of cholera and small-pox in the jungle. They have no medicines, but in surgical cases apply herbs.

When a man dies his brother takes the widow to wife. There is no limit to the number of wives a man may have.

Cultivation.—Tobacco, paddy, red pepper, Indian corn, *dhal*, yams, pumpkins, poppies, sesamum, rhea, and rice are the chief crops. *Jhuming* is extensively carried on, and much of the Ranga valley is terraced and irrigated.

Costume.—A wicker-work helmet with a plume of magpie feathers is generally worn, but some of the Chiefs wear a cylinder of thin silver round their heads. A cloth is worn tied crossways in front and round the waist and between the legs. Many wear a number of cane rings also round the waist, arms, and legs as a protection against sword cuts; except for these rings the arms and legs are bare. A knapsack of wicker-work is worn on the back and a small basket slung on the left side. The sword is worn slung round the neck by a piece of string.

Arms.—A long straight *dao*, bow and arrows, the arrows with barbed iron points, and occasionally a long spear.

Villages.—The houses are sometimes from 40 to 60 feet long, built on *changs*, as many as 150 people often living in one house, but many families live alone in small houses. The Daphlas are cleaner than other hill races, and keep their villages less dirty than either the Miris or Mishmis. The villages vary in size from 10 to 200 houses. In consequence of requiring new *jhum* land villages constantly move about. There is no attempt made to fortify the villages, nor are the sites selected with a view to defence. The only measures of defence adopted by the Daphlas are as follows: first, to collect large heaps of stones on the path leading up to a village; those are bound with cane bands and on the approach of the enemy the severing of the cane band launches the heap of stones on to them; second, the Apa Tanungs place cross-bows in position at different points likely to be attacked; third, to *panji* the approach to villages.

Government.—Each village is independent to the extent of local self-government; but in certain localities a number of villages acknowledge the leadership of the Chief or Gam. Thus, in the last raid made upon us, Nana Gam headed the warriors of several villages, and Pakfi Gam was the acknowledged leader of all the warriors from his portion of the country. Each Gam is the head of a household, and the council of Gams of a village give the laws to the whole community. A Gam of proved wisdom in council and conduct in the field will occasionally obtain, not only power over his own village, but over many of the neighbouring villages. Even when he attains this power he does not, however, act independently of the council of the different villages.

Slaves.—There are two great classes in the community, free men and serfs. The latter live in the houses of the free men, but can hold property and have a voice in the government of their village, though they do not intermarry with the free class. One of the free class can be reduced to a serf by his own act, but a serf can never become a free man. From any class of free men a Gam, or head of a household, can be elected; but certain of the free classes are more esteemed than others, though they all live together and intermarry. The serfs are called Hatimorias and are divided into two classes, Beta and Nera. Murder is punished by the confiscation of the murderer's whole property, which is made over to the relations of the murdered man. Theft is punished by severe corporal punishment.

The Nera class are said to be Daphlas by birth. The others are purchased slaves of other tribes.

Chapter VII

EARLY VISITS TO THE APA TANIS

1

THE APA TANI PLATEAU

(From a report by R. B. McCabe in 1897)

THE sight is one I shall never forget, as we suddenly emerged on a magnificent plateau some ten miles in length, laid out in highly cultivated and artificially irrigated terraces well watered by the Kali river, a sluggish stream some 45 to 60 feet in breadth, with low alluvial banks. The valley was dotted with isolated hillocks, and low pine-clad spurs ran here and there into the valley from the Eastern ranges. No crops were on the ground, but the stalks gave ample evidence of the beautiful character of the recent paddy harvest. Our hearts warmed at the sight of primroses, violets, wild currants, strawberries and raspberries, and I felt disposed to almost believe some of the wonderful stories we had heard of the fabulous wealth of this country.[1]

[1] The Apa Tani plateau was first visited by H. M. Crowe of the Joyhing Tea Garden, who went again four years later to escort Captain Dun. Both his visits were apparently very successful. On the other hand, when the German explorer von Ehlers went to the valley in 1895 he was met with an inhospitable reception and was robbed and turned out of the country.

'In 1896, a party of Ankas put up at the house of one Podu Miri near the Kadam Tea Estate, and when the family had peacefully lain down to sleep, killed Podu and his stepson, and carried away four captives. Three months after, a small expeditionary force was dispatched into the hills, which reached the valley of Hong, rescued the prisoners, and punished the Ankas by compelling them to release six persons whom they had carried off a short time previously from a friendly Dafla village. The comparative leniency of this punishment was due to the fact that the Ankas seem to have had a genuine grievance against Podu.'—B. C. Allen, *Assam District Gazetteers: Lakhimpur* (1905), p. 75 f. R. B. McCabe, a member of the Indian Civil Service, ultimately became an Inspector-General of Police. He accompanied the expedition (which was led by Captain G. Row) as Political Officer.

2

CHRISTMAS AMONG THE APA TANIS

(H. M. Crowe, *Account of a Journey to Apa Tanang Country*,[1] 1890, pp. 1 ff.)

I HAD long intended making a trip into the lofty hills north of Lakhimpur, the high range which towers above my garden. The lower ranges I knew well enough. Few game paths between the Ranganadi and the Subansiri were unknown to me.

Early in December an old friend, Tajang, a Ghasi Gam of the Subansiri, came to see me, and while he was at Joyhing I had a visit from some hillmen, who asked me to fix the date and fulfil my promise to visit them in their homes, saying that there was no time to be lost, as later in the year the passes would be covered with snow. I thought old Tajang's presence auspicious, he had been in the hills with me before, and he was very pleased when I asked him if he would go with me to the mysterious Aka Miri country, the home of the red-tailed Apa Tanangs. We accordingly got ready and arranged to get off at once.

I left Joyhing tea-garden at 12 o'clock on December 16th (1889). I had with me a boy, Tajang and his Ghasi boy, a Dafla named Tara, and a few hillmen, Daflas, to carry my things. I took three maunds of salt, fourteen rupees' worth of blue beads, and some *eria* silk cloths. These formed the treasure, and with a few loads of stores, we started marching up the Joyhing river. The Joyhing divides itself into two streams about a couple of miles above the Joyhing garden. We took the stream to the left, and went along over stones and big boulders, gradually ascending until it became dark. We camped for the night on a space, which was cleaned and had evidently been used for the same purpose before.

December 17th.—Early up, the elephants packed, and started. We went straight to the west, climbed over a hill, and descended to the Ranganadi, reaching it about 11 o'clock a.m. The elephants went by a long and easier route, and did not arrive till 4 p.m.,

[1] Parts of Crowe's report were included without acknowledgement in the *Preliminary Notes on Daphlas* by G. W. Dun, published as an official document in 1897.

so that little progress was made this day. Camped a short distance above a *pung*, or salt lick, much frequented by game. Near this was a weir made by the hillmen to catch fish.

December 18th.—Dismissed the elephants. Collected the necessary baggage, and followed the eastern bank of the Ranganadi (Paniarpoba of the Daflas) all day. The path lay over huge boulders and nasty rocks, and occasionally along the almost vertical side of the hill, with the river foaming at an uncomfortable depth below. I nearly lost one of my party at one of these places; a stone came crashing down the hill-side, and struck my boy, who lost his balance and fell, clinging to the side of the precipice. He was extricated by a couple of Daflas, who climb like monkeys. These small streams come from the north-east. Reached a small Dafla settlement in the evening, headman Seje. Camped in the *jhums*, or clearances. I do not think we travelled far as the crow flies, but the march was so stiff that we had all had enough. The hamlet, Seje's, where we encamped, only consists of a few small houses scattered about in twos and threes on the face of the hill above.

December 19th.—We spent the whole of the 19th going from house to house up the hill, getting coolies to replace the Daflas who had accompanied us thus far, and who returned to bring up the things left at the camp where we parted with the elephants. Had much difficulty in getting men, as the villagers were just finishing their harvest-home festivities. It was only by presenting silk cloths and salt that I could induce them to assist me. Their reluctance was due simply to their not wishing to leave their liquor, and not to any unfriendly feeling towards, or fear of, the next village. The result was that we only got to the upper houses of the scattered village that evening. The hill-side was very steep, and the only camping ground a threshing floor, which had been artificially levelled, and was about 10 feet × 20 feet. It was so steep that the Daflas put up bamboos to prevent us from falling over the verge in the dark.

December 20th.—Made a late start, as the Daflas had been carousing. The path led straight up the hill through bamboos, which had been burnt in previous years. The loose soil, more ashes than earth, and the angle at which we climbed made progress very tedious until forest was reached on the top of the hill, when the path was flatter and easier, but almost obliterated and difficult to find, being only a game track. We gradually ascended along a spur of the high hill, marked in the map 20, until nightfall. Water was very distant, but was found in small quantities, sufficient for our party of twenty, from the *khud* to the left of the path. Throughout the day we looked down on the deep valley of the Per river on the right, with a higher range beyond, along the watershed of which is a path, which, I was told, the Apa Tanangs use on their way to Joyhing.

December 21st.—Started at daylight. Climbed without stopping a very precipitous hill-side along a faint track till 12 a.m. We then found ourselves on a knoll covered with white rhododendrons, which were just coming into flower. I fancy we must have been at the height of about 7,000 feet above sea level. To the south there was a glorious view of the Assam Valley, on the north I could see below me the broad flat cultivation of the Apa Tanang villages, and beyond, low hills covered with grass and patches of forest extending as far as the eye could reach. I could see no snow peaks, owing to the haze which prevails at this season of the year. Not far off and to the north-east lay a high peak.

We continued our march along the watershed to the westward. The trees on the north side of the hill were covered with moss. The ridge was very narrow, in many places not more than four feet broad, with precipices on either side. The vegetation consisted of oak and rhododendron. At about 2 p.m. we came to a high peak, of which we skirted the side along a narrow track, gradually descending to a little stream. From the stream we ascended to the top of the next spur, and found open ground with scattered trees, a species of oak, the acorns of which covered the ground. The path seemed to be more frequented, and the tracks of tame *mithan* told us that we were nearing a village. At 3 p.m. we descended rapidly till it became too dark to proceed further. We camped on a small open space on the hill-side without water; some of my men went down to the Dafla village below, and brought up some of the villagers with loads of firewood, rice, hill beer (*apong*) and water. In the evening many of the villagers came up to my camp, they appeared to be very friendly.

December 22nd.—Descended to the Dafla village marked Takhas on the map, below my camp. The headmen are Nipak and Chiring. I was shown a spot for my camp, the same place where someone of the survey party had encamped thirteen years ago. The place was very small, and the hill-side very steep on either side. Above me lay the two sections of the Dafla village, there are about 100 houses in all. Each house was about 100 feet long, and contained three or four families, or about 16 people. The village was formerly much larger.

We stayed here today, and met a number of Apa Tanangs who had come to trade with the Dafla, with whom they seemed on excellent terms.

December 23rd.—Started with some men of the Dafla village as carriers led by Tada, brother of Nipak Gam, and went straight down to the valley below. We were preceded by some of the Apa Tanangs, who had been staying in the Dafla village, and who went on to announce my arrival. In the road met a number of Apa Tanangs, who had been trading, exchanging rice for cotton, and who met us with friendly demonstration. The road from Takhas onwards was very fair, but hardly fit for laden mules. Crossed a river called the Pangi, about 60 feet broad and three feet or four feet deep, a rapid mountain torrent. A felled tree thrown across formed the bridge. From the river we ascended through land which had been cultivated and abandoned, to a low pass, and then descended through dense bamboo jungle, and camped on the bank of a small stream. Some Apa Tanangs came in to tell me that I would be well received in their village. The camp was placed under some magnificent pine-trees.

December 24th.—Started early and reached open country covered with ferns and coarse grass. White with hoar-frost. Proceeding through undulating grass land, crossed a stream, a tributary of the Ranganadi, flowing through the Apa Tanang country. About half a mile from this we came to an open pool about 20 feet in diameter, the water of which was warm and brackish, so warm that the men ran in to warm their feet after walking through the hoar-frost. We then came to some flat rice-fields after crossing the stream again. The crop had been reaped apparently in November. About 11 o'clock we reached the Apa Tanang village of Hong Nampo. It consists of about 500 small houses and a great number of granaries.

The village lies among groves of the dwarf bamboo-like China bamboo. It is entirely undefended. There seemed to be very few goats or pigs, a striking contrast to the Dafla villages I had come through. We halted outside the village, and had a talk with the people through Dafla interpreters. They objected to the Dafla carriers coming into their village; saying they had had differences about *mithan*, &c., but at the same time offered to take on my things themselves, and to give me everything I required. They said they would build me a house, and escort me back when I wanted to go, if I would dispense with the Daflas. I made up my mind that it would not be politic to part with the Daflas, who had seen me so far, and after stopping some hours at the Apa Tanang's village, I returned to Takha's village, which I reached at about 10 p.m. In the course of conversation we discussed the reasons for my visit, which I stated to be pure curiosity. I was also asked about their loss of two women and four men, who, they stated, were detained in Dafla villages in the plains in the North Lakhimpur subdivision. They complained that the women had been enticed to the plains by Dafla refugees living in their village. They said they were anxious to trade with the plains, but had difficulty in doing so, owing to the jealousy of the hill Daflas on our frontier and those living in the plains. I told them they would be perfectly safe in coming down, and that if they would represent any injuries which had been done to them to the civil officer at North Lakhimpur, they would be certain to get redress, and that they would be protected from outrage in the plains in our territory. I did not accept their invitation to stay some days, as I could not spare the time. Personally, I did not distrust them, as they were evidently harmless and inoffensive savages. There were no skulls stuck up in the village, or any signs of warfare; but the Daflas frequently insisted that they were treacherous, and the Chief, Takha, was evidently afraid of them: possibly his conscience made him a coward, and there is no doubt that unsettled disputes exist.

The frontier tribes are interested in preventing the remoter clans from visiting the plains, as they make a profit out of hillmen and plains traders by acting as intermediaries. The Apa Tanang are dependent on the plains for their supply of salt, and the Daflas could easily deprive them of their supply. Each tribe, however, is averse to extreme measures, and the bloodthirsty outrages, common among Nagas, are unknown in these hills, reprisals being confined to capturing or kidnapping isolated individuals, who are detained to force on the settlement of disputes. When I passed through

Takha's village, I saw an Apa Tanang woman with a log fastened to her leg, evidently a prisoner, but at the same time there were a number of Apa Tanangs bartering rice with the Daflas and apparently on the best of terms with them. The Apa Tanang is a keen trader, and, if they could come down to the plains in perfect safety, would do so in great numbers and develop considerable trade. I may mention here that since my visit to their country, they have come down to Lakhimpur in considerable numbers, though only in large parties.

As a substitute for salt they boil down the ashes of burned ferns and other plants they find in the forest, and make a cake of a kind of potash. I could see three villages and their cultivation, which I estimated at about 3,000 acres of level ground. The Apa Tanangs appear to occupy only the flat land near the stream which runs through their valley, and the Daflas the higher ground above. The whole valley drained by the Ranga appears of a very considerable extent. It is formed of low swelling hills covered with ferns and grass, with patches of oak and pine forests. The hills bounding the valley on the north appeared to be some 50 miles distant. I met two men on the road between Hong and Takhas, evidently Daflas, tall, well-built, clean-limbed men, who said they came from a village five days distant, and I believe within the drainage of the Ranga.

The Apa Tanang are small men, not particularly powerful, and evidently as peacefully inclined as their state of existence will allow them to be.

December 25th, Christmas Day.—I marched back to the camp of the 20th from Takha's village, and on the 31st I returned to Joyhing, marching by the same route. The road throughout was a difficult one, and not that generally used by the Daflas, who come down usually by the Pansnoi route. Comparing them with Daflas, the Apa Tanangs are smaller and rather darker men. Some of them are tattooed like Daflas, they wear cane helmets of the same shape, and tie their hair like Daflas in a knot in front with a brass skewer passed through it. The knot is tied round with black hair. I note this as it is a point of distinction between the Daflas and Apa Tanangs. The Daflas tie the *poodoom*, or knot of hair with a yellow cotton thread.

The Apa Tanangs usually wear dark blue cloths of the same shape and size as those worn by Daflas, but striped yellow and red. The cloth is a simple square sheet, with a loop and button on one side about 18 inches apart. This loop and button fasten the cloth around the man's neck. The most distinctive feature, however, is a kind of tail. It is made of strips of fine cane bent into the shape of a horse-collar with an elongated end. These strips of cane are loosely fastened together, and the loop of the horse-collar goes round the waist. The elongated end hangs down behind, and is plaited loosely. The whole is dyed red with *manjhit*, in which it is boiled. I was not able to form any theory of the practical value of this strange appendage unless it was intended to take the place of a portable cane-bottomed chair. The women are tattooed with broad blue streaks down their chins and down their foreheads, they wear peculiar pieces of black wood inserted on either side of the nose about an inch in diameter, which do not, according to our ideas, add to their beauty. They wear their hair rolled up into two balls on the top of the head, with a brass skewer through each knot. They had few beads, if any, in contrast to their Dafla and Miri cousins, who trade direct with us, and have consequently added to their wealth in trinkets. A Dafla woman frequently wears eight or ten pounds of beads round her neck. They seemed very industrious as they walked along the paths with loads on their backs, spinning cotton with the ordinary Assamese takari.

A good deal of labour had been spent on cultivation, both in draining and irrigating their land. Aqueducts had been made with hollowed-out trees to convey water when it did not flow naturally. I saw a good many cattle about the size of Assamese cattle, but much sleeker. They don't use them for ploughing, only using hoes, which they get through the Daflas from Assamese, apparently of Garo manufacture. They had plenty of *mithan* and poultry.

The Apa Tanang differ from any hill people that have come under my notice in the following respects: Their houses are small, and they live in isolated families. Sons and daughters marrying are given homes to themselves. Polygamy is not practised, as among other hill tribes. Slavery exists in a very mitigated form; slaves are simply servants, fed and clothed by their masters and sharing the vicissitudes of their masters' fortunes. I understand that their language is the same or similar to that of the so-called Doi and Ridi Abors, or the people inhabiting the valleys of the Khru and Upper Kamla as far as the snows of Thibet.

3

ADMIRABLE SITE FOR A CANTONMENT

(From a note by Captain G. W. Dun, 19th April 1893, printed as a footnote in *Preliminary Notes on Miris*, 1897)

IN 1893 Captain Dun visited a tribe living in the upper part of the Kal stream, an affluent of the Ranga. The people in the southern villages of this valley more resembled Daphlas; those in the northern villages were more like Miris. They had been previously called Apa Tanungs by Mr Crowe, but Captain Dun maintains that these people, or at least some of them, the northern villages, are Ankas. It is also possible that the southern villages only are Apa Tanungs.

This open upper portion of the Kal valley is important, as it supports a comparatively large population and supplies rice to the hill villages all round. There are probably other similar valleys in the neighbourhood, notably the Ranga. The people there, however, are said to live upon the pith of a palm which grows wild there, but the upper Kal valley is a place where troops could at once find almost all they required.

The stream—for it is nothing more—flows down the western side of the valley, and from the eastern slopes plateaux project, all of which offer good sites for camps or stations. The streams come down from the eastern side and irrigate the rice fields which are laid out in terraces round the feet of the plateaux.

The village of Hong is placed on the north side of a low spur which runs almost across the valley. It is not defended, but is hidden by groves of bamboos, carefully fenced in to protect them from the ravages of cattle, and pine-trees (*pinus excelsa*). North of Hong there is an admirable site for a cantonment. Nearly all the other villages lie on the western side of the valley and at the northern end, and can be seen from this site. . . . These villages were not visited, and it is probable that there are errors in nomenclature and position.

The following is another list of villages received. There was no time or opportunity for making a correct map and list:

Hong	Niche	Haja
Hari	Tajang	Diretta
Reru	Niti	Kalo
Bamin	Dota	Hao

It is probable that some are Chiefs' names. Captain Dun estimated that Hong contained 800 houses. It is said to be the largest village in the valley. Only one family lives in each house, and they are densely packed together, so that a fire is a most serious occurrence.

Men from the upper end of the valley were taller, cleaner, and more civilized in appearance, though they had never come in contact with Europeans and did not know what money was.

The Hong people are almost perfectly unsophisticated. Most of them till their fields with sharpened bamboos; a few only have acquired iron hoes. The valley lies at an elevation of 5,000 feet and the size of the trees attests the excellence of the soil, which, however, varies very much in character.

The lower slopes of the surrounding hills are covered with grass and bracken, then comes a belt of pines, then the forest trees, all the higher hills being densely clothed with forest.

There were no signs of very heavy rain. It would appear to be lighter than on the outer fringe of hills immediately above the Assam plain. The hills surrounding the valley on the north, east, and west are comparatively low, and not so high as the barrier range on the south which is so remarkable a feature in this part of the Himalayas. The people of the valley appear to be perfectly peaceful. We (Mr Crowe and Captain Dun) hardly saw any arms, and only bows, arrows and long Tibetan swords were occasionally carried by visitors from other villages. The Hong people do not arm themselves when they go down to the plains. There were no traces of head-taking as amongst the Nagas, and the people appeared to live in peace with their neighbours. They are certainly not so suspicious or naturally hostile as the Abors. Captain Dun could not discover what the system of government was. There were no outward signs of reverence paid to the men who figured as the headmen in the receipt and distribution of presents. The most important personage appeared to be an individual named Hyang. The next two were called Tupi and Riku; but whether these men were the heads of clans, or whether they had obtained their position between the European and the other villagers simply by being more intelligent could not be ascertained. There was certainly no village council house or general assembly as among Abors, Nagas and Lushais. Want of time and the fear of creating suspicion prevented

Mr Crowe from making any inquiries on this subject or upon customs of burial and marriages.

The women, naturally ugly, are disfigured to an extraordinary degree by the wooden plugs they insert into their nostrils. Put in as small pegs when they are little girls, the peg is gradually increased in size till it becomes a disc 2–3 inches in diameter.

The people are good-natured and well-behaved and require no coercion to behave well.

4

THE APA TANIS: ANOTHER VIEW

(From R. B. McCabe's Report of 1897)

MY impressions have been derived from personal observation and from information received from the Apa Tanangs themselves and from Daflas who had resided for a long time in the Apa Tanang country. The first point to which I would call attention is that the name 'Apa Tanang' is a complete misnomer. Throughout the Expedition I never once heard this name used by a single Miri or Dafla; the tribe was referred to only by the names of Ankas, Apas and Akas, the first name being that in most common use. Captain Dun agrees with me that these people are best described under the name of Ankas, but goes on to state that they are more allied to the Miris than to the Daflas. I totally disagree with this last dictum. I had the opportunity of seeing plains Daflas, Abor Daflas and Miris side by side with the Apa Tanangs, and while the latter differed most markedly from the Miris they bore a most striking resemblance to the Daflas. The principal points of difference are:

1st—They wear no cane helmets.
2nd—They carry no bows and quiver.
3rd—They wear a tail.
4th—Their cloths are of distinct patterns.
5th—They tattoo their faces differently.

The Miris did not seem to be able to make themselves understood by the Apa Tanangs, while I noticed that my Dafla coolies chatted away with them without hesitating for a word, and as far as I could judge they appeared to be speaking one and the same language. I have no hesitation in concluding that the Apa Tanangs are merely a tribe of Abor Daflas who have developed a few distinguishing characteristics from their isolation and from the special physical features of the country they inhabit. They are somewhat smaller and of less robust build than the Daflas, but this is easily accounted for by the fact that while the latter have to cultivate steep, sterile mountainsides, the former are favoured with a fertile, level, well-watered plateau yielding a maximum out-turn for a minimum of labour. The male Apa Tanang only tattoos below the mouth; a horizontal line is drawn across the underlip, and straight lines are drawn downwards from it to the point of the chin. The women are tattooed with broad blue lines from the top of the forehead to the tip of the nose, and from the lower lip to the base of the chin. To add to their original ugliness they wear wooden plugs inserted in the sides of the nostrils, expanding the nose right across the face. Both the Daflas and the Apa Tanangs wear strips of cane around the waist, but the latter specially distinguish themselves by the addition of a tail. This tail is made of loosely plaited strips of cane dyed red, and gives the wearer a most ludicrous appearance. In reply to my inquiries as to the meaning of this appendage, I received nothing but the stereotyped answer—'Our fathers wore it, and so do we.' It must be left to some scientist to determine whether it is used as a portable cane chair, or for the sake of decency, or again perhaps with the idea of inspiring awe in their enemies. I would describe the Apa Tanangs generally as a 'timid, good-natured, industrious and loquacious people far inferior in pluck and physique to the Hill Miris'. It would be interesting to ascertain the sources of information from which previous reports on this tribe were derived. There are no four-feet wide roads, no stone granaries, and no bullocks and ploughs. The Apa Tanangs only possess a few hoes which they obtained through the Daflas, most of the work of tilling the land being done with sharpened bamboos. Each village has its granaries built outside the circuit of houses. These granaries consist of small bamboo sheds with roofs, either of thatch or of pine shingles, and are usually half hidden in clumps of bamboos.

The houses are very large and commodious. I would roughly estimate the total population of this tribe at 15,000. As all the villages are within half a day's journey of one another, the Apa Tanangs can in a few hours concentrate a large force to repel any invasion, and it is due entirely to this fact that they have been carefully let alone by the neighbouring Miris and Daflas. On the other hand, their inferiority in arms and physique reduce them to a comparatively low level as an aggressive power. It is quite possible, nay even probable, that this tribe was at one time in regular communication with Tibet, and even at the present moment articles of Tibetan manufacture find their way into the country; but from the evidence I have collected I feel justified in stating that the intercourse is very limited, and that Tibet exercises absolutely no authority in Apa Tanang land. The present tendency is to seek trade relations with the plains of Assam, and instead of bartering Tibetan rock-salt and swords, the Apa Tanangs show a strong leaning towards salt, hoes and *daos* imported from our district of Lakhimpur.

Chapter VIII

FIRST IMPRESSIONS OF THE ABORS

1

HISTORICAL PRELUDE

(A. Mackenzie, *History*, 1884, p. 34 ff.)

THE Abor or Padam country was visited in a friendly way in 1825–6 by Bedford and Wilcox, and by Dalton in 1855. The right bank of the Dihong was found occupied by the Pashi and Meyong Abors, the left by the Paddo, Siboo or Silook, Meybo, and Goliwar Abors. Membo was the most important of the settlements. This village was built on a range of hills rising from a small stream called the Shiku, about four miles from its confluence with the Dihong, and numbered probably over 300 houses.

The Hill Miris, commanding by their position the cultivated tracts of Bordoloni, Sisi, and Damaji, had acquired an acknowledged right to *posa* similar to that asserted by the Duphlas, Akas, and Bhutias. So far as can be gathered, the Abors, though much more powerful than any of these tribes, had no such rights. This was owing no doubt to their comparatively remote situation, cut off as they were by the great river Dihong from the cultivated country along the Brahmaputra Valley. Rights, however, they had of a somewhat different kind, which were more difficult to settle even than those arising out of the *posa*.

The Abors claimed, as I have said, an absolute sovereignty over the Miris of the plains, and an inalienable right to all the fish and gold found in the Dihong River. The Miris for many years acknowledged the Abors as their masters. They were quite ready to accept their position of go-betweens of the rude hillmen and the Assamese traders. It was on the whole a profitable one, and the more so while the unsettled state of Assam under its Native Government made simple agriculture a somewhat precarious pursuit. The Assamese Government also, anxious to conciliate their highland neighbours, had long since relieved these Miris of all revenue charges, acknowledging thereby the subjection of that tribe to the Abors, whose interpreters they were officially recognized to be. During the Burmese invasion, and after the British annexation of Assam, more than one community of Miris found it to their advantage to move away from the vicinity of their Abor lords, and one of the earliest notices of the Abors outside of geographical memoirs is an account of a demand made by the Dubba tribe of Bor Abors in February 1830, that the British authorities would send back a village of Miris who had moved away to the detriment of the Abor trade. The Government of course could not coerce the Miris into returning, but it sanctioned certain expenditure by the Political Agent, with a view to induce these or kindred tribes to settle where they could minister to the wants of the Abors in the way of trade. Eventually the original Miri village returned to its old site, and the Agent induced the Bor Abors to undertake to leave them free of exaction for two years, two Chiefs of the lower Abors becoming surety for their good treatment. The Abors are curiously enough described in the correspondence as 'far the best disposed of the hill tribes, though the most powerful, and never known to commit an act of unprovoked ravage or outrage on the villages of the plains'.

The first impression made on the Abors by our local officers would seem to have been also favourable, for early in 1836 a body of 200 Abors came down and offered to settle on the Dihong. They were willing to submit to our criminal jurisdiction, but objected to pay taxes. The local officers were afraid that they might prove dangerous neighbours, but the Governor-General's Agent, viewing them as little other than Miris, a tribe which had long since proved itself amenable to order, overruled the opposition. Two years later he urged upon Government, without success, the deputation of a special officer to conciliate the Hill Miris and Abors. It is probable that the Abors, as a warlike race, were expected by the local officers to act as a counterpoise to the Khamptis, Singphos, and Mishmis, who at this time were giving cause for anxiety. In 1840, indeed, the Abors did take the side of Government unmistakably, when the Khamptis, in alliance with the Mishmis, were fighting against us.

Besides asserting their sovereignty over the Miris, the Abors claimed, as above stated, a right to all the fish and gold found in the streams that flowed from their hills. In the islands of the Brahmaputra, and along the lower courses of its northern feeders, were numerous villages of Hindu gold-washers and fishermen called Beeahs or Beheeahs, who had, perhaps, themselves originally been driven from the hills by the Abor-Miri advance. In the pursuit of their avocation these Beeahs were wont to frequent the Dihong, Dibong, and other tributaries of the Brahmaputra, and from them the Abors were always in the habit of receiving, if not regular blackmail, at least frequent conciliatory offerings and acknowledgments of superiority. The Assam Government, which derived no small portion of its revenue from the gold-dust of the rivers, had an interest in keeping stationary these Beeah settlements, even when the occupation of gold-washing became much less remunerative than it once had been. Under British rule the Beeahs became their own masters, and many of them, like the Miris, moved lower down the valley. The few who remained soon found out that the new Government had different ideas on the question of protecting its subjects from those of the imbecile administration it succeeded, and they began to repudiate the claims of the Abors to restrict their movements on the Dihong and elsewhere. The Abors in revenge carried off to the hills such of the refractory Beeahs as they could lay hands upon.

Their feelings towards us do not appear to have as yet been actively hostile for in 1847 Captain Vetch, the Political Agent, had a most friendly conference with the Pashi, Meybo, and other Padams, who to please him voluntarily released all the captives they had taken. Negotiations for the establishment on the Dihong of a trading store under Government protection were at this time set on foot, with a fair prospect, as it seemed, of ultimate success.

Unfortunately, however, this promising commencement of intercourse was never regularly followed up, and a year or so later we were brought into hostile collision with a neighbouring tribe of Dhobas or Dubba Abors lying west of the Dihong. The facts were these: Captain Vetch had gone to the hills with a small party of troops to demand the restoration of a body of Cachari gold-washers carried off by these Abors. The captives were restored, but his camp was attacked by night, and the Abors were only beaten off after hard fighting. To punish this treachery, Captain Vetch burnt their village—a step which led to the submission of the offending tribe, but which, however righteous an act in itself, tended greatly to disturb the generally harmonious relations hitherto subsisting between the Assam officials and the wild tribes in this quarter. Not that friendly intercourse was openly broken off, for early in

1851 a large body of upper Abors came down and settled on the Dirjmoo, advances being made by Government to enable them to purchase implements of husbandry. But from this point we begin to find frequent notice of outrages committed by the Abors and of remonstrances offered by the British officials.

At the very time of the settling of the Abor village on the Dirjmoo, the clans on the Dihong were renewing their depredations on the gold-washers. As Government now farmed out the right of gold-washing (for the vast sum of Rs 80 per annum), it felt bound to protect the Beeahs from such encroachment, and orders were given that an escort should accompany them to the Dihong, and a guard be permanently stationed at the mouth of that river. An effort was still, however, to be made to establish an annual fair for the conciliation and profit of the Abors; and a proposal to tax the Miri villages near the Dihong, north of the Brahmaputra, was negatived as being likely to annoy the paramount tribe. These measures were designed to combine the advantages of a strong and of a conciliatory policy; but they were not fully or fairly carried into action. It is doubtful whether their intention was ever properly made manifest to the tribes concerned. The guard only remained on the Dihong for one season, and the Abor trade was lost sight of amid the pressure of other more urgent matters.

In 1855 (as already noted) the village of Membo was visited by Dalton, then Principal Assistant to the Governor-General's Agent in Assam.

In 1858 occurred the first serious Abor outrage. On the 31st January of that year the civil station of Debroogurh was startled by the news that the Beeah village of Sengajan, only six miles distant from the station, though on the north of the Brahmaputra, had been cut up by Abors from the hills. Inquiry soon made it tolerably certain that the Kebang clan of Bor Meyongs were the perpetrators of this atrocity. It was designed apparently to punish the Beeahs for having some years before deserted their village, and for a recent refusal to pay the dues or tribute which the Abors demanded of them. An attempt was made to follow up the raiders to the hills, but, owing to the extremely inaccessible character of the country and various mischances, which need not be specified in detail, the troops did not succeed in overtaking the Abors or in reaching the village of Kebang. It was indeed with difficulty and with some loss of credit to those in command that they got back to Debroogurh. Emboldened by their impunity, the Kebang men took up a more advanced position threatening the plains; and it now became evident to Government that if it wished to prevent a state of chronic outrage along the border, a serious effort was necessary to convince the hillmen of our power to punish. An offer of the Meybo Abors to act as mediators had no practical effect. Government could only accept an unconditional submission, which the Kebang people were in no mood to offer.

Preparations for an expedition into the hills upon a somewhat imposing scale were put in hand with vigour. No doubt was entertained as to the propriety of invading the Abor territory to punish the authors of a crime so flagrant as the massacre of Sengajan. The safety of our own civil stations was at stake. Indifference would, it was felt, lead only to more daring attacks.

The civil officers of Debroogurh spared no pains to get together the information necessary to render the military operations successful; and if the results of their inquiries proved eventually of less value than was anticipated, that fact may serve as a warning and a lesson for future enterprises of the kind. While the military authorities were settling the character and strength of the force to be employed, the Deputy Commissioner of Luckhimpore had, as he believed, fixed the precise locale of Kebang, and the best way of reaching that village. From the report of a Pashi Abor scout, it appeared that Kebang lay on the Yembopani, a tributary of the Dihong, only four and half days' direct journey from the plains. Such, however, was the difficult character of the country that it was considered better to convey the force in canoes by the route of the Dihong than to attempt the trackless hills between the Brahmaputra and the Yembopani. This determined, the Deputy Commissioner went on in advance to make arrangements for food depots, and to conciliate, if possible, the intermediate clans. At Pashighat, opposite the junction of the Sikoo with the Dihong, deputations from the Pashi, Meybo, and Pado communities presented themselves, professing friendship and promising not to oppose the advance of troops. The Deputy Commissioner appears to have relied too confidently upon these protestations. He conversed freely about the approaching expedition, and gave, it was afterwards feared, by far too many indications of the route which it was intended to follow.

By the 19th March a force had arrived at Pashi under the command of an officer of the rank of Captain.

On the morning of the 20th the advance began into the Abor Hills. As far as Pangee, an Abor village fifteen miles upstream, the force proceeded in boats. The guns were for some distance carried on elephants along the bank, but the hill ranges between Pashi and Pangee proved to be so precipitous and came down so close to the river that this mode of conveyance had to be abandoned, and the guns were eventually taken on board the boats. At Pangee it was discovered by the civil officer that the coolies supplied by him at Debroogurh for carrying food had through some mistake of the military commander been discharged soon after leaving that station. He had, however, a body of 70 coolies with him, and these were pronounced sufficient for commissariat purposes as the guns were to be left at Pangee to guard the boats, which had there to be abandoned owing to the occurrence of dangerous rapids that could not be stemmed. On the 22nd March the troops, numbering with officers 104 fighting men, broke ground at Pangee, marching by the left bank of the river over a steep hill four miles to Ruttoomi Ghat, a point above the rapids, where the river had to be crossed on rafts of bamboo. These, it was found, the Ruttoomi Abors had, as a measure of conciliation, prepared in anticipation, though not in sufficient numbers. The Ruttoomis also offered to find guides, and professed the most remarkable hatred for the Kebang Abors, the object of attack.

The Deputy Commissioner, who had accompanied the force so far, remained with a guard of twelve men at Ruttoomi Ghat, while the rest set out on the morning of the 24th for the final advance on Kebang, supposed to be only 12 or 14 miles distant. Next morning two messengers came back to Ruttoomi Ghat with a note from the Commanding Officer asking for meat and liquor for the Europeans to be sent by the bearers, and containing in a postscript the words 'Rice, rice'. The meat the Deputy Commissioner sent at once, while he proceeded to hurry up supplies of rice from Pangee and Pashi, at the same time sending coolies with two respectable Assamese acquainted with the Abors to ask rice from the villagers of Ruttoomi. In a few hours two of this party came running back, crying that the rest had been set upon and made prisoners by the Abors. Other signs of hostility soon manifested themselves. A party of twelve bringing up provisions was attacked between Pangee and Ruttoomi, and seven were killed.

Meantime nothing had for two days been heard of the advance force. At last, on the morning of the 27th firing was heard, and the little column appeared on the heights under Ruttoomi hard pressed and pursued, but keeping the enemy fairly in check. The force had failed altogether to reach Kebang, though there was afterwards reason to believe that it had got within 800 yards of that village. The troops had had to fight almost every step of the way; had lost a European and three Native soldiers besides coolies, the only wonder being that the losses were so small; and had had to retire without effecting the object of the advance, owing as it seemed to the entire want of any proper arrangements for keeping up a supply of provisions from Ruttoomi Ghat. In the end the officer in command had become distrustful of his guides, would not believe that Kebang was anywhere near, and turned back at the very moment when a little perseverance would probably have carried everything. The only excuse for his action is that in the absence of reliable information it is very difficult on such expeditions to say how far perseverance should be carried.

The whole of the Abor villages round, seeing the discomfiture of the expedition, now made common cause against it; and without attempting to punish Ruttoomi for its treachery, the force returned as fast as possible to Pangee, Pashi, and the Brahmaputra.

The relations between the civil officer and the officer in command of the troops had unfortunately, from the outset, not been cordial, and the return of the expedition in this ignominious plight was the beginning of much recrimination, fruitless correspondence, and departmental bickering. The Government could not but hold that both parties were in fact to blame. The Deputy Commissioner had been too ready to trust to his powers of negotiation, and believed that he was in this way winning allies when he was only revealing his plans to enemies. The military commander did not see that his supplies were secure, but recklessly led his men into the hills, trusting to the civil authorities to provide all that he required. But, above all, it was clear that for an advance into a hostile territory, physically difficult and quite unknown, the detachment of troops sent was altogether inadequate, either to cover its own communications or to force its way. But for the individual bravery of those concerned—

a quality which is nowhere more conspicuous than in these frontier expeditions—the troops would never have returned to tell the tale.

The Bor Meyong Abors of Kebang and other villages (rendered bold by the repulse of the expedition) took up a still more advanced position towards the plains, stockading themselves at Pashi, with which village they were now in offensive and defensive alliance. After much anxious consultation, it was held by the local officers and by Government that it was absolutely necessary to devise some means of punishing their insolence and protecting the district from outrage and attack. Proposals for establishing a line of posts from Sisi to Pobah Mukh were taken into consideration, but the plan which commended itself to all as politically essential was that of another expedition on such an effective scale as should infallibly command success.

Rumours that some such step was contemplated soon reached the hills, and a deputation from the Meybo Abors (a neutral clan) came to the Deputy Commissioner, professing their own feelings of friendship, and offering to become mediators with the Meyongs. They were civilly treated, but their overtures were on this occasion not entertained.

While the expedition was preparing, the orders of the Secretary of State upon the former fiasco arrived in India. He forbade the undertaking of any second expedition, 'save upon trustworthy information, and with an adequate force'. This instruction was not held to interfere with the course of action already determined upon.

The expedition was upon this occasion of the strength shown [below].

Indian Navy Brigade
- 2 Buglers
- 60 Men
- 4 European Officers

Native Artillery
- 3 Havildars
- 2 Naiks
- 1 Bugler and 50 Men
- 2 12-pounder howitzers
- 2 4-2-5 mortars
- 1 European Officer

Assam Light Infantry
- 6 Native Officers
- 13 Havildars
- 14 Naiks
- 5 Buglers
- 211 Sepoys
- 1 European Officer
- 1 European Non-commissioned Officer

On the 26th February 1859 it reached Pashi, where the Abors had entrenched themselves in great force. On the 27th the troops stormed the village, which was perched on a hill, and defended by eleven stockades, nine of which were obstinately held by the hillmen till they were driven from each successively at the point of the bayonet. The neighbouring village of Kingkong was taken in like manner. Our loss was one killed and 44 wounded, chiefly by poisoned arrows. After halting for a few days to show that they were complete masters of the position, the troops burnt the villages and retired leisurely to their boats.

Later in the year a strong reconnoitring party passed along the whole Abor frontier between Sisi and Lallee Soota; but no attempt at hostile demonstration was made by the tribes.

The Pashi Abors, with other clans in their neighbourhood, would seem after this to have made up their minds not to provoke the Government further, for in July 1860, they came in to make formal overtures of friendship, which were of course accepted. The Meyongs still continued hostile, and towards the close of 1861 they again cut up a Beeah village, situated this time on the further or south side of the Brahmaputra 15 miles from Debroogurh. These Beeahs were part of a body of *ryots* who had deserted the north side of the river after the former Meyong massacre in 1858, and the present raid appears to have been designed partly to show them that they were not yet beyond the reach of their Abor lords, and partly to take vengeance for aid rendered by the Beeahs to the troops in the campaign of 1859. Inquiry seemed to show that the Abors had been assisted in planning these daring attacks in the neighbourhood of a military station by information received from the Miri villages lying between them and the Brahmaputra, and a proposal was brought forward by the local authorities that all the Miris on the line of the Booree Dihing should be deported far south of the Brahmaputra, in order thereby to deprive the Abors of the covert help rendered them by these allies. The Miris of this neighbourhood were however, it was admitted, by no means dangerous in themselves. They had for years been quietly cultivating the soil and paying rent to Government for their fields. Their extreme subservience to the Abors was the result not of love but fear; and Government, seeing clearly that its duty lay rather in giving them efficient protection than in punishing them for a very natural timidity, refused to move them from their village sites, one reason for leaving them alone being that their labour was necessary to carry through any works of frontier defence that might be resolved upon.

The question of defending the country from further raids was then anxiously discussed. Those who best knew the frontier advocated the opening of a line of road and the establishment of fortified posts between Sisi and Lallee Soota, or along the face of the Abor tract. Others maintained that no merely defensive line of the kind would be sufficient, but that, until roads were run into the hills themselves, making the hill villages accessible at all times, no hope of security could reasonably be entertained. The occupation of the Abor hills for a whole season by a strong military force was, as a still more thorough scheme, advocated by some. A chain of forts had in fact been sanctioned by the Local Government after the first Abor massacre; but their erection was stopped on financial considerations by the Public Works Department of the Supreme Government. The present repetition of outrage had the effect of compelling the Local Government to act irrespectively of such formal sanctions. The Lieutenant-Governor of Bengal, as now advised, held that he was bound either to abandon the extensive tracts in Luckhimpore lately assigned to tea planters, or to give efficient protection to an industry already directly encouraged by the State. The cost of compensating the tea interests would, it was argued, to put the case on the lowest possible grounds, be more than the cost of organizing a proper frontier defence. Accordingly, the local Public Works Department was ordered to complete the forts at once by convict labour. The road along the frontier to Pobah Mukh was to be opened and maintained; and a scheme was laid before the Supreme Government for 'retaining by means of troops, forts, and roads, effective military command' of the whole Abor marches.

The bustle of all this preparation and defensive energy did not fail to attract the notice of the Abors, who, doubtless interpreting matters by the light of their own fears, made overtures for general reconciliation. The Government directed that any such advances should be favourably received, and endeavours made to bring the Chiefs to enter into a binding agreement for the preservation of order along the frontier. Small stipends were to be allowed to those who would undertake to prevent hostile aggression by their own or kindred clans, to keep up a tribal police for the prevention of marauding, and to surrender criminal refugees. An annual meeting between the civil officers of Luckhimpore and the covenanting clans was suggested as an important matter to have secured. No relaxation of military preparation was permitted during the pendency of these negotiations. After what had happened in 1859, the Government could only afford to conciliate while it was materially strong. At length, in November 1862, the Deputy Commissioner met the Meyong Abor deputies in solemn conference at Lallee Mukh, and after a prolonged palaver extending over seven days, an agreement was concluded between the British Government and eight communities of Meyong Abors. In lieu of money stipends to Chiefs, the treaty provided for payments in kind of articles that could be distributed among the whole community. The democratic nature of the Abor system of government made this course advisable, and the plan has the advantage of giving each leading member of the clan a personal interest in keeping the peace. Numerous other societies of Abors have given their assent to similar engagements. Among others our old enemies of Kebang executed an agreement of this nature in 1863.

Since these forms of agreement were instituted, the Abors have given but little trouble. They are a sulky, intractable race, and it is possible that some day they may break through the restraint which self-interest at present puts upon them. But it is reasonable to hope that every year of quiet, every visit paid by them to the markets of Sadiya, renders this more improbable. New wants are being created and new ideas imbibed, which cannot fail to have effect. At the same time the local officers feel that they must be ever on their guard lest opportunity lead to outrage, and the fruit of years be lost in a moment of unbridled savagery. Much tact is required in dealing with them. They are in manner insolent and rude beyond all other tribes of this frontier. In 1863, for example, the Meybo Abors went off in a temper from the annual meeting, refusing to take their presents, because the Deputy Commissioner would not allow them to treat him with impertinent familiarity. Again in 1865 the Meyong Abors absented themselves from the meeting, alleging as an excuse the prevalence of small-pox and cholera on the plains. It transpired, however, that they were really indignant because the price of salt had risen in the Sadiya bazar, and that they had in spite eaten the agreement entered into with the Deputy Commissioner, and shown in various indescribable ways their low opinion of that officer and his superiors. In 1866 they were again absent, but sent in a demand that the posts at Pobah Mukh should be abandoned. Of course this only led to the stockades being strengthened, and the Meyongs by degrees came round to a better frame of mind. The Bor Abors, a very influential clan, attended the meeting of 1866, and entered into agreements. This may have had a good effect on the rest, for there has been no open disturbance or dissatisfaction since. There is reason to believe that the Miris form very unsatisfactory agents between the local authorities and the Abors. It would be of great advantage to secure some Abor lads to educate as interpreters.

In 1876–7 the tribe showed symptoms of hostility consequent upon the advance of a Trigonometrical Survey Party into the hills, and it was thought expedient to discontinue these operations. The local authorities subsequently proposed a military demonstration along the frontier to overawe the hillmen, but this was negatived by the Government of India. The aggressive attitude taken up by the Bor Abors towards the Chulkatta Mishmis led, however, in 1881 to a forward movement on our part: the fear being that if the Bor Abors were once allowed to cross the Dibong, they would establish themselves in the plains and seriously threaten Sadiya. Troops were advanced to Bomjur and Nizamghat, and the object in view was attained without opposition, the Bor Abors withdrawing to their own hills. The occupation of Nizamghat has served up to date to impose a salutary check upon the Bor Abor villages. But the Assam Report for 1881–2 contains an account of an outrage committed by Borkheng, the Chief of Pado, upon two Miris and a Native sepoy, which had not up to the close of the year been properly explained.

It is to be regretted that the effect of direct and unofficial intercourse with these Abor clans in their own villages has not been more thoroughly tried. They are not unamenable to kindly treatment, for in 1855–6 the Reverend Mr Higgs, a worthy clergyman of Debroogurh, obtained a considerable influence over them, and was wont, it is said, to pay annual visits to their hamlets under the escort of their young men. He also settled some Abor immigrants near Debroogurh. It would perhaps be now a desirable thing to procure and educate some Padam youths who might hereafter become missionaries of civilization and of higher things to their uncouth brethren in the hills. The Abors, however, still want their Cleveland.[1]

2

FIRST VIEW OF THE ABORS

(R. Wilcox, 'Memoir of a Survey of Assam and the neighbouring Countries, executed in 1825–6–7–8', *Asiatic Researches*, Vol. XVII, 1832)

22ND NOVEMBER, 1825.—After tolerable progress, Captain Bedford arrived in the evening near Pasial, an Abor village, which is half a day's journey inland from the river, on the right bank. This was the limit of his excursion, as on various pretences the Abors of that place opposed his further progress. One plea urged was that any-one having met them on friendly terms would no doubt be very ill

[1] The last two decades of the century were unhappy. At the end of 1884, J. F. Needham, who was then Assistant Political Officer at Sadiya, visited Membu, Balek and other villages, meeting everywhere with a hospitable reception. In the following year he went to a number of Bor Abor villages and at the beginning of 1886 returned to Membu with the object of throwing a suspension bridge across the Siku river. But now the Abors showed themselves less friendly; they declined to allow the work to be undertaken and put forward many grievances against Government. They objected to the establishment of outposts near the hills and to the orders which prohibited them from coming armed to Sadiya. They complained that the allowances paid to them were insufficient, that runaway slaves who succeeded in escaping across the Inner Line were not returned, and that the Mishmis were better treated than the Abors when they visited Sadiya.

In 1889, four Miris were decoyed across the Inner Line by the Minyongs of Yomsing and Ledum and were cruelly put to death. A blockade of the Pasi-Minyong country was forthwith established and so great was the inconvenience caused to everyone that the powerful village of Kebang compelled the offenders to present sixteen *mithun* to Government in compensation.

In November 1893, the Padams of Damroh killed three military sepoys who were on patrol and in the following month attacked another police party. To punish this, in January 1894, a large force of five hundred sepoys and military police advanced on Dambuk and met with very stiff opposition. Before the village could be occupied, a huge stockade of trees, eighteen hundred yards long, on which the mountain guns made no impression, had to be captured. Three men were killed and twenty-seven injured in this operation. Sipu and Silluk were also captured at a cost of eight casualties, and it was then decided to proceed to Damroh. The bulk of the rations were left at Bordak with a small

received by the Abors higher up, with whom they were at enmity. It was therefore necessary to return after a stay of two days, and with such information as was to be obtained from the natives, who, though obstinate on the score of a further advance, and troublesome, from their rude habits and childish curiosity, were on the whole amicable and communicative.

The hills on the right bank belong to the Pasial and Mayong Abors, and those on the left to the Padoo, Siboo and Meeboo, and Goliwar Abors.

The Pasial Abors were armed respectably enough; every man had a bow and quiver of arrows, part of the latter of which were poisoned. They also carry light spears, or the sharp heavy sword (*dao*) of the Singfos. The Abors are not particular in their diet, and eat the flesh of the elephant, rhinoceros, hog, buffalo, kid, and deer, as well as ducks and fowls, but they expressed an abhorrence of feeders on beef. They exhibited also a marked predilection for brandy, although some of them pretended to give a preference to a fermented liquor prepared by themselves. Salt, cloth, and tobacco were in great request amongst them.

The dress of the Abors consists principally of a *choonga* (Assamese name for *dhoti*) made of the bark of the *uddal* tree. It answers the double purpose of a carpet to sit upon and of a covering. It is tied round the loins and hangs down behind in loose strips, about fifteen inches long, like a white bushy beard. It serves also as a pillow at night. The rest of their dress is apparently matter of individual taste; beads round the neck are not uncommon. Some wore plain basket caps, some had the cane caps partly covered with skins, and others wore them ornamented with stained hair, like our helmets,

detachment of sick and weak troops while the remainder of the force went on into the hills. The party got as far as the Yamne river but were unable to reach Damroh and returned. On their arrival at Bordak they found the camp gutted, the rations stolen and the unfortunate guards lying dead on the ground. Altogether thirty-five persons were killed in this attack. In punishment for this the villages of Kumku, Padu, and Membu (which had so often been visited in the early years) were destroyed.

A blockade was now proclaimed and the payment of *posa* was discontinued. In 1896, however, the blockade against the Pasis and Minyongs was raised, but that against the Padams was maintained till 1900.

For fuller accounts of the 1894 Expedition, see L. W. Shakespear, *History of the Assam Rifles* (1929), pp. 116 ff., and R. Reid, *History of the Frontier Areas* (1942), pp. 193 ff.

and resembling the head-dresses of the Singfos. Almost every man had some article of woollen dress, varying from a rudely made blanket waistcoat to a comfortably and tolerably well-shaped cloak. One of these, of a figured pattern, was made with sleeves; it was said to come from the country of the Bor Abors. The texture was good, though coarse, as was that of a red cloak worn by the Chief of the village.

The Abors seem to have been in the habit of levying contributions on their lowland and less martial neighbours of Assam, and to have resented any irregularity in their payment by predatory incursions, carrying off the people as prisoners. Several Assamese captives were found amongst the Abors of Pasial, some of whom had been so long amongst them as to have become completely reconciled to their condition.

3

AN ABOR CHIEF

(R. Wilcox, 'Memoir of a Survey of Assam and the neighbouring Countries, executed in 1825–6–7–8', *Asiatic Researches*, Vol. XVII 1832)

After our return to Shigaru Ghat we halted to allow time for the arrival of the Bor Abors. From the neighbouring villages we had constantly visitors, who come to exchange their yams or fowls for salt.

The Duku Chief had been down during our absence, and he now made his appearance again,—a fine-looking, well-dressed fellow, with very good manners, and a number of followers. When he stopped in front of our tent, he saluted us with a shrill whoop, more like the crowing of a cock than any other sound I can think of, and without appearing to take notice of us, he continued a long speech, during which he exalted his voice, as if calling to people at a distance, and never ceased beating his right foot on the ground, but every now and then the extraordinary whoop was renewed. When this was over he good-naturedly informed us that he had given us a specimen of the ceremony of meeting at councils amongst the Abor tribes. We were very much pleased with this man, but could not get anything from him either in the way of information or assistance in our project. He refused to take us to his village, on the plea that his authority would prove insufficient to protect us from the unpleasant familiarities of his people. He presented some rock-salt from Thibet in the shape of large crystals. I think that their possessing this article at so short a distance from our side is a collateral proof that they cannot have to travel very far for it.

We had little more success with the Bor Abors when they arrived, though they seemed equally well-inclined towards us. They assured us that they could not venture to take us to their villages without having prepared the people for our reception by the Miris. They promised, however, to exert their influence, and did not doubt but they should be able shortly to send us down an invitation. They appeared to me to be sincere in professing their inability to answer our inquiries about the Dihong; they remarked that they were no travellers, and had little curiosity about remote countries. Whereas we, on the contrary, seemed very inquisitive in such matters, and it would therefore be infinitely better that we should travel and gain from actual observation the information we sought, as it could be but imperfectly acquired from those who did not understand our purposes. They could only hold out hopes of our being able to visit their own villages; they assured us that they had no influence with the next tribes, and that we should certainly experience much difficulty in treating with them, and should we gain a footing amongst the Simongs or Regas, it would be but one step in moving towards the accomplishment of our wishes.

While the Bor Abors remained, we had a specimen of their skill in shooting with the bow, which was not particularly creditable to them. The object was a trunk of a tree, at the distance of one hundred yards, which they always shot very near to without hitting. Lieutenant Burlton then indulged and astonished them by firing at a mark placed at the extreme distance to which their arrows would range.

4

A HOSPITABLE AND SOCIAL RACE

(J. M'Cosh,[1] *Topography of Assam*, 1837, pp. 142 ff.)

THE Abors, Bor-Abors, and Mishmis inhabit an extensive range of mountainous country, along the southern exposure of the great Himalayan chain, from the 94th to the 97th degree of east longitude, and border with Thibet and China. It is difficult to form a conception of the extent of these tribes, but they are not to be despised; for during the insurrection of the Muamarias, no less than 17,000 Abors joined to drive that tribe out of Assam. It is probable that at no ancient period these two tribes were unconnected, but the Mishmis are now considered by the Abors as dependent upon them, and treated as slaves. Besides the Mishmis here mentioned as subservient to the Abors, there are several tribes of them, such as Muzu-Mishmis and Taen-Mishmis inhabiting the extreme branches of the Lohit or eastern channel of the Brahmaputra, who are probably independent. These tribes possess one of the lowest grades of civilization; they occupy numerous villages along the precipitous shores of the two great northern branches of the Brahmaputra, the Dihong or Sampo, and the Dibong.

Their houses are so constructed that the perpendicular side of the rock forms one wall: the floor is made of bamboos, with one side supported on the rock, and the other on beams driven into the ground. The space underneath is inhabited by the cattle, and the interstices in the floor afford the double advantage of showering down all the offal to the herd below, and preventing the accumulation of filth and nastiness.

Though the snows of their mountain-home have narrowed their means of subsistence, and limited their intercourse to their immediate neighbours, yet they are a hospitable and even a social race; and a constant round of festivity is kept up from one end of the year to the other. Each Chieftain kills the fatted bullock in turn; all his associates are invited to partake of the good cheer: the host is in his turn a guest at the next feast; and thus a reciprocity of entertainment is insured.

[1] At this date John M'Cosh was a lecturer in Clinical Medicine in Calcutta.

Nor are these hospitable rites allowed to be forgotten; the skull of every animal that has graced the board, is hung up as a record in the hall of the entertainer; he who has the best stocked Golgotha, is looked upon as the man of the greatest wealth and liberality; and when he dies, the whole smoke-dried collection of many years is piled upon his grave, as a monument of his riches, and a memorial of his worth.

These people, accustomed to a temperature at and about the freezing point, seem to dread an exposure to the heat of the low countries during the summer, and make their descent to their markets at Suddia only in the cold weather, and take their departure to their snows as soon as the Simla-tree puts forth its blossoms.

They bring along with them a few bags of musk, and musk-deer skins; some ivory, and a few copper pots, which they obtain from the Lama country; and a considerable quantity of a vegetable poison called *Bisa*, used in poisoning arrows. These they exchange for glass beads, of which they are very fond, and cattle, for the purpose of eating. The musk is for the most part adulterated; a portion of the genuine musk being abstracted to make into artificial bags, and its place filled up with dried blood.

5

AS BRAVE AS THEY ARE SAVAGE

(J. Butler, *A Sketch of Assam*, 1847, pp. 110 ff.)

Of the three classes of Bor Abors,[1] Abors and Merees, the first reside on the loftiest and most remote mountains north of the valley of Assam. The second class on a lower range, and the third at the foot of, or on the plains immediately leading up to, the hills. Several parties of Abors visited me frequently at Saikwah to barter a few fowls, eggs, ginger, chillies, yams, &c., for salt, and other necessaries of life. They appear to be descendants of the Tartar race; and are

[1] In 1912 it was decided, as a result of the new information gained during the Abor Expedition of the previous year, that 'Padam' should be used instead of 'Bor Abor' in official correspondence.

large, uncouth, athletic, fierce-looking, dirty fellows. The hair of the women is cut short, like that of the men: in a circle round the crown of the head it is two inches long, but the hair in front and behind, below the upper circle, is only about half an inch long. The ears of the men and women are perforated, the aperture, one inch in diameter, being distended by a piece of wood, worn as an ornament; and the necks of the Abor women are loaded with innumerable glass bead necklaces of all colours. Their arms are likewise adorned from the wrist to the elbow with brass rings; the legs are exposed from the knee downwards, the calf of the leg being bandaged with cane rings to the ankle. The Abors are feared and respected by all the neighbouring tribes for their martial spirit; nevertheless they are in great dread of the highland or Bor Abors, who are said to be as brave as they are savage. Like all the hill tribes of Assam, the Abors are void of beards: invariably plucking them, and leaving only scanty moustaches. They can neither read nor write, and their language sounds extremely harsh. The dress of the Abor Chiefs consists of Thibetian woollen cloaks, and a simple piece of cotton cloth, about a foot square, which is passed between the legs and suspended by a string round the waist: but not so effectually as to screen their persons from exposure every time they sit down. Of delicacy, however, the Abors are as void as they are of cleanliness. They wear three kinds of helmets, one of plain cane, and others trimmed with an edging of bear's skin, or covered with a thick yellow skin of a species of deer. A more formidable looking covering for the head could scarcely be worn.

In December 1835, an Abor Chief, with two hundred followers, descended from the hills, and begged permission to locate on the Dehing, within a day's journey of Suddeah. The Political Agent asked the Chief whether he was aware that the land in that quarter was within the Company's jurisdiction, and that settlers necessarily became subject to our police administration. He replied he was aware of that, and would readily give up any of his people guilty of criminal offences, but demurred to the introduction of our police officers for the apprehension of offenders. He was then asked whether he and his people would agree to pay taxes. His answer was that they had never been accustomed to do so, and could not submit to it.

From various reports, the Abors are deemed a very rude, barbarous people, but of open manners and warlike habits; their bluntness of expression is more manly and pleasing than the base servility and sycophancy of the Assamese. As they have been accustomed to levy contributions from the inhabitants of Seesee, and other districts in Assam, they would be dangerous neighbours, if located in the immediate vicinity of the Suddeah people.

Not acceding to the terms on which we were disposed to acquiesce in their application, the Abors returned to their hills. Scarcity of the means of subsistence was, it is supposed, the cause of their visit; and they evidently meditated replacing the Merees, who formerly laboured for the Abors on the Dehong quarter, but have since emigrated to Upper and Lower Assam, to escape the exactions of that tribe.

It appears that the Abors are not allowed to emigrate to Assam; for in 1844 two young men having eloped with two damsels to Saikwah, and the latter claiming protection from the British authorities, an inquiry was made as to the cause of their deserting their own country; when one freely confessed that her father had given her in marriage to an old man, but preferring a young Abor, she had determined on living with him in the Company's territory and disobeying her father's commands. The other stated that she had been given in marriage to a young man, who died, and she was retained for his younger brother, a mere boy; but not being disposed to wait until he had reached the age of puberty, she had fallen in love with an Abor youth, and trusted they might be permitted to pass their days in peace in the forests adjoining Saikwah. If their prayer was not granted, the girls affirmed, in the most earnest manner, that they would be tortured and sold to another tribe; while their young husbands would be cast into the Dehong river with their hands bound, to suffer death by drowning.

To the present day, little is known of the Abor country, Europeans never having been permitted to penetrate any very great distance into the interior.[1] The eminent astronomer and adventurous traveller, Lieutenant Wilcox, in 1827, endeavoured to ascend the Dehong

[1] How little was known may be seen from the account given by Francis Hamilton in his *An Account of Assam,* compiled in 1807–14: 'On the side of the Brahmaputra, opposite to the Miri or Dophlas immediately beyond the Dikrong river, are said to dwell a people called Abor, and further up another tribe called Tikliya Nagas, both of whom are extremely savage. They are indeed said to be cannibals, and to have little intercourse with the people in Assam, although the two territories are adjacent.' This, of course, is nonsense.

river with the view of proving that this stream was the celebrated Sampoo river; but after a few days' journey he met with insuperable difficulties, from the rapidity of the current, the closeness of the country, and the absolute prohibition of the Abors against his proceeding farther. Since that period, no strenuous endeavours have been made to acquire further information regarding these rude barbarians. The Merees speak the Abor language, and a friendly intercourse exists between the tribes; though the Merees have ceased to bear the yoke of slavery or be subordinate to the Abors. Their chief occupation is husbandry, and they are generally considered a quiet and tolerably industrious race.

6

THE MEANING OF THE TATTOOED CROSS

(Major H. Vetch, Political Agent, Upper Assam, in a letter dated 3rd January 1848)

THE Bor Abors appear to be a blunt, independent, and warlike race, who, while they have no objection to carry off cattle or what they can lay hands on belonging to other Abors or Meeshmees, make common interest with all those of their own clan.

They acknowledge the authority of a Chief approved by themselves for his ability, but almost every question of consequence appears to be settled in assembly. Some of the villages are large and populous, and all those of the same clan (although wide apart) are prompt in sending them quotas of armed men to any point where danger is apprehended by a part of their community. Their arms are a long spear, long strait sword, dagger, and bow and arrows. Many wear a sort of helmet, made of cane, plaited and ornamented with the hair of the yuk, dyed red, as well as by any trophies of the chase they consider suitable to produce a wild or warlike appearance. Many of them have the mark of the cross tattooed on their forehead, but I could get no satisfactory account of the origin of affixing this emblem. They said it was intended to stand in the place of the brass utensils and other articles buried with them at their funerals, in case they should die poor, and not be able to afford them.

(Father N. M. Krick, in a letter dated 1st September 1851, from *J.A.S.B.*, 1913, Vol. IX, pp. 114 f.)

On the 26th September I landed at Saikwock, situated along the eastern bank of the Brahmapootra. Captain Smith, commander of the frontier troops, received me very kindly.

On the 19th November, Captain Wath, who was organizing an expedition for the protection of the Dihong gold-washers, invited me to join him, and offered to introduce me to the Abors. We started with an escort of 200 soldiers and 9 elephants. After a five or six days' march, we met about 600 Abors all armed with bows and arrows, and lances measuring some fifteen feet in length. Captain Wath, after a friendly talk, asked them to receive me and see me safe to Tibet. 'We can't do that,' they replied; 'he would come to grief,—and we are responsible for our guests.'

What struck me most during the conference was, besides their savage dress, the typically European physiognomy of those people.

But I soon noticed, at a closer examination, most extraordinary tattoo marks: it was a cross neatly designed and painted in blue on their faces. Most of them wore it on the forehead, others on the nose; some of these crosses had a double horizontal beam, the vertical line running from the forehead down to the tip of the nose; others had only one single cross-beam running either across the nose or above the eyes.

The savages were unable to explain the origin of this symbol; but they believe that any man who is marked with this sign, is protected in this life, and taken straight to heaven in the next, and that none but these are called to share God's felicity.

I made them understand I was a priest, a teacher of prayer, and that I had come to explain to them the mysterious power of the Cross. I then took my crucifix, kissed it, and let them kiss it each in turn.[1]

[1] See also p. 242.

Chapter IX

VISITORS TO MEMBU

1

THE FIRST VISIT TO MEMBU

(R. Wilcox, 'Memoir of a Survey of Assam and the neighbouring Countries, executed in 1825-6-7-8', *Asiatic Researches*, Vol. XVII, 1832)

We arrived (Lieutenant Burlton was now with me) at Singaru Ghat without any remarkable occurrence on the way, and immediately sent Agakong (a Meeshmee Chief, resident on the Dihong) to the Membu village to show the beforementioned stone[1] and remind them of their invitation. He brought back one of the two influential men of the place, with information that we were expected at the village, and that they should be happy to see us. In the meantime people had been with us from Padu village to express the wishes of the Gam and commonalty of that place that we would remain on the sandbank where we were, and there receive their visits and hold a grand conference, which the Abors seemed to understand at the only reasonable purpose of our coming, or, at any rate, as the only admissible mode of communicating our intentions.

We held to our first resolution, but before we could set out the next day, more messengers arrived from Membu to inform us that they were aware of the endeavour made by the Padu people to detain us, and begging that we would pay no attention to them. This manoeuvring exhibits the difficulty of treating with people who do not acknowledge one common head, but, on the contrary, are all jealous of one another, and united only in cases of general application to the common welfare.

We started and marched two hours through a dense tree-jungle, by a path admitting, as usual, but one man at a time. We then came out upon a fine path of cultivation, extending four or five miles, and passing through a part of it we entered a path eight or ten feet wide, and perfectly even, which continues in a direction nearly

[1] The Membu people had sent a round stone as 'an emblem of the stability of their friendly inclination'; until, they said, 'that stone crumbles into dust, shall our friendship last'.

north to the Shiku. Near this rivulet we found a slight rise in the ground, which terminated on the river's bank in a perpendicular conglomerate. We were quite astonished at the skill and labour shown in the construction of the cane suspension bridge thrown over at this point; it was such as would do no discredit to the department for similar works in Calcutta. Groups of trees at either end are so conveniently situated for making fast the canes, that the idea occurs of their having been planted for the purpose. The canes are passed over pegs in the supporting posts, and separately stretched and fastened to the different trees. There are two good main suspenders, and on these hang elliptical coils of cane at intervals of a few yards, supporting at the bottoms of them the footway, which is not more than twelve or fourteen inches wide. The ellipses are further connected by canes running along the sides, protecting the passenger from the fear of falling; but though considerable stability is thus given to the whole structure by connecting its several parts, there is still a very unpleasant swinging and waving during the passage. The span between the points of suspension is full one hundred and twenty feet.

The road from the bridge to Membu village ascends a low hill, and is stony. In one place, where the natural form of the rock with some artificial defences narrow the path, we found a doorway recently built of green boughs, intended, as we understood, to keep out those evil spirits who might chance to travel in our company.

On both banks of the Shiku are cliffs of conglomerate, the faces fresh from recent slips, caused perhaps by the undermining of the river in the rains (as the quantity of rubbish at the base is trifling). The peaks of this conglomerate ridge are remarkable for their sharpness. Approaching the village, we first passed a great number of granaries, built apart for security against fire. The village may consist of one hundred houses, built near each other in the midst of a stony slope of easy ascent. In the middle is the Morang, a large building which serves as a hall of audience and debate, as a place of reception for strangers, and as a house for the bachelors of the village generally, who, by their laws, are not entitled to the aid of the community for the construction of a separate dwelling. It was intended that we should lodge here, but the effect upon our olfactory nerves of certain appendages of convenience was so appalling, that we made good a very hasty retreat from it, and we had luckily received hints from the Luri Gohayn on this subject, which had induced us to bring our small tent....

I informed them that I was the bearer of presents, to be divided according to their own custom amongst the Abor villages, and I requested that they would take charge of them and give notice to the Bor Abors that the concurrence of that more powerful tribe might be had for an equitable division. They declined the office, and in return begged that I would make my own division. I had been given to understand that the influential men would not dare to accept anything for themselves in public, but I felt the difficulty of satisfying each in private, not only from the numbers, but from my ignorance of the relative claims of each to consideration. It was therefore by open dealing, and by the magnitude of the present offered to the whole, that I hoped to succeed.

It suffices now to say that our visit was not attended with any advantageous result; they would not consent to our proceeding further by land, and they assured us of the utter impossibility of our going on by water.

I seized a moment during the conference, when all appeared in perfect good humour, to put questions about the course of the Dihong, and could only learn that it comes from the west or north-west, but the Abors of this place are evidently unacquainted with it beyond a very short distance, since their country, or rather that of the Abors, which they visit, lies away from the banks of the river in a northerly direction. Beyond the Bor Abors, on the opposite bank of the Yamuni river, are the Simong tribe, from whom the former receive the Lama goods. The Reiga tribe are on the western side of the great river, beyond the Pasi and Mizong tribes. Some of those present were of opinion, from what they had understood, that both Reigas and Simongs have but a short distance to go to reach the Lama country. All agreed in affirming that the Dihong is not navigable, and that it would be absolutely impossible to proceed along the banks.

The Membu people promised to inform the Bor Abors of our arrival. A hog was voted us by the Council, and also a supply of rice, but neither was given with that hospitable feeling which marks the friendly tribes of the Meeshmees. It seemed as if they voted their gifts in the necessary observance of a custom, and afterwards gave them with great reluctance. These singular people acknowledge no other authority but that of the Raj, or people generally, who make laws at the Councils, assembled in the Morang, where everyone has an equal vote; but though not acknowledged by them, it is evident that some few, either through their superior wealth, hereditary esteem, or real ability, exert a very strong influence on the rest, and can readily sway them to any measure. It would be supposed that this would greatly facilitate the gaining of any point at issue with the Abors, but the extreme jealousy of the Raj, and vigilant watchfulness to preserve their democratical rights, render it a matter very difficult to manage to bribe these influential men, and my want of success amongst them I attribute entirely to my insufficient knowledge of their habits, and consequently of the proper mode of intriguing with them. It is singular to observe in them such different shades of extreme rudeness and civilized observance of laws enacted and allowed by them to be necessary for the good of the community. The purpose of the primary article of their clothing (which consists of a triangular piece of coarse cloth six inches long and four or five broad at the end, by which it is suspended to a string tied round the loins), is vitiated every time they sit down; but of this they seem perfectly careless. Indeed, as we discovered in the evening, when prompted by curiosity to enter the Morang again, the bachelors are in the habit of basking by the side of their wood-fires without any covering at all, and during the day I had remarked that in the midst of a crowd of both sides the men did indeed avoid wetting their next neighbour's leg, but observed no other of the ordinary precautions of decency. However, while many others of the mountain tribes seem superior to them in some points, I have not elsewhere seen them equally ready for a labour like that of constructing the cane suspension bridge. There is more order than usual also in the regular mode of building their granaries. They have equitable laws to make public burdens (such as the presentation of a hog voted us that day, or erecting a new house for any member, when assistance is required), fall equally on all.

Of their religion, I learned no more than that, like the Meeshmees, they occasionally sacrifice to a deity supposed to reside in the woods and mountains. The conical mountain, called Regam, they believe to be the abode of a rather malignant demon; for they assert that anyone who should attempt to pry into the secrets of his dwelling, on the summit, would surely die, as they know from experience.

It was not a little remarkable that though the Abors are said to be the source whence the strange tales of the Sri Lohit are derived, we heard nothing about it from them; on the contrary their geographical ideas are reasonable enough. They declare the Dihong to come from a very great distance, and that it can nowhere be crossed but by boats or rafts, being always too wide for a cane bridge. The Lama country, with which they have intercourse, is situated on the right bank of the river evidently, because after crossing it from east to north to reach the Reiga tribe they entirely lose sight of it in their progress to the north-west.

While on the subject, it may be as well to allude at once to information derived from other sources, particularly from another tribe more to the westward. It is said that one route to the Lama country is by the Kalapani (or black river), which falls in beyond Meyong; it is followed up to its source, and then some snowy mountains are crossed to the inhabited country. Chokies are there placed, and they cannot visit the interior; but the town where they exchange commodities is situated on the south bank of a very large piece of water, which, as they speak of a feature in it so very remarkable to them, of its 'having no current', must be a lake. The Governor of the town is named Gendu, and he wears a shirt of mail and rides a horse—so they say. They insist that the Dihong has nothing to do with the lake, and they conclude it to be distant from it.

Here we have apparently the origin of the strange reports current in Assam, to which allusion has been made, of the large and magnificent river; or what is quite as likely in my estimation is, that we derive our story from those tribes who are in contact with the Bhotiyas on the west, and that the Bhotiyas allude to the veritable Sampo passing their country to the north. All the more wealthy Abors have cloaks of Thibetan woollens; indeed scarce a man is seen amongst them without some article of the manufacture of Thibet. They wear large necklaces of blue beads, which they esteem very highly, and they profess that they are not procurable now; they look exactly like turquoises, and have the same hue of greenish blue; but a close examination discovers in them minute bubbles, marking the agency of fire. They are extremely hard, but the only one I could get possession of I broke with a hammer, and it had exactly the fracture of fine Chinese porcelain.

The very rude tribes, of the existence of which the Assamese have an idea, and mention by the names of Bibcrs and Barkans, and are mentioned by the Subanshiri Abors under the latter name as residing to their north, may perhaps be the Lho-ptra of Father Georgius, whose account is completely corroborated by a singular note in Persian on a map from Nepal, which I have recently seen; they were to the south of Takpo, where the Capuchins had an establishment.

2

FATHER KRICK AMONG THE ABORS

(Father N. M. Krick, 'Account of an Expedition among the Abors in 1853', translated by Father A. Gille, S.J., *J.A.S.B.*, 1913, Vol. IX, pp. 108 ff.)

SINCE the English first occupied Assam twenty-nine years ago, several agents of the East India Company have tried to gain access into this country, with a view, if possible, to enter into commercial relation with Thibet, and to ascertain whether the Siang, known to the English by the name of Dihong is really the famous Zang-po, which crosses Thibet from East to West, and which has been such a puzzle to the geographers of the last centuries. But the Padams knew the *timeo Danaos et dona ferentes*. 'If we allow,' so they said, 'any Englishman to penetrate into our country under what pretext soever, he is sure to have an army at his heels.'

In their opinion, any white skin, any nose somewhat protruding is of English make. This will make you understand the trouble I had in getting their consent to receive me. My cross so similar to theirs and my reputation of a French priest were my only passport. My reception was accompanied with ceremonies peculiar enough to find place in this letter.

Eighteen young men met me at the foot of the mountain. No sooner did I move on, than the two youngest of the band proceeded to cover my body with leaves, whilst singing words utterly unintelligible to me. They meant of course to purify me and deliver my body from all diabolical influence. This exorcism was soon to be followed by a second performance more weird and threatening. As I emerged from the forest, I was made to pass under an arch bristling with bows and arrows, and decorated with all sorts of devilries and monsters pierced with arrows, and in striking attitudes that baffle description. This piece of architecture was fearful to behold, as well it might be, for it was to expel from my body the more stubborn devils who had been daring enough to cross the first obstacle. The women rushed to their doors to watch me passing by, and it was amidst a throng of curious onlookers, squalling children and howling dogs that I was conducted to the common building, where I found the men waiting for me. My arrival was hailed with a thunder of savage and dinning cheers sounding through the house like a discharge of artillery. It was a last assault on the evil demons who should have forced their way through the first barricades; the most vicious devils would retreat before such a terrific uproar. The spirits being thus settled to everybody's satisfaction, I had now to lend myself to the curiosity of the crowd.

In an instant, I was surrounded by a circle of eager men and women, studying every detail of my figure. I was repeatedly obliged to go out into the street to show myself to the public. Lorrain, with his long shaggy hair, his tail drooping low, and his flabby ears, went in for a fair share of the public admiration. The crowd kept watch the whole night; fleas were no less anxious to get to my skin; with so many guests, sleep of course could not be very long.

Next day, general meeting, to which the whole village was convoked. The six Chiefs sat down in a circle, right in the centre of a spacious hall. The president of this uncouth senate invited me to come and sit at his right, and without previous warning donned my head with a reed helmet of monstrous size, crowned with a red painted tuft of goat's hair, and another of bear's fur, two bear's tusks crossing each other on my forehead. This was the signal that opened the meeting. After several speeches, the members were asked to cast their votes; the Chiefs then withdrew for deliberation, soon returning with a favourable answer. 'Migom (king),' so they said, 'we are convinced that your intentions are peaceful; we therefore allow you to advance through our country.'

But as I was expecting the arrival of a new confrère, who was to accompany me, I demanded permission to wait for him. 'Yes, yes,' they all replied with one voice, 'and if you cure our sick, we shall keep you for ever, and we shall build you a house,' and in evidence of their sincerity, the Chiefs put the guardhouse at my disposal.

No sooner was I settled down in my new home, than invitations poured in from all sides requesting me to go and look after the sick: being a priest, I must needs be a physician too. The only remedy these people ever heard of is religion. They have recourse to neither drugs nor medical treatment of any kind; even the use of simples is unknown. Such things are according to them perfectly useless, as all diseases, both internal and external, are directly caused by either bad spirits, or good spirits having some good reasons to show their dissatisfaction. Exorcism is therefore the only remedy, and the only doctor is the priest: the bad spirit must be expelled, or the good one propitiated by sacrifices. If the complaint is proof against these superstitious practices, it is because the spirit is unrivalled in malice and power: there lies the secret of all mortal diseases. As I am writing to you,[1] my room exhibits the appearance of a hospital of incurables: here is a young woman whose arm is covered with a horrible ulcer. 'When did you get that?' 'Three years ago,' she replied. 'I killed a rat; my disease dates from that time.'

Further on there lies a young man suffering from scrofula; his legs are swollen, his body is covered with ulcers,—a dying skeleton. 'How long have you been ill?' 'Migom, I used to be nice and fat, a stout and brave warrior; but last year the evil spirit got hold of me, and he has done his work.' Another patient has his stomach swollen to awful dimensions. I see nothing but suffering all about me. All these patients are somewhat trying to my medical skill; they are draining my dispensary, whose deficiency beats that of my capacity. However it was God's will that several patients should recover perfect health; hence there was a rush for the French Hippocrates. Everybody wanted to fall sick for the sole pleasure of being looked after by such a learned man. It was no good my pretending to be unable to cure certain diseases; if I did not cure them, it was because I did not want to; willy-nilly, I had to give them remedies, were it

[1] This account was originally sent to Dr Bousquet, surgeon at the Necker Hospital, Paris, under whom Father Krick had taken some lessons in medicine.

but a few drops of water. A few purgatives, some ointments, a little care, had worked all these marvels. Such was the enthusiasm that those people wanted to carry me in triumph on their shoulders. It was no use for me to tell them that Almighty God had given to my remedies the virtue that cures; they would not believe me. My power was in the touch of my hand. And so they went on repeating: 'You are the most powerful Dondai (priest); no spirit can resist you; your hand cures everything.' Of all this the practical consequence was that I had to touch everything with my hand, even the most disgusting wounds. I was not given a minute's rest. At every moment someone came rushing to me: 'Father, some medicine!' At early dawn I went out to see my patients only to return at midday thoroughly fagged.

However, my great reputation was very near causing my ruin. One evening, I was startled by loud clamours issuing from the common-house. The next morning, the president came to inform me of what had happened. 'Migom,' he said, 'some Meris (an Assamese tribe subject to the English) have spread the rumour that you are an English spy; that you should not be trusted, as you possess the power, so they say, of turning our food into poison by a single act of your will. If we keep you any longer, our country will suffer great calamities. Last night our people insisted on setting fire to your house, but they refrained from carrying out their design on my promising them to force you to leave the country.' There was no time for deliberation; so my departure was fixed for the next day.

Towards ten o'clock in the evening, another Chief came to me at the head of a party of men, who evidently objected to the loss of my medical powers. The Chief then spoke: 'Migom, we have at last made those cowards understand the folly of their behaviour, and that, instead of expelling you, we ought to keep you to look after our sick. Besides, are you not our father? Did you not, at an early period, bring us the blessing of the cross? And now, after having been round the world, you have been restored to us. When you will have mastered our tongue, who knows what new benefits you will have to bestow on us? Therefore stay, it is the wish of the whole village.'

But the devil, who has no worse enemy than the missionary, was not to be so easily beaten. Two days later, whilst the villagers were away working in the fields, the village took fire. On hastening to the spot, what was my surprise to see standing on the top of each roof one or two men brandishing long swords, and endeavouring to kill the fire-demon. 'Fetch water,' I shouted; but, they were obviously too busy with their quixotic performance against the devil to hear me; so I told off the women, who were quietly admiring the valiance of their husbands, and forced them to fetch water; and as they saw what the water could do, they all rushed back to the torrent. Even our Don Quixotes, seeing that their sabres were not half as effective as water, soon exchanged their weapons for the water-jars. All the houses, save two, were rescued from destruction. I was proclaimed the hero of the day: all acknowledged that the demon of fire dreads the water, though some felt inclined to blame me for not having foreseen and prevented the accident.

The next thing to do was to imprison the spirit of fire on the scene of the disaster. The burnt houses were hedged in and surrounded with devil-scaring emblems. In spite of these precautions, it was feared that the devil might escape and take refuge into some odd corner of the village, so the very next day all the men, armed to the teeth, with beating of drums, and fearful howls, set out in pursuit of the devil, far into the jungle.

The two families whose dwellings had been burnt down, were banished for one year, for if any of their members were to set foot in a house within those twelve months, the building would not escape from the flames.

Useless to add that my presence was made responsible for all those accidents. The loss of two *mitous* (wild cows) sustained by my next neighbours increased the public distrust. Great, however, was the embarrassment of those poor people; on the one hand, they had found in me a friend, ready to do anything to bring relief to their bodily as well as to their spiritual ills; on the other hand, fright chilled their attachment to me. The diplomats of the village could not bear to see me settling so close to Assam; as for me, I delayed my departure as much as I could, as I was anxious to give to my confrère, Mr Bourry, sufficient time to join me.

Eventually, on Good Friday, whilst all the huntsmen were gathered at my house for a hunting-meet, Lendemk, the great Chief, said to me: 'I order you to leave the village tomorrow.' 'All right,' I said. 'I had come to give you my affection, and to offer you my services, but as you refuse my benefits, I will carry them elsewhere.'

'Oh! I don't mean that,' he exclaimed, 'you misunderstand my words. Stay for some few days more, but if any accident were to happen, I should be made responsible for it.' 'That is just the reason that induces me to go,' I answered. 'The very first accident that happens in the village, you will attribute it to me.'

All I could do was to secure the assistance of the president of the Council in finding out a direct route into Thibet during the next season. The following day, before leaving, I visited the sick once more, dressed their wounds and at once set out on my journey with Ibang, the second Chief, as my guide. My heart was heavy, though it was a considerable relief to shake off at last the innumerable hosts of fleas that devoured me. We pitched our tent in the forest for the night. The next morning a violent storm burst over our heads. I took the altitude of the sun; I registered on the 11th March 1853, 115°44′. As I had not the declination of that day, I could not make the calculations. The longitude was about 95°20′ (Greenwich).

Then I cast a long parting glance towards the village of Mimbo which I was so sorry to leave.

The village was situated at a height of 600 ft. above the plains of Assam, and spread out on the curved flanks of a magnificent mountain, that was encircled by a belt of peaks rising to a prodigious height. To the West rose the sacred Orega peak, the rendezvous of all the spirits of the country. The small river Sikan flows from East to West along the foot of the mountain. Towards the South, the eye rests on the smooth plains of Assam, where the famous Siong or Dihong of the Assamese shoots up, reflecting the rays of the sun across the sky.

Now a few words on the race to which the Padams belong and on the marvellous signs which I have discovered among them.

The Padams stand midway between the Mongolian and the Caucasian races. They are beardless; hair and eyes are black; the skin is brown; the eyes stand at right angles with the nose. The forehead is flat, the face broad, the nose short, the cheek-bones somewhat prominent, and stature moderate.

This is how they account for their origin: 'When the earth was but a mass of mud, God came down from Heaven; with a handful of mud he made two brothers and two sisters. The Padams descend from the elder, and the Miris from the younger brother. Hence the

Padams are a privileged race, living in plenty and invincible on the battlefield.'

The males are tattooed at the age of eighteen; the pattern is, in my opinion, of evidently Christian origin.[1] The majority wear on the forehead a perfectly shaped Maltese cross of bluish colour ✠; others wear the ordinary cross † with the vertical beam running along the nose, and the cross-bar above the eyes. Others wear the Lorraine cross ☨, with the upper cross-beam on the forehead, and the lower lying across the bridge of the nose. Others again wear the Maltese cross on their calves. The women have the Maltese cross tattooed on the upper lip, and on their legs the Lorraine cross with two St Andrew's crosses drawn on either side, as shown in figure.

X X ☨ X X

The men have as a rule their chin tattooed with three vertical and parallel lines; the women have five or seven of them, as the case may be, on the chin, and four on the upper lip, two on either side of a cross, and the whole set is bracketed.

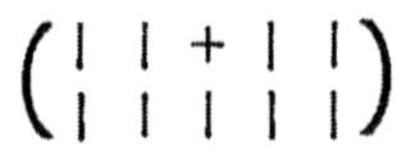

I have often questioned the Padams as to the origin and meaning of these signs. Some answered that God at creation had given them to the Padams as a distinctive mark of the elder tribe; others asserted that they had received them from a northern tribe; several confessed their ignorance in the matter, but all agreed as to its being the sign of God, and a most beneficial badge too, as 'he who wears it', so they said, 'is acknowledged and protected by God; if he dies, he is at once received into heaven'. 'But what, if he has not the sign?' I asked; 'Where is he to go?' 'God will disown him and cast him off.'

I may be allowed to hazard here a suggestion with regard to the origin of these signs. It is my opinion, and all those who have come

[1] 'We venture to suggest that in this explanation of Abor tattoo marks Fr Krick was unduly influenced by his zeal as a missionary. There is, we believe, no reason to attempt the derivation of these symbols from Christian sources, as the cross—one of the simplest designs imaginable—is found in some form or another in all savage ornamentation. The designs found nowadays tattooed on Abor men or women are far more varied in character than Fr Krick's observation would lead one to suppose, and all will be found fully detailed in Sir George Dunbar's forthcoming memoir on the anthropology of the Abors and Galongs.'—Original footnote by J. Coggin-Brown and S. W. Kemp (1913).

in contact with the Padams agree with me, that the pattern, as I have described it, is the Christian cross. These are briefly my reasons:

1. No other marks are tattooed on their bodies.
2. Their crosses are altogether similar in shape to our four crosses: the ordinary cross, the Maltese, the St Andrew's and the Lorraine cross.
3. The spiritual meaning attached to them by the natives strongly confirms my conjecture.

What then would be the meaning of the vertical lines, always numbering 3, 5 or 7, with which they tattoo their chins? Might not the number 3 be a reminiscence of the Blessed Trinity, the number 5 a reminder of the five wounds of Our Lord, and the number 7 a figure of the seven Sacraments? Whereas the four lines on the upper lip might with some plausibility represent some virtues or mysteries.

But when were these emblems adopted by the Padams? Fr Athanasius Kircher in his in-folio bearing the title *La Chine Illustrée* mentions several missions established in Thibet, China and Tartary from the time of the Apostle St Thomas. This book was printed at Amsterdam in 1665. He also published a map, roughly drawn, but giving accurately enough the chief towns and districts; on it he traced the route followed by Frs Francis Dorville and John Grabere from Peking to Goa, through China, Tartary, Thibet and Bengal. These Fathers travelled from Lassa to the North of the Padam country, whilst according to their information Fr Andrada went as far as the Thibetan town Radoc. Now we are told that in this country they discovered evident traces of the Christian religion, proving to a certainty that the Gospel had been preached to those tribes. They speak of three men who bore the names of Dominic, Francis and Anthony.

In 1826 Colonel R. Wilcox, on discovering the use of the cross among the Padams, made attempts to trace its origin, and found in Hindostan a map on which it was stated that since the twelfth century there existed a mission in the South of Thibet among a tribe called Shokhaptra.

Now, I have entered Thibet by the South-Eastern frontier, without coming across any traces of our holy religion; several other travellers entered it by the South-West with no greater success. So, it is quite possible that the Shokhaptras be a tribe occupying the South of Thibet, in the vicinity of the Padam country. As a matter of fact, I have often been told by the Padams that there existed towards the North, before reaching Thibet, a tribe which shunned all intercourse with the Padams, and from which they pretended to have received the cross. The Padams, being their next neighbours, must have been struck by the importance those people attached to the cross, and may have adopted it for their own use without guessing much of its meaning. Or it may be that the missionary, in order to bring home to those uncultured minds and hearts the truths of our faith, advised his catechumens to tattoo themselves with the cross; or anticipating, perhaps, that the missionary's death would leave them without a pastor, the natives may have wished in this manner to preserve a precious deposit of their faith.

I once met a Thibetan who was marked with the same sign; on my asking where he had learned to wear it, he pointed towards the Padam country, adding that he had received it from the savage mountaineers.

The dress, government and customs will not be devoid of interest for a Frenchman; so a few details on that subject will, I expect, be welcome. I have very little to say about their mode of dressing, as their clothing is reduced to a minimum somewhat too primitive; however, the full dress sometimes worn by men deserves a short notice.

It is composed of eleven pieces: 1st, a loin cloth. 2nd, a long loose mantle open in front, and sprinkled all over with designs of shining colours such as stars etc. 3rd, a cuirass painted black and made of camel hair; it covers the chest and the back, the head passing through a hole in the centre, and is used as a defensive covering against the thrust of the lance. 4th, a steel helmet painted black, with a tuft of bear's or goat's hair on top; two boar-tusks cross each other in front, like the two guns on the shako of an artillery-man. The three last articles are imported from Thibet. 5th, an edge-tool bearing a common resemblance to the hatchet and the sword. 6th. a long Thibetan sword. 7th, a small basket. 8th, a bamboo shield, turned into an umbrella when it rains. 9th, bow and arrows. 10th, a long knife. 11th, a pouch containing tobacco, a pipe, a flintstone and similar articles.

Neither women nor men are fond of long hair; they do not allow it to grow beyond two or three inches in length.

The women wear heavy yellow necklaces, iron or copper bracelets; but the most peculiar article of their ornamental apparel is their ear-rings; these are long spirals of wire about two inches thick, sufficiently heavy to tear the ears, and stretch them out of shape, so that the ornaments dangle on the shoulders. The men wear but one kind of necklace; it is composed of blue stones strung together, of unusually neat cut. This article is highly valued, and transmitted from father to son, as they pretend to have received it directly from God. Some stick into their ears silver or wooden (bamboo) tubes.

The Padams are not a nomadic people, but possess large and fine villages. Their system of government is democratic and republican, the strictest dependence being tempered by the most absolute freedom. Every man is his own master. But, if a question of common interest arises, the point at issue is settled by a council, under the presidency of the Chiefs of Bor-abor, this village owing its privilege to the fact that God placed in it the elder of the two brothers he created.

Excepting the case just mentioned, each village is self-governing and independent. It has its own administration, both legislative and executive. Women have no share in the government; they cannot even set foot in the council-room.

Every male, reaching the age of reason, is by right active member of any assembly. Each commune is ruled by five or six Chiefs elected for life by the people; they control all affairs of greater importance. If any of them dies, his son, if capable, succeeds to his office; else, he remains a common citizen, and another election supplies the vacancy.

Laws are framed by the people, sanctioned by the council, and promulgated by the president. Every decision is supposed to come from the people; the Chiefs have no right but to approve and enforce it. Hence, the people propose, the council sanctions, and the president promulgates.

Every evening, all the men gather in the spacious council-room to discuss the topics of the day, which means: (1) to inform one another of what has been seen or heard; (2) to discuss the political questions put forth by one of the Chiefs; (3) to settle what the village will do on the next day, for it is understood that no one is free to dispose of his time as he thinks fit; his daily work is cut out, discussed and officially decreed by the majority of the council. Hence, every evening, between 10 and 11 o'clock, boys are sent about the village shouting at the top of their voices: 'Tomorrow, tiger hunt! Tomorrow fishing! Tomorrow, field labour! Tomorrow, *genna*!' i.e. obligatory holiday.

These injunctions are obeyed to the letter, for this people is as law-abiding and respectful to the powers that be, as it is proud of its liberty. To call a Padam a slave is an insult that would make this proud mountaineer gnash his teeth and grasp at his bow.

The council-house is also used for extraordinary gatherings convoked to deal with a sudden emergency, such as was my arrival; sometimes, especially on rainy days, it is turned into a rendezvous of gossip and handiwork. Everybody takes his tools and passes the time as pleasantly and as usefully as he can.

The tribe has its army or civic guard, composed of young men above 17 or 18. All of them, except the married men, sleep at the barracks.

The Padams are hunters by taste, and farmers by necessity; yet, they are excellent cultivators. The roads are planted on both sides with fruit-trees. The only farming-tools they know are their arms and their hands, and their backs are their only means of transport. Yet their granaries are well stored with rice, gums, maize, *bobossa* and several other products.

The bow is their favourite weapon, and they use it with great dexterity. It is their vade-mecum, the first toy of the child, who shoots from morning till night.

Arts and trades are scarcely known. The women weave their cotton with rough yarn by means of an appliance which no man in his senses would ever think of calling a loom. The worker in iron can be called neither a blacksmith nor a farrier: his anvil is a stone, a bamboo stem serves as a substitute for the bellows, and the work is as wretched as the tools. Architecture has not had much of a chance. Planks planed with a hatchet compose the flooring and walls of the Padam hut, and the roof is thatched with plantain-tree leaves. The inside is so dark that it requires some caution to feel one's way in it. But if their dwellings are roughly built, their bridges deserve our admiration. Their construction is solid; the floor is a light network of rattan palm twigs, and so elastic that it yields to the pressure of the foot and rises like a spring.

Commerce is insignificant. The following are the domestic animals: 1st, the *mitou* or wild cow, domesticated and exclusively reared for the slaughter-house; 2nd, small black pigs, much appreciated by the Padams; 3rd, fowls; 4th, dogs, small and lean, but excellent hunters.

Rice and herbs form their staple food; they are eaten without either salt or butter. Meat and fish are the most popular dishes. The ordinary drink is fermented rice beer or *bobossa* water; pure water is never used at meals.

The Padams are naturally hospitable; the guest is first expected to give a present to make friends with his host, but it is the meal that sanctions and seals friendship for ever; as soon as you have touched food, 'you are friends till the sun falls', as these savages are wont to say.

Respect for old age is pushed to its extreme limits, and surpasses whatever has been recorded of old Lacedæmon. Old people are exempt from all work, and constitute a separate class by themselves. Whilst the young are out in the fields, the old gather in the council-house and make merry. No calamity is dreaded as much as the curse of an old man. One day, as I called on the Chief Leudouck, I saw an old man whom the Chief had called in to the sick-bed of his child. I asked him whether he was a priest. 'No,' said the Chief, 'but the words of an old man are a powerful blessing; God endows it with a divine efficacy.' Old age is, as you see, a most desirable condition among the Padams; all honours are due to it, and priests are taken exclusively from its ranks.

On my travels I have come across many superstitious people, but really the Padams beat them all. Here everything is done, everything explained by invisible agencies. Their spirits number millions. Each forest, each tree of unusual size, water, chiefly when it eddies round or murmurs in its fall, mountains and villages, are all crowded with divinities good and bad, great and small, weak and powerful. They are held in such fear that nothing could induce a Padam to violate what he considers to be a manifestation of the god's will. If a stone rolls from the mountain, if a leaf drops from a tree, it must be a spirit on a stroll; if the wind blows through the forest, the gods are indulging some healthy exercise; if the wind shakes the trees and howls through the valley, the *deos* or spirits are quarrelling.

The priest makes it his constant business to appease the wrath of the good spirits and to fight it out with the bad ones.

The soul survives the body and is in its future life rewarded for its virtues and punished for its crimes. Priests and priestesses alone have the power to sacrifice to the gods and enter into communication with them. It is God who chooses the priests from all classes and gives them their mission. The wonders a man works, the events he predicts, are so many signs of his vocation to the priesthood.

The priest expels the spirits and forces them to restore the soul to the dying man. This is how this extraordinary feat is performed:

Amidst a crowd of singing and howling attendants all standing around the patient, the officiating priest, armed with a long sword, performs a wild dance. Without ceasing to whirl rapidly round, he throws in the air a handful of rice, the grains of which go in search of the soul of the patient. As the grains drop on the blade of his sword, this skilful performer catches the soul in its flight, proudly shows it to the onlookers, fastened on the point of his sword in the shape of an unfledged bird, and runs to tie it on the top of the patient's head. If the soul returns to the body, the patient will not die; but he would be hopelessly lost, should the bird succeed in freeing itself and fly away on its miraculously acquired wings and feathers.

My informants were sorely disappointed at my incredulity and swore that every single word of theirs was the truth pure and simple. 'We have often witnessed the facts as we describe them,' so they said, 'and we can't understand how, being a priest, you can doubt them, as they are in every priest's power. The first time a man will fall sick in the village, we shall take you to him, and you will see the truth for yourself.'

What appears more certain and more tangible are the penances and privations these people are ready to undergo to propitiate or appease the spirits. They unhesitatingly suffer any mortification and trial, except that of visiting the sick; for to see a sick man, or to have anything to do with him would be running into the jaws of a bad spirit.

When I was staying at Mimbo, the villagers went out cutting rattan twigs for the construction of a bridge; before commencing the work, they sacrificed a dog to the spirit of the mountain, so that he should have no leisure for mischief whilst he was feasting on this delicacy.

The bridge was placed under the protection of a good spirit who received sacrifices to his heart's content. To give proof of still greater generosity, the whole village made *genna*, i.e. took a three days' holiday in honour of the spirits. A three days' *genna* is also observed after a burial, a two days' *genna* for a still-born child, and one day for a dog dying a peaceful and natural death, as the dog is a victim in odour of sanctity with the *deos.* At the birth of a child, the whole family is impure for a number of days varying according to the sex of the child.

Adults do not marry before the age of 18, though it may happen that a younger bride be received into the bridegroom's family and treated as a daughter of the house. For the first five or six years of her marriage life, the wife continues to stay with her parents, unless she begets children in the meantime and is thus entitled to set up a separate household. Should the parents disapprove of the alliance, the girl may leave them and marry lawfully without their consent.

The Padam is very active, jolly, a lover of freedom and independence, generous, noble-hearted, plain-spoken, more honest than the average Oriental, not over-moderate in eating and drinking, at least as far as quantity is concerned. I have not lived long enough among them to be able to speak of their morality. I confess I have never been able to discover what they understand by modesty; they seem to possess much of the child's simplicity, and Mimbo is undoubtedly less corrupt than Paris.

3

CAPTAIN DALTON'S VISIT TO MEMBU

('Correspondence and Journal of Capt. Dalton, of his Progress in a late visit to a Clan of Abors on the Dihong River', *Selections from the Records of the Bengal Government*, 1855, No. XXIII, pp. 151 ff.)

In the able *Memoir*, by Lieutenant Wilcox, of the Survey of Assam, and the neighbouring countries in 1825–6–7 and 8, published in the 17th Vol. of the Asiatic Society's Researches, there is an interesting account of a visit paid by him to the Membu Abors on the

Dihong River. This I had not read when I wrote the Journal from which the subjoined Notes are transcribed, but though I now find that my information is not altogether new, I have not omitted any observation, or incident, I had previously recorded, as the two accounts will show how very little this singular race have changed in more than a quarter of a century of time. I am, moreover, in hopes that my Notes on the habits, customs, and characteristics of the Abors may not be without interest, as very little information on these points has been published.

The term Abor, signifying barbarous, rude, independent, is, by the Assamese, applied very indefinitely to all the independent hill clans on both sides of the valley of Assam, but it is more peculiarly the appellation of the hill races on the southern slopes of that portion of the great Himalayan range between the Dihong and Soobunsheri Rivers.

There are five settlements of Abors, or as they call themselves 'Padam', in the lower ranges bordering on Assam, in the vicinity of the Dihong River, viz. Membu, Silook, Padoo, Pashee, and Bomjeer. In regard to their relations with our Government, they might be called the united or confederated Padam States, but each community in its internal affairs is governed by its own laws, devised and administered on purely democratic principles.

It has been assumed that they are in some measure dependent on the kindred clans occupying the loftier ranges behind them; but I believe that the villages of the Padam, bordering on Assam, are larger and in all respects more flourishing than those in the interior; and I am inclined to think that they consider themselves as independent of their northern as of their southern neighbours.

Though the most accessible, they have hitherto been the least known of the hill tribes bordering on Assam. We have had little direct intercourse with them and the Meerees, through whose intervention the Abors have maintained some trade and communication with the plains, and have done all in their power to keep us apart. The Abors have kept clear of all the outbreaks of other clans that have at different times disturbed the frontier of Upper Assam, maintaining, on all occasions, a strict neutrality; nevertheless, on their own account, they have once or twice been on the brink of a quarrel with us, in consequence of their asserting and our refusing to admit their exclusive right to the Dihong River, its fish and its gold; and because we turn a deaf ear to their demands to have the Meerees, whom they consider their slaves, restored to them or made to live where the Abors could coerce their services.

Membu is the largest of these neighbouring Abor settlements, and is reported the most influential in the confederate councils. For several years, from mistrust arising out of the dispute above alluded to, its inhabitants have seldom been seen in the stations of Assam; but having received an assurance from some of its chief men that if I went to their villages, in a friendly and confiding manner, I should be well received, and impressed with the conviction that the mischief-making propensities of the Meerees could be counteracted in no better way, I determined to avail myself of an opportunity of paying them a conciliating visit, and Lieutenant F. G. Eden,[1] of the 1st Assam Light Infantry, volunteered to accompany me.

We proceeded up the Dihong in boats, and on 31st January 1855, reached the point near the foot of the hills, about sixteen miles from the junction of the Brahmaputra and Dihong, whence it was necessary to continue our journey to Membu by land. Up to this point the navigation of the Dihong presents no difficulties. The rapids are mild in comparison with those met with on the way to the Brahmakund; and the Saikwah boatmen think nothing of them. We found ourselves here in sight of the villages and cultivation of the Pashee, Padoo, and Membu Abors. I sent off a party to give notice of our approach; they very soon returned with three Membu Abors whom they had met on the road, who offered to take us up at once with them, and assured us a hearty welcome. One of them, an old man, named Jowlung, thought it necessary to call the sun and moon to witness the sincerity with which this was asserted. Another amusingly added that the Abors were trusty, but were we so? As, however, we had to wait for elephants, it was eventually decided that two of them should go before and prepare for us; and that we should start for their village on the 2nd, under the escort of the third.

[1] Father Krick, author of the preceding extract, was murdered in 1854, and in February 1855, immediately after the visit to Membu described here, Lieutenant Eden was deputed to lead the first punitive expedition into the Mishmi Hills to avenge the crime.

We marched at 9-30 a.m. Road or pathway skirting the river for three miles, then plunges into a magnificent forest and proceeds due north. At the edges of the forest, and overlooking a fish-dam thrown across a white-crested rapid of the Dihong, the Abors have a halting place, a long shed capable of containing 100 men, with racks for drying fish. The forest contains fine timber of good growth. Noticed Nahi, Amari, and Hilika, and a good sprinkling of *cautchouc* trees. It is intersected by a small stream called the Sidee, said to rise from a spring close by. A few Abors from the village met us here and returned with us. After traversing about six miles of forest, we emerged on Abor clearings, though we understood we were not yet half way to the villages.

Their cultivation is almost all in the plains and they have gradually extended it to a distance of about seven miles from their villages. They cultivate rice, cotton, tobacco, maize, ginger, red pepper, a great variety of esculent roots and pumpkins; they have also a good kind of sugarcane for which their soil, a rich black loam, appears admirably adapted. Of late years they have added opium to their crops, and the use of the drug is rapidly spreading amongst them. Against unnecessarily breaking up new lands, they have a wholesome prejudice, which I should be glad to see adopted by our own *ryots*, when the land has been for ages fallow. Under this system, the whole space from their villages, to the most distant point of their cultivation, about seven miles, has been cleared and appropriated, and the whole forest is spared. The boundaries of each man's clearing are denoted by upright stones; and property in cultivated and fallow land is recognized. For implements of husbandry, they have only their long knives or swords, crooked bamboos to scrape the earth, and pointed sticks to make holes, into which they dexterously shoot the seed grain. It is thus they rear their principal crop of rice, and it gives them a good return. Industry and the richness of the soil make up for all deficiencies, and seasons of scarcity are rare with them.

The remainder of the march was all through cultivation or fallow land. It was intersected in various directions by well-cleared paths; that on which we were travelling looked as if it had been recently swept.

The country became undulating as we approached the hills, and after one steep ascent we suddenly found ourselves overlooking the little valley of the Shikoo and arrested by a formidable barricade, constructed, however, not to oppose our progress to the village, but to keep the village *mitheens* from straying to the cultivations.

Here we met another deputation of Abors who readily consented to remove the barrier sufficiently to admit of our elephants passing. All owners of cattle have a deep interest in the preservation of this fence. The penalties exacted for trespasses by cattle are rigorous and perhaps deserving the notice of the Indigo Planters' Association and Legislative Council! The sufferer without troublesome intervention of judge, magistrate or jury, estimates himself the amount of damages, gives a decree in his own favour, and proceeds forthwith to execute it by helping himself from the granary of the owner of the trespassing *mitheen*. With the *mitheens* which have been often described, pigs and poultry complete the number of their domestic animals.

As we looked down on the Shikoo, the scene that opened on our view was very beautiful and interesting. The river flows through a deep glen meandering amongst crumbling cliffs of gravel and conglomerate, mixed with layers of coarse sandstone. In the bed, breaking the streams into noisy rapids, alternating with still pools, are vast fragments of the cliffs and of a steeped and mottled quartzose rock, pink and white, of which the next hills are composed; one hill rising from the stream looks as if it had been cleft from top to bottom. The entire section of the hill is exposed and it is one mass of gravel and boulders. Across the glen and stream, there is a high-level suspension bridge of cane, of simple and ingenious construction, and a low-level temporary bridge of timbers. The latter is composed of planks thrown across piers of loose stones, and cradles of bamboos, girded with cane rails on both sides, render the passage of the bridge easy and safe to the most nervous person.

The canes forming the main support of the suspension bridge are thrown across beams supported partly on triangles of strong timber, and partly on trees opportunely growing where required. These trees have stays to counteract their flexibility, and they and all the sustaining canes are made fast to other large trees or to piers of loose stones like those supporting the low-level bridges. The roadway is also formed of cane, attached to the main and minor suspenders by elliptical girders of the same material.

The suspension bridge sways considerably, but there is no danger or difficulty in the passage across, and the smallest children that can toddle, and men and women with heavy loads are continually using it. I am told that some portion of it is repaired every year, so that in three or four years it is all renewed. On both sides of the Shikoo, in the vicinity of the bridge, there are some indications of a taste for landscape gardening. The low brushwood cleared away, all fine trees carefully preserved, clumps of bamboos evidently planted in effective positions and fenced in, and groves of jack-trees similarly guarded. The paths though rugged, are well cleared, and some labour has been bestowed to render steep descent as easy as circumstances admitted.

We took the shortest and steepest road to the village which is about a mile and a half from the bridge, sending the elephants round by a more circuitous but easier road. An ascent of about 300 feet brought us to the first houses, a group of granaries, wisely kept apart from the village to preserve them in case of fire; then came the houses of the inhabitants closely huddled together, and except that they all face the same way, built without order at the discretion of the inhabitants.

Our entrance excited some curiosity but no alarm. We passed one or two scowling faces, and it is possible that some observations were mentioned, which, had we understood them, could not have been considered complimentary; but generally the inhabitants, male and female, appeared to look upon it as great fun. They pointed to the *moorung* or town hall as our destination, and when we reached it, finding that I was not pleased with the quarters allotted to us, I was told that Wilcox sahib and Neufville sahib, the only British Officers they had previously seen in their village, had thought them good enough. This was a snub for me; however I selected another site where there was more space and less dirt.

We were now introduced to the Gaums or leading characters (Chiefs they can scarcely be called in a community so essentially democratic as we found this to be) and made known our wants. Curiosity had collected around us all the idlers in the village; but they showed little inclination voluntarily to assist or to obey the orders of their Gaums to do so, till Lieutenant Eden set them the example of lifting and removing ponderous stones from the space required for our tents; and seeing one of us thus at work, they gave some assistance without fear of compromising their dignity as independent citizens. As the villagers came in from their cultivations in the evenings, the crowd about us increased. Our friend Jowlung had prepared us for the ordeal, and we submitted ourselves patiently to the scrutiny of the rough and dirty, but good-humoured mob. The approach of night did not drive them away, and we had to make a solemn appeal to the good feeling of the Gaums for a respite, whilst we dined. They addressed the crowds in tones of loud expostulation and it had for a time the effect of partially dispersing them. After we had dined, the headmen came again and the crowd reassembled in front of the tent. Eden gave them some tunes on the cornopean, which excited great admiration, and more encores than the weary performer could attend to; but without the stimulus of music, they were quite content to stand outside in the cold so long as they could see what was going on inside the tent. At last pleading fatigue, we shut up, put out the lights, lay down to rest, and after a little murmuring, and one or two attempts at intrusion, we were left in peace. A section of the villagers adjourned to the *moorung* close by where they caroused till midnight, and thus went jovially home. Shortly after, shrill-voiced boys were heard going through the villages, in different directions, repeating some words in a clear monotone, like a street cry, and then, with exceptions to the occasional grunt or squeak of an obtrusive pig, or the crying of a child, all was still.

3rd February.—A wonderful chorus of cocks announced (much before the proper time) the approach of day. At earliest dawn the monotone cry of the preceding evening was repeated all through the villages. This we subsequently learnt was an order proceeding from the citizens in *moorung* assembled, proclaiming a holiday in honour of the visitors, consequently everyone remained at home. At an early hour we perambulated the villages under the escort of our friend Jowlung. He introduced us to all the families of distinction and at each house a jorum of *mhud*, as a cup of good fellowship, was proffered, and the ceremony of tasting it conformed to. Our guide made up for our deficiencies in the quantity imbibed. The beverage is a kind of small beer, palatable and innocuous in moderation when fresh brewed, but exceedingly disagreeable both in taste and in its effects when at all stale.

More than once during the morning walk, the owner of the house we were visiting, suddenly struck with the thought of swearing eternal friendship, made known his resolve by an offer to exchange coats. Before the purport of this extraordinary proceeding had been explained to us, it was somewhat startling to see a brawny Abor violently gesticulating, and at the same time working himself out of his upper garment as if stripping for a pugilistic encounter, but as the offer, though perfectly disinterested, as far as regarded the value of the respective raiments, involved a transfer of certain other property (live-stock) which I had no desire of possessing, I was obliged to decline fraternization after this classical model. The village occupies some twenty acres of rocky, craggy ground, at different elevations, varying about 200 feet. It is sheltered by lofty peaked hills, that as you look towards the North embrace it on three sides. To the South, from the most elevated sites, a fine view of the plains of Assam is obtained. The whole course of the Dihong River, from the hills to its junction with the Brahmaputra, and many miles of the combined rivers, are discernible.

The houses are nearly all the same size, about forty by twenty feet each, with a veranda or porch, one hearth, and no inner enclosure. They are apparently not intended for the accommodation of more than one married couple; and in practice it appears that when a man marries he leaves the paternal roof and builds a house for himself. In this he is assisted by the community, and all the component parts having been previously collected, prepared and arranged, the house is framed, floored, thatched, and ready for his reception in four-and-twenty hours.

In trimming and fitting the framework of timber, some trouble is taken; the flooring of bamboos is four feet from the ground; the walls and doors are of planks, and the thatching, which comes down on all sides as low as the flooring to keep off the high winds, is of grass, or more commonly of dried leaves of the wild plantain. We had an opportunity this morning of seeing a house commenced and under construction; next day it was completed and occupied by the family.

As we could only see a portion of the village at one view, I found it difficult to estimate the number of houses, and from the Gaums, whose notions of arithmetic are of the vaguest kind, I could get little information. From one crag I could count about 150 houses, the lower and most compact part of the town. There are probably as many more in the outskirts. All round bamboos and jack-trees are planted and carefully fenced, and one of the most influential men has near his house a grove of beautiful palms, surrounded by a loose stone wall.

The inhabitants are well supplied with water. There are several springs, and the discharges from these are collected and carried to different parts of the villages in aqueducts or pipes of bamboos, from which it constantly flows. In the Garrow villages, where the same method for the supply of water is adopted, I have seen the inhabitants washing themselves by squatting under the spouts; but I am sorry to say that my friends, the Abors, never avail themselves of their water privileges for ablutionary purposes; they consider dirt an antidote to cold, and positively cherish it.

There is a burial-ground at one of the entrances to the village. Over the graves are constructed miniature houses, in which every day, for one year of mourning, a fire is lighted and fresh food is placed. Beneath this is a small underground chamber made with planks or bamboos; the body is burnt, bound in a sitting posture, a practice common to all the clans having affinity with the Abors. Some of these clans bury with their dead arms and equipments that they may appear in the next world as great warriors. This I was given to understand is not the custom of the Padam Abors.

Returning to the tent, we found it surrounded by women and children, prepared to make the most of the holiday allowed to them for the express purpose of making our acquaintance. We did our best to gratify them. All the curiosities, including ourselves, were freely submitted to their scrutiny. As the docility of the elephants had, whilst unloading the previous evening, excited great interest, they were sent for again and made to exhibit, and finally all were made happy by a distribution of glass beads and salt.

Amongst the females goitre seemed to be a common disease, and numbers were further disfigured by bad sores and cutaneous disorders, the concomitants of filth. In general, however, they are a strong healthy-looking race, comparatively free from the epidemic diseases that occasionally decimate the Assamese; and from all the information I could collect on the subject, the population is an increasing one. The village must have doubled in size since seen by Lieutenant Wilcox, but this is partly owing to the emigration to it of Abors from the interior. For savages, the adult females are decently clad; and their demeanour, though free from timidity, levity, and unconstrained, is totally devoid of any appearance of immodesty.

Their dress consists of two cloths, generally tinted blue and red, manufactured by themselves from cotton grown in their own farms. One round the loins forms a petticoat just reaching to the knees; it is retained in its position by neat girdles of cane-work. The other is folded round the bosom, but this is often dispensed with; and the exposure of the person, above the waist, is evidently considered no indelicacy. Their necks are profusely decorated with strings of beads reaching to the waist; and the lobes of the ears are, as usual with the hill races, enormously distended for decorative purposes. Round the ankles, so as to set off to the best advantage the fine swell of the bare leg, broad bands of cane-work are tightly laced; and some of the belles, most particular about their personal appearance, wore these anklets of a light blue tinge, but the most singular article of their attire remains to be discovered. All young females, till they become mothers, wear, as an undergarment, suspended in front from the loins, a row of from five to a dozen round embossed plates of bell-metal, which rattle and chink as they move. Very young girls, except for warmth, wear nothing else, but the smallest of the sex is never seen without these appendages.

The Abor women, in features and complexion, approaching nearer to the Chinese than to any other known type, are not much distinguished for beauty; but amongst the forest of happy faces, massed in front of the tent, were some merry youthful ones that were almost pretty and would have been quite so with a freer use of water and more becoming coiffure. They are hard-worked, but the whole burden of field labour is not thrown upon them, as is the custom amongst most of the hill tribes. Wives are treated by their husbands with a consideration as marked, as it is singular, in so rude a race; but then, in marriages the inclinations of the parties most concerned is consulted, and polygamy is not practised. This is a notable characteristic. I do not say it is the rule, but it certainly is the prevailing practice of the Padam only to have one wife. They spoke with contempt of those who had a plurality, and I was assured both by Membu and Silook Abors that the Padam generally repudiated the custom as leading to jars and dissensions. In the Membu village, there is, I am informed, only one individual with more than one wife. On all sides of them a different practice prevails. Amongst the Abors, bordering on Sisee, a man may have as many wives as he can afford to buy; the wealthy thus monopolize more than their share, and if another revolting practice, that of polygandiaism, did not obtain, many of the poorer classes would probably be debarred from all share of conjugal felicity. It is not unusual amongst these Abors for two brothers to have one wife between them. Amongst the Chulikattas, to the East of the Padam, great Chiefs have been known to have had as many as sixteen wives at a time. The Digaroo and Tyung Mishmees are equally unlimited in their uxorious propensities. One of them, well known in Assam, appears in the plains every year with a new wife!

Marriages are sometimes, amongst the Padam, arranged by the parents, but more frequently I believe, the young people settle these affairs for themselves; and from all I could learn a feast is the only ceremony required to ratify and declare the happy event, but it is customary for the lover to present his mistress and her parents with such delicacies as field mice and squirrels.

In a society where all are equal in rank, and where the productive industry of a man and his wife is sufficient to maintain them in all necessaries and luxuries enjoyed by their neighbours, and where the community assist the young couple at starting by building a house for them, fathers and mothers have little occasion to manoeuvre matches. It is a fact, that amongst the Padam they seldom interfere; and to barter their child's happiness for money, would be regarded as an indelible disgrace.

The Abors, however, view with abhorrence the idea of their girls marrying out of their own clan; and I was gravely assured, that when one of the daughters of Padam so demeans herself, the sun and moon refuse to shine; and there is such a strife in the elements that all labour is necessarily suspended, till by sacrifice and oblation, the stain is washed away.

The hair of both males and females is close cropped, which is done by lifting it on a knife and chopping it all round with a stick. The practice of tattooing is resorted to by both sexes. The women have peculiar marks about the mouth. In the hollow of the upper lip, immediately under the nose, is figured a cross; and on both sides of it, above and below the mouth, are stripes, generally, but not always, seven in number. . . .

The men all wear a cross on the forehead, between the eyebrows; the peculiarity of these marks and their resemblance to Christian symbols have led to various conjectures regarding them; but the Abors themselves have no traditions that would warrant the belief of their being the remnant of early Catholic teaching.

In regard to male costume, the smallest particle of covering is all that is considered necessary for purposes of decency; but when full dressed, an Abor is a very imposing figure, coloured coats, without sleeves, of cotton of their own manufacture, or from the manufacture of their neighbours the Chulikattas, are commonly worn. Some wear long coloured cloaks, with loose sleeves, of woollen cloth, obtained from Thibet and they make themselves warm jackets of, and use as wrappers and blankets, white cotton cloths of their own manufacture with a long fleecy nap. For war and on state occasions, they wear helmets of very formidable and picturesque appearance. The foundation is a strong skull-cap of cane. The best are obtained from the Chulikattas, who, in making such things, are more ingenious than the Abors. It is adorned with pieces of bearskin, *chowry*, tails dyed red, boars' tusks, and to crown all, the beak of the buceros. For arms they have cross-bows and common bows, with arrows, the latter used with and without poison; very long spears, daggers, and long straight-cutting swords. By their own account, it is on the latter weapon they chiefly rely in warfare, and they are fond of exhibiting their skill in using it. I believe they consider themselves quite competent to meet our troops in the open field on equal terms; and as they have never felt the effect of fire-arms, it is probable that their first experience will be dearly purchased. They laughed at the Manual and Platoon, that the small guard we had with us were made to go through for their edification, and showed how they would run round and cut them in bits with their claymores, whilst the sepoys were loading. That such would be their tactics in their first engagement with our troops, I think highly probable, but they would not try them a second time.

The only fighting that the present generation of Abors has been personally engaged in has been a long war with the Chulikattas who are armed the same way. Peace, ratified by a feast, has recently been declared between the Chulikattas and the Abor clans next to them, but the Silook and Membu Abors look with suspicion on all Chulikatta professions of amity. They pronounce them to be a treacherous race who would eat your salt today and cut your throat tomorrow.

In the afternoon we were invited to take our seats in the *moorung* to confer with the citizens there assembled. The *moorung* is in the same style of architecture as the private houses, but it is 200 feet in length and has sixteen or seventeen fire-places, round all of which were seated groups of citizens. On our first entering, there was an attendance of 180 adult males, but when the debate was at its height, there could not have been less than 300 present, besides small boys who took up observing positions on the rafters. We placed our chairs opposite the central fire-place, round which the headmen congregated. There was first, Bokpang, a short stout, jolly-looking individual, who, from the influence he exercised generally in the assembly, especially when a call to order was necessary, and from his manner of opening the debate, I was inclined to consider as the Chairman or President, and in charge of the Foreign relations of the State; second, there was Looitem, the Nestor of the republic, who made the longest speeches, going extensively into early history and precedents, and expatiating with spirit and strong enthusiasm on the ancient renown, virtue, and valour of the Padam race; third, Jewlung, the War Minister, a young man of stalwart frame, tall and well-built, with a fine open countenance. I think he would prove, on occasion, the most trusty friend or most dangerous foe of all the Membu notables. His father Kiri, who is still alive, a retired statesman, had at one period of his life more influence in Membu than is now possessed by any single Gaum. Jewlung is, I think, working himself into the same position and may be looked upon as the 'coming man'. Of the other Gaums I can only give the names as given to me; fourth, Junkoor; fifth, Sabdook; sixth, Bomood; seventh, Bamad. I had no means of estimating their respective influence or merits; but I found, with regard to the position of one or two of them, there was a difference of opinion; all agreed that there were seven Gaums, but all did not appear agreed as to the individuals who just then constituted this august body; and it is both possible and probable, that the list was increased with an eye to the distribution of presents.

The conversation commenced by a blank speech from Bokpang, which, on being interpreted, proved to be an inquiry as to what possible object we could have had in visiting them. It was not easy to persuade them that there was nothing reserved, no *arrière-pensée* in the assurance that the visit was solely intended to inspire confidence and friendship. When they were tired of questioning on this point, we had to listen to a succession of long harangues, arrogating, at the outset, very extravagant pretensions on the part of the Abors; but all these were disposed of in reply, dwindling down to more reasonable claims. At one time the debate was rather stormy and disorderly, a factious demagogue, named Jolook, arose and declared it was all humbug to talk of friendship, if no concessions were to be made to the Abors; and that for his part he was not going to fraternize on such terms. A hot debate ensued, but it ended in Jolook's discomfiture; and a fresh brew of *mhud* having been introduced, we all drank to good fellowship, including the turbulent Jolook. We had not exactly come to an agreement upon all the questions discussed. The Membu Padam would not take upon themselves to resign the claims of the Padam confederacy, but they disclaimed all idea of ever attempting to enforce them. The finale was a proposition that, in accordance with Padam custom, the friendly alliance should be sealed by a solemn feast called Sengmung, in the estimation of the Abors, inviolably binding on the high contracting parties. They were to eat what we provided, and we were to eat what they provided. The republic would give a *mitheen* and some pigs; and they suggested that if we slaughtered one of our elephants for them it would suit their taste exactly. To this we demurred, but admitting the propriety of cementing friendship in the manner proposed, I offered to buy a *mitheen* for them and this was agreed to. I then gave them some tobacco and salt which was divided amongst all present by a portion being sent to each hearth.

No presents are openly received by the Gaums for themselves. Everything given on public grounds is lodged in the common treasury to be disposed of for the benefit of the whole body corporate. Belonging to the *moorung* are public pigs, poultry, and other possessions to be used as occasion requires. Fines, forfeitures, and escheats are similarly appropriated; but in regard to punishments, their system is one of the most extraordinary that was ever devised. After some study of the matter, I find that feasts and sacrifice are expiation for everything. The crime of an individual is treated as a public disgrace to be atoned for by all. The culprit has eventually to bear the expense of this; it may therefore be regarded as a fine; but the process of realization is a most singular one. Suppose it is decreed that in expiation of the offence a pig is to be sacrificed; the Raj, that is the community, appropriate for the purpose the first animal of the kind, in good condition, and private property that comes to hand. The owner is at liberty then to fix his own value upon it, and recover as best he can from the culprit. It may be said that it would have been simpler to have proceeded in the first instance against the property of the offender, but where all are judges, who will condescend to act as a mere Sheriff's officer? The system adopted provides an executive without any trouble to the Raj or expense to the State.

There is no power vested in the community to take life or inflict corporal punishment on a free-born citizen, but like another model republic, they have their 'domestic institutions', and the law of the master is not the law of the slave. I heard of a slave having been put to death by his master by order of the Raj for having seduced a free-born girl.

I was right glad, at the conclusion of the conference, to emerge from the fetid atmosphere of the *moorung* and breathe the fresh air. What with tobacco smoking, *mhud* drinking, loud talking, pestering, questioning, and the vicinity of the public pigsties, I never had a more troublesome and unpleasant diplomatic duty to perform.

The necessity of interpretation made the long harangues all the more tedious; and as great importance was attached to every word spoken, great care was required to have the speeches on our side correctly rendered.

The *moorung* is occupied every night by all the adult males in the village, free men and slaves who are not married; and I am informed that with them a certain proportion of the married men are nightly on duty, so as to constitute together a sufficient available force for any contingency of attack, fire, or other public necessity.

That night the orders issuing from the *moorung* proclaimed that next morning the women only were to go to work in the fields. The men were to remain for further conference with the visitors.

As the arrangements for the feast of Sengmung were likely to delay our departure till the afternoon, we determined on making a short march from the village to the Shikoo, where we hoped to spend a quiet evening. Before leaving, we paid another visit to the *moorung* and had more long speeches to listen to, but though some of the discussions of the previous evening were reopened, the debate was carried on in an orderly manner, the principal speaker being Bokpang who assumed a placid conciliating tone. They pressed us greatly to make a longer stay, and considering the amusement we had afforded them, the presents that we had made them, and that our people bought up all their spare cloths and curiosities, I dare say they were perfectly sincere in the desire they evinced to see more of us; but we had had quite enough of their uncouth society and declined trespassing any longer on their hospitality.

On our way down to the river, we met, returning from their day's work, groups of merry girls, with most of whom we had made acquaintance on the preceding day. One was the bearer of two fine pieces of sugar, one of which she gracefully presented to Lieutenant Eden and the other to me, as she bade us a smiling farewell. When they found we were to halt at the Shikoo, several returned with us to the encamping ground and supplied us with fuel and yams, receiving guerdons of salt in exchange. We pitched our tent in a grove of trees between the *mitheen* barricade and the river, in sight of the two bridges, a most desirable spot for a small encampment, which we might have availed ourselves of at first; but in trusting yourself in the hands of savages it is good policy to take up quarters in the very midst of them and their families. In such a position, if you can attain it, the most barbarous tribe is not likely to attack you. They feel answerable for your safety and dare not abuse the trust reposed in them. If you camp at a distance, you are not so safe; you appear to evince less confidence in those you are visiting, and your position affords hope of being able to shift responsibility in case of harm befalling you.

We had plenty of spectators from the village whilst we camped, bathed, and dressed, but as evening closed, they dispersed. We were left to ourselves; and our servants and the guard who had not had a comfortable meal since we quitted the boats, cheerfully betook themselves to the task of preparing one. Our own culinary operations were performed in a manner rather more appetizing than they could be in the midst of the pigs, dogs, and dirty mess of the village, and soon all were engaged in cooking or eating, and in talking and laughing over the adventures of the two preceding days. Suddenly all sounds of mirth ceased; a cry of alarm arose; we rushed out to ascertain the cause and found everyone outside gazing in mute astonishment and terror at the spectacle that was presented and which certainly was most startling.

The opposite heights were illumined by the glare of not less than a hundred torches, moving rapidly down, and marking the windings of all the paths that led from the villages to our camp. They were borne by armed men who advanced swiftly towards the bridge, crossed it, and were soon beside our watch-fire. They were headed by a woman who pressed on eagerly, not pausing to notice us; and it was explained that the object of the expedition was to search for two children of hers missing since morning. Some of the party relighted their torches at our fire, then hurrying on, all disappeared behind the *mitheen* barricade. Group after group succeeded. The place was alive with torches appearing and disappearing amongst the rocks on the opposite side of the river, and illuminating the valley, and reflected from the river as they crossed the suspension bridge. Our people were greatly alarmed, but after questioning different parties, I saw no reason to doubt, as they did, the cause assigned for this eccentric proceeding; and after satisfying ourselves that the Abors did go in the direction they professed to be going, we gave ourselves no further trouble about it.

But we were destined to be disturbed again. Shortly after midnight, I was violently aroused from my slumbers by someone calling out, 'Sahib, Bor Sahib, Captain Sahib,' in a voice that could only belong to an Abor or an Ophicleide. Notwithstanding the expostulation of the sentry, the *purdahs* of the tent were gently raised, and a head appeared. It was that of the demagogue Jolook. 'We have been sent,' he said, 'to stay and watch with you lest you should be alarmed by the incursion of the searching party and its return late at night.'

I got up and went out and found Joulung, Jolook, the Deodar or village priest, and others seated at our fire, and entered into conversation with them. In regard to the torch-party they stated, that a woman, a widow, with two children, one an infant at the breast, the other a boy of three or four years, had gone to the farm early in the morning. She tied the small child on the back of the boy and proceeded with her work. When she gave over for the day, and was preparing to return, the children were missing; she searched till evening without success, but was not much alarmed as she concluded they had gone home; but when she reached home and found no children there, she made her cries heard all through the village 'How could we sit still and listen to them ?' A meeting was called; the young men all equipped themselves, and, as fast as they could get ready, started for a search.

I thought this little incident highly creditable to the Padam republic. Rough and rude as they are, their hearts must be in the right place, when at one poor woman's sorrowing cry, a whole community arise and go forth into the cold damp air prepared to pass the night in searching for an infant. No mandate was sent forth; no apathy was shown; no excuses were made. The widow's grief was as a spark to a train of honest sympathy, and it at once burst forth in a train of active benevolence. The torches are prepared and the young men go forth. The next thought of the elders is given to their guests on the Shikoo; and surely nothing could have been kinder, or in better taste, than the determination they came to. They reflected that the sudden rush of a large body of men, through our camp, in the middle of the night, might give us occasion of an alarm and mistrust. They therefore sent a deputation of their own body to stay with us and inspire confidence. The deputation constituted themselves into a watch; and though it rained heavily towards morning, and there was a shed close by to which they might have retired for shelter, they would not give up their exposed position in front of our tent.

Losses of children, in the manner described, are said to be of frequent occurrence. They are most probably kidnapped by other clans, but that this is the most likely solution they were not disposed to admit. They asserted that the *Deo* spirits hid them. This they could prove, as, in the event of the first search proving unsuccessful, it was their practice to cut down large trees in the forest. This mode of retaliation immediately caused a commotion amongst the *Deos*. 'What's the row now,' says one. 'Oh,' replies another, 'the Padam have lost a child.' 'Then who has got it, give it up quick, or the rascals won't leave us a tree.' Then the child is found in the fork of a tree or some other out-of-the-way place.

We sat some time with the watch. A bottle of rum was produced and under its influence they became very communicative and musical. The Deodar sang songs purporting to tell of the creation of the world and the origin of the Padam race. These, which would have been worth knowing as containing the Padam tradition, were very imperfectly rendered to me by the Meeree interpreters, though the priest gave a meaning commentary on each stanza for its more easy solution.

The human family are all descended from the common mother. She had two sons, the eldest was a bold hunter. The younger was a cunning craftsman. The latter was the mother's favourite; with him she migrated to the west, taking with her all the household utensils, arms, implements of agriculture, and instruments of all kinds so that the art of making them was lost in the land she deserted; but before quitting the old country, she taught her first-born how to forge *daos* and to make musical instruments from the gourd, and she left him in possession of a great store of blue and white beads. These beads, and the simple arts known to him he transmitted to his posterity, the Padam, and from him they received the injunction to mark themselves on the forehead with a cross. The western nations are descended from the younger brother and inherited from him and the continued instructions of the mother their knowledge of science and art.

The above is a very imperfect synopsis of the long legends sung by the Deodar. I hope, on some future occasion, to be able to give a fuller account of these ballads which appear to contain all their traditional history.

The religion of the Dihong Abors appears to be much the same in practice and belief as that professed by kindred tribes to their west, an account of which may be found in a former number of the Asiatic Society's proceedings.[1]

They believe in a future state as one of reward or punishment for the actions of this, but acknowledge one Supreme Being as the great father of all. They adore and offer sacrifices to a great number of Jyloun deities, whom they invest with attributes, each with one, from all that their course of life leads them to reverence or fear.

Thus they have no medicine for the sick; for every disease there is a spirit, and a sacrifice to that spirit is the only treatment attempted.

[1] See pp. 136 ff. of this book.

A mountain called Regam, is, as the abode of one or more spirits, a place held in great awe. No one can return from its summit; consequently its mysteries are undisclosed.

In regard to their sacrifices one trait is particularly worth noticing; generally, with hill clans, a sacrifice to the gods is nothing more than an excuse for a debauch.

In cases of sickness or deaths, when an animal valued as food, a *mitheen* or a pig, is offered by the Padam, no one is allowed to share the feast with the gods except the very old men who, as poor and superannuated, may be regarded as on the 'parish', and who live in the *moorung* at the public expense.

The Abors do not acknowledge any direct trade with Thibet, though they have and use many articles of Thibetan manufacture. Thence come their sword-blades, tobacco pipes, woollen cloths, and copper cooking vessels, and the blue and white beads, to which they assign a celestial origin, are no doubt imported from the same quarter. They tell wild stories of the agency employed to supply their wants from Thibet, and I think their intercourse with that country must rather have diminished than increased since we first became acquainted with them.

We know for certain, that to the east of the Abor the Chulikatta and Meeshmee clans extend across the range from the Assam Valley to the frontier of Thibet, and the representatives of these clans in close proximity to the Lamas differ in no essential respect from those bordering in Assam. But the Abors tell you of the existence of barbarous tribes with whom they have no affinity in the higher ranges behind them and you meet with no one of the clan who acknowledges to have passed this barrier of savages.

The requirements of the Abors are at present very trifling. All they take from Assam is salt, iron, brass cooking pots, a few silver ornaments, and *erin* cloths. They give in exchange their long-napped white cotton cloths which are much prized as rags or quilts, ginger, red pepper, and sometimes rice.

Early this morning all the Gaums, and a large deputation from the villages, made their appearance in our camp, bringing the *mitheen*, a very fine bull, as their offering to us for the Sengmung. Mine, which I had paid for the day before, but had not seen, they acknowledged having received, and it was to be slaughtered and eaten that day. This done, we stood in the relation to each other of sworn friends; and I took the opportunity of our being out of the village to visit each of the most influential of our new friends.

Joulung and Bankong escorted us to our boats and a party of Abor boys were sent in charge of the *mitheen* which reached Saikwah in safety.

The results of this visit proved most satisfactory. Return visits were made to us by all the Gaums, who for the first time appeared at Saikwah and at Debroo with their wives and daughters to see us and to trade; and I received invitations from the Pashee, Padoo, Bomjeer, and Silook Abors; requesting me to visit them as I had visited the Membu.[1]

4

MEMBU THIRTY YEARS LATER

(*Report on the Visit of Mr Needham to the Abor villages beyond the British frontier*, 1884[2])

I WAS met close to the entrance of the village by Bapok, one of the senior Gams, who told me that he was glad to see me, and that I might stay as long as I liked. He is a thin, wizened, old man, with rather a nice expression, partially blind and scarcely able to walk. We were then conducted to a spot close to the village Morong, or Dekhachang (called Mosup in Abor), and there we pitched our

[1] This account, rewritten and condensed, forms part of Dalton's chapter on the Abors in his *Descriptive Ethnology of Bengal*, pp. 21 ff., published seventeen years later.

[2] This was in October 1884. Needham 'accompanied by a private gentleman' also visited Gina, Romkong, Balek and Monku (as the names were then spelt), taking seven days for the whole tour. Balek was then a small village of about thirty houses. The *Report on the Administration of the Province of Assam* for 1884–5 comments on this expedition as follows:

'The visit, on the whole, proved successful in several respects. It added to our geographical knowledge of the position and accessibility of the villages which Mr Needham entered, and the strength and character of the Abors who inhabit them. For a long time the men of this tribe have kept sullenly aloof from British authority. They have not been visited by any officer since 1854, they do little trade, though they come down in numbers to buy salt, and they have seldom had any formal communication with any officer, except when

tent, and while the work was going on, crowds of women, children, and men began to form around us, some taking hold of this, others examining that, and all asking for *aman* (Abor, for present). I told them tnat I was very sorry that I had brought nothing in the shape of presents with me, but this they would not at first credit, and as soon as they did they showed unmistakable signs of dissatisfaction. They said that Dalton, Bivar, and Nabin Sahebs had each brought numerous presents with them when they visited their village, and that they could not understand therefore why I had come up empty-handed. I explained that I did not know that it had been usual for Sahebs when visiting their villages to give them presents; that I had come up as light as I could possibly travel; that I was not sure whether they would admit me into their village, &c., &c., but no amount of, even legitimate, excuses appeared to satisfy them, for they growled out: 'Oh! you are a pretty Saheb to come up here in this manner. Other Sahebs that came up brought three or four elephant-loads of things, and everyone got a present.' Just then the Kotokis suggested a walk through the village, and thinking this was a good way of getting rid of the majority of my persecutors for a time, I jumped at the suggestion, and Mr Mellor and I started off at once to explore the village. I must here premise that this report is entirely from memory, for I considered it very

their representatives appear to receive their *posa*. In their reception of the party they showed themselves, according to their light, to be amicable and hospitable, and, their grievances having been listened to with patience, they now know that there is at Sadiya an officer who does not regard them with hostility and contempt. By these steps some advance has been made towards a better understanding with the Abors. On the other hand, certain elements of difficulty and possible danger have been brought to light by this visit. It has shown the overweening self-confidence and pride of the tribe and the exorbitant demands they are inclined to make. The haughty spirit and the belief in their own power of attack and defence displayed by these savages make the Chief Commissioner doubtful whether any course of amenity and justice will have a beneficial effect until they have been compelled to recognize the overwhelming strength of the British Government. There can, however, be no question that the line of policy which is now being followed is the right and only one under present circumstances and that it ought to be persevered in.

'Mr Needham paid a second visit to Membo in March 1885, accompanied by an Assistant-Engineer, in order to erect a wire suspension-bridge over the Siku. The Abors had themselves suggested the erection of the bridge in October 1884, but on the arrival of the engineer, they refused to allow him to put up the bridge, alleging as a reason the insufficiency of the materials, the real motive being distrust of the intentions of Government in undertaking the work.'

impolitic to walk about with a notebook and pencil in my hand lest the people should think I had visited them with some hidden ulterior object in view. The Kotokis in fact warned me against using a notebook. While walking through the village I made notes mentally, and I will now attempt to jot down a few, and thus not only give you as correct an account as I can of all we saw and did, but likewise endeavour to give you some idea of the village itself, the construction of the houses, and the people (women in particular, because we are continually seeing the men at Sadiya) in it, &c., &c. The village is apparently built upon a very broad and stony spur, and the houses lie on terraces, in batches of 60 or 80, one terrace above the other, so that those on the upper terraces are several hundreds of feet above those on the lower ones. It is an excessively large one containing at least from 250 to 300 houses, which, with 10 people to a house—and I do not think I am overestimating the number, for I entered several houses, and found families in them numbering from 12 to 20—would give a population of between 2,000 and 2,500 souls. The ground upon which the houses in each terrace are erected is strewn with loose stones, some of a large size, and is extremely uneven, so that in some places 10 or 15 houses may be seen upon tolerably even ground, while around these again the roofs only of others are perceptible; but as each house is on a *chang* every available space has been occupied, for no ground is too uneven to build upon. The houses are all fine massive buildings (I did not see a single mean-looking house in the village) from 60 to 80 × 20 feet, something after the style of the Angami Naga's house, except that the front veranda is covered in like the sides, the roof coming to within 2 feet or so of the front *chang*, and the latter is then carried on, though on a slightly lower level, outside all for some 15 or 20 feet further. This is very convenient in many ways, for on a rainy day there is a large sheltered veranda to sit in, while if sunshine is required the occupants of each house can squat about on the outer *chang*. No thatching grass is available, and so all the houses are thatched with a kind of plant called *Tara* by the Abors. It is very like the *Toko-pat* used in many parts of Assam, but the lower stem of the *Tara* is excessively thorny. This is split in half and laid on when dry and it is alleged that it will last from five to six years. The fronts of the houses are made of huge boards (like the Angamis), some of which are 3 or 4 feet wide, but they are not, as far as I could see, carved. The heads of all game killed in hunting, as also of those killed at feasts, are arranged on shelves fixed to these boards, and under the roof in the veranda there are numerous bamboo shelves used as receptacles for all sorts of miscellaneous household goods. The eaves of the houses come down close to the ground, and each house has a back, as well as a front, but they are nevertheless naturally very dark inside, and as each house has from two to five large fire-places, each about 4 feet square, in which fires appear to be kept constantly burning, they are not comfortable places, for a stranger at least, to sit in for any length of time. The fire-places are made (like those in Miri houses) of planks resting on posts covered over with 6 or 8 inches of earth, and over each one there is a bamboo framework suspended from above for drying meat, &c., on. None of the houses have any partitions inside, so that there can be no privacy of any sort. Fowls do not appear to prowl about much inside the houses. For laying and sitting purposes they are supplied with bamboo baskets fixed in the front veranda, and they also roost there at night. The pigsties are at one side of the house. They are partitioned off for each pig and are boarded, and as the pigs are well fed and cared for, they are fat and really nice eating, and as the boards upon which they rest are laid down with a slope outwards, most of the filth runs outside and is carried off by the rain. The whole village is strewn with dirt of sorts, but I did not experience a single bad smell while I was in it. I was told that there are regular places set apart outside the village where the people ease themselves. There are a very large number of jack trees in the village, and I am told that the Abor jack is much prized. I also saw some magnificent lime and orange trees, and I tasted the fruit of both and found them very juicy and good. The majority, however, of these had recently been hacked down owing to cholera having been raging at Padu. These trees are, I am told, periodically so treated, i.e. whenever any serious stomachic disease makes its appearance. Why the jack trees escape upon such occasions I could not find out. Goitre is very prevalent in this village, and I was repeatedly asked for goitre ointment though I had none with me. I should say that at least two-thirds of the men, women, and children have it, and some of those I saw were abnormally large, and yet the water appears to be beautifully clean and pure, and the village is plentifully supplied with it from a huge spring which comes out of the rocks at the top of the spur, and the distance from the spring to the lower end of the village must be at least three-fourths of a mile, or a mile, in length.

We were about two and a half hours walking through the village, and upon our returning to the spot where our tent had been pitched we found some 700 or 800 people, men, women, and children, round it and the spot where our cook was busy getting our food ready, and as soon as we got inside we were completely hemmed in by a sea of heads.

The sides and back were lifted up, and the heads were popped in here, there and everywhere, and everything seized and examined *nolens volens*, especially a looking and burning glass I had with me, the magnifying power of the latter tickling their fancies greatly.

About 5 o'clock we were asked to go and see the Morong (Mosup in Abor) or Cutcherry. Abors are excessively proud of their Mosup, and the Membo men were continually impressing upon me the fact that all important topics are talked over and disposed of in it I paced the place and found it 80 yards long and 10 yards wide, and I counted 24 fire-places in it. It is built on the same plan as the houses, except that it is entirely open along the whole of one side in addition to having the usual front and back exit, probably to allow of its occupants jumping out speedily in case of an attack, or fire, &c. In this house all the single men warriors reside, and it is also used as a council room. The side walls are crammed with the heads of every description of animal, and all down the centre of it are to be seen the bows, arrows, fishing-gear, hats, spears, &c., &c., of the warriors on bamboo trays. The Mosup is close to the entrance to the village. I should say the place would hold about 500 men. After sitting there for a short time we returned to our tent and called for dinner, for as we had carried no lamp with us we decided to dine while it was daylight. We placed three or four Miris at either entrance to the tent, and these men endeavoured to keep back the crowd as also to explain that the 'Sahebs' were not in the habit of being stared at at meals, but all their endeavours to keep off the crowd were futile. In fact, the more they were told to keep back the worse they were. They said—'Why did you come here if you object to be looked at? We want to see you,' and so the pushing and straining for places of vantage from which a good view of us could be had went on while we were eating, and fingers were unceremoniously popped onto, and into, anything strange, such as corn beef, mustard, pepper, &c., &c. We finished our dinner as soon as we could, and then went outside, as we were being stewed inside the tent, but it was quite as bad there. Our hats were pulled off our heads and went the round of 100 heads in as many minutes, handkerchiefs the same. Each and everything we wore was felt, and then we were asked to take off our things. We took off our coats and explained that we had got nothing on under our banians, but until we had opened these also the gaping crowd were incredulous, and they appeared to disbelieve their eyesight, as they put their hands on our skins and felt our chests. Then we had to take off our boots and socks, as they declared we had no feet, and when we had done so, the girls got hold of our feet and petted them as an old maid would a friend's pet lap-dog that she had not seen before. The women, I may here remark, are excessively rollicky and jolly, and the unmarried girls have apparently any amount of latitude given to them. They are also utterly shameless. The women are plain, but the majority of them have jolly, laughing faces. They are squat and heavily made, and are likewise big-limbed. They wear their hair cropped (as also do the men) like the Chulikatta Mishmis (called Dumteng in Abor), and have their breasts bare, their only article of clothing being a very short petticoat, fastened round their waists, which reaches to about two inches above the knee. Many of them are tattooed with perpendicular lines over the lips and corners of their mouths, which does not improve their looks, as also on the back of their legs, right under the bend of the knee, above the calf.

The unmarried girls wear five or six flat circular plates of brass, one slightly overlapping the other, called *Boiop*,[1] fixed to a plaited band of thin cane, under their petticoats, and while working in

[1] 'The women's costume consists in all of three pieces. These are the *beyop*, the skirt and the breast cloth. As soon as they can walk the girls wear a disc or two about the loins, or perhaps some metal charm, or a few shells. This, in a few years, expands into the *beyop*, the girdle worn by every maid and woman from the Dibang to the Subansiri until the birth of her first child. The *beyop* consists of locally-made discs fastened on to a band of cane, screw pine or a strip of hide. These discs vary in size. The larger, averaging about three and a quarter inches in diameter, are worn in the centre of the girdle and the remainder graduated in diminishing size towards the hips. Although as a general rule skirts are worn from early childhood, girls of about fourteen may occasionally be seen with no other covering save the *beyop* and a cloth about the shoulders (generally supporting a younger brother or sister), but the number of discs on

their fields or in the village on a hot day, it is the only article they have to cover their nakedness. They also wear little gaiters of plaited cane, coloured, about six inches wide, on each ankle, called *Essong* in Abor. They are excessively fond of necklaces, earrings and bracelets, in fact finery of all sorts. Their teeth are as black as a coal from continually chewing tobacco and lime (the latter the Abors make themselves out of a shell which they find in their river beds), and many of them also smoke pipes like the men do. They are very fond of singing and dancing, and they treated us to two exhibitions, and did their utmost to get us to sing and dance too. There is nothing either graceful or pretty in their dancing. Some 15 or 20 hold one another by the arm above the elbow, and after one of their number has sung a line or two, in an almost inaudible and very plaintive voice, the rest join in a chorus moving round slowly in a ring the while. Sometimes they open out the chain to its full extent and run up against one another face to face, singing all the while, first one way, then the other. . . . During the conversation, Bapok happening to make some very disparaging remarks about the Miris in general, a young Miri who was sitting in front of him said something, which I did not quite catch, in vindication of his brethren,

the Minyong girdle give it enough weight to fall in a graceful curve that entirely fulfils its purpose.

'The number of discs varies in the different tribes. Minyong Abors wear seven, eight, or even nine discs on the girdle, and Galong girls three or four. To the north the Janbos are satisfied, it is believed, with two discs, and the still less chary maids of the Boris are said to be content with one. The *beyop* discs are not worn during the period of menstruation. The mythical origin of the *beyop* is that a spirit, Gingor-Shingor, fell in love with a woman, and whenever he had intercourse with her he gave her a *beyop* disc. When a child was born she took off the girdle of discs; and that is how they first were worn, and why they are discarded on the birth of a woman's first born.

'Both skirt and breast cloth are wound tightly round the body, the skirt being held in its place by cane rings. The wearing of the breast cloth is not habitual, for a hill woman does not consider the exposure of the upper part of her person to be immodest.

'Married women, whether Dafla, Galong or Abor, frequently wear waist bands studded with metal bosses. These are very much smaller than the average *beyop* discs and are generally made of brass. Girls and women wear rings of cane round their waists whether they wear metal-studded bands or not; and they weave for themselves very fine belts of cane in white, relieved by patterns of black interwoven through the material. The women wear, sometimes in great profusion, necklaces similar to those worn by the men. Their brass bracelets are of a lighter stamp than those of the men.'—G. D. S. Dunbar, 'Abors and Galongs', *Mem.A.S.B.* (1915), Vol. V, pp. 30f.

when Bapok jumped up and made two furious prods at him about the pit of the stomach with the farreled end of his spear, remarking—'How dare you interrupt me.' I mention this incident merely to show how arrogant the Abors still are towards their late Miri slaves, as they frequently styled them. After this we sat down to a hasty breakfast, for one of the Dekha Gàms came up while we were conversing, and in a loud and impertinent voice said—'What do you mean by holding a Darbar here, the cutcherry is full, and that is the ònly place where topics of this kind are allowed.' I then said that I had hoped that out of deference to myself they would say all they had to say under the shade of a tree as it was very hot inside their Mosup (cutcherry) and the fires hurt my eyes, but I had no sooner thus expressed myself, than there was a derisive howl from the crowd in substance as follows:—'I like your cheek. Our Mosup is our cutcherry, you have your cutcherry, and you don't listen to cases outside it, neither do we Abors, so to the Mosup you will have to go whether you like it or not.' Accordingly, at a little before 11 a.m. we adjourned to the Mosup. I have already mentioned that there are 24 fire-places in this place, and as they are all nearly always kept alight, I leave you to imagine what a comfortable place it was to sit in on a warm afternoon, surrounded by some 6 or 700 not over-sweet people, all puffing the most filthy tobacco, and drinking a nasty, sickly, sour-smelling grog, some of which we were compelled to drink ourselves, around one. We were kept in there till a quarter to 4 p.m., and during the whole time by either Bapok or Pokpang. Pokpang is also an old and very influential Gam. He is also partially blind, and with the most hideous expression of countenance I ever remember seeing. On the afternoon of our arrival in the village he was pointed out to me, on the occasion of our visit to the Mosup, and the Miris, Kotokis, all spoke of him with bated breath, remarking—'That man is the most to be feared in Membo. He holds the lives of every man visiting it in his hands.'

October 14, 1884.—I pitched my tents on the right bank of the Dihong nearly opposite the spot where our troops were encamped in 1859, just before the assault on Romkong. We could see the Padu village smoke curling up above the forest trees, but we could not see the houses (this village is more easily reached from the spot where the Siku empties itself into the Dihong than from Membo), and the different shades of green from the village *arrahs*, all on the slopes of the hills, looked very pretty about sunset. From the centre of these, as it were, rises the sugar-loaf looking peak called Regam by the Abors. The Padu people declare that it is the abode of a mighty spirit, and none of them therefore ever dream of going up there. It is alleged that there is a *bheel*, covering about a *purah* of land, very near the top of it, in which there is a very large *Buku* fish without any tail and that two black divers swim about the water and guard the fish. The legend was started by the Pasi Abors. They declare that years and years ago some of their people when searching about for a new village site came upon the *bheel* and saw the fish and divers in question.

Chapter X

THE ABORS AT THE END OF THE CENTURY

1

MOST NUMEROUS AND POWERFUL

(G. W. Beresford, *Notes on the North-Eastern Frontier of Assam*, 1881, pp. 15 ff.)

OF the above tribes, the Abors are the most numerous and powerful. They occupy the hills from the Dibong north round to the Miri and Duffla Hills west. It is not known how far north they extend, but it is believed up to the frontier line of Tibet, with which country they evidently trade and communicate, as most Abors wear dark red woollen coats and other articles of clothing and ornament of Tibetan manufacture. Very little is really known of these people. They have always had the credit of being a fierce and warlike race, but little is on record to justify this opinion and estimate of their character, for, with the exception of two or three small punitive expeditions against them for raids committed on British subjects, which did not add much to our knowledge of them, their country, manners, customs, or resources, no one has succeeded in penetrating their country and habitat proper beyond the nearest villages, and therefore very little is known of them.

The Abors are divided roughly into two divisions. Those living on the left or east bank of the Dihong river up to the Dibong are called Bar Abors, or 'great' Abors, and are said to be the origin of those called Pasi and Meyong, and of the whole tribe. Those living on the right or west bank of the Dihong are called Pasi-Meyong, formerly only Meyong, but owing to some tribal dispute many years ago some of the Pasi Abors of the large and important village of Siku fled across the Dihong, settled in the Meyong country on the right bank, and are to be found yet distinct and separately known as Pasi in most of the Meyong villages, hence the term Pasi-Meyong, which has caused endless mistakes and confusion in the misapplication of the term, and ignorance of what Pasi and Meyong really mean. In published records of official correspondence of recent date the terms Pasi and Meyong are used to denote separate villages of those names; but, as a fact, it will be found that no such villages exist, but other villages of different names inhabited by Pasi and Meyong Abors. There are some villages on the west of the Dihong inhabited only by Meyongs, but most of them by Pasis and Meyongs combined. A native of the district, when questioned, will probably not mention the real name of the village at all, but say it is Pasi or Meyong, simply according to the tribal distinction of its inhabitants.

The real habitat of all the Abors is the lofty mountain ranges between Assam and Tibet, in the interior hills and beyond the front or nearer intervening ranges from whence their superabundant population, for the want of room and land, have overflowed into the valley of Assam through the gorge of the Dihong, and thence, spreading to the east and west, have occupied the lower ranges of hills to the borders of the plain country south. These latter Abors might be considered more in the light of plainsmen in contradistinction to those who inhabit the higher and interior ranges from 8,000 to 12,000 feet elevation, and with whom we have next to no communication.

It is said that all the Abors, whether Pasi or Meyong, acknowledge a common origin from the Bar or Pasi Abors, and they have overflowed, as it were, from a common centre, Damloh Padam, situated on a high snow-clad range of mountains, 12,000 feet elevation, three days' journey up the Dihong gorge above Pasighat and Syquaghat. It is now their chief stronghold and most important settlement, as it ever has been. It may be useful to explain here that the range of hills 5,000 feet elevation, immediately over the Assam Valley, is not generally inhabited, owing to the steepness of its southern slope. Therefore, when the first immigrants left Damloh Padam, they could not occupy or utilize this range but were forced to come out of the higher ranges by the gorge of the Dihong and spread themselves over the lower ranges, from east to west, bordering on the plain. The Bar Abors and Pasi Meyong, although cognate races, seem to keep apart as if they were separate tribes, and the Dihong, which separates them, is considered their natural boundary. Up to very recent times, the river Sessiri was considered the eastern boundary of the Bar Abors, and beyond that to the east was Mishmi territory; but within the past few years the same irruptive tendency that compelled them to leave Damloh Padam and the interior hills, to seek for pastures new and fresh land to cultivate in a southerly direction towards the plains, where they established a settlement so far back as 1837, called Bomjur on the banks of the Dibong between Sadiya and Nizamghat, led them also to push forward settlements in an easterly direction across the Sessiri almost up to the Dibong, the latest of which, the Damphuk, was established only in 1878, and is now a large and important village, constantly reinforced from the older Abor villages near the Dihong. It is said only a few months ago ten or twelve families removed from Pandur to Damphuk. All the hill country between the Sessiri and Dibong was formerly Mishmi territory and largely inhabited by them, but the latter, being the weaker or less warlike community, are being gradually forced across the Dibong and dispossessed of their former lands. If the encroachments of the Abors and their irruptive tendencies were likely to stop short at the Dibong, not much harm would be done, as a great number of the Mishmis west of that river have already moved across to the east bank. But it is stated that it is the openly expressed intention of the Abors to push across the Dibong and annex the whole Mishmi country as far east as the Diphu, and in view of this they have established Bomjur, commanding the line of communication of the Chulikatta Mishmis with Sadiya and the plains, which they have interrupted already by the slaughter of a party of Mishmis some years ago at a place called Mishmi Katta (slaughter) on the Dikrang. It is said the Abors are now only waiting till they have established themselves in sufficient strength at Damphuk, when the move across the Dibong will take place. Hence, the anxiety of the Political Officer for the establishment of the strong military outpost at Nizamghat, for the protection of the Chulikatta Mishmis and their trade route against further encroachments of the Abors. The Mishmis are very friendly with the British Government, and just the opposite to the Abors; it therefore seems expedient that something should be done for their protection. If this is not done, there is not much doubt but that in a short time the Abors will push their way across the Dibong and annex as much of the Mishmi country as they require, and the Mishmis will be forced either to retire further into the hills to the north and be cut off from the plains altogether, or if they succeed for a time in stemming the tide of Abor invasion, will not be so friendly towards us as they now are at present. The choice seems to lie between our having the hills to the north and east of our frontier held by friendly

Mishmis or by inimical Abors. The Mishmis are most anxious for the establishment of an outpost at Nizamghat. The question is what is to become of the Abors. Their leaving their own part of the country is apparently only the result of natural causes, an ever-increasing and overflowing population and want of land to subsist on. No outlet is to be found for them further north, so they are forced to the south, east and west.

The Abors, like all other hill tribes, are agriculturists and keep *mithan* and other cattle. It is said their villages are open and undefended, but their sites are chosen on the most inaccessible spots. They are all armed with bows and poisoned arrows and cross-bows, and are said to be fair marksmen. They also carry spears, heavy short swords, or Khampti *daos*, and long knives. They wear strong helmets made of cane, ornamented with skins of beasts and birds. Each man seems to choose his own particular fancy as to shape of helmet, dress, and ornament in general. As a rule, most Abors wear a long dark red woollen coat of Tibetan manufacture, which readily distinguishes them from the Mishmis, whom they otherwise very much resemble in appearance, dress, manners, and customs. But unlike the Mishmis, whose houses are very long and large, containing many families under one roof, the Abors live in smaller houses, each containing only one or two families. They are, as a rule, of good physique and a powerfully-built race of men particularly those from the interior of the hills; but they appear of a morose and sullen disposition when brought into contact with Europeans, which is perhaps attributable to the numerous grievances they think they are labouring under at the hands of the British Government; but if an Abor can be drawn out of his habitual reserve he is just as lively and good-tempered as most other hillmen. The word 'Abor' in Assamese is synonymous with fierce, savage, and warlike, and is used generally in Assam to denote savage and unknown tribes. A Naga in the middle of the Naga Hills will point out some distant and unknown village or country as inhabited by Abors; and this has perhaps led to the undoubted dread these Abors are held in by all the plains population in this part of the country. They are of a predatory nature, and come down annually into the plains after they have gathered in the harvest, to trade and levy tribute on any villages beyond the Inner Line, or wander about hunting and fishing, and there is no doubt if it were not for the present outposts and force they would soon be in possession of the whole country on the north bank, east of Dibrugarh; and not a trader or Assamese would be found there. The Abors are not supposed to possess firearms, or know the use of them.

2

CYNOPHAGISTS

(*Assam Census Report*, 1881)

THE mountain region occupied by the Miris is situated midway between the country of the Abors on the east and that of the Daphlas on the west. . . . The Assamese word *abor* means independent (*bori* means 'subject or dependent' and *bor* is the root of the verb meaning 'to submit or own allegiance') and the Abors may have been so called by way of contrast with the vassal Miris. So closely are Abors and Miris connected that the names of some of their tribes (Rottom, Beni, Talen, Hepu, Laha and Chimirr) are the same, but the Abor branch of Chimirr is said to be distinguished by the custom of eating dogs; in fact, they are cynophagists.[1] Occasional intercourse is still

[1] The tribesmen of the North-East Frontier Agency and indeed the tribal people throughout Assam are greatly attached to dogs, possibly on account of the great importance this animal has in the life of the hunter, warrior and herdsman. The dog is often regarded as a member of the household, eats at the common meal, is petted and cared for, and buried after death. I have seen a Minyong carry a dog across a stream to save it getting its feet wet.

The fact that many tribes eat dogs may seem at first sight to be incongruous with this attitude, but it is not really so. The Lhota Nagas, for example, sacrifice and eat dogs because they are regarded as the most intelligent of all animals and so specially gratifying to the spirits. The Angamis regard dog's flesh as an excellent tonic and it is taken specially at the Sekrengi Festival which aims at preserving the health of the village in the coming year. The Rengmas regard the flesh as healing for wounded men, and the eyes may be swallowed as an antidote to poison. In Tuensang I found that a dog was buried at the foot of the central pillar of a *morung* by the Phoms and Konyaks, possibly so that it could act as a watchman.

A learned note by J. H. Hutton on Cynotherapy (*Man in India*, 1932, Vol. XII, pp. 69 ff.) describes how dog-flesh has been used all over the world as medicine. 'It may be,' he says, 'that there is, or has been, an idea that the soul matter

maintained between them and Miris long settled in the plains. In one of the houses of a Miri village of the Majhuli, I found a young Abor girl who had been purchased from her parents for Rs 60 by a Miri on a trading visit to the hills. He had brought her up as one of his family, but she was easily distinguishable from them by her fairer complexion and more strongly marked Mongolian features. The Abors have only just begun to settle in our territory, mostly between the inner and outer lines of the frontier, and consequently beyond the limit of the census.

3

AN AGREEMENT WITH THE ABORS

(A. Mackenzie, *History*, 1884, pp. 43 ff.)

WHEREAS it is expedient to adopt measures for maintaining the integrity of the British Territory in the District of Luckimpore, Upper Assam, on the Meyong Abor Frontier, and for preserving peace and tranquillity; and whereas, by virtue of a letter, No. 11 of 11th October 1862, from the Officiating Commissioner of Assam, transmitting orders from the Government of Bengal, conveyed in a letter, No. 256T, dated the 8th August 1862, from the Officiating Junior Secretary to the Government of Bengal, the Deputy Commissioner of Luckimpore has been authorized to proceed in this matter, and an engagement to the following effect has been entered into with the Meyong Abors this 5th day of November A.D. 1862, at Camp Lalee Mukh:

First.—Offences commenced by the Meyong Abors in a time of hostility towards the British Government, and for which the

of human beings and of dogs is of similar quality and that the latter can usefully be substituted for the former for that reason.' If an Angami kills a hunting dog, he must leave the village for five days and is treated as a sort of homicide. Canine have been substituted for human sacrifices in the Naga Hills. The Lushais, Thados and Chins used to regard dog sacrifice as specially efficacious in case of illness. Hutton suggests that the notion of the medicinal power of the dog may have arisen from observation of dogs licking and so curing their own wounds, and he refers to a family in England who as recently as 1921 attributed their recovery from scabies to the licking of a pet dog.

assembled heads of villages have sued for pardon, are overlooked, and peace is re-established.

Second.—The limit of the British Territory which extends to the foot of the hills is recognized by the Meyong Abors, who hereby engage to respect it.

Third.—The British Government will take up positions on the frontier in the plains, will establish stations, post guards, or construct forts, or open roads, as may be deemed expedient, and the Meyong Abors will not take umbrage at such arrangements, or have any voice in such matters.

Fourth.—The Meyong Abors recognize all persons residing in the plains in the vicinity of the Meyong Hills as British subjects.

Fifth.—The Meyong Abors engage not to molest or to cross the frontier for the purpose of molesting residents in the British Territory.

Sixth.—The communication across the frontier will be free both for the Meyong Abors and for any persons, British subjects, going to the Meyong villages for the purpose of trading, or other friendly dealings.

Seventh.—The Meyong Abors shall have access to markets and places of trade which they may think fit to resort to, and on such occasions they engage not to come armed with their spears and bows and arrows, but merely to carry their *daos.*

Eighth.—Any Meyong Abors desiring to settle, or occupy lands, in the British Territory engage to pay such revenue to Government as may be fixed upon by the Deputy Commissioner, the demand, in the first instance, to be light.

Ninth.—The Meyong Abors engage not to cultivate opium in the British Territory or to import it.

Tenth.—In event of any grievance arising or any dispute taking place between the Meyong Abors and British subjects, the Abors will refrain from taking the law into their own hands, but they will appeal to the Deputy Commissioner for redress, and abide by his decision.

Eleventh.—To enable the Meyong Abors of the eight *khels* or communities who submit to this engagement to keep up a police for preventing any marauders from resorting to the plains for sinister purposes, and to enable them to take measures for arresting any offenders, the Deputy Commissioner, on behalf of the British Government, agrees that the communities referred to shall receive yearly the following articles:

100 Iron-hoes
30 Maunds of salt
80 Bottles of rum
2 Seers of *Abkaree* opium
2 Maunds of tobacco

Twelfth.—The articles referred to above, which will be delivered for the first year on the signing of this engagement, will hereafter be delivered from year to year to the representatives of the eight *khels* or communities of the Meyong Abors, as aforesaid, on their meeting the Deputy Commissioner at Lalee Mukh, or at any other convenient place on the Meyong Dwar side.

Thirteenth.—On the occasion of meeting the Deputy Commissioner, the Meyong Abors, in earnest of their continued friendly feeling, engage to make a tribute offering of a pig and fowls, in exchange for which they will obtain usual suitable acknowledgements.

Fourteenth.—In event of the Meyong Abors infringing, or failing to act up to any of the provisions of this engagement, it will be considered void and will no longer have effect.

Fifteenth.—The original of this engagement, which is drawn up in English, will remain with the Deputy Commissioner of Luckimpore, Upper Assam, and a counterpart or copy will be furnished to the subscribing Meyong Abors.

Sixteenth.—In ratification of the above engagement contained in 15th paragraph, the Deputy Commissioner of Luckimpore, Assam, on behalf of the British Government, puts his hand and seal, and the recognized Headmen or Chiefs of the eight *khels* or communities of the Meyong Abors affix their signatures or marks this 5th day of November in A.D. 1862.

H. S. BIVAR, *Major,*
Deputy Commr., First Class, Luckimpore, Upper Assam,
and Agent, Governor-General, N. E. Frontier

[Here follow the signatures of 34 Chiefs on account of eight different *Khels.*]

4

ABOR ETHICS

(From a Tour Diary of J. F. Needham,[1] for May 1886)

CASES of adultery are very rare, though not altogether unheard of amongst us. The punishment is by fine, the delinquent having to give the aggrieved party from four to eight *mithon* (worth Rs 40 each) according to the nature of the case. If it transpires that the adulterer was entirely to blame, viz. that having taken a fancy to the woman, he so worried or coaxed her as to get her eventually to consent to allow him to cohabit with her, he will be ordered to pay the aggrieved party six or eight *mithon*; but if, on the other hand, it should turn out that the woman was as much to blame as the man, that even if she did not actually court his temptations, she did not spurn them as she should have done, he is only mulcted of four *mithon*, and the woman is likewise punished, viz. stripped and tied up in the Moshup, and, a chillie having been inserted into her vagina, she is kept tied up until she is almost hoarse from roaring on account of the pain it causes, and this is done in the presence of the whole village. Sometimes a chillie is put up her anus and rubbed into her eyes likewise. After she is let loose, she goes home and carries on her work as of yore. In all cases of adultery, too, the aggrieved party commences proceedings by going to the adulterer and giving him a severe crack on the head with the back of his *dao*, and custom forbids the latter's retaliating, but the aggrieved party is forbidden to kill the adulterer.

Theft. This offence is also punishable by fine, the number of *mithon* which the thief is ordered to pay being proportionate to the value of the property he has stolen. If the thief denies the theft, he is ordered to go through the following ordeal in the presence of the whole village, and thus endeavour to prove his innocence.

A large fire having been kindled, it is fed until the flames reach to the height of two or three feet. A bamboo *chunga*, about one *hat* long and not large enough to admit a man's fist easily, is then filled

[1] At this time, Needham was an Assistant Political Officer and posted at Sadiya.

with water, and, into it an egg having been dropped, the *chunga* is placed on the fire. The culprit then sits down by the fire in the company of one of his uncles (mother's brother), and carries a fire-screen about two feet square, made (by his uncle) from the leaves of a creeper called *au kun yar* by the Assamese (*ta-lo* by the Abors), which contain a large quantity of watery sap, and are consequently not inflammable. Just before the water in the *chunga* commences to boil, he (the culprit) rises to his feet, and repeating: 'Hear me ye heavens and ye sun! If I have really stolen this man's—whatever it may be—cause my hand to be burnt, and do not permit the egg to leave this *chunga.* If, however, on the other hand, I am not a thief, do not burn my hand, but permit me to take out the egg unscathed,' he proceeds to endeavour to take the egg out of the *chunga*, protecting his face and chest from being burnt by means of his fire-screen, and all Abors assert and verily believe that if the experimenter is telling the truth, the egg will appear at the top of the *chunga* as soon as the water boils; but that if he is lying, it will not, and he will consequently be unable to secure it. It is, of course, excessively lucky that all Abors believe in the infallibility of this test, especially that it is possible for an innocent man to take it out; for otherwise anyone might, out of spite, accuse his neighbour of thieving, and thus mulct him out of a few *mithon* without the accused having a chance of proving his innocence. If the accused person succeeds in taking the egg out of the *chunga*, he is at once declared innocent, and his accuser is ordered to make him ample amends in the shape of either eight or ten *mithon* for all he has gone through.

5

A PROPHYLACTIC AGAINST DISEASE

(From a Tour Diary of J. F. Needham, for May 1886)

LEAVING Ngapok-ghat at 1-45 p.m. we continued until nearly 4 p.m., several showers falling during the interval, when we again halted for fifteen minutes or so, a short distance from the village (Siluk), to enable the elders to finish the indispensable green arch or bower called *motor* by the Abors, which is invariably made ere any outsiders are allowed into a village. It consists of a number of green boughs placed in the ground a short distance from the entrance to the village, so as to form an arch, with a number of split pieces of bamboo plaited together in fanciful shapes stuck about it, and some roughly-made bamboo *panjis* are generally stuck into the ground on either side of the arch, parallel to and facing the path by which the incoming party are advancing. The Abors thoroughly believe that this proceeding will effectually keep away sickness from the village in case anyone about to enter it should have come from a sick-stricken place. Sometimes fowls are sacrificed and placed on a spot on top of the above, but upon this occasion I did not notice any fowls.[1] Soon after we commenced to move again, I was met by Karmut and Pogi, two of the head *gams*, and they conducted me up a narrow, tolerably steep, and very stony spur, from the top of which a very fine view of the plains to the south and south-east is to be had, into the village to a beautifully level spot close to the Moshup, where I subsequently pitched my tent under the shade of a very fine jack-tree.

[1] The custom of erecting a ceremonial arch as a prophylactic against disease will be noted in the narration of Father Krick and it has persisted down to the present day. The following passage occurs in a diary by Reverend L. W. B. Jackson who went to Kabang with Williamson in 1909 shortly before the latter's murder. He describes how at Kalek he 'reached a gate over which were festooned large leaves and in the centre of which was suspended a small dead pig with its intestines exposed and made to look as horrible as possible. This, they said, was to drive away the evil spirits of cholera and, as it had been recently placed there, I assumed that it was feared that the evil spirit would enter with us and this sort of demon worship was done against our coming'.

On leaving the village, Jackson had a similar experience. 'After we had got free of most of these and were well started down the hill, we heard a great shouting up in the village and ere long a crowd of young men and boys came running down the path behind us, shouting and throwing small pieces of bamboo stalk in our direction. Most of these pieces landed in the jungle, but occasionally one would come uncomfortably near our party. I had seen these small pieces of bamboo stalk cut and strung together up in the village before we started, but then supposed that they might be for food. All this shouting and throwing was for the purpose of driving away the evil spirit which they supposed accompanied us and which they thought, unless scared away, might return to their village.'

6

SQUIRRELS AND MARRIAGES

(From a Tour Diary of J. F. Needham, for May 1886)

WHEN a young fellow takes a fancy to a girl, he asks her if she will live with him as his wife, and, after obtaining her consent, he sends his father and elder brother, if he has one, or his uncle (mother's brother) to negotiate with her parents. As a propitiatory offering, it is usual for them (the lover's father and brother, or uncle, as the case may be) to take a little liquor and four small squirrels, called *kere ketua* by the Assamese, *lupo* by the Abor. I have seen one dried specimen, and as far as I can ascertain this *lupo* is the small species of squirrel so common in the plains. I can, in fact, think of no other animal so like the specimen I saw. The Abors are excessively fond of these little animals, and they are everlastingly setting traps up trees for them. In cases of sickness, and, in fact, in all special cases in which it is necessary to propitiate the evil spirits, these same *lupo* are largely used, so that it appears to be the aim of everyone to have a few always at hand in the dried state with them, and there is rarely, if ever, any opposition offered to the match by the girl's parents, though some amount of parleying takes place regarding the total number of *lupo* (the only gift given to the girl's parents) which the bridegroom's relations have to agree will be given to the parents of the girl ere the bridegroom can, according to Abor custom, claim her as his wife, and remove her from her father's house. The number required is, I am told, proportionate to the wealth of the bridegroom, that is to say, more would be required from a rich than from a poor man. From the latter 30 to 40 would be considered sufficient, while from the former 200 or 300 would not be considered excessive. The question 'Why is there this great difference in numbers when the article sought for can be trapped as easily by a poor as by a rich man?' is, it seems to me, answered as follows—because the rich man has (presumably) much more leisure, or he has slaves whom he can utilize to trap the squirrels. Trapping these little animals is, to an Abor at least, more an effort of labour than skill, and the demanding of a fixed number of them in each case in which a girl is given in marriage is the test employed by the Abors to prove that the young lover is willing to undergo a certain amount of trouble in order to repay the people who have ungrudgingly given him their daughter to wed.

They are not very difficult to trap, for I am informed that anyone setting about the work in earnest can catch a large number in a month, besides, it is not necessary that the full number demanded should be paid up at once. After the girl's parents' consent has been obtained, the young man sleeps regularly in his father-in-law's house, and the girl whom he has sought and obtained is recognized as his wife from that time.

The young couple, however, separate during the day, and each one continues to work, as of yore, for their respective parents, and this sort of thing continues until their first-born is six or seven years old, when, if the whole of the *lupo* originally demanded have been paid up, the young couple go off to live in a house of their own which has been previously erected by their friends. Generally, one year before the time fixed for this exodus, the husband's relations brew large quantities of liquor, and a day having been set apart as a holiday, the young couple's relations meet and have a big drink together, and from that time the former (viz. the young couple) start cultivating on their own account, and work no longer for their parents. The fact that the young husband and wife continue ungrudgingly to work for their parents for so long a time after their marriage shows conclusively that there is much real mutual fondness between Abor children and their parents, for otherwise, although the latter might consider that having had the trouble and anxiety of bringing up their children in their youth, they have a just claim to their labour as long as it is possible to utilize it, such a claim could only be enforced where an innate fond feeling for their parents, and likewise the spirit of obedience on the part of the children, existed.

7

A SYLVAN SPRITE

(From a Tour Diary of J. F. Needham, for May 1886)

ABOR women will never pick the fruit growing on plantain-trees in deserted *khets* after they have become enveloped, or even partially so, in jungle, as they fear the Nyipong, a sylvan sprite whose habitat is alleged to be the plantain-tree (it likewise lives in a large sting-nettle called *pagigitak*, which has a very pretty white-looking seed and which the Abors affirm is the food of the Nyipong). This Nyipong is believed to be an evil genius, essentially bent on harming females, and so almost all the ailments which women suffer from, but especially such mishaps as occur at the time of giving birth, or ailments during the menstrual period, are attributed to it. A black hen is the usual propitiatory offering to this spirit, though in some cases a pig or a dog is required to appease it; but although this sprite is, as I have said, chiefly a harmer of females, it is nevertheless believed to harm males likewise at times and all cases of haemorrhage which occur, or severe stomach aches which necessitate a man rolling about like a woman in travail, are attributed to it. The Miris residing about Sadiya similarly dread this Nyipong, but their fears appear to be slightly less than those of the Abors, for their women do not hesitate to pick the fruit from the trees standing in deserted *khets*, even though they be overgrown in jungle.

Chapter XI

THE MISHMIS

1

HISTORICAL PRELUDE

(A. Mackenzie, *History*, 1884, pp. 47 ff.)

THE first mention of the Mishmis in the Bengal records dates from 1825, when Lieutenant Burlton, in exploring the upper course of the Brahmaputra beyond the Noha Dihing, reported that the 'Mishmah' Hills were occupied by tribes 'who were very averse to receive strangers'. In 1827 Lieutenant Wilcox succeeded in persuading the Tain Mishmis to pass him through their villages on to the country of the Mezhos.[1] He found that there were then three Chiefs (brothers) ruling over the Tains, by name Krisong, Ghalum, and Khosha. Of the Mezhos, one Chief, called Ruding, gave a certain amount of assistance to the travellers; but the principal Chief, Jingsha, would not receive them, and they only escaped from a treacherous attack by a hasty retreat overnight. They succeeded in penetrating 'to the point where the Brahmaputra in its hill course, after flowing nearly due south from Thibet, suddenly changes its course and flows in a westerly direction'.

In October 1836 Dr Griffith paid a visit to the Mishmi Hills; he only succeeded in penetrating to the village of Ghalum on the Lohit, and though he was kindly received by the Tains, they absolutely refused to pass him on to the Mezho-Mishmi country, stating as their reason that, just before his visit, the Mezhos, aided by a force of seventy Lamas, had invaded their country and done much damage. He found that the Singphos, and especially the Duffa Gam, had considerable influence over the Tains. They were most anxious to come to Sadiya to trade. The Mezhos, Dr Griffith thought to be descended from the crop-haired Mishmis of the Debong, but, like the Tains, they preserve their hair. The Tain population he estimated at 460 only in the seven villages he saw near the Lohit. Ghalum, Khosha, and Prinsong were now the principal Chiefs.

[1] It is now customary to classify the Mishmis in three groups—the Idus (of whom the Bebejiyas are a subtribe), the Taraons and the Kamans, who are called by the plains people Chulikattas, Digarus and Mijus respectively.

With the Chulkattas it was said both the other tribes were at constant war.

In 1845 Lieutenant Rowlatt penetrated to the Du, and up that river in a northerly direction to the village of Tuppang, where he met Thibetans.

Early in 1848 Government received intelligence of the murder, by Mezho Mishmis belonging to Jingsha's and other villages, of a *fakir*, Permanund Acharjya, who had tried to make his way from Assam to Thibet. Rewards were proclaimed among the neighbouring tribes for the apprehension of the murderers, and it was afterwards reported, or rumoured, that the Lamas or Thibetans had punished the guilty persons, but no reward has ever been claimed on this account.

In 1851 M. Krick, a French missionary, made his first journey into these hills under the guidance of a Khampti Chief of Sadiya, the Choukeng Gohain. Avoiding Jingsha's village, he reached in safety the Thibetan settlement of Oualong, where he was well received. Beyond that village, as far as Sommen, he found extensive cultivation and a well-peopled tract along the open valley of the Upper Brahmaputra. On his return he stopped at Jingsha's village, where he would have fared but badly had it not been for his medical skill. In 1854 he returned to the hills with a colleague, M. Bourri, and, under the escort of the Tain Chief Khosha, was brought safely through to Thibet. He was, however, followed across the border of that territory by a Mezho Chief of the Menong clan, named Kai-ee-sha, who murdered both the missionaries and carried off their property and servant in utter disregard of the Thibetan authorities of Rima, a small post near which the travellers had encamped. The news reached Assam in November. It seemed almost hopeless to attempt to punish the murderers. But both the local officers and Government felt that, if possible, something in the way of retribution should at least be attempted. Lord Dalhousie, moreover, was not the man to trifle with such a matter. The neighbouring Mishmis, who appreciated our bazars and dreaded their closure, undertook to assist the passage of any avenging force, and their offer was accepted. In the end of February 1855 a small party of twenty Assam Light Infantry, with forty Khampti volunteers and a few hill porters, marched from Sadiya under the command of Lieutenant Eden. For eight days this little band pressed on by forced marches, swinging across dangerous torrents on bridges of single canes, climbing for hours at a time without water and in bitter cold, till in the grey dawn of a misty morning Kai-ee-sha was surprised and captured in his village on the Du, his elder sons slain in open fight, his people dispersed, and the murdered Frenchmen to the full avenged. Such an exploit did not fail to astonish and awe the tribes around. Kai-ee-sha was hanged at Debroogurh, but not before he had in prison killed two of the guards appointed to watch him. A son of his named Krosho, who had, owing to his youth, escaped the fate of his brothers, was present, a peaceful purchaser, at the Sadiya fair of January 1871.

The Tain Mishmis are keen traders, and they appreciate so highly the advantages of our markets that they never give any trouble to the authorities of Luckimpore. That they have intertribal feuds with the Mezhos has been already noted; but they suffer most from the ferocity of the Chulkattas, who have also been to us most unpleasant neighbours, and to whom the narrative must now refer.

Between Sadiya and the hills inhabited by these savages, lie twenty or thirty miles of dense forest through which run the paths used by the hillmen when frequenting the markets of the plains. The Chulkattas were wont to take advantage of these routes to surprise frontier villages and travellers and carry off captives. In April 1855 they took away three servants of Lieutenant Eden's. When the hue and cry was raised, the Bomju Abors sent in to offer their aid to intercept the raiders, but the message was received too late to be of any practical good. Some information was, however, at this time gathered about these Mishmis from the other tribes. There were, it appeared, at least four clans of Chulkattas known as Apelong, Ahompo, Nossa Mega, and Goroi Mechai. The offenders in the present case were Apelongs, who had acted apparently without any concert with the rest, for the Nossa Mega people as well as the Alundi section of the Tains gave information against the Apelongs, and the former eventually succeeded in recovering the captives for us. These savages thus seem to be more under the influence of intertribal jealousy than bound together by any common bond of union. It is right to mention, however, that some pressure was no doubt brought to bear upon the whole of the clans in this instance by our closing all the paths leading to our markets, save two adapted only to the convenience of notoriously friendly clans.

Towards the close of the same year the Apelongs made a sudden attack upon a village near Sadiya, killing two and capturing others of the inhabitants. Again friendly Mishmis undertook the task of recovering the captives and, curiously enough, of punishing the aggressors. In January 1857 a third daring foray was made by the Apelongs who cut up a village within earshot of the sepoy guard at Sadiya. Fear or carelessness prevented the sepoys from making any attempt at rescue or pursuit. Measures were upon this concerted for a punitory expedition, but the Sepoy Mutiny broke out in Upper India, and all such petty matters were put on one side for a time. The last raid was instigated, it was reported, by relatives of Kai-ee-sha.

In October 1857, the Chulkattas again sacked an outlying homestead, and in the month following they massacred the women and children of a village belonging to the Khampti Chief, Choukeng Gohain, while the male inhabitants were absent with the Assistant Commissioner establishing outposts to check these very Mishmis' raids. The excuse which they took the trouble to put forward for this atrocity was that some of their clan had died of cholera when visiting the Gohain. This outrage roused the spirit of the Khampti villagers in their own defence. They armed, and shortly afterwards drove back with loss a body of Chulkattas whom they detected stealing down upon their settlements.

In 1861, and again in 1866, these Mishmis attacked Choukeng Gohain's village on the Koondil, and though beaten off with loss, yet did some damage. The Khamptis had by this time received arms from Government, and proved as a rule quite able to defend their own. The frequency of these Chulkatta raids, which threatened the prosperity of the settlements round Sadiya, induced the local authorities to inquire whether an extension of Khampti colonies would not form a screen round that important frontier post. Further supplies of arms were accordingly promised, and a monthly payment of one rupee was guaranteed to each Khampti who accepted arms and took up a site for cultivation to the north of the Brahmaputra. This frontier militia proved a success. A strong colony occupied a position towards the Dikrang, and the Chulkattas have not since attempted to give trouble.

In March 1868 Kalood, a Chulkatta Chief, came to visit the Deputy Commissioner at Luckimpore. He was taxed with the numerous raids committed by his tribe since 1841, but with cool effrontery denied them all. He said that he was at feud with the Tains and his other neighbours, and was anxious to settle under our protection in the valleys of the Dikrang, Koondil, and Diphoo, two days' march from Sadiya. After some discussion he was allowed sites for his people at Habba in the Koondil Valley, where he would be fairly under supervision, and he undertook forthwith to bring down 200 houses of his clan to this place.

In February 1872 the Chulkattas visited the Sadiya fair in large numbers bringing india-rubber, wax, and skins for sale. They behaved well but on their way home murdered a worn-out Naga slave of their own, whom they had hoped to dispose of at the fair and did not think worth taking back when they failed to sell him. The inquiries consequent upon this led to the discovery of the fact that an extensive system of slave dealing prevails among the hill tribes, in which the Singphos are understood to take an active share. The Tains (or, as they are now generally called, Digaru) and Chulkattas, have given no serious trouble of late years. Occasional offences by individual members of the clan must of course be expected; but the Chiefs as a rule do their best to maintain order and assist in the apprehension of criminals. During the cold season of 1878–9 some Mishmis of the Bibegia clan committed two small raids into the plains during the cold season, killing in one instance, two Assamese of the village of Potia Pathar, and in the second killing two Khamptis and carrying off four others whom they found cutting rubber in the country twenty miles beyond Sadiya. The captives were afterwards ransomed by their friends. The reason alleged for the murder of the Assamese was an old feud dating from 1865, when the Mishmis stated that some of their people had been killed by British subjects, and in the other case it was stated that the Khamptis had on some previous occasion killed some of their people; but the Deputy Commissioner thought that plunder was quite as much the object of these outrages. The raiders were promptly pursued by the Frontier Police, with some men from the military guard at Sadiya, as far as Jerindamukh, where the dead bodies of their victims were found, but the murderers were not overtaken.

The advance of our frontier outposts to Nizamghat and Bishemnagar, and the opening of a patrol-path between them, will, it is hoped, put a stop to such marauding expeditions for the future, or at least will afford greater facilities for promptly punishing the offenders.

In 1880 Kaladoi, one of the leading Chiefs of the Chulkattas, formally professed allegiance at the Sadiya fair. Fighting between the Digarus and the Thibetans in the interior hills was reported during the cold weather of 1879–80.[1]

2

THE MISHMIS IN 1826

(R. Wilcox, 'Memoir of a Survey of Assam and the neighbouring Countries, executed in 1825–6–7–8', *Asiatic Researches*, 1832, Vol. XVII)

WE saw several Meeshmees, wild-looking but inoffensive (rather dirty) people. The dress of the labouring men being as scanty as

[1] During the last decade of the century, relations with the Mishmis were disturbed by two main incidents.

'A British subject was murdered at Dikrang, his death, so rumour reported, being indirectly due to an attempt made to tame the savage hillmen by showing them the might and majesty of civilization, or so much of it as is represented in Calcutta. The headman of the Medakhel was taken to the Calcutta Exhibition, and on his return incontinently took to his bed and died. The British Government, sad to say, was held responsible for this unfortunate event. It was accordingly decided that a *sarkari* head must be buried with the body of the travelled Mishmi, to propitiate his spirit, and the nearest head available was forthwith taken. A blockade was at once proclaimed against the Chulikatta Mishmis, and they were excluded from our markets, but as they were still able to obtain supplies from the neighbouring hillmen who were allowed to come to Sadiya, the blockade was not effective. In 1887-8, the matter was settled by the payment of a fine of Rs 2,000, and the blockade was raised, as there seemed to be little hope that even if it were continued it would lead to the surrender of the culprits.'

In 1899, a party of Bebejiyas, a subtribe of the Idus, attacked the small Khampti hamlet of Mitaigaon, killing some of the inhabitants and kidnapping three children. An expedition was sent out six months later and succeeded in rescuing the captives.

Towards the end of the century it became necessary to restrict the movement of the Digaru Mishmis. 'The men of this tribe are keen rubber tappers, and it has been found necessary to forbid them crossing the Brahmaputra and entering British territory from the south side of that river, as they try, whenever they can, to tap the trees in the Government forests and pass the product off as rubber brought from their hills.'—B. C. Allen, *Assam District Gazetteers: Lakhimpur* (1905), pp. 57 ff.

that occasionally used by Bengalee boat-men, and perhaps not quite so decent, scarcely deserves that name. The richer have coats of Thibetan coarse woollens, generally stained of a deep red, and sometimes ornamented with white spots, which are preserved from the action of the dye by tying. The most remarkable article of their equipment is the ear-ring, which is nearly an inch in diameter, made of thin silver plate, the lobes of the ears having been gradually stretched and enlarged from the age of childhood to receive this singular ornament. A pipe, either rudely made of bamboo or furnished with a brass bowl, imported from China, through the intervention of the Lamas, is never out of their mouths, and women and children, of four or five years of age, are equal partakers of this luxury. The men are generally armed with a spear or straight sword.

3

RUDE FRIENDS

(R. Wilcox, 'Memoir of a Survey of Assam and the neighbouring Countries, executed in 1825-6-7-8', *Asiatic Researches*, 1832, Vol. XVII)

WE were most heartily welcomed by our rude friends, particularly by old Ghalum, who seemed delighted with our visit, and we were (or rather I was) surrounded by the inmates of his house and a few of the neighbours the whole evening, all anxious to satisfy their innocent curiosity, excited by the odd fashion of my apparel and the magic art of the invisible musician of my snuff-box.

The next day at daylight there was a great hustle without much noise, which I found was caused by the pursuit of one of their hill cattle called *mithun*, which was to be slain for a feast in honour of our arrival. Company began to arrive at an early hour from the neighbouring villages, and when the feast was ready, we had a very numerous assembly. A large quantity of the meat was minced and mixed with flour of the *marua*, then made up into cylinders of leaves, into which it was pressed and cooked. These were handed about in trays of plaited bamboos, with plenty of *madh*, or fermented liquor, prepared also from the *marua*; but they presented me with an entire hind-leg, to cook after my own fashion, and to the better Khamptis of my party they also presented separate portions. The Luri Gohayn alone forbore to eat of it, thinking that it too nearly resembled beef, which, not from the maxims of his own religion, but from a wish to cultivate the good opinion of Hindus, he had long discontinued to taste of. I was constantly thronged and made to exhibit my curiosities, as my gun, pistols, and musical snuff-box, which last was kept in constant requisition.

The lower class of the Meeshmees are as rude looking as can well be imagined. Their ordinary clothing consists of a single strip of cloth, which is as narrow as its purpose possibly permits, and they wear on occasions of ceremony the jacket which I have already described as fashioned with so little art. It comes half-way down the thigh, and is made of a straight piece of blue and red striped cloth, doubled in the middle, the two sides sewn together like a sack, leaving space for the exit of the arms at the top, and a slit in the middle, formed in the weaving, admits, in like manner, the passage of the head. The hair is turned up and tied in a small knot on the crown, and this custom serves to distinguish them from the Digbong Meeshmees, whom they always designate 'crop haired'; a narrow belt of skin over the right shoulder sustains a large heavy knife with its sheath. The knife serves for all purposes of agricultural and domestic economy; it is applied, in the same way with the Singfo *da*, to open a passage through jungle. The other apparatus appertaining to dress consists of a broader belt, worn across the left shoulder, carrying both before and behind plates of brass, which may be termed back and breast plates; they are of four or five inches diameter, and beaten into a curved or spherical form, but they appear to be rather ornamental than useful. A pouch of monkey's skin at the girdle is also suspended to a belt containing tobacco, the small pipe and the case for flint and tinder armed on one side with a strong steel. Both this and the pipe are commonly of Chinese manufacture, and are frequently engraved with letters. The Chinese of Yunan readily interpreted the characters upon one to signify, 'made at the shop of—' and 'should it prove bad, please to bring it back to the maker, who will exchange it'. A spear is constantly carried in the hand, the head of which is manufactured by themselves, of soft iron, procured from the Singfos; the shaft is of a porous and brittle wood, and it has little resemblance of a weapon fitted for war. Their swords are Chinese made, very long and perfectly straight, and of equal breadth, ornamented sometimes with a kind of red hair. They have excellent cross-bows.

The Chiefs are seen wrapped in long cloaks of Thibetan woollens or in handsome jackets of the same, generally dyed red or striped with many colours. The head-dress is not remarkable; in the fields it is merely a hemispherically shaped cap of split cane, and in their homes they prefer to wear a red strip of muslin, encircling the head as a turban. Their ear-rings differ according to their wealth; those most esteemed (and when the lobe of the ears had been sufficiently extended) are formed of a cylinder of thin plate silver, tapering in diameter to the centre, the latter being often one inch, and the former one inch and a half.

The wives of the Chiefs are habited in petticoats, brought from the plains. They wear a profusion of beads, frequently a dozen strings; and when they are of a sort of white porcelain, their equipment must weigh at least ten pounds. Other necklaces are of colourless glass, mixed with oblong pieces of coarse cornelian, and all of Thibetan or Chinese manufacture. The ornament for the head is a plate of silver as thin as paper, gore-shaped, and long enough to cross over the forehead. One sort of ear-ring had a remarkable appearance; it is a brass wire ring, three or four inches in diameter, put through the top of the ear and having suspended to it a triangular plate of silver, which remains in the direction of the shoulders.

Polygamy is allowed—the limit is only the inability or disinclination of the Chief to exchange more hill cattle for new wives. My host, Ghalum, had then ten,—two or three in the house, and the remainder, to avoid domestic quarrels, have separate houses assigned them at some little distance, or live with their relations. As has already appeared, they suffer no sort of restraint, but young and old mix with the men in the performance of every kind of labour except hunting.

Ghalum's riches were evident in the embellishments of one wall of the interior of his dwelling; there, on bamboos extending the whole length, were rows of the blackened skulls of *mithuns*, Thibet cows and those of the plains, some hogs, and a few bears, deer and monkeys. The estimation of wealth is to be guided by the number of the skulls of the *mithuns* and cattle of the Lamas, which are of the greatest value. I was in the course of my journey in the house of one man who is accused of the shabby trick of retaining on his walls the skulls of his father's time, thereby imposing on all but those of the neighbourhood. I understood that they were generally piled within a little palisade, which marks the spot where the Chief lies buried. Of their religion I only learnt that they sacrifice fowls or pigs to their sylvan deities whenever illness or misfortune of any kind visits them, and on these occasions a sprig of a plant is placed at the door to inform strangers that the house is under a ban for the time, and that it must not be entered. Ghalum's house is about one hundred and thirty feet long and eleven wide, raised on posts sufficiently high to give plenty of room below to the hogs.

The morning after the feast a number of visitors still remained, curious to see what I should produce as presents, and anxious themselves to share, though without pretensions. It had been at first intended that we should depend on Krisong, the elder brother of the three Tain Chiefs, for arrangements in furtherance of my scheme. He is esteemed as being the more martial and decided character, and his influence in his own tribe, and with the Mizhus also, is consequently greater; but he was absent with a party of men to assist the Chibong Gam against an incursion of the Dibong Meeshmees at the village of the former, distant two days' journey in a northerly direction. Had this man been present, and had he entered into our views, success would have been more probable, from the operation of fear with the Mizhus.

In his absence it only remained to engage the services of his brothers, Ghalum and Khosha. I presented them with jackets of scarlet broadcloth, large silver ear-rings, and red handkerchiefs, with a few other trifles, and did not omit to send to Krisong's house a similar present, though of less value. Immediately after the distribution, I observed a number of the visitors quit the house with a rather discontented air. Those who had received gifts were long busy in admiring them and while discussing their merits I perceived great deference was paid to the judgement of Ruding, a Chief of the Mizhu tribe, whose intercourse with the Lamas is frequent, and who laid down the law on this occasion with all the dignity and authority becoming so experienced and enlightened a traveller.

The Meeshmees differ with the other hill tribes in their habit of trafficking—every man among them is a petty merchant. They did not seem to comprehend why I should be unwilling to part with any of my stores for an equivalent, and I was amused at their exhibition of cunning in attempting to draw me into making a bargain.

4

DISCOMFORT AMONG THE MISHMIS

(R. Wilcox, 'Memoir of a Survey of Assam and the neighbouring Countries, executed in 1825–6–7–8', *Asiatic Researches*, 1832, Vol. XVII)

A LITTLE Meeshmee boy led the way, clambering up the face of a perpendicular rock, assisted by a hanging cane, made fast for the convenience of passengers to some tree above. All that I could surmise of our direction was that we were travelling towards the east, but whether north-east or south-east, it was impossible to say; and owing to the sharpness of the ascent, the distance got over was equally uncertain. In the evening the Thathutheya mountain defined the limit of our movements towards the east by the help of a bearing on it; but instead of having a ridge-like form, it was now a high sugar-lofted peak, and the name only enabled me to recognize it. We had crossed one ridge, and to our north, at the base of the hill, could hear the Brahmaputra rolling along. The view was limited to the extremities of two sharp bends of the river; the hills, clothed in black forest, rose above us on each side, and Thathutheya above overlooked them. Although we had advanced but a few miles beyond the Kund, yet it was nearly dark before we halted. Not a bit of level ground large enough to spread a blanket could be found, and with great labour and perseverance my people scraped away a part of the hill's face, where the trunk of a large tree, acting as a support to the ground behind it, favoured the operation, and over my bed-place, as the sky looked threatening, I had a few branches placed as a shelter.

A new scene opened on us when we surmounted the next ridge. We gained a much more extensive view, but much of its grandeur was lost on the hillside by the clouds enveloping the mountains, depriving us of a sight of their summits. On our east we were glad to see low green hills, with patches of cultivation, and here and there an assembly of three or four houses: beyond a deep, wide, dell sunk, of which the bottom was hidden, but on its opposite side a large mountain rose from an extended base and hid its head in the canopy of dense vapours. The chasm of the Brahmaputra could be seen extending to the north-east, but its crookedness limited the view and closed it abruptly.

On the side of Assam the bird's eye-view was extremely beautiful. The mountains beyond the Dihong were distinctly visible, yet distant as they were the undefined horizon rose far above their level, intersecting the plain. The silver river here and there exhibited its bright white light, and on the right the bases of the high northern mass were seen one beyond another projecting out into the level surface of the wide plain; hovering between us and the depth below, were white curled clouds in innumerable little patches.

While standing on the ridge the clouds which had looked threatening began to annoy us with a shower, which soon increased to a heavy fall of rain; and anxious as we were to move on, or at least obtain good shelter, we were compelled to take refuge in a small field hut built for the accommodation of labourers who come some distance from their homes to cultivate the more favoured spots. The thermometer in the middle of the day in the plains had latterly stood at 83° or 84°; at twelve o'clock today it was at 61°, and we found it excessively cold. The effect of a sudden change of temperature to the amount of 20° is felt much more than would be imagined or has often been noticed by travellers.

The rain continued and confined us to our hut, but we were visited by a party of women who had been out with their long conical baskets on their backs to bring in a store of grain and roots from a distant field, and they promised us assistance from the village in the few trifles we required. In the coldest weather they are very scantily clothed. A coarse thick petticoat of blue cotton, wove by themselves, is their common dress; it reaches to the knee, and has merely a slit in it to admit the head through. They are excessively dirty, and at all times and seasons have a short pipe in their mouths.

We could perceive one or two large houses at the distance of but half a mile on the face of the next hill, and were informed by our visitors that we might there shelter our whole party as they were empty. The next day the rain still continued to fall heavily, but we took advantage of a slight intermission to go round the hollow to the opposite side, and were well pleased to make the exchange for a large house well sheltered from the boisterous wind. At intervals of a few feet the Meeshmees cut a square hole in their bamboo floors, and formed a hearth there of earth, supported by cross-beams below. These, to the number of eight or ten, were quickly covered with burning faggots by my shivering people, and the smoke, having no exit through the wetted roof, soon became an almost unbearable nuisance. I have remarked that a great number of the Meeshmees have their brows habitually contracted from the custom of half shutting their eyes against the penetrating gas arising from their wood fires. The house we were in had been deserted on account of two or three deaths of members of the Gam's family having happened in it.

The Gam of Dilling, with his daughter, a young damsel, the calf of whose leg would have measured more in circumference than both mine,[1] came to see the white man. Though dignified with rank, their appearance was no better than that of commoners. The lady was highly pleased with a string of red glass beads, and not only gave me a fowl in return, but by informing her acquaintance of the beauty of my wares, procured me other offers of barter.

Three days we remained confined to this hovel, and on the fourth, the 25th October, were well pleased at the prospect of a change. Heavy masses of white clouds rolled along the dells below, and rising up the hill's face, enabled us to see that on the peaks to the north snow had fallen in considerable quantity. The sun's influence helped to dissipate the mists and discovered to us our situation. On the west we had a narrow glimpse of Assam; to the north we saw the Brahmaputra, deep in its narrow chasm and white with foam. The majestic peak Thathutheya closed the view in that direction, and on the east we were separated only by the deep ravine

[1] W. Griffith also, a few years later, was impressed by the enormous calves of Mishmi women. R. G. Latham, in his book *Ethnology of India* (1859), quotes Wilcox's remarks about the size of the damsel's calf and asks, 'What was the size of the captain's? Was the enlargement natural? In more than one savage country artificial means of thickening the legs are resorted to. Men should remember this, and make inquiries accordingly, when the legs of young ladies are twice as thick as their own.'

of the Disu rivulet from the large mountain Thematheya. Snow gathers on the summits of both these in the colder months, but on Thematheya it does not remain long. We descended to the bed of the Disu by a very rugged path, admitting but of slow progress, and traversing the base of Thematheya, we approached the Brahmaputra in a northerly direction. Several waterfalls were passed, and amongst them one of singular beauty, though the stream is small. It first shoots clear over the brink of a high rock, which is nearly perpendicular and quite smooth, and then, dividing into mist, almost disappears from sight till caught again near the bottom.

5

A WILD SITUATION

(R. Wilcox, 'Memoir of a Survey of Assam and the neighbouring Countries, executed in 1825–6–7–8', *Asiatic Researches*, 1832, Vol. XVII)

THE Brahmaputra was visible at no great distance on the right, emerging from a long narrow chasm in the hills. On its northern banks the low hills, the tops of which had been visible from Chala, were seen running along its edge; thence stretching away to the right, and varying in size and character from the mere wooded ridge to the towering naked peak resplendent in its clothing of snow and glittering in the sunbeams, until they gave place to spreading plains.

Our host for the night was the Chief of Thethong, of which village we saw but two huts, and imagination can scarcely picture a situation more wild than they were placed in. The slope of the hill where they were built was full thirty degrees; the huts were of great length, and about twelve feet broad; the beams of the floor resting on one side on the hill's face, and on the other upon stakes driven into the ground below. The roof is of the lightest materials, in order that the smoke may have free egress, and it hangs down, projecting on each side to near the floor, to give protection against the wind. Within, on one side, rows of bamboos extend horizontally, the entire length laden with the blackened skulls of all the animals on which the owner had, in the course of his life, feasted his friends. Cross fences of bamboo-mat divide it into small apartments, in each of which are one or more hearths glowing with burning faggots. Both house and inmates were black with dirt and smoke. Outside the door it is but necessary to turn the back on the hut to suppose that we are far removed from the habitation of men, in the depths of some wild forest—so little does the immediate vicinity of the dwelling display any sort of care.

In the evening a storm of wind and rain came on, and the thunder rolled in awful peals, echoed by the surrounding walls of mountain. On the morrow heavy and continued showers forbade exit from the house, and on the third day we were in the same way involuntary prisoners. I was assured that it would be necessary to wait some time after the cessation of these heavy rains before the rivulets between us and the Tain hills could possibly be crossed, and I was also reminded that if they should continue we should very soon find the Laih so swollen as not to admit of our fording it on our return; and as to procuring provisions, however hospitable our host seemed, I found that he watched his very slender store with great and jealous vigilance. The poor fellow indeed could have ill afforded to feed my people for one day. Under these circumstances I felt well pleased that some intermission of the weather permitted me to regain my more comfortable habitation at Chala on the fourth day. Here again I was detained by the state of the Karam, which could not be forded.

6

ENORMOUS CALVES

(W. Griffith, 'Journal of a Trip to the Mishmi Mountains', 1836[1])

WE were met by the Gam, or Chief, before any signs of the village there were visible. The population is small; the people fair, but

[1] Published in a 'Selection of Papers', covering the years 1825–70, by the Bengal Secretariat Press in 1873.

begrimed with dirt: the dress consists of a loose jacket without sleeves. The primary article of clothing is indeed so scanty, that the less one says about it the better. The women are decently clothed, and have generally enormous calves, certainly bigger than those of the men: their favourite ornament seems to be a band of silver, broadest across their forehead, which encircles their head. This village is close to the hills and within a day's journey of the Koond, at least for a Meeshmee. One Assamese slave is among the inhabitants, who was sold when a boy. A few of the men have Singfo *dhaos* or swords, others miserable knives, and some the usual spear so general with the tribes on this frontier, but in general the weapons of these people are most insignificant. The view of the hills is not fine from this place; it is too close to see any of great height, and they soon disappear to the westward. In the evening that of the Koond, which bears E.N.E. by N. is fine, particularly one mountain, which is known at once by its numerous cascades or appearances of waterfalls, which, although they appear like streaks of white to the eye are distinctly visible through a telescope. The bed of the Karam is almost entirely stony, and the immediate banks are clothed with grass. The jungle is of the usual thick description. The Gam, whose name is Jingsha, is a respectable-looking man, fair in his dealings, and willing to oblige. They all have tobacco pipes. . . .

At our old halting place, and which is near Dee-ling, another *Ahum-metta Ghas* was shewn me. This attains, I am told, a large size: it is not very unlike in habit a Melanorrhaea, and its young leaves are tinged with red, the mature ones are coriaceous. I have not seen it in flower. The juice, at least from small branches, is not very abundant, and at first is of a whitish colour. It is, *on dit*, after drying that it assumes the black tint. At any rate it is excessively acrid, for one of my servants who cut it incautiously had his face spoilt for a time. The swelling, even after four days had elapsed, was considerable. With this as well as the *Rhus* they dye the strings of the simple fibres of *Sawar*, which they all wear below the knee. If not properly dried, these strings cause some inflammation. The strings are ornamental, light, and when worn in small numbers, graceful; but when dozens are employed and all the upper ones loose, they deform the figure much. Some of the women, perhaps anxious to restrain the protuberance of their calves, tie two or three lightly across the calf.

7

MISHMI WIVES

(W. Griffith, 'Journal of a Trip to the Mishmi Mountains', 1836)

WANT of means forms the only limit to the number of wives of a Meeshmee. A rich man, who has at his disposal numerous cattle, &c., will give 20 *mithuns*; but the wife appears to bring with her slaves, &c., as a return. A poor man will get a wife for a pig. Whatever the number of wives may be, each will have a separate *khetee* (field), and each *khetee* has a separate granary. All the wives live in the same house; in fact one house forms the village. Theft is punished by a fine inflicted by a meeting of all the Gams; if the fine is not paid, or the offender refuses to pay, he is slain in a general attack. Murder is punished in the same way, but by a heavier fine; adultery against the consent of the husband, or at least elopement, is punished by death. If with the consent of the husband, the delinquent is fined. There appears to be no regular law of succession, the favourite son succeeding without reference to age.

8

EARLY COMMERCE WITH THE PLAINS

(W. Robinson, *Descriptive Account of Asam*, 1841, pp. 243 f.)

THE Mishmis, a tribe occupying the hills to the north of Sudiya, are in the habit of frequenting the markets at that place. They bring with them a few Lama swords and spears, *Mishmi tita*[1] and a

[1] 'The Meeshmee name for the *Teeta*, is *Yoatzhee*; of Bee, *Th'wee*; *Ghe-on* is the Meeshmee name for the smelling root, which the Assamese call *Gertheon*. The smell of this is a compound of Valeriana and Pastinaca; it is decidedly aromatic, and not at all disagreeable; it is white inside and abounds in pith, but has scarcely any taste.'—W. Griffith, 'Journal of a Trip to the Mishmi Mountains'. Nevill also describes the *Mishmi tita*: 'This plant is well known as *Coptistita* belonging to the natural order of *Ranunculacae*. The root is called *Mishmi tita*, it is a drug of great repute as a tonic and febrifuge. The active principle is the alkaloid berberine of which the root contains as large an amount

considerable quantity of vegetable poison, used in poisoning arrows, and *gertheana*, much esteemed by the natives for its peculiar, and rather pleasant smell. They also bring a little musk, a few musk-deer skins, and some ivory, which they obtain from the Lama country. These they exchange for glass beads, of which they are very fond, cloths, salt, and money, to which last they begin to attach great value. When a sufficient sum of money is procured they lay it out in purchasing buffaloes, and the country cattle.

The Abors and Miris bring down pepper, ginger, *manjit* (madder), and wax, which they exchange for the produce of the plains.

The only valuable article of trade with the Singphos is ivory, which they bring down in considerable quantities.

The Nagas occasionally frequent the markets at Nagura and Kacharihath, and other spots along the borders, where they barter their cotton and ginger for a few minor articles. They also manufacture and sell a little salt, the produce of the brine springs in the vicinity of their hills. This seems to be the only intercourse held with them by the inhabitants of the lowlands, who rarely ever venture to visit their haunts on the hills.

9

INTO THE MISHMI HILLS

(E. A. Rowlatt, 'Report of an Expedition into the Mishmee Hills to the north-east of Sudyah', *J.A.S.B.*, 1845, Vol. XIV, pp. 477 ff.)

ON Thursday, the 21st of November last (1844), I quitted the port of Saikwah by water, and on the following day being joined by two Sudyah Beekhyahs, Deena Hazaree and Baleah Boca, who were to accompany me during the trip. At the mouth of the Koondil

as seven or eight per cent. Several maunds annually are sold in Sadiya and this quantity is brought down to Calcutta, whence it is shipped to China. Also a large quantity is sold by the Mishmis to the Tibetans of Ruipo and Alupu. The plant grows pretty generally through the country and is found on the higher slopes of the hills. It is interesting to note that the Mishmis have of late taken up the cultivation of the plant.'—G. A. Nevill, *Report on the Dibong Survey and Exploration Expedition, 1912–13.*

river, where I had remained the night, we took our final departure, myself in a small *khail-boat*, and the rest of my party in the small fishing boats of the country, which, for the sake of ascending the rapids of the Burhampooter, are made particularly light and handy.

As it was our first day, we were not able to start very early; and I found that the evening was drawing to a close before we had long passed the mouth of the Tainga-panee. Up to this point the stream continues pretty tranquil, although a perceptible difference is observable in the rate at which it flows; and as from this point upwards the banks and islands are almost entirely formed of stones washed down from the mountains, the water from hence is most beautifully clear and transparent.

November 23rd.—In pursuance with the directions I had given the previous evening, the boats moved off by sunrise, and by 9 a.m. we reached the Khamptee village of the Kaptan Gohain at Choonpoora, where I stopped for a short time, and again moving forward, arrived by the evening within a short distance of the mouth of the Dhollee river, which I got to early the next morning. Being anxious to see a copper temple that is situated on a branch of this stream called the Sutrung, I ascended the river in the smaller boats, and finding that the water in the Sutrung was only a few inches deep, I was obliged to wade up this stream; but from the jungle having become excessively dense, and having no person with me who knew exactly the position of the temple, I was obliged to give up the attempt and return to the mouth of the river, unsuccessful and disappointed.

The erection of this building is ascribed to a demi-god, named Purahoutan, who, falling in love with the goddess Khaisa Kattee, undertook at her commands to build her a temple in the space of one night, which if he succeeded in completing he was to obtain her hand in marriage, but failing in his task was to give himself up to be devoured by her. On these terms, Purahoutan commenced his undertaking, and had completed the temple with the exception of the doors, when the sun being made to rise before its time he was obliged to fly to the woods; but, being soon after overtaken by his beloved, was then and there devoured as a morning repast.

The temple is called the Tama-suree, being partly made of copper and at so late a period as a little upwards of twenty years ago, two human beings were sacrificed yearly at her shrine to propitiate the good auspices of this sanguinary goddess.[1] Near the mouth of the Dholee are yet visible the remains of the residence of the Chutteeah Rajas, whose rule is said to have extended over the whole valley of Assam as far as Gowalpara, but which was terminated by the invasion of the Ahoms, who crossed the hills from Moonkong.

November 25th.—As we had now fairly got into the rapids of the Burhampooter, where it was necessary for the boatmen to be constantly in the water, I stopped to cook before setting off, as the weather being cold the men did not like wading, until they had fortified themselves with some food. I managed, however, to get off by 8 o'clock, and before midday had passed the mouths of the Khairam and Degoroo rivers. The banks of the Burhampooter are here principally wooded with the Sissoo tree, intermixed with Hallecks which, from the beautiful red flower that blossoms on it at this time of year, imparts quite an autumnal tint to the landscape.

This day the patches of cultivation in the hills became quite apparent, and the landslips on some of the moutains appeared of such magnitude that the fact of a village being occasionally swept away ought not to be wondered at, and I was told that the village of Macrusu was so destroyed last year, and that many of its inhabitants together with the Chief of the village were involved in the destruction. By evening we arrived at the mouth of the Sidroo, where we remained the night.

November 26th.—From this point the river becomes a succession of rapids, so that during the day our progress was but slow. The scenery is, however, very magnificent, and the river abounds with a great variety of the best sorts of fish, amongst which I mention the Silghurreah, Boca, Maikhan, Liun, Sandoees, Advee, &c. which when fresh caught are most delicious eating.

At the foot of one of the hills that approaches the Burhampooter at this part, is observable a high white cliff, which the traditions of the natives affirm to be the remains of the marriage feast of Raja Sisopal with the daughter of a neighbouring king, named Bhismak; but she (Rookmunee) being stolen away by Krishna before the ceremony was completed, the whole of the viands were left uneaten, and have since become consolidated into their present form.

[1] There is a detailed account of the Tameshwari Temple in an article by S. F. Hannay, 'Notes on Ancient Temples and Other Remains in the vicinity of Sudyah, Upper Assam', *J.A.S.B.*, 1849, Vol. XVII, Part I.

As we had now arrived within a short distance of the Khamptee village inhabited by the sons of the Rannah and Jow Gohains, I sent in some of my people to inform them of my arrival, and in the meantime made as much progress in the boats as the nature of the stream would allow, but found that the current was too rapid to admit of my reaching the mouth of the Dura river; a short distance from which I therefore remained for the night.

November 27th.—About 10 o'clock this morning, the party I had dispatched to give information of my arrival made their appearance, bringing with them the sons of the Rannah and Jow Gohains, together with several Mishmee Chiefs, and a numerous train of followers both Khamptee and Mishmee, when all were assembled and a conference took place. It was arranged that I should proceed into the hills guided by these Khamptee Chiefs, who appearing to possess a good deal of influence over these Mishmees, I was glad to accept of their escort. I therefore left my boats, and after passing over three or four miles of pebbly beach that lines the banks of the Burhampooter (or Lohit as it is usually called by the people in this part), I reached the road which, leading through the jungle that intervenes between the river and the hills, ascended up to the village which is situated a short distance up the acclivity on a level piece of ground well adapted for such a purpose. The village of these Khamptees consists of fifteen houses, and is placed on a spot of ground that some years ago was the site occupied by the Mishmees, who then called it Maboling, and is watered by a small hill stream named the Toolooah. Their cultivation, which is rather extensive, is scattered around the village, both on the side of the hill and in the plain beneath. This position has now been occupied by these people for the last three years, and in consequence of the protection they afford to the Mishmee tribes in this quarter from the inroads of the Chullee-Cuttia and Myjoo Mishmees, a great many of the more influential Chiefs, amongst whom I may more particularly mention Prum Song, the head of the Muroo tribe, have settled in their neighbourhood which, being much more productive than the hills in the interior and nearer to the plains, with which they are anxious to extend their trade, they find it much to their advantage to cultivate the goodwill of these Khamptee Chiefs; for, should these Khamptees remove from this place, the whole of the Mishmees who have settled in their vicinity must again flee to the sterile mountains beyond the river Tiding, and forego all the advantages of trade, which from their proximity to Assam they are at present enabled to prosecute with considerable gain to themselves. During my stay in this village I ascertained the height at which the Burhampooter issues from the hills to be 2,049 feet above the level of the sea.

By the 3rd December all arrangements having been completed, and the necessary number of people collected to carry the baggage, I left the Khamptee village, and again passing down the descent entered on the stony beds of the Burhampooter; over these we passed for some miles, and found the passage along them anything but pleasant walking. On arriving at the mouth of the Damai river we ascended that stream, and by evening had reached the path that leads up the first range of mountains. On producing my store of beads, salt, &c., I found that half a rupee's worth of these articles was demanded for every day's work, and as I could not have proceeded without the assistance of the Mishmees, I was obliged to agree to their very exorbitant demands.

On the morning of the 4th, after a hasty meal had been dispatched, and the several loads adjusted, we quitted the spot we had occupied during the night, and for some time ascended and descended the small hills that line the banks of the Damai. After an hour or two we arrived at the foot of the large range that bounds the view from the plains; the ascent was rather abrupt, and the path but a bare track up the face of the mountain. By midday we reached a small level piece of ground, where a little water was procurable; and as the mountain air seemed to sharpen our appetites, a few eatables that we had with us were devoured with great gusto.

By 4 p.m. we reached the summit, from which a splendid view of the plains and the surrounding hills is visible: on the right are seen the towering mass of immense mountains that form the country of the Myjoo Mishmees; and in the plain beneath, the prospect is only bounded by the far distant horizon, within whose limits the endless sea of forest that characterizes this part of Assam is the only object that meets the eye. From this point we again descended for a couple of hours, and as the evening was drawing to a close, arrived at a small hill rivulet where, as water is the principal requisite to be sought for in a place for encamping, I determined to spend the night, although nothing but the stony bed of the stream was available to rest on. The weather being cold we found our night's repose rather uncomfortable, and were glad when the morning broke to arise and set about procuring some breakfast: this being soon accomplished we again set out, but found the road worse than the previous day, as it led over numerous landslips that in this part are met with on every slope; part was therefore over broken ground, and every now and then we had to pass onward by means of single trees that had accidentally fallen across the chasms that intersected the path. As the greater part of this day's march was descending the mountain we had ascended the day before, and the road improving as we advanced, by 12 o'clock we entered on the scattered cultivation of Saloomgoom, from which the Burhampooter is distinctly visible winding its tortuous way around the foot of the hills beneath. As we approached the village, here and there the houses of the Mishmees became apparent, and as it is the custom of these people to build separately on the land they cultivate, a village is spread over a large space, although confined to a few habitations. On reaching the house of the Gam Abasong, I found that the whole of his people were employed in making preparations for the reception of myself and party, and doing all they could to make us welcome.

By 10 a.m. of the 6th we left this village, and there being a scarcity of people to carry the baggage, I here deposited everything that it was possible to dispense with: after passing some cultivation the road led down by a steep descent to the banks of the Tiding river; some distance up this stream a large number of Mishmees, principally of the Malo and Moree clans, are located, who cannot be reckoned at less than a thousand persons. As the river was low, we crossed over by means of the fishing weirs, which extend across the stream; but the usual method adopted by the Mishmees themselves, is by fixing a hoop of cane round the waist, which passing over a single rope of the same material stretched from bank to bank, enables them to propel themselves forward with their hands and feet, and whatever articles they may have with them are suspended to the bottom of the hoop: in a similar manner both cows and buffaloes are conveyed from bank to bank, being dragged over by other ropes attached to the hoops in which they are carried.

In the bed of this river are to be found a great variety of the different primitive rocks: lime is here met with in immense blocks, and granite, serpentine, &c. with numerous metalliferous stones, are mixed together in the greatest profusion. On leaving the bed of the Tiding, the road leads over the spurs of the mountains that continue down to the banks of the Burhampooter, and for some distance passes under the perpendicular cliffs of primitive limestone, from which are visible the pendulous stalactites that are peculiar to this formation; after passing the limits occupied by this rock the soil becomes micaceous, and in a few places I observed mica slate to cross out from the surface. Arriving on the banks of the Burhampooter, the only path was from block to block, which being of great size and worn to a smooth surface from the action of the water, the passage over them was thereby rendered both arduous and difficult.

The mountains in this neighbourhood are mostly covered with dense tree-jungle, of great magnitude, for about two-thirds of their height, above which is grass, and near the summits bare rock; and in the dells between the mountains, small hill streams, of beautifully clear water, flow along the hollows until lost in the large rivers that intersect the country. By sunset we reached a Mishmee house, and were glad to avail ourselves of the shelter offered.

December 7th.—As rain had continued falling during the night and the greater part of the day, I was unable to proceed further than a few miles; but contrived to reach the house of a Chief, named Heasong, to whose residence most of my baggage had been taken on by mistake the previous day.

December 8th.—On leaving this place, and passing through much low jungle where formerly cultivation had been very extensive, we reached the Loolooah rivulet, and crossing which the road lay skirting the banks of the Burhampooter, to the bed of which we occasionally descended; for the most part the road for these hill tracks was tolerably good, except one place that ran along the side of a low rocky mountain where the footing was unsafe and precarious, from which had anyone fallen, he would have been precipitated some thousand feet into the boiling stream of the Burhampooter, the noise of whose waters was just audible from the height we were passing. During this day's march we passed by an elevated lake of small extent, as well as many streams of minor size, and by 4 p.m. arrived at the house of Rumling, who is the Chief of the Taen tribe of Mishmees, and has established himself near the Pass leading from the country to the south of the Burhampooter, which being inhabited by the Myjoo Mishmees, with whom the tribes to the north of the river are at war, affords thereby a protection against the inroads of these people. As a large pig had been slain by this Chief in honour of our coming, a part of which is usually reserved for the inmates of the house, I was much amused to see the manner in which these people cook and feed themselves. The animal being killed, the blood is all carefully collected, and with the grain *babosa* is made into a kind of black pudding; the meat is boiled in a large chaldron, and being cut up into pieces is distributed in leaves amongst those in the house; these pieces being taken up in the hand are forced as far as possible into the mouth, and the remainder cut off close to the lips: when this is disposed of, the mixture of *babosa* and blood is stuffed down their throats as fast as they are able to swallow it. In this manner their meals are completed in a few minutes, when they again take to their pipes, which are seldom out of their mouths from morning to night. Many of the cooking utensils used by these people are made of stone; but they also possess some of copper, which are brought over from the Lama country; in these they boil their water, cook their victuals, and make the liquor of which they consume large quantities; but as it is drunk in an unfermented state, and therefore is of little strength, a great many quarts are necessary to produce the slightest intoxication.

As I was informed by this Chief that some people of the Lama country were at a village some distance further on, I determined to proceed to the place they were remaining at, and sent forward a messenger to inform them of my intention. It was therefore the morning of the 11th December before I quitted this Chief's house, and after proceeding some distance we arrived at the Dillee river, which is a stream of considerable size, having its rise in the snowy range bordering the Lama country, along whose banks a path to that country exists. After crossing this river we proceeded along the verge of the Burhampooter, and by 4 p.m. reached the mouth of the Doo river, which, although a stream of some magnitude, is yet much inferior in size to the Dillee, and rises also in the same range of mountains as that river, a little more to the eastward, and is one of the routes by which the trade with the Lama people is carried on. From this point the Burhampooter has a south-easterly direction, and, winding between the mountains, passes through the snowy range beyond which the valley of Lama is situated. By the route of the Dillee river the road leads out at the village of Glee, and by the Doo at that of Lamai in whose vicinity are also many other villages of the Lama people, all of which are described as situated on the Burhampooter. The village highest up this river is named Lisko, where the Burhampooter is said to be but a mountain rivulet, and on the west side of the same mountain from which this issues likewise proceeds the Dehong river.

December 12*th.*—After quitting our halting-place we proceeded up the bed of the Doo river, over large boulders of granite and serpentine, and where from the river passing between perpendicular scarps of rock we were unable to continue along the bed, it was found necessary to ascend the banks of the river, which as they were very precipitous, was found to be difficult to be accomplished, and in many cases extremely dangerous to pass. By 3 o'clock our party reached a flat piece of ground overlooking the river, where it was considered advisable to remain during the night.

The several clans in the neighbourhood of this stream consist of the Manneah, Tshee, Dhah, Tummaih, and Mlee, who altogether are a numerous people, but in appearance most indigent and ill provided both in food and clothing, and are as wild a set of unwashed savages as may perhaps be met with in any part of the world.

The water of the Doo is by no means good, having a disagreeable taste, and has the property of giving goitre to all those who drink it.

December 13*th.*—On leaving the bed of this river, the ascent up the Dagoom range of mountains is very steep, and in many places where the rain had cut the side of the mountain into deep chasms, the path could only be passed by means of trees thrown from point to point, beneath which a perpendicular scarp of rock was all the resting-place that would have been found had an unlucky step or a rotten bough caused anyone to fall at any of these places.

On arriving at the village of Tuppang, I and my party put up at the house of the Gam, and as the Lama people were staying at a house not far distant, during the afternoon I had an interview with them. It appeared they had come across the snowy range for the sake of trading with the Mishmees for *teeta* ; but from the snow having fallen unexpectedly, had not been able to return to their own country.

In appearance these people much resemble the Chinese, and are dressed in a loose robe that falls in folds around the waist, and are a fair and tall race of men; some wear the hair plaited in the Chinese manner down the back, while others have the head shaved; and from their description of themselves, it appears that those who trade with the Mishmees are likewise a hill tribe, and in their manner of life differ very little from the Mishmees themselves. I should however imagine that the country they inhabit is not very rugged, as on all the cattle brought from thence I observed the marks of the plough distinctly visible on the neck. After conversing with them for some time, I found they were prohibited by their own Government from visiting the plains of Assam, and not having been to Lassa the capital, were unable to give me any precise information regarding the Tsampoo; but said that, according to all they had heard, the river flowed into the valley of Assam after quitting the country to the north of the mountains, and is therefore in all probability identical with the Dehong.

The view from this village is very grand, as the distance from the snowy range, which was immediately opposite, was only two days' journey to the summit, and from this point (Tuppang), I was told by the Mishmees that they were able to reach the village of Lamai in the Lama country in three days.

As no further population is to be met with on this side of the snowy mountains, I determined to retrace my steps from this point, as no advantage could, I conceive, take place by my proceeding any furtner in this direction; I therefore on the following morning again left this village, and, varying my route so as to allow of my getting a sufficient set of sights to complete my survey, I arrived again at the Khamptee village on the 22nd of December.

From hence I set out to visit the celebrated Teeruth of the Hindoos, called the Brahma Kund, which I reached, and returned from, in two days. This place I found to be merely a bay or inlet of the Burhampooter, into which falls a small stream, that issues from the side of the hills immediately above it; this is considered the holy water in which all the devotees who visit the place bathe themselves, and is reported to have the virtue of washing out all the sins that the person may have previously committed. During the time of the Ahoms, it was necessary for the king on his ascension to the throne to be washed in water brought from this place, and until this ceremony was completed he was not considered fit to take upon himself the reins of government: to insure the benefits of absolution, it is considered necessary that the person should ever after forego the use of some kind of food; but as this is left entirely to the person's own choice, such articles are commonly selected as are either not particularly liked by them, or such as are not often procurable. At the point where the water first shows itself, the large stone that covers the orifice as well as those on either side of the stream, were formerly gilt by a Khamptee Raja, a portion of which gold is yet visible. The water of this streamlet is warmer than that of the Burhampooter, but is of a disagreeable taste. I was told by my guides, that the rains of 1843 considerably altered and damaged the place.

On my arrival at the Khamptee village I left by boat, and again reached the post of Saikwah, on the 30th December.

10

MISHMI DRESS IN 1844

(E. A. Rowlatt, 'Report of an Expedition into the Mishmee Hills to the north-east of Sudyah', *J.A.S.B.*, 1845, Vol. XIV, pp. 488 f.)

Dress and Arms

THE dress worn by the Mishmees consists of a cloth bound round the loins, which passes between the legs, and is fastened in front, and a coat without sleeves that reaches from the neck down to the knees; two pouches made of fur are used, in which to carry their pipe, tobacco, flint, steel &c., and on the back is carried a flat-shaped basket, which is covered with the long fibres of the Sinwa tree, and ornamented with the tail of a Lama cow; below the knee is bound a quantity of finely split cane. The dress of the women is made of exactly the same material as that of the men, and consists of a bodice which barely serves to cover the breasts, and a skirt that reaches from the waist as far as the knee; on the head is worn a tiara of silver, and a profusion of beads are suspended around the neck.

The principal weapons used are the spear, and a straight sword of Lama manufacture, to which is occasionally added a matchlock or cross-bow, from which are projected poisoned arrows. When proceeding on any expedition of danger, a strong coat of sufficient thickness to ward off the force of an arrow is added to their costume, as well as a cap of fur, or split bamboo.

In person both male and female are disgustingly dirty, and, with the exception of a few of the Chiefs, are seldom washed from one year's end to another.

Manufactures

The clothes worn by these people are for the most part made by themselves, and consist of cotton which is cultivated by them for the purpose, and a few woollen articles made from the fleece of the Lama sheep, and in appearance seem to possess great durability both as to colour and material. The hills, however, beyond the first range of mountains bordering Assam not being capable of producing cotton, the people beyond these limits are therefore entirely dependent for dress on the Mishmees bordering Assam, and the Lama people on the north side of the snowy range. In all other branches of manufacture, these people seem to be very deficient, and with the exception of spear heads and a few articles of this description, are capable of producing no kind of utensils that might prove of use to them in ordinary life.

11

AN IMMENSE, DESOLATE, ALMOST IMPASSABLE TRACT

(J. Butler, *A Sketch of Assam*, 1847, pp. 115 ff.)

THE Mishmee tribe reside in the hills on the north-east extremity of the valley of Assam. They are divided into several distinct clans. The Dibong Mishmees are called Chool-Kutta or Crop-haired, and the others are known by the appellation of Tains and Mezhoos.

They are a very wild, roaming race of people, constantly engaged in petty war amongst themselves and their neighbours, the Abors and Singphoos, when the most remorseless reprisals and massacres are committed. They have no written language, and appear to belong to the Tartar race. They are of diminutive stature, but stout, active, and hardy; very dirty in their persons, and little encumbered with clothing. The Chiefs wear the coarse red coloured woollens of Thibet, and the dress of the lower orders is extremely scanty. The women, however, are more decently attired; wearing a striped or coloured petticoat, or cloth folded round the waist, extending to the knees, and a kind of jacket or bodice, with a profusion of necklaces of several pounds weight, composed of porcelain, glass, and pieces of cornelian. The hair is bound up in a knot on the crown of the head, with a thin band of silver passing round the forehead. The lobe of the ears is hideously distended to an inch in diameter, to admit of the silver ear-ring being inserted: this mutilation of the ear evidently having been gradually effected from early youth. The Mishmees are not restricted in their number of wives; each man taking as many as he can afford to support. A curious custom is said to prevail as a preventive to the constant bickerings and jealousies natural to this system; each wife either has a separate house or store-room, or she lives with her relations.

The Mishmees, women and children, as well as men, are inordinately fond of smoking; and use a roughly-made Singphoo bamboo pipe, or a brass China-made bowl, with a bamboo tube. A bag made of monkey's skin is suspended from a belt for the express purpose of carrying the tobacco pipe, flint and steel, with a leather case containing tinder. The men wear a long, straight sword, of China manufacture, ornamented with a tuft of coloured hair; and a lance, manufactured by themselves, is constantly carried. They also use the cross-bow and poisoned arrows. Their head-dresses are composed of dog skin, fastened under the chin by strings. Like all savages, they are superstitious; invoking an unknown spirit supposed to reside in the inaccessible mountains or dense forests; and on being afflicted by famine, sickness, or other misfortunes, they invariably sacrifice fowls and pigs, that the evil may be removed, and the wrath of the invisible spirit appeased by their offerings and submission. We are led to believe that the authority of the Chiefs, though respected, is not absolute: they are obliged to abide by the decisions of the people, duly assembled for the purpose of settling disputes and arranging the amount of amercements to be imposed for offences committed. For all heinous crimes remission is said to be procurable by the liquidation of a fine; but adultery, if the husband be not privy to the offence, is punished by death, which is inflicted by the people purposely assembled for the trial.

The Mishmees, like the Abors, are most skilful in the construction of cane bridges; which they throw across rivers of eighty yards breadth. Three large cane ropes are sufficient to pass a person over in safety; but the transit, to any but a Mishmee, would be impracticable: for few would hazard the risk of falling into a rapid river below, or of being suspended midway on these ropes, unable to retire or advance. Accidents, however, rarely occur, and the Mishmees cross over their rivers in this manner without difficulty or apprehension.

In the year 1836, it was said that the Mezhoo and Tain, or Digaroo Mishmees had a serious quarrel about a marriage: for though at enmity often times with each other, and speaking a different dialect, they have not been debarred from intermarrying. Blows having been exchanged, the Mezhoo Chief Rooling determined on speedily overcoming his enemies by an overwhelming force, and for this purpose he invited the Lamas to come to his assistance; which they did, and entered the Mishmee country with a force of seventy men, armed with matchlocks. The Tain Mishmees were totally defeated by the Lamas and Mezhoo Mishmees, and lost about twenty men. After this success, the Lamas returned to their own country about September 1836, and from that day we have had no similar invasion of this portion of Assam in favour of the Mezhoo Mishmees. No precise information is obtainable as to where these hostile operations occurred; but the conflict evidently took place several days' journey in advance of the villages visited by Lieutenant Wilcox in 1826–7, and by Dr Griffith in 1836–7. However, such was the heart-burning of feud between the Tains and the Mezhoos in 1836–7, that the late Dr Griffith, in his visit to the Mishmee country, could not by promises or bribes induce the Tains to furnish him with guides, even to the nearest village of the Mezhoos, or there can be little doubt that he would have succeeded in making good his way into the Lama country. In justification of their conduct.

the Tains remarked, 'If we give you guides, who is to protect us from the vengeance of the Mezhoos when you are gone? And who is to insure us from a second invasion of the Lamas?'

The Mishmee tribes were formerly obedient to the Assam Governors, the Suddeah Khawa Gohains: if they were not totally dependent, they at least gave small presents as tokens of submission, and attended to the orders of the Khamtees and Singphoos. In 1835, for example, the Duffa Gaum received considerable assistance from gangs of Mishmees sent down to erect his stockades. If under any pretence, therefore, the Thibetians, being a branch of the Chinese empire, should be permitted to establish their supremacy over the hill tribes in allegiance to the British Government in this quarter of the valley, our interests would be affected; but in the present rude state of society in this region there is little to be apprehended on this score. An immense, desolate, almost impassable tract, intervenes, so as to render ingress or egress from Assam to Thibet impracticable, excepting at certain seasons of the year. Traversing such a country, when the route follows the course of rivers, must naturally be difficult in the extreme. The hills are invariably characterized by excessive steepness, and as the greater portion of the route winds round them at some height above their bases, marching is excessively fatiguing, difficult, and dangerous. In many places a false step would be attended with fatal consequences: precipices must be crossed at a height of a hundred feet above the foaming bed of a river, the only support of the traveller being derived from the roots and stumps of trees and shrubs, and the angular character of the face of the rock. The paths are of the very worst description; always excessively narrow and overgrown by jungle in all directions. In very steep places the descent is often assisted by hanging canes, which afford good support, but no attempt is ever made to clear the paths of any obstruction: in fact, the natives seem to think the more difficult they are, the greater is their security against foreign invasions.

Notwithstanding these impediments to a free intercourse, some little trade, it is supposed, is carried on between the Mishmees and Lamas; the Mishmees exchanging their *bih* (poison), *gathewan* (an odoriferous root), *manjeet* (madder), and *teethah* (a bitter root, greatly esteemed for its medicinal qualities) for Lama cattle, brass pipes, gongs, and copper vessels; and if a friendly feeling of confidence could be established between the people of the plains of Assam and the Lamas, it is impossible to calculate to what extent the commerce between the two nations might attain. Once every year in the cold weather, that is between November and March, the Mishmees visit Suddeah for the purpose of bartering the only export produce of their country: namely, *bih*, *teetah*, *manjeet*, *gathewan*, gongs, brass pipes, and copper vessels; in exchange for which they invariably take, in preference to English merchandise, cows, buffaloes, and a quantity of small, coloured beads. Their cultivation is scanty: apparently not sufficient to supply their wants, and is, moreover, carried on in a very rude way. The ground selected as most favourable for cultivation lies on the slopes of hills, or on the more level patches occasionally bordering rivers. Some villages produce a good sort of hill rice, but their chief cultivation is *ghoom dhan* (or Indian corn), *Konee dhan*, and two or three other inferior grains. The villages situated at low elevations produce excellent yams and *aloos* of several kinds. They are not acquainted with wheat, barley, &c., nor have they taken the trouble to grow potatoes, but that esculent is obtainable at Suddeah in great abundance. Of opium, a small quantity is cultivated, chiefly for sale to the Singphoos; though many of the natives are great opium-eaters. A small quantity of inferior cotton is also cultivated for the manufacture of their own clothing, and tobacco is in great request among them; they are likewise very fond of spirituous liquors.

We have no authentic data whereby to judge of the amount of the population, but from the following rough census of the followers of a few Chiefs, it would not appear to be extensive.

No. of Chiefs	Names of the different Chiefs	No. of followers
1	Jengsha	50
2	Japan	80
3	Deeling and Yeu	80
4	Ghalooms	80
5	Khoshas	100
6	Primsong	70
		460

The number of villages among which the above population is distributed, is seven; but there are two other villages, Muresas and Roolings, close to Khoshas. By far the greater number of villages appear to be located near the banks of the Lohit; one only has been observed on the Lung. The villages of Jengsha, Japan, Deeling, and Yeu, consist of several houses each; neither, however, exceeding ten in number. Ghalooms, Khoshas, and Primsong, consist each of a single house, capable of containing from eighty to one hundred and sixty persons. These comprehensive residences are divided by bamboo partitions into twenty or more rooms, all opening into a passage, in which the skulls of animals killed during the possessors' lifetime are duly arranged. The houses are all built on raised platforms, and the roofs are formed of the leaf of the arrowroot plant, or the leaves of cane, which are found in great abundance in all the forests. Khosha's house is one hundred and sixty feet in length; each room possessing a fire hearth; but as there are no chimneys, or any outlet for the smoke, excepting the door, a Mishmee dwelling is scarcely endurable.

Of Mishmee habits and customs little is known; feuds and misunderstandings having hitherto obstructed a freedom of intercourse indispensable to the acquirement of correct information. Several European officers have visited the Mishmee country for a few days, and have been desirous of proceeding by this route over the mountains north into the Lama country, or Thibet; to ascertain whether the celebrated Sampoo river flows into the Burrampooter from this quarter, or debouches into the Dehong, below Suddeah, or takes its course, as has been surmised, through China.[1] This interesting inquiry, however, has not yet been solved; though little or no doubt appears to exist that the Sampoo joins the Burrampooter at one of these points. The British Government have hitherto, from prudential motives, abstained from giving offence to or exciting the jealousy of the Chinese, by permitting any of our officers to attempt to enter Thibet from the extreme north-eastern quarter of the valley

[1] It was, however, Asiatic enterprise that solved the mystery of the Tsangpo (Sampoo). Intrepid Indian explorers such as Sarat Chandra Das and Krishna, with the Lama Ugyen Gyatso and later the celebrated Kintup, succeeded despite enormous difficulties in charting a great part of the course of the river, which is now known to flow through south-east Tibet and finally into the plains of Assam as the Dihang. For an interesting account of the Tsangpo and its explorers, see F. M. Bailey, *China-Tibet-Assam: A Journey, 1911* (1945).

of Assam. This is a sacrifice of geographical knowledge to policy; for there can be no question that a scientific traveller would obtain much information respecting the character of the country, and bring us acquainted with a people at present unknown to the civilized world.

12

THE RELIGION OF THE MISHMIS

(E. T. Dalton, *Descriptive Ethnology of Bengal*, 1872, pp. 16 f.)

THE religion of the Mishmis is confined to the propitiation of demons whenever illness or misfortune visits them. On these occasions the sprig of a plant is placed at the door to intimate to strangers that the house is for the time under taboo. They appear to have no notion of a supreme and benevolent deity. They worship Mujidagrah as the god of destruction, Damipaon as the god of the chase and of knowledge, and Tabla as the god of wealth and disease, and a great many others without name. It appears both from Lieutenant Rowlatt and the Abbé Krick's notes that the Mishmis have priests, but they are few in number and have to be brought from a distance when required. Monsignor Krick describes one that he saw at a funeral ceremony.

This took place over the remains of the wife of a Chief who had been dead and buried three months. The tomb was near the house covered with a roof, under which were suspended the deceased's clothes and her drinking cup. For several days previous to the arrival of the priest, an attendant was employed singing a mournful devotional chant to the accompaniment of a small bell. There was also a preliminary sacrifice of a red cock and hen, the blood of which was received in a vessel containing some other fluid, and the mixture carefully examined, as it is supposed to indicate if the result will be fortunate or otherwise. At last the priest arrived, dressed like an ordinary Chief, but he wore a rosary of shell and, attached to the front of his head-dress, two appendages like horns.

For two days, at intervals, the priest and his son employed themselves in singing chants, marking the time by waving a fan and ringing a bell; on the third day he put off his Chief's Tibetan robe and assumed what may be regarded as his pontifical dress,—a tight-fitting coat of coloured cotton, a small apron, a deer skin as a mantle; from his right shoulder descended a fringe of long goat's hair dyed bright red, and over his left shoulder he wore a broad belt embossed with four rows of tiger's teeth and having attached to it fourteen small bells. On his head he placed a bandeau ornamented with shells and, round the knob of hair at the top of his head, a movable plume which turned like a weathercock.

This was followed by a wild demoniacal dance, but whether a *pas seul* by the priest, or one in which the people generally joined, we are not informed. The object was, however, to make as much noise as possible to frighten the devils. After this, lights were all extinguished, and the party remained in darkness, till a man suspended from the roof obtained a fresh light from a flint. He was to be careful not to touch the ground as he produced it, as the light thus obtained was supposed to be fresh from heaven.

When the burial is of a person of note, animals are slain, and the skulls arranged round the tomb; and under the shed built over the grave, raw and cooked flesh with grain and spirits are placed (the share of the dead), and all the arms, clothes and implements he was in the habit of using when living. The poor, it is said, burn the dead without much ceremony, or throw the bodies into the river.

13

AS IF TICKETTED FOR SALE

(E. T. Dalton, *Descriptive Ethnology of Bengal*, 1872, pp. 17 f.)

THE dress of a Mishmi is, first a strip of cloth bound round the loins and passing between the legs and fastened in front; a coat without sleeves, like a herald's tabard, reaching from the neck to the knee—

this is made of one piece of blue and red or brown striped cloth doubled in the middle, the two sides sewn together like a sack, leaving space for the exit of the arms, and a slit in the middle, formed in the weaving, for the passage of the head;—two pouches covered with fur attached to leather shoulder-belts, with large brass plates before and behind, like cymbals; a knapsack ingeniously contrived to fit the back, covered with the long black fibres of the great sago palm of these hills, and further decorated with the tail of a Tibetan cow; a long straight Tibetan sword; several knives and daggers, and a very neat light spearhead of well-tempered. finely wrought iron attached to a long thin polished shaft.

The head-dress is sometimes a fur cap, sometimes a wicker helmet.

The women wear a coloured cloth fastened loosely round the waist, which reaches to the knees, and a very scanty bodice which supports without entirely covering the breasts. They wear a profusion of beads, not only of common glass but of cornelian, agate and some of porcelain. On their heads they wear a bandeau of a very thin silver plate, broad over the forehead and tapering to about half an inch in breadth over the ears, thence continued round the back of the head by a chain of small shells. Both men and women wear the hair long, turned up all round and gathered in a knot on the brow secured by a bodkin. They are thus distinguished from their neighbours, the Chalikatas or crop-haired Mishmis.

Small girls go naked about the villages, but wear a little billet of wood suspended from a string round the loins, which hangs in front and serves as a sort of covering, especially when they are seated in their favourite position in the porch on the edge of the raised floor of the house. They look as if they were ticketted for sale.

The Mishmi men and women are inveterate smokers. They commence at the earliest possible age, and when they are not sleeping or eating they are certain to be smoking; they use brass pipes, many of them of Chinese manufacture.

14

THE CROP-HAIRED MISHMIS

(E. T. Dalton, *Descriptive Ethnology of Bengal*, 1872, pp. 18 ff.)

THE hill country bordering on Asam, between the Digaru and Dibong, and on both banks of the hill course of the latter river, is occupied by a tribe nearly allied to the people last described as Mishmis, called Chalikata Mishmis by the Asamese in consequence of their habit of cropping the front hair on the forehead. Their country lies to the north of Sadiya, and their villages extend across the Sub-Himalayan range to the borders of Tibet. The hills being loftier, it is more rugged and difficult of access even than the country of the Tain Mishmis. So difficult indeed, that though we have had aggravation enough, an expedition into the interior of their country has never been attempted. I have been informed by the Khamtis that one route to the plains traversed by the Chalikatas is along the cliffs of the Dibong river. The path is generally a narrow ledge winding round a precipice, but in one place there is no ledge! *only holes in the face of the rock for the hands and feet*. The proper name for the Chalikata clan is, if I recollect right, Midhi. They are greatly detested and mistrusted by their neighbours, the Abors and Tain, and they are much dreaded by the Sadiya population in consequence of the prowling expeditions to kidnap women and children. They are full of deceit. They come down in innocent-looking parties of men and women to the plains, apparently groaning under the weight of the baskets of merchandise they are importing for barter. They proceed thus till they find an unprotected village, then throwing aside their fictitious loads, they pounce on the women and children, and carry them off to the hills. They thus attack villages of Tains and Digaru Mishmis, as well as Asamese villages, but they are afraid of the Abors, who are always on the alert.

The Midhi have some villages situated in low hills, about 16 miles to the west of the Dibong gorge, which are accessible, and which I have visited. I much regret that I have lost my journal of this expedition undertaken in company with Captain Comber in 1856, as we have no published account of the Midhi, and I have now nothing but my memory to trust to.

The inhabitants of the villages I visited were, in those days, in habits of intercourse with the plains, and frequented the Saikwah market. Wilcox tells us that they opposed Captain Bedford in his attempt to ascend the Dibong river in 1826. The attempt to visit their villages had been made by that officer, but the people came lown in large numbers to the river, and showed themselves so unfriendly, that Captain Bedford deemed it expedient to retire.

The villages belonging to the people then so hostile are those we visited, and we found them very friendly. I recollect being much struck with a considerate act of delicate attention on the part of the women of the first village we came to, Anandia I think. The march from the river to this village was a long one, and there was no source of water on the road. When we got rather more than half way, and our people were suffering greatly from thirst, we came upon a group of girls with delicious spring water in new vessels made of the great hollow bamboo, called the *kaku bans* who had come thus far to meet, welcome, and refresh us.

The villages contained from 10 to 30 houses, each very lightly framed; they were long and narrow, about 60 feet by 12. One side was a narrow passage from end to end, the remainder was divided into small apartments in some of which were seats,—a sign of civilization not often met with in Indian huts.

The Gams rejoice in very sonorous names as Alundi, Alunga. They are hereditary Chiefs, and have considerable influence over their clansmen, but no power over their persons or property, and no authority to punish crime or even to take notice of it. The notions of the Midhi on this subject are truly savage. If an injury is inflicted on one of them by a member of another tribe, it is incumbent on the tribe of the injured party to avenge it; if one of his own tribe offend, it is the business of the person offended only. He has no law except that which he can take in his own hands, and between people in the same village feuds are thus perpetuated for ages.

I was told of some very large villages in the interior, and I have heard from released captives of Chiefs of great wealth in cattle and slaves. One or two of these great men occasionally visited us, but generally there was cause of quarrel between us that kept them in their hills. The number of wives a man possesses is with them, as with the Tain, an indication of wealth, some Chiefs having as many as sixteen. Marriage ceremony there is, I believe, none; it is simply an affair of purchase, and the women thus obtained, if they can be called wives, are not much bound by the tie. The husbands do not expect them to be chaste; they take no cognizance of their temporary liaisons so long as they are not deprived of their services.[1] If a man is dispossessed of one of his wives, he has a private injury to avenge, and takes the earliest opportunity of retaliating, but he cannot see that the woman is a bit the worse for a little incontinency.

The Midhi, like the Mishmis previously described, are a trading people. Large parties are continually on the move trading with Tibet. On such occasions, men send their wives if they cannot go themselves, and to anyone who has seen how the men and women promiscuously bivouac at night, the exceeding complaisance of the husband will not appear wonderful.

The colour of the Midhi varies from dark brown to the fairness equalling that of a European brunette. Some amongst them have rich red lips and ruddy complexions, and I have seen Midhi girls that were decidedly good-looking, but their beauty is terribly marred by their peculiar method of cropping the hair. The front hair is combed down on the brow, then cut straight across from ear to ear, giving them foreheads 'villainous low' and they are generally begrimed with dirt. The back hair is collected in a knot behind, and secured with long bodkins of bone or porcupine quills. The men wear wicker helmets that come down in front right to the eyebrow, and unlike modern bonnets are large enough to cover the chignon behind. This gives them the appearance of having very large heads (they have not got small ones) and very scowling countenances. Their features are in fact of a coarse Mongolian type. The faees flat and broad, the nostrils wide and round, and the eyes small and oblique, but these characteristics, though stronger in the Midhi than in the Tain Mishmi, are less marked in the former than they are in the faces of their neighbours—the Abors. It has always struck me that the Midhi women are comparatively taller and finer creatures than the men.

Notwithstanding the bad character that I have given them (and I would not venture to have done so on any authority but their own), they are the most ingenious of the family; they have learnt

[1] This is certainly not true today.

to utilize for clothing many of the fibrous plants that grow wild in their hills, as well as cotton and wool.

They were probably the first people on this side of the Himalayas to discover the valuable properties of the *Rhea nivea*, and many others of the nettle tribe; with the fibre of one of these nettles they weave a cloth so strong and stiff that, made into jackets, it is used by themselves and by the Abors as a sort of armour. They supply themselves and the Abors with clothing, and their textile fabrics of all kinds always sold well at the Saikwah market. It was very interesting to watch the barter that took place there between these suspicious, excitable savages and the cool, wily traders of the plains. The former took salt chiefly in exchange for the commodities they brought down, and they would not submit to its being measured or weighed to them by any known process. Seated in front of the trader's stall, they cautiously take from a well-guarded basket one of the articles they wish to exchange. Of this they still retain a hold with their toe or their knee as they plunge two dirty paws into the bright white salt. They make an attempt to transfer all they can grasp to their own basket, but the trader, with a sweep of his hand, knocks off half the quantity, and then there is a fiery altercation, which is generally terminated by a concession on the part of the trader of a few additional pinches. In addition to the clothes, the Chalikatas bring to market large quantities of bees-wax, ginger, and chillies.

The costume, with the exception of the head-dress, is very similar to that of the Tains, but the jackets worn by the women are larger and are sometimes tastefully embroidered. This garment is generally worn open, exposing an ample bust heaving under a ponderous weight of agate and glass beads. Their favourite weapons are straight Tibetan swords, daggers, bows and cross-bows, and they are the only tribe who always carry poisoned arrows. They have neatly-made oblong shields of buffalo hide, attached to which, inside, is a quiver full of finely-made poisoned *pangis*; with these they invariably garnish the path by which they retreat with their prey.

By an exchange of weapons, warriors become sworn comrades, and if one falls, it is the duty of the other to avenge his fate and recover his skull.

For the entertainment of their guests, the people of one village that we visited got up a very characteristic dramatical entertainment.

The first scene represented a peaceful villager with his children hoeing the ground, and singing and conversing with them as if utterly unconscious of danger. A villainous-looking crop-head glides in like a snake scarce seen in the long grass, takes note of the group, and glides away again. Presently armed savages are seen in the distance. They come gradually and stealthily on, till within a convenient distance they stop and watch their prey like so many cats, then there is a rush in, the man is supposed to be killed, and the children carried screeching away.

This was followed by a dance. The Gam dressed himself in robes similar to those worn by the Mishmi priests, described by Monsignor Krick, and danced a stately measure with a young woman also similarly robed. I recollect being much struck with the imposing appearance of the dresses worn on this occasion, but I am unable to describe them accurately.

The robe of the female was ampler than usual and had a fringe of more than a foot in breadth. She bore aloft, as she moved, a small drum which gave forth its sound at every motion. The male performer had a head-dress with horns, a broad belt round his waist with an enormous brass buckle, according with the popular notion of a bandit's girdle, and across the body was worn the singular embroidered shoulder-belt with its peal of small bells. This was a religious dance, used at funerals and other ceremonies. They bury their dead in the wood away from the village: a place is cleared in the forest in which the grave is made, and the remains of the deceased and his arms and clothes are deposited in it. They then dance over it.

I have met with no people so entirely devoid of religious feeling as are the Chalikatas. I had long conversations on the subject with several of the Chiefs, and they utterly rejected all notions of a future state, or of immortality of any kind. The spirits they propitiated were, they declared, mortal like themselves, and though they admitted there must have been a creator, they flatly denied that the being who called into existence their hills, rocks, rivers, forests, and ancestors could still be alive. Men die and worms eat them, is their creed, but when I suggested that their custom of placing in the grave, with the dead, weapons, food, and clothes must have originated in some idea that the spirit would regain such things, they said, it was nothing of the kind; it was done as a mark of affection to their departed relative,—a feeling that indisposed them from using what he had used, and thus benefiting by his death.

15

MISHMI CUSTOMS

(T. T. Cooper, *New Routes for Commerce: The Mishmee Hills*, 1873, pp. 236 f.)

UNTIL they have become the parents of grown-up children, the men and women never eat meat in each other's presence, nor can a man (except on very solemn occasions) eat meat in a father-in-law's house. This peculiar custom, when a man has many wives (and he always keeps as many as he can afford), often prevents him from eating flesh in any house in the village save his own. Poor younger sons have to work very hard for a wife, for they get no help from their father, but have to trade sometimes for years before they can bring their wives home to a house of their own; but on payment of a part of the purchase-money the youth may marry and visit his wife at her father's house, though she and her children can never leave it until every head is paid. This custom is a great stimulus to the young men in their musk-hunting and trading excursions, for until they pay for their wives they hold no position, and their wives and children have to work for the benefit of the wife's family.

The two most important ceremonies of the Mishmees are undoubtedly those attending deaths and marriages. In the case of sickness a soothsayer is called in, and he generally prescribes the sacrifice of fowls or pigs, according to the state of the patient. These sacrifices he orders as a propitiation to the demon who is supposed to be instrumental in causing sickness. When death ensues, particularly in the case of a Chief, *mhittons*, pigs, and fowls are killed without stint, and all the old men and women feast to their hearts' content, hospitality being considered a great virtue. They eat in honour of the departed, talking the while of his great and good qualities. The body is burnt after two days and the ashes collected and placed in a miniature house, created close to the family residence. This unique tomb is then surrounded by some of the skulls collected by the Chief during his lifetime, which serve as a monument to his past hospitality, whilst the rest of his treasures are divided amongst his sons, the son-and-heir taking the lion's share. When there are no sons the skulls go to the nearest male relations. The eldest son takes the title of *gam*, or Chief, and holds a yearly feast in honour of his deceased father, which is considered one of the most sacred observances amongst them.

The laws which regulate their social system are simple but most effective. In case of murder a council of Chiefs is held, and on proof of guilt the nearest male relative cuts up the culprit at pleasure, or takes heavy compensation. Should, however, the victim be a slave belonging to another person a fine of five *mhittons* settles the matter if paid; if not, the offender is punished, generally by reprisals, against which there is no remedy. Any owner may kill his own slave at pleasure.

As to religion, their notions are very vague. Polytheism, encumbered with all the rites and ceremonies of fetishism, is their true creed. The yearly sacrifice and feast in honour of the deceased parents shows that they have some idea of a future state, but I could not find out their particular ideas, as death is a disagreeable subject of conversation among them, and Chowsam (a Mishmee) always declined to interpret questions relating to it.

16

THE MISHMI HOUSE

(T. T. Cooper, *New Routes for Commerce: The Mishmee Hills*, 1873, pp. 189 f.)

THE interiors of the Mishmee houses more resemble cowsheds than human habitations, while from the outside they might be mistaken for fowl-houses. They are built on bamboo piles, the floor being raised, while the roof of dry grass projects in long eaves reaching down to the level of the floor, and hiding the walls which, with the floor, are some six feet from the ground, and made of bamboo wicker-work, and admit a strong current of air. They are about twelve feet wide, while the length varies according to circumstances, generally regulated by the number of wives of the owner, each of whom has a separate stall or room for herself, so that in the case of a rich Chief the houses are often forty yards long. The door, about five feet high, situated at the end, is reached by means of a balk of timber, with notches cut in it. On entering, a long passage presents itself, from which the rooms open just as stalls in a stable. The first, or the strangers' room, has in it a movable stove, such as are found in the Khamtee houses. The most striking feature of the interior is the number of skulls of *mhittons*, bullocks, buffaloes, bears, tigers, deer, monkeys, and *takins*. In the house of a powerful Chief several hundreds of skulls are hung up along the walls of the passage, and his wealth is always calculated according to the number of these trophies, which also form a kind of currency among the tribes, slaves and knives being purchased for so many heads each. The word 'head', as expressed in the Mishmee tongue, also means anything which is given in exchange; for instance, if a Mishmee buys a *mhitton* for two *mhittons*' heads, one bear's head, one iron pot, and one piece of cloth, each article will be reckoned as a head; so that this term among them has a very wide significance. . . .

At some distance from every house a number of little storehouses are erected, each on four uprights, and from the number of these buildings one may count the wives possessed by the owner of the house. Each wife has a storehouse of her own, in which she stores all the grain and other produce she is able to raise by her own industry. . . .

Mhittons, pigs, and fowls form the principal livestock in the Mishmee country, but only the Chief possesses these riches, which even with them are scarce. Nearly every house swarms with rats, which live in the skulls ornamenting the walls, and one or more cats in every house live on these vermin. Dirt and filth abound, and the people never wash, so that their otherwise fair complexion is generally begrimed with soot.

17

THE NEED OF NATIVE EXPLORERS

(G. W. Beresford, *Notes on the North-Eastern Frontier of Assam*, 1881, pp. 28 f.)

THE Digaro or Eastern Mishmis inhabit the hill and mountain ranges up the sources of the Brahmaputra from the Brahmakund as far as the Chinese or Tibetan frontier east, and round to west as far as the Digaro river, and extend north as far as the frontiers of Tibet. The Digaro river is considered the boundary between them and the Chulikattas. Very little is known of the Digaros, owing to their living so much further from Sadiya that the Chulikattas and a smaller number come down to the plains of Assam to trade. They are easily distinguishable from the Chulikattas by wearing their hair very long and tied in a knot on the top of their heads, and, instead of the cane helmet, most of them wear caps made from the skins of martens, hill foxes, &c., and also a species of waistcoat or sleeveless jacket made from the skin of the *takin*, an animal only found on very high snowy ranges and resembling a cross between domestic cattle and a goat. It is about the size of a medium-sized cow or large deer, with head and horns similar to that of the goat. It is a reddish brown colour. Hardly anything is known of this animal, and it is believed that only a few skins of it have ever been secured as specimens. The Digaros use the same arms, and their manners, customs, and style of villages are much the same as those of the Chulikattas. They are, however, wilder-looking, and are supposed to inhabit the highest ranges just below the snow line. The furthest tribes that visit Sadiya take a month or more in making the journey. The Digaros have directly or indirectly some trade and communication with Chinese Provinces, as they are in possession of Chinese coins, metal tobacco-pipes with Chinese inscriptions on them, and other articles of Chinese manufacture. They are just as averse as the Chulikattas to allowing strangers to travel through their country or to approach the Lama or Chinese frontier. Both Wilcox and Griffith made the attempt to trace the sources of the Brahmaputra, east of the Brahmakund, but without success, fifty years ago, and Cooper since, with a like result. Since then, no attempts seem to have been made towards exploring this part of the country. The only chance of success in penetrating and exploring such countries as that of the Abors, Chulikatta, or Digaro Mishmis is by means of native explorers, such as those that have recently started from Sadiya towards Batang via the Dibong and Chulikatta country, by the lavish expenditure of money and presents in bribing the different villages which explorers would have to pass through, a doubtful experiment, owing to the jealousy of the different villages of each other. It is said the native explorers who lately left Dibrugarh and Sadiya for Batang had to pay Rs 1,000 to certain of the Chulikattas to be guided only as far as the frontier line of Tibet, so it is very uncertain whether they will succeed in penetrating much further north, for, as has been explained, the Mishmi villages on the Tibetan frontier are said to be in the pay of the Tibetans to prevent strangers or travellers passing through them. An armed party, independent of local carriage or supplies, would make its way in any direction required.

18

INNUMERABLE CLANS AND VILLAGES

(G. W. Beresford, *Notes on the North-Eastern Frontier of Assam*, 1881, pp. 23 ff.)

The Chulikattas, by which name they are universally known, occupy the hills commencing from the Sessiri river to the north-west of Sadiya up to the Digaro river to the north-east; formerly they occupied the whole of the lower ranges on the right bank of the Dibong up to the Sessiri river west, which was considered their boundary in this direction from the Abors, but within the past few years the Abors have dispossessed them of this tract by establishing settlements at Damphuk, between the Sessiri and the Dibong, and lower down on the right bank of the latter at Bomjur, and it is said the Abors openly declare their intention of still further encroaching on Mishmi territory by crossing the Dibong. The

Chulikattas, who were dispossessed of their lands on the low hills where Damphuk now is, had to cross the Dibong and settle on the left bank, and they are alarmed lest the Bar Abors should eventually cut them off entirely from the plains. The Abors have before this interrupted their trade route to Sadiya via the Dikrang, and cut up a large party of them some years ago at a place now known as Mishmi Katta, on the Dikrang. Formerly both Chulikattas and Digaros received tribute from the Assamese of the Sadiya district, for which they now receive instead *posa*, or an annual subsidy, from Government. It is said the Chulikattas acknowledge a common origin with the Abors, whom they very much resemble in most particulars, such as clothing, dress, ornaments, arms, and mode of living. They eat together, and their religion is the same. The Chulikattas are easily distinguishable from the Abors or Digaros by having their hair cut short in a line over the eyebrows. They wear cane helmets and hats of different patterns, ornamented with skins of birds and beasts. Their arms are bows and arrows (poisoned), spears, short swords, *daos*, and knives, in fact, just the same as Abors. Their houses are built in hill fashion on piles, but are unusually long and large, eight to ten families living under one roof. Thus, a village might be described or shown on the map to consist of only four or five houses, whereas it might consist of 40 or 50 families and contain 200 to 250 inhabitants. It is said that the Mishmis do not stockade or artificially defend their villages. The Mishmis are broken up into innumerable clans and villages, and recognize no common head or form of government, each village or group of villages being independent of the others, their headmen, or *gams*, being their nominal Chiefs or leaders. They come down in large numbers throughout the cold weather to trade with the plains. Those living on the right of the Dibong cross by the well-known ford at Nizamghat, and both they and those on the left bank of the Dibong use the dry channel of the Dikrang as a route to Sadiya; those living more to the east, on the Ithu river, come down by the Diphu. They trade indirectly with Tibet, and wear articles of dress or ornament of Tibetan manufacture, but do not know or confess to much knowledge of that country or routes thereto. It will be found most probably that the dealings of the nearer tribes to us with Tibet are confined to the intervening tribes. The men of the interior and higher ranges are of good physique, and some of them very fair, with a strong Mongolian cast of features. Cane bands below the knee are worn by a great number, similar to those worn by the Angami Nagas. All are inveterate smokers, both sexes included, and smoke bamboo pipes very similar to the Lhota Nagas, and, like most hill tribes, are very dirty and filthy in their habits. Slavery is not an institution among them, at least not to the same extent as among the Abors; neither do they want or lay claim to the plain country at the foot of their hills, and hence there is no difficulty in our dealings with them, as compared with the Abors. The Chulikattas altogether appear to be an inoffensive and peaceable race, though formerly they gave a good deal of trouble. In 1854–5 they committed two outrages, in 1857 four or five, but since 1857 have not raided or given trouble. It is said they greatly fear the Abors, and are anxious for the establishment of an outpost at Nizamghat for the protection of their territory and trade route from the encroachment of the Abors. There are large herds of wild elephants in the low hills and plain country bordering their territory on the east of the Dibong, in the capture of which they say they would gladly assist. The Chulikattas appear to have very little connexion or in common with the Digaros. The best known and most friendly of the Chulikattas are those of Lako's village, over Nizamghat, who, from more constant intercourse with us and civilization, are getting very civilized ideas. Lako himself, locally known as the Raja, who understands and speaks Assamese very fairly, might be and is fully depended on in any dealings with the Chulikattas. Kalidoi, whose village is two or three marches further north of Lako's in the interior of the hills, is another Chief who appears to be very friendly, and might be depended on. The Chulikattas, although not a warlike race, ought to be able to hold their own in their own part of the country. A few of them of Lako's village have old smoothbore muskets and ammunition presented by Government; perhaps if more were issued, and they were encouraged more to defend their own territory, less would be heard of the encroachments of the Abors.

19

A UNIQUE EXAMPLE OF SELF-DENIAL

(J. Errol Gray, *Diary of a journey to the Bor Khamti Country, 1892–3*, 1893, pp. 12 f.)

At the mouth of the Tungan we met a party of Digaru Mishmis: they were camped there and had their women and children with them. They had come on a fishing and hunting excursion, living only a day's journey from here on the Tieng-pani. The men spoke Singpho fluently. The women were rather pleasant looking, inclined to be slim, with small waists, very exceptional in hill races. I am told that the women are not allowed to eat flesh of any kind, though fish is not forbidden: the men are under no similar restriction. The self-denial practised by the women in abstaining from meat which they have constantly to cook and prepare for the men is probably an unique example among savage races.

20

A MALIGNED RACE

(J. F. Needham, *Report on the Bebejiya Mishmi Expedition, 1899–1900*, 1900, pp. 13 ff.)

During my sojourn in the hills I became gradually agreeably aware of the fact that the Bebejiyas are, as a whole, very desirous of being on friendly terms with us, and I have almost begun to believe that they are a maligned race! There are, of course, bad characters among them, as there are amongst every nation under the sun, but I do not believe that the tribe, as a whole, is nearly as black as it has been painted.

For generations past the Assamese, and plains people generally, including Khamtis, Singphos, Dowaniyas, &c., residing on the north bank of the Brahmaputra have learnt to look upon them as a bloodthirsty and dangerous race, and all works of reference on the tribes on our North-East Frontier speak of them as such, *vide* page 47 of Mackenzie's *History of the relations of the Government with the Hill Tribes*, and page 328, Volume I of W. W. Hunter's *Statistical Account of Assam*, and this opinion has been materially fostered by the Chulikattas themselves, who have hitherto succeeded in converting even me to their ways of thinking.

I do not, however, mean that the Chulikattas have ever purposely tried to mislead me regarding the character of the Bebejiyas. The fact is that during my incumbency here they (Chulikattas) have oftener than once suffered grievously for the sins of the Bebejiyas, and have not only been accused of committing outrages which we now know was the work of the Bebejiyas, but have likewise been blockaded and fined for the same, on the plea that Mishmis are all alike, and that even if their (Chulikatta) tribe were not the actual perpetrators of the outrage, they nevertheless connived at it, and could, if they wished, arrest and bring in the guilty party; hence they have never lost an opportunity of running the Bebejiyas down before me upon all and every possible occasion, and as there are no Bebejiyas who can speak Assamese, and I hitherto honestly believed them to be the deceitful and bloodthirsty devils everybody declared them to be, my dealings with them, during my long incumbency at Sadiya have, naturally, not been as frequent or as cordial as they might have been.

Had they possessed intelligent Chiefs, able to talk Assamese, such as the Chulikattas have, I might long ago have got at the true state of affairs, as I have recently, by the merest chance, done while halting in their country.

The fact is that both tribes are very quarrelsome, and given to taking life for very trivial differences (the Bebejiyas are, if anything, worse in this respect than the Chulikattas), and their creed is 'an eye for an eye'. Amongst themselves, therefore, no serious injury can be wiped out with honour until the injurer, or some relative, and it is immaterial whether it be a female or a child, has been killed, hence blood-feuds are very common among them.

The Bebejiyas are nothing like as large a tribe numerically as I have hitherto been led to suppose they are; I do not believe the whole community numbers more than 3,000 to 4,000 souls, if as many, and I do not think they could turn out more than 1,500, at the outside, fighting men.

They have only 31 villages; many of these are mere hamlets, containing some 520 houses. Some of the Chiefs' houses are over 300 feet long, with 8 or 10 rooms, or spaces partitioned off, and these undoubtedly contain a goodly number of men, women, and children, but the majority I saw were not more than 80 or 100 feet long, containing, I calculated, at the outside, from 8 to 10 souls (including women and children).

By multiplying the total number of houses by 8, therefore, we get a population of 4,000 odd only for the whole tribe, and in calculating 3 adult males for each house, their fighting strength would be but 1,500 men.

The tribal name of the Bebejiyas is Mithun, and the Chulikattas Midu. The Chulikattas say they sprang from a man called Tara and the Abors from Tara's own brother (by the same father and mother) called Tani (Tani means a human being in Abor); they thus claim relationship with the Abors. The Bebejiyas, they declare, are of Digaro origin, and they insist upon impressing upon me—as they have always hitherto done—that they are in no way related to the Bebejiyas, though the two tribes appear to me to be identically the same, for they live in exactly the same manner, their customs are similar, they are clothed alike, and their language is undoubtedly the same, and although a Chulikatta never marries a Digaro girl, and a Bebejiya does, the two tribes (Chulikattas and Bebejiyas) intermarry freely.

21

A SACRED NECKLACE

(J. F. Needham, *Report on the Bebejiya Mishmi Expedition, 1899–1900*, 1900, pp. 16 f.)

BOTH tribes are exceedingly superstitious, and like the Abors, or Padams, each village or clan has its sorcerer (called Igu in Bebejiya and Chulikatta, Miru in Abor, and Dondai in Assamese), who is gravely consulted when anything untoward happens in the village. These men wear fantastic articles of dress, and feign to possess miraculous powers.

While at Hunili, a huge necklace, consisting of tiger, bear, pig, and monkey's teeth, and claws, together with a headband of plaited cane, studded with cowries, and with coloured feathers waving at the sides, was discovered in the adjoining jungles, and brought into camp, and these turned out to be the village sorcerer's charms, which had been hurriedly hidden when the people first fled into the jungles. Old Arati, hearing that they were in our possession, begged that they might be returned to him as he himself had shot the animals whose teeth and claws adorned the necklace, and he had presented it to the village sorcerer, and his request was granted, to his extreme delight.

22

BEBEJIYA MANNERS AND CUSTOMS

(J. F. Needham, *Report on the Bebejiya Mishmi Expedition, 1899–1900*, 1900, pp. 19 ff.)

WHEN a man wishes to marry, he asks the girl's parents' consent, and makes them a few propitiatory presents. When consent has been obtained, and presents suitable to the bridegroom's means, in the shape of *Sikra daos, kanhis*, pigs, or what not, have been given to the parents, the villagers build a new house for the pair to live in, and the girl goes off and lives with her husband. The parents of the girl then give the bridegroom a few cheap presents in return for those received by them. There is no intermarrying amongst the several clans.

Polygamy is common among the men, who may have as many wives as they can afford.

Adultery is rare. Whenever a case occurs, the village sorcerer is called by the aggrieved party, and he proceeds to search the woman's armpits, and (if guilty, I suppose) finding a very tiny bird there, he proceeds to devour it, and pronounces that all will now be well.

The aggrieved party then claims compensation from the adulterer in the shape of *mithan*, *dankis*, pig, &c., according to his means, and if not complied with, a blood-feud ensues. Barren women are at a discount. If a woman turns out barren, the village sorcerer is consulted, and he is alleged to know the reason why, and the cure.

When a grown-up person dies, the whole village does *gena* (taboo), not so if a child dies. The latter is buried at once without any ceremonies, but in the case of an adult the body is not interred until the third day. Until that time relatives sit round it, and cry, and if the weather is hot, fan the body. On the third day, the body, wrapped in the clothes usually worn by the deceased when alive, is put into a rough coffin hewn out of a tree and carefully lined with matting and leaves, and carried to the grave, which is generally three or four feet deep. After the above mentioned coffin has been put into the grave, two planks are put over it, and these being covered with leaves and mats the hole is filled in. Money is rarely, food never, put into the grave with the body, but a man's spear, *daos*, &c., are generally buried with him. Sometimes other articles, such as extra clothes, &c., in a basket or a *danki* are put into the grave, and these may be subscribed for by the villagers for this purpose.

If a man dies an accidental death, he is buried near the spot where he died, though always a good distance from any frequented path, for the spirit of the dead is greatly feared. Graves are generally dug below the village.

Women are delivered in a squatting posture (that is in the position in which all natives sit to eat, smoke, or talk, &c.). There is no village *gena* after a child is born. The mother continues unclean for ten days, and then returns to her ordinary work.

Twins occur occasionally. There is a superstition that if a boy and a girl are born, the pair lives; if twins are, however, of the same sex, that is, two boys or two girls, one is almost sure to die.

The diseases most common are goitre, skin diseases, ophthalmia, stomach complaints, and fevers. On every occasion, the sorcerer is consulted, and he invariably recommends the propitiation of some malignant spirit by means of fowls, pigs, &c.

Bebejiyas use the *corydalis* plant (which grows wild in their country), and likewise *Mishmi teeta* (called *aron* by Bebejiyas) from Thibet for stomach-ache.

If a man is wounded by a poisoned arrow, the sorcerer is called in, and he proceeds to cut the wound open and suck out the poison, and after several incantations, the patient is left alone.

23

MISHMI TRADE IN 1899

(J. F. Needham, *Report on the Bebejiya Mishmi Expedition, 1899–1900*, 1900, pp. 15 f.)

THESE people cultivate *Mishmi teeta* and take it to Thibet, where it is said to be in great demand. They likewise take musk-deer pods and dyed cloths, and all descriptions of skins, viz., tiger, leopard, deer, bear, otter, &c., and these, together with the *Mishmi teeta*, they barter for *dankis, Sikra daos*, cattle, guns, pistols, powder, caps.

Noga Chulikatta tells me that during the last two years the Thibetans are selling cap-guns, as good as our own, to the Mishmis, and he declares he has seen several of these guns among the Chulikattas. He also tells me that the sale of guns, double as well as single barrel, and pistols by Thibetans to Chulikattas is increasing yearly, and that a good single-barrel gun can be got in Thibet for a good-sized bundle of *Mishmi teeta*. He tells me that the Abors and other tribes will, if this goes on, soon have lots of guns. I have asked Noga to try and bring me in a gun purchased from the Thibetans, as I should like to know where they come from. If all Noga tells me is true, this trade in fire-arms is a serious matter to us, and it behoves us, I think, to try and find out more about it.

Neither the Bebejiyas nor the Chulikattas are as well-to-do as Abors (Padams) or Passi-Minyongs, and this is due to their inordinate love of giving feasts! A Mishmi (Bebejiya or Chulikatta) is never happy, except when feasting his relatives and friends; the consequence is that as soon as he has acquired any money, he at once disburses it on *mithan* and pigs. Feasting is, in fact, a mania with them, and the heads of all animals slain during each successive generation are carefully set apart in different rows along the passage inside their houses as mementos of the wealth and hospitality of past and present occupants. Of course, the wealthier a man is, the larger and oftener his feasts.

I am informed that a Chulikatta Chief called Diju, of the M'taiu clan, whose village lies high up the Dibong near the Thibetan frontier, has been known to kill 100 *mithan* at one feast! Notwithstanding these continual feasts, however, the people seem fairly well off, as they appear to possess numerous pigs and poultry, and have heaps of *bobosa* (a millet) and Indian corn, their two staple foods.

24

AN ANNUAL FAIR

(G. W. Beresford, *Notes on the North-Eastern Frontier of Assam*, 1881, pp. 35 f.)

AN annual fair, or *Mela*, is held at Sadiya at the full of the moon which occurs about the end of January or beginning of February, to which all the hillmen and frontier tribes resort for the purposes of trade, to receive the annual *posa* or subsidy from Government, or have their difficulties and disputes settled by the Political Officers. The Deputy Commissioner of the district attends, and the annual race meeting of the planters living on the Sadiya road is held at the same time, besides athletic sports for the hill and other tribes. It is estimated that four to five thousand hillmen attend this fair, and the amount of trade done by them amounts to nearly Rs 50,000. The imports at this fair are principally rubber, madder, wax, cotton, musk, cloths, mats, Khampti *daos*, and ivory. The exports are Assamese and English cloths, salt, brass, iron, and bell-metal utensils, silver ear-rings and ornaments, beads, brassware and opium. All the hill tribes are inveterate smokers and addicted to ardent spirits, and the dealers in tobacco and spirits must also drive a thriving trade. In a political point of view alone this fair must have an excellent effect, bringing together, as it does, to a common rendezvous all the hill and frontier tribes of the district, who have the opportunity of coming into contact with civilization and the great ruling power, and who otherwise most probably would never see or hear of each other, except perhaps as enemies. When the present known, though undetermined, routes to China and Tibet are opened up Sadiya is likely to become a very important place and a starting-point to them.[1]

[1] A number of such fairs were held from the middle of the century onwards and were attended by large numbers of tribesmen. One of the most important was at Udalguri which was visited by what are described as 'Tibetan Bhutias of Tawang': they were probably Sherdukpens and Akas, for the Tawang Monpas have always been reluctant to come down to the plains: indeed in 1876, the Sherdukpen Rajas of Shergaon and 'Rupraigaon' were specially invited to the Darbar at Tezpur when Queen Victoria was proclaimed Empress of India. In 1875, 2,000 and in 1876, 3,600 tribesmen were present: they brought ponies, sheep, dogs, salt, a little gold, blankets, yak's tails, musk, chillies, spices, wax, madder, oranges and walnuts. They took in exchange English and Assamese cloth, thread, rice, betel-nuts, brass and iron utensils, bar-iron, hoes. Another fair was at Doimera: it dates back to the days of the Assam Rajas and was on a smaller scale: in 1876, the first year in which statistics were collected, imports did not exceed Rs 13,000, while at Udalguri they amounted to over Rs 25,000, exports being double that amount.

The Sadiya Fair catered to the needs of the Miris, Mishmis, Khamptis, Singphos and Abors, though for some years the Abors did not attend. In 1876, 3,000 tribesmen were present and the numbers rose in later years. In 1874, they brought down over Rs 25,000 worth of their own articles and took home goods to the value of Rs 17,630. In 1876, the turnover was much greater: they sold Rs 49,100 and bought Rs 44,475 worth of goods, though the amount fell off considerably in the next few years.

The Sadiya Fair was clearly a great occasion. In 1881, Mr McWilliam with Major Peet, to whom he was handing over charge of the area, crossed the Brahmaputra at Saikwa in boats decorated with gilt standards and gorgeous flags. The following day there was a procession headed by the officers on a large elephant and followed by the principal Singpho and Khampti Chiefs also on elephants, a Miri band and several parties of dancing-girls. The Mishmis would not join the procession, prefering to march in a body of their own parallel to the main one. In 1883, there was a display of fireworks for the first time and it is reported that 'although they showed to some disadvantage on account of the dampness of the weather and the brightness of the moon, they were, nevertheless, much appreciated by the Abors and Mishmis who saw them, and many wonderful stories have since been circulated regarding them'.

From this year onwards the Abors began to attend the Fair and by 1885 there were 900 Abors, nearly half the total number of tribesmen, attending it. It is interesting to note that the Abors sold a large quantity of their own hand-woven cloth to the visitors from the plains. The Digarus bought more finery in the shape of beads than the others and the Khamptis and Singphos, who 'wove the pretty tartans which they wore', bought English thread and also affected English pottery. Rubber stood at the head of the list of articles sold by most tribes and the Singphos and Khamptis brought down for sale elephant tusks and rhinoceros horns. In 1884, the Chief Commissioner objected to the distribution of rum as a political present to the tribesmen during the Fair, and in that year the quantity of opium sold came down from Rs 30,300 to Rs 9,757. It is said that salt, brass pots and iron were in great demand by the Abors while the Singphos were the chief dealers in more sophisticated goods such as tea, sugar, oil and gur.

The *Report on the Administration of the Province of Assam* for 1878–9 notes that in 1879, 'about 40 Europeans were present, and the usual barter went on between them and the hill people, the latter disposing of all they possessed in the way of arms and ornaments, and of most, indeed, of their clothing. Articles of this nature commanded prices which must have surprised the owners'.

Chapter XII

THE KHAMPTIS

1

HISTORICAL PRELUDE

(A. Mackenzie, *History*, 1884, pp. 57 ff.)

THE Khamptis were originally immigrants from Bor-Khampti, the mountainous region which interposes between the eastern extremity of Assam and the valley of the Irrawaddy. They are of Shan descent and adhere to the Buddhist religion. When they first came to Assam they settled on the Tengapani, but in 1794, during the troubled reign of Gour Sing, probably in consequence of pressure from the then invading Singphos, they crossed the Brahmaputra, ousted the Khawa Gohain, or Assamese Governor, of Sadiya, the Khampti Chief usurping his titles and dignity, and reduced the Assamese *ryots* to a position of subservience if not of actual slavery. The Gowhatty Government was compelled to acquiesce in the arrangement, and, after the annexation, the British Government found the Sadiya tract entirely under Khampti management.

Mr Scott, the Governor-General's Agent, recognized the Khampti Chief 'Chousalan Sadiya Khawa Gohain' as the local officer of the Assam Government, permitted him to collect the poll-tax of the Assamese of the district, and entered into arrangements under which the Khawa Gohain, instead of himself paying taxes, undertook to maintain a contingent of 200 men, to be armed by the British Government. In 1824 the Khamptis rendered such material aid in the campaign against the Singphos, that Mr Scott was led to urge upon Government that in any arrangement made for handing over Upper Assam to a Native prince, the country inhabited by the Khamptis should, with that of the Muttucks, be kept apart.

The relations which subsisted between the Sadiya Khamptis and their brethren in Bor-Khampti led, however, at times to much uneasiness and doubts as to the loyalty of the former. In 1830, for instance, a body of Singphos and Bor-Khamptis invaded the tract south of the Brahmaputra, but were dispersed by troops under Captain Neufville. The current rumour in Assam at the time was that the Khawa Gohain was in league with these, though the local officers discredited the report. It certainly appeared to be the interest of that Chief to cultivate our friendship, but it is impossible to trust absolutely to *a priori* argument of that kind where semi-savages are concerned.

In May 1835, a fresh immigration of 230 Moonglary Khamptis took place. They came wishing to settle under the British Government, and asking for arms and exemption from taxes for ten years. They were refused fire-arms, but were told that they would be allowed to live free from all dues for three years. The Government seems at this period to have been much impressed with the advisability of inducing colonists to take up land at the head of the Assam Valley, provided that their doing so did not interfere with the area reserved for tea cultivation. What was wanted was a cheap and effective barrier against future invasion from Burma, the dread of which long continued to trouble the Government and explains much of the policy in regard to Upper Assam, Manipur, and this frontier generally.

It was unfortunate that just about this time the arrogance of Chowrangfat Sadiya Khawa Gohain (the son of the man we had found in office, who died early in 1835) compelled the Government to remove the Khamptis from the position of pre-eminence which they had hitherto occupied, and which had doubtless acted as an attraction to their tribe in Bor-Khampti. A dispute had arisen between the Khawa Gohain and the Bor Senapati, or Chief of the Muttucks, in regard to a tract of land called Chukowa, on the south of the Brahmaputra. The British officer in charge of Sadiya, to prevent collision, attached the land, and ordered both parties to refer their claims for his consideration. The Khawa Gohain in defiance of this order took forcible possession, and treated all remonstrances with open contempt. The Governor-General's Agent was compelled, in vindication of his authority, to order first the suspension, and thereafter the removal of the Khampti Chief from the post of Khawa Gohain, which had indeed come to be looked upon by his tribe less as a dignity conferred or ratified by our Government, than as an inherent attribute of their Chief as a tributary power. If any proper control was to be maintained over the Sadiya tribes, the authority of Government certainly needed at this time to be reasserted. The Khawa Gohain was therefore removed to a station down the river out of the reach of temptation to intrigue, and his post was abolished, the duties being made over to the British officer stationed at Sadiya in charge of the troops, who was to collect the capitation tax from those cultivators who paid it, and to administer justice to the Assamese either directly or by a punchayat. As regards internal management, the Singphos and Khamptis were left to their own Chiefs. No change was made in their relations to Government, and no taxation was in fact ever imposed on them. The British officer in charge was, as far as they were concerned, left to interpose or mediate only in serious cases or where members of different tribes were parties to the dispute.

At first the minor Khampti Chiefs seemed satisfied with these arrangements. They did certainly good service immediately afterwards against the Singphos—so good indeed that the Government rather rashly rewarded them by permitting the ex-Khawa Gohain to return to Sadiya in a private capacity to live among them. They were not, however, really content. They had lost their profitable position of control over the Assamese. Their slaves had been released. They knew that proposals for bringing them under regular assessment had been more than once mooted. Many incentives to revolt were secretly rankling in their minds. In 1837, the local officers were warned that the ex-Khawa Gohain was intriguing to form a combination of tribes to attack Sadiya, but no tangible proof was obtained, and the warning was disregarded.

At length in January 1839, the long meditated plot developed itself in action. On the evening of the 19th of January, Colonel White, the officer-in-command at Sadiya, had held a durbar at which the Khampti Chiefs attended, to all appearances as friendly and loyal as they had hitherto outwardly shown themselves. That very night, a body of 500 Khamptis under their Sadiya Chiefs advanced upon the post from four different directions, surprised the sentries, and made for Colonel White's quarters and the sepoy lines, firing the station as they rushed through. The surprise was complete, and their enterprise was fatally successful. Colonel White was butchered, eighty others were killed or wounded, and all the lines but two were burnt to the ground.

Had the Khampti Chiefs now shown resolution equal to their skill in combination, they might have done serious damage to our position on this frontier. As it was, their hearts failed them after the capture of Sadiya. They retreated with all their adherents without waiting for attack, and deserting their villages took refuge with their leaders, the Tao and Captain Gohains, among the Dibong Mishmis. A rising among the Khamptis south of the Brahmaputra was put down by the troops. The Singphos, Muttucks, and Abors at once offered their aid in punishing the insurgents. The Khamptis had no friends among those they had so long oppressed. Treachery too was soon at work in their ranks. One Chief, the Chouking Gohain, came in and surrendered, and then led a party of troops into the hills who drove the Tao and his followers from their Mishmi refuge. This defeat of the rebels set free a number of Mooluck Khamptis, 200 in all, who had been compelled by the Tao to follow him into the hills after he had murdered their Chief for refusing to join in the attack on Sadiya. Soon after, about 900 Khamptis laid down their arms and were removed from Sadiya to sites in Luckimpore lower down the river. In the cold weather of 1839–40 a second and a third expedition into the Mishmi hills again and again dispersed those who still remained in arms. But it was not till December 1843 that the remnant came in and submitted. These were settled above Sadiya to form a screen between the Assamese and the Mishmis.

In 1884 the position of the Khamptis in Assam was this: one body had been settled at Choonpoorah above Sadiya under the Captain Gohain, cousin of the late Khawa Gohain. The few Moonglary Khamptis formerly on the Tengapani were located near Saikwa to the south of the Brahmaputra. A third party under Chowtang Gohain were settled at Damadji, while a fourth was placed under Bhodia, son of the late Khawa Gohain, to the west of Luckimpore. By this dispersion they were effectually prevented from doing any further mischief. They ceased from that time to be of any political importance.

2

THE KHAMPTIS AND THEIR METALS

(W. Robinson, *Descriptive Account of Asam*, 1841, pp. 372 ff.)

THE religion of the Khamtis is Buddhism, and their customs appear precisely the same as those of Ava. Their priests every morning hurry through the village or town, preceded by a boy with a little bell, each priest holding a lacquered box, in which he collects the offerings of the people, presented generally by the women, who stand waiting at their respective doors with a portion of their ready cooked meal.

The first appearance of the Khamti houses usually excites the surprise of those who are not accustomed to their style of building; the floor on which the family live, is completely hid under the low projecting eaves, and all that appears to view is the open and dirty ground floor, crowded with buffaloes and pigs.

Few of the women boast of much beauty; they are in general plainly dressed, and make a very neat appearance. The men turn up their hair, and form a large knot with it on the centre of the head; the women, either from the natural profusion of their tresses, or from their taking more care of them, far excel the men in the height of their topknots, which they wear nearly in the same fashion, but divide it with silver ornaments and small glass beads. Their petticoats accord better with our notions of female delicacy, than the odd dress of Burman ladies.

It is a singular custom amongst the Khamtis, that the principal amusement of their Chiefs is working in metals; in which, practice renders them infinitely more skilful than the lower classes, who perhaps cannot spare much time from their labours in the fields. They readily employ themselves in fashioning ear-rings for the purpose of barter, the workmanship giving a double value to the silver. A couple of hammers and a few punches are all the tools requisite, and these they carry with them in their travelling bag. The silver is melted and poured into the hollow of a bit of bamboo, when repeatedly heating it, it is beat with great patience and perseverance into plates almost as thin as paper; by a proper management of the hammer, they make it spread in the required direction till long enough to bend into a cylinder; the edges are then cut even with a pair of scissors, and the parts to be soldered are notched in a castellated form, the alternate projections inserted, and a little borax with a very thin bit of plate laid over the joint, which the application of a little heat readily unites; a curve is then given to the sides of the cylinder, when the top only is required to finish it. The top is of course a circle, and when beat thin enough, it is laid on a bed of lac softened by heat, and with blunt punches an embossed pattern is then given; both the silver and lac being repeatedly heated to prevent the latter from becoming brittle, and to soften the former sufficiently to cause it to assume readily the indentations of the punch. In this way, with the aid of sharper punches and some of small size, very pretty patterns are often given. The ordinary silver pipes of the Khamtis are of very neat workmanship.

There is a silver mine in the Bor-Khamti country, but it has never produced more than 8,000 rupees a year. It might be turned to much advantage, but the possessors are afraid of increasing its revenue, lest by doing so, they should excite the avarice of their neighbours.[1]

3

THE KHAMPTIS AS A SOLDIER SAW THEM IN 1847

(J. Butler, *A Sketch of Assam*, 1847, pp. 57 f.)

In stature the Khamtees are middle-sized, in countenance resembling the Chinese more than any other tribe on the frontier, and possessing the same kind of complexion: perhaps a shade darker. They are an active, intelligent, shrewd, warlike-looking race of men, but there is a sinister expression, mixed with a peculiar severity, pervading their countenances, that leaves anything but a favourable impression of the benevolence of their dispositions. Vindictive and cruel natures would infallibly be imputed to them by the physiognomist, and experience has shown that this would prove a just estimate of their general character. The Chiefs of this tribe are fond of mechanical employments, and with rude instruments most ingeniously work up iron and silver into a variety of forms for arms, ornaments, and pipes. With a little European instruction they would probably become skilful workmen in this art. Their wearing apparel consists of a simple dhoti or sheet folded round

[1] The account of silver-work is taken word for word from Wilcox's *Memoir* (1832).

the waist and falling below the knee; this, with a dyed blue cotton jacket extending below the waist and well fitted to the body, gives them a smart, tidy appearance. Their long hair is bound up in a high knot on the crown of the head, and sometimes a white cotton cloth is used as a turban. The principal food of the Khamtees consists of rice and vegetables; but meat, when procurable, is never refused. They also enjoy spirituous liquors; and their creed, Boodhism, seems to have imbued them with few prejudices debarring them from the unrestrained indulgence of their natural inclinations.

4

A VISIT TO THE KHAMPTIS IN 1850

(E. T. Dalton, *Descriptive Ethnology of Bengal*, 1872, pp. 7 f.)

In 1850 a large colony of fresh settlers from Bor-Khamti—between three and four hundred individuals—under a Chief, a scion of one of their best families, migrated to Assam in a body. He was a young man of remarkably good address and unusually fair and good-looking. He had two wives, one a pure Khamti, the other half Asamese, both good-looking girls. They settled a few miles above the old outpost of Saikwah on the left bank of the Brahmaputra not far from the Nao Dihing, and when I first visited them about six months after their arrival, I was surprised to see how rapidly and admirably they had after their own fashion established themselves.

The Chief's first wife had frequently visited me at Dibrughar, and transacted business with me on behalf of her husband and his people, for which she showed great aptitude. As I entered the village I saw her at the head of the women returning from their farm labour; each woman bore an axe and a faggot of wood, but that borne by the Chief's wife was a tiny little ornamented implement, and her faggot a miniature bundle of little sticks neatly cut and tied together, evidently emblematic rather than useful. She received me smilingly, and leading the way to her house did the honours with grace and dignity.

I was lodged in a part of the newly raised priests' quarters, and in the evening was entertained by a very creditable display of fireworks and fire balloons, all of their own making.

5

THE HISTORY OF THE KHAMPTIS

(E. T. Dalton, *Descriptive Ethnology of Bengal*, 1872, pp. 5 f.)

THE Shan or Tai or Thai race have exercised a powerful influence over the fortunes of Asam. The Siamese are now the most important branch of this family. They are called by the Burmese Shangyai, or eldest branch of the Shans; but there was once a great nation of this people occupying a tract known to the historians of Manipur as the kingdom of Pong, which touched Tipperah, Yunan and Siam, and of which the city called Mogong by the Burmese, and Mongmarong by the Shans, was the capital.

In the reign of Sukempha, the thirteenth sovereign of the empire of Pong (who succeeded his father A.D. 777), his brother Samlonpha, who was the general of his forces, having subjugated Cachar, Tipperah and Manipur, pushed across the hills to the valley of the Brahmaputra, and commenced there a series of conquests by which these Shans gradually reduced the whole country, from Sadiya to Kamrup, to subjection. It is probable that this was effected by several inroads extending over several centuries, as the Asám annals give the year, corresponding with A.D. 1228, as that of the commencement of the reign of Chukupha, who is said to have been the first to assume for himself and people the name Ahom, the 'peerless', and to have given this name, now softened to Asam, to the country. His successor Chatamla in A.D. 1554 adopted the Hindu religion and changed his name to Jaiyadhaja Singh, and from his time the Asam Kings always took Hindu names and favoured Brahmins, and the Ahom Shans, adopting the language and customs as well as the religion of the conquered people, grew to be regarded as a new division or caste of the Hindu Asamese population, rather than as intruders of an alien race.

The kingdom of Pong was finally broken up by the Burmese King Alompra about the middle of the last century, and on its dismemberment other branches of the Shan race migrated to and settled in Asam.

The Phakis or Phakials on the Dihing river, the Kamjangs of Sadiya, and the numerous settlements of Khamtis are all colonies of this race, retaining the costume, customs and religion they brought with them into the valley. It will be sufficient to describe the latter, who are the most numerous and important.

Whatever may have been the original seat of this people, they emigrated to Asam, within the last hundred years, from the country known to us as Bor-Khamti near the sources of the Irrawaddy, which was visited by Wilcox in 1826, and according to their own annals they had occupied that country for many centuries. Captain Wilcox found them a divided people. Two great clans had been at feud for fifty years, and it was partly owing to these dissensions that horde after horde continued to flow into Asam.

Their first settlements in the valley were, by permission of the Asam Rajahs, on the river called the Tenga-pani, but during the civil wars in Rajah Gaurinath Singh's time (A.D. 1780 to 1790) they pushed on to Sadiya, ousted the Asam Governor of the Province, called the 'Sadiya Kowa Gohain', and gave that title to their leader; and the people of the country acquiescing in the arrangement, the Asam Government was too weak to disturb it. The Khamti Chief was acknowledged by the Asam, and subsequently by the British Government, as Sadiya Kowa Gohain. But in A.D. 1839 the Khamtis rebelled against the latter Government, and, having been expelled from Sadiya in consequence, they for some years lived the life of the hunted, scattered on the frontier, but were eventually allowed to settle somewhere in the vicinage of their old villages.

The Khamtis are not a handsome race. They are of rather darker complexion than the other Shans, and of coarser feature; the Mongolian peculiarities being more strongly developed in them than in their reputed brethren. It may be on this account that Mr Klaproth supposes them to be of Tartar origin; but, as observed by Wilcox, if it be so, the period of their migration to the Shan provinces must be very remote, since all traces of their original language have been lost. He (Captain Wilcox) nevertheless found them in Bor-Khamti as an isolated people, a very extensive district inhabited by Singpho tribes intervening between them and the other place where the Shan language is spoken. Moreover, the country they occupied was not peopled solely by Khamtis, but also by Muluks, Khalongs, Kumongs and others, cognates of the Singpho, and the mass of the labouring population were Khapoks, whose dialect is closely allied to the Singpho. These lower tribes were apparently the remains of the earlier population who had been subjugated by the Khamtis.

After settling in Asam the Khamti Chiefs frequently took to themselves Asamese wives, and in some families the effect of this mingling is very marked in softening and improving the features of the generations that follow it.

6

RELIGION AND CULTURE OF THE KHAMPTIS

(E. T. Dalton, *Descriptive Ethnology of Bengal*, 1872, pp. 6 ff.)

THE Khamtis are very far in advance of all the north-eastern frontier tribes in knowledge, arts, and civilization. They are Buddhists and have regular establishments of priests well versed in the recondite mysteries of their religion, and a large proportion of the laity can read and write in their own language.

The houses built by the leading Khamtis in Asam are precisely similar to those that Wilcox saw in Bor-Khamti. For the residence of a Chief and his family two large houses are built, framed of strong timber with raised floors and thatched roofs, contiguous to each other, a trough of wood being fixed under the junction of the two roofs to carry off the water. As each roof covers a breadth of 18 to 20 feet, and is 80 or 100 feet in length, great space for the family and retainers is thus obtained. The interior is divided into chambers, private and for reception, and the whole terminates in a railed open balcony, a prolongation of the raised floor beyond the eaves affording a convenient airy place for the family to sit and work or lounge in. The roof of the houses comes down so low that externally there is no appearance of wall. The people of the common order have similar houses, but single instead of double.

The temple and priests' quarters are also of timber and thatched, but the temples are elaborately carved, and great neatness and taste are evinced in the arrangement of the internal fittings. The priests have shaven heads and amber-coloured garments and rosaries. The office is not hereditary; any person may enter upon it after the necessary novitiate and instruction in the *bapuchang*, as the priests' quarters are called, but they must, so long as they wear the sacerdotal habit, renounce the world and devote themselves to a life of celibacy.

Every morning the priests move quickly through the villages preceded by a boy with a little bell, each holding a lacquered box in which he receives the offerings of the people, generally presented by the women, who stand waiting at the door with a portion of their ready cooked food.

The priests in their hours of relaxation amuse themselves by carving in wood, bone or ivory, at which they are very expert. In making ivory handles of weapons they evince great skill, taste, and fecundity of invention, carving in high relief twisted snakes, dragons, and other monsters with a creditable unity and gracefulness of design.

It is customary for the Chiefs also to employ themselves in useful and ornamental arts. They work in gold, silver, and iron, forge their own weapons and make their wives' jewels. They also manufacture embossed shields of buffalo or rhinoceros hide, gilding and lacquering them with skill and taste.

The women are skilled in embroidery; they make elaborately worked bags for their husbands and for sale, embroidered bands for the hair and other pretty things, and are not the less capable of bearing a very severe share of the outdoor farm work.

The Khamtis have two great religious festivals in the year—one to celebrate the birth, the other to mourn the death, of Gautama. At these ceremonies boys dressed up as girls go through posture dances, for which, I believe, Burmese women are celebrated, and at the anniversary of the saint's death the postures are supposed to be expressive of frantic grief; but as a more distinct commemoration of the birth, a lively representation of an accouchement is acted. One of the boy-girls is put to bed and waited on by the others. Presently something like infantile cries are heard, and from beneath the dress of the invalid a young puppy dog is produced squeaking, and carried away and bathed, and treated as a new-born babe.

It will be seen by what I have stated above that Khamtis are not restricted to one wife. I do not, however, recollect having met with more than two to one husband, and though the second wife may be the favourite companion of her lord, the supremacy of the first wife is always maintained. The Shan tribes have no idea of a *purdah*, i.e. of secluding their females; they all go to market and pay visits in a very independent manner, and the Khamti women have not suffered in character from the freedom allowed to them. The ladies of the Ahom families in Asam are equally unrestricted; indeed, till the occupation of the country by aliens of our introduction, the seclusion of even well-born Hindu maidens was not enforced, and to the present day, I believe, the ladies of the ex-royal family are in the habit of visiting the officials when they have an opportunity of doing so.

The dress of the Khamti is simple and neat: the men commonly wear tight-fitting jackets of cotton cloth, dyed blue, a white muslin turban so twisted as to leave exposed the topknot into which their long hair is twisted, projecting somewhat over the forehead. The nether garment is of coloured cotton of a chequered pattern or of silk, more or less ample according to the rank of the wearer. The upper classes wear the Burmese *patso*, a piece of parti-coloured silk.

They are seldom seen without the useful weapon the *dao* hanging in its sheath, plain or ornamented according to the condition of the wearer, by a sling made of split rattan. It is worn somewhat in front, so that the hilt is readily grasped in the right hand; this and the defensive round shield of buffalo hide are sufficient for a Khamti to take the field with, but many of them now carry muskets or fowling-pieces.

When they rebelled in 1839, their combinations for attacks were well planned, but they lacked the courage to carry them out. They are, however, wonderfully useful auxiliaries in mountain warfare, capable of enduring great fatigue, of subsisting on any kind of food, and full of resources. They will start on an expedition, each man carrying his own provisions for ten days and all necessaries. These generally include a small cooking vessel; but a Khamti can cook his rice in a fresh-cut joint of a bamboo. If it be a dash at a particular point, and they are to return by the same road, they lighten their burden by making a cache of food for one day at each halting place. If they come to an unfordable river, they construct rafts in a very short space of time, solely of bamboo. They will navigate rock-broken rivers on these rafts, skilfully shooting the rapids, and often thus pleasantly breaking a journey.

The costume of the women is like that of the men, plain but neat. They wear their hair drawn up from the back and sides in one massive roll, which rises four or five inches, so much in front as to form a continuation of the frontal bone. This gives an appearance of height to figures that require an artificial addition. The roll is encircled by an embroidered band, the fringed and tasselled ends of which hang down behind; the lower garment, generally of dark-coloured cotton cloth, is folded over the breasts under the arms, and reaches to the feet. This style of wearing the principal garment, common to the Shans and Manipuris, appears to have been introduced into Asam by the former, as the Asamese women of the lower classes have all adopted it; but the Khamti women wear in addition a coloured silk scarf round the waist, and a long-sleeved jacket. The chief ornaments are cylindrically shaped pieces of bright amber inserted in the lobes of the ears, and coral and other bead necklaces.

The burial ground of the Khamtis is generally a tidily kept spot apart from the village. The graves are surmounted by conically-shaped tumuli which, when first constructed (to the best of my recollection) diminish from the base to the apex in a series of steps, the earth being kept in position by bamboo matting round each step. The Ahoms, notwithstanding their conversion to the Hindu faith, retained this method of sepulture to a recent date. The tumuli constructed over the graves of the Asam (Ahom) sovereigns are very extensive, and when opened the remains of the dead have been found in coffins of massive timber with gold and silver ornaments, and outside the coffin various utensils, arms, and implements of agriculture.

7

INVETERATE TRADERS

(T. T. Cooper, *New Routes for Commerce: The Mishmee Hills*, 1873, pp. 149 f.)

THE Khamtees are inveterate traders, and to their industry Northern Assam is much indebted for the best rice and vegetables, especially potatoes. Although the Chief is lord of the soil, the whole community till it on the co-operative system, the Chief having his portion allotted to him; after which the produce is equally divided between each house, according to the number of hands in it who have helped in the cultivation. As slavery is an institution among them, well-to-do Khamtees never labour. Besides the common land, small plots are also cultivated by individuals. Free-born people also possess numerous herds of tame buffaloes and oxen used for tilling the ground, and also as a means of barter with the Mishmees.

All the grain produced by a village is kept in public storehouses always built on the river bank so as to be near water in case of fire; and the Chief's man of business, or tax-collector, attends at one of these houses at daybreak every morning to serve out the paddy to every house, a member from which attends to receive the daily supply, and the produce of all grain sent to market from these stores is accounted for by the Chief, who distributes it *pro rata* among the different houses.

As a rule, all the freemen are hunters, very few of them doing manual labour, and in this they are very expert, both on land and water, handling a boat among the rapids in an unrivalled manner. They are also the soldier guardians of the clan, as well as the merchants who trade with the Assamese, and other tribes, while the older men, who are beyond leading such an active life, assist the Chief as counsellors of the community. In physique, the Khamtees are superior to any of their neighbours, and conspicuous for their light complexions. Their national characteristic seems to be an exceeding restlessness. Where unchecked, predatory habits are the delight of the warriors, and the murderous readiness to use their knives makes them much dreaded, while their mode of warfare, which consists of early morning surprises, with fire and sword, has caused them to gain a deserved name for treachery.

8

THE HOUSE OF THE VIRGINS

(T. T. Cooper, *New Routes for Commerce: The Mishmee Hills*, 1873, pp. 147 f.)

SOME of the social laws (of the Khamtees) are very curious. At either end of the village there is a large house set apart for a singular purpose. At the age of puberty all the girls are sent from the house of their parents to one of these buildings called the *House of the Virgins*, and reserved entirely for the dwelling-place of unmarried women. From the time that the young girl enters this place she never sleeps anywhere else until married. Rising at daylight in the morning, she repairs to the house of her parents, spends the day there assisting in the household duties, and returns to her sleeping-place with other unmarried females at sundown. As with the girls so with the boys. They occupy the house at the opposite end of the village, and every youth, though he spends the day in the house of his father, at night must return to the bachelors' sleeping-place.

The 'Virgins' House' is sacred, and no man is supposed to enter there; indeed, the vigilance of the old maids who have outlived the age of romance prevents any proceeding which might be termed scandalous, and the morality of a Khamtee village is a pleasing contemplation.

9

KHAMPTI RELIGION

(T. T. Cooper, *New Routes for Commerce: The Mishmee Hills*, 1873, pp. 145 f.)

THE great stronghold of the Khamtees is in the neighbourhood of the Irrawaddy, in the extreme north of Burmah, the Khamtees of Assam being emigrants from the country under the leadership of Chowsam's father. In religion they affect to be strict followers of Burmese Bhuddism, but, excepting among the priests, their religion is little more than polytheism under a thin veil of Bhuddist pantheism, the beauty of Gautama's teaching being utterly unknown amongst them, while many of their customs are altogether opposed to Bhuddism. They kill and eat all animals, and use the flesh and milk of cows and buffaloes without scruple. Their priests are men of great importance, and their influence is greater even than that of the Chiefs. No undertaking is commenced without first consulting them, and by pretended divinations they select and announce an auspicious day. They are also the schoolmasters, every free-born Khamtee youth being compelled to attend school in the temples, where he learns to read and write his own language, and often Burmese, using the Burmese written characters for both languages. These priests receive their office from Bhuddistic institutions in Burmah, and are, without exception, strictly orthodox among themselves, although they seem to indulge the whims of the Khamtees in many religious forms and ceremonies foreign to Bhuddism. I was very much surprised to find no trace of monotheism among this people. To all appearance they seem to have been converted by followers of Bhudda from polytheism direct to pantheism, and in this present a striking example of the strength of Bhuddism when preached to polytheists.

The Khamtees are divided into innumerable clans, each clan having its own village and Chief, or Gohain, and curiously enough each clan is recognized by the pattern of the waist-cloths worn by the men. The villages vary in size according to the strength of the clan. . . . The houses are all built on bamboo piles as in Burmah, and entered by a ladder.

10

AN INTERVIEW WITH A KHAMPTI RAJA

(J. Errol Gray, *Diary of a journey to the Bor Khamti Country, 1892–3*, 1893, pp. 25 ff. and 66 ff.)

18*th January*.—Today I had an audience of the Langnu Rajah. He has only been recently raised to this position: the former Rajah died last year, and the present man is his nephew. About midday couriers came to our camp, which was on a piece of grassland close to the bank of the Namlang and some three hundred yards to the north-west of the village, to announce that the Rajah was ready to receive us. We entered the village which is surrounded by a double palisade through a narrow gate. The palisade was from 12 to 14 feet high made of split trees roughly hewn to the shape of planks and interlaced with bamboo plinths, it did not appear very strong but doubtless answers the purpose for which it is erected to stave off a sudden rush of an enemy in the dark. From the entrance of the gateway to the Rajah's house there was a continuous one-plank bridge raised about a foot above the ground, this was to avoid soiling the feet in the mud dirt caused by the numerous pigs and cattle, which roam about the inside of the stockade enclosure. I noticed the houses were large commodious structures built on piles 4 to 5 feet above the level of the ground, and far superior to the buildings I had seen on the Assam frontier in the villages of either Khamtis or Singphos. The Rajah's house did not differ materially from the others surrounding it, except that it was larger and more solid looking and was raised on higher piles. The approach to the audience chamber was up a very massive flight of stairs made of squared logs; the chamber itself was a room some 35 to 40 feet wide and 45 to 50 feet in length with a half dome-shaped roof; it had two large fire-places, in both of which fires were burning. Opposite the door by which we had entered and on the other side of the room there was an enclosed space in which was situated the Rajah's throne. The entrance to this enclosure was by a narrow gate on either side of which were stands containing guns, spears, swords, shields, helmets, and other warlike paraphernalia. The throne was merely a raised dais covered over with a rug on which was embroidered the design of a tiger. A stool had been placed close to the fire-place in front of the throne enclosure, and it was expected that I would sit on it, but as I had brought one of my camp-chairs with me I preferred to use it instead of the stool. The room was crowded with men, women and children to such an extent that in the entrance of our party the strain on the floor was so great that one of the supporting beams gave a loud crack, and the floor there sank down a foot. This temporarily scattered the crowd, and we found a passage to the fire-place in front of the throne gate.

All this time a large Burmese gong situated at one end of the room was sounding with monotonous regularity. As soon as I had taken my seat the gong ceased beating and Chownoi Chowsai, the Rajah's brother, coming in from a door leading from the interior of the house, seated himself on a large round stool on the opposite side of the fire-place. He was dressed in a Chinese coat of black silk very full in the sleeves and a kilt of red silk reaching a little below the knee. In his mouth was a long pipe at least three feet in length, the bowl of which was made of some metal alloy I could not recognize, the stem of the root of the *maichu* bamboo and the mouth-piece of silver. He was quickly followed by the Rajah himself dressed in a very similar fashion, his Chinese coat being of a blue colour instead of black and his kilt a silk tartan. His pipe was somewhat longer even than his brother's. He immediately entered the enclosure and seated himself cross-legs on the dais. I opened the conversation (speaking through my interpreter) by saying I had come by the orders of the Maharani to visit the Khamti country and make the acquaintance of the Rajahs; afterwards I was to try and make my way to the Chinese frontier, and I would be very pleased if they could assist me in getting there. The Rajah answered in a speech which lasted over ten minutes, its purport was as follows. 'They had heard rumours of the approach of the English up the Irrawaddy valley, also of the expedition into Hukong, and it was said that a force was coming into Khamti from Assam this cold weather. These various rumours had somewhat disconcerted them, not knowing to what extent they were true, and the sudden arrival of our party yesterday had not tended to allay their feelings of anxiety, for though we professed to come on a peaceable errand they had no guarantee that we were not the advance guard of a larger party to follow us in a few days. He saw many Khamtis of the Lunkieng caste in my party; now the Lunkiengs were enemies of the Lukkuns and it was possible that the former had deeper designs in accompanying me than I had given out. When Woodthorpe and Macgregor visited them seven or eight years ago, though only staying four days in the valley, they had sent word of their coming some time previous to their arrival, but I had given no notice whatever, and this had somewhat excited their suspicion.' To this I replied that I had come straight out from England and had no time to give them intimation: that Woodthorpe had slowly worked his way up from

Assam, surveying, and consequently had plenty of time and opportunity to communicate with them. I had no other design than that of seeing the country and people and all I required was the friendship of the Khamti Rajahs and their permission to pass through their territories. The Langnu Rajah replied saying: 'In this part of the world friendships could not be formed by mere words, it was customary in contracting such bonds to give a more practical proof of sincerity in the shape of gifts. If I was earnest in gaining their goodwill I must be prepared to "recognize" not only the Chiefs but the people, for without the consent of the people the Rajahs themselves could do nothing to help me.' I said I had come prepared to 'recognize' both Chiefs and people and would be pleased to know what form of present would be preferred. The Rajah said this was a wild country, and they had dangerous neighbours in the Singphos, therefore no present would be so acceptable as guns. I answered: 'I was sorry I had not brought any large number of these: two I had given away at Khomang, one I had presented to Chownoi Chowsai yesterday, and the few I had left were needed for my own protection. If they insisted upon having guns they must wait until my return to Assam, when I would have no further use for those I was now retaining and could then part with them.' The Rajah said he was afraid of accepting promises, as a very similar promise had been made to his brother by Woodthorpe (in 1885), but had not been fulfilled. I inquired the particulars and was told that Woodthorpe's emissaries, whether with or without his authority, had promised each of the Khamti Rajahs a present of a gun and Rs 100 in cash; that only three Rajahs had received anything, two of them only getting guns; the third, the Langtao Rajah, merely receiving a few trifles such as a pair of boots, a telescope, and a cloth or two; in no case was the money present received. However in spite of this disappointment when Woodthorpe's party was returning to Assam, the then Langnu Rajah hearing that the Namyak Singphos were preparing to attack him, sent Chownoi Chowsai with an armed party to escort him past the dangerous part of the path. In return for this escort Woodthorpe had given his brother a letter saying that whenever he came down to Assam by presenting this letter before the authorities he would receive a double-barrelled gun as a present. On their way back after having safely seen Woodthorpe's party across the Phangmai they met a large party of

Singphos who were going in pursuit of Woodthorpe, but Chownoi Chowsai dissuaded them from going on any further by saying that Woodthorpe was three days' journey ahead, and that he had been met by a large force from the Assam side which was of course false information and told in the interests of the Englishmen who might otherwise have lost their lives. Subsequently his brother had visited Assam and presented Woodthorpe's letter to the Deputy Commissioner at Dibrugarh who told him that he knew nothing about it and to apply to Woodthorpe himself, but as this gentleman had left Assam, his brother had to come back empty-handed and was greatly shamed. This made them chary of accepting promises, and if I had no guns to give, a cash present would be taken instead. I said I was willing to give this, and if some responsible person was sent to my camp in the evening I would make over the sum I intended to give. I then opened the question of the Singpho country, and asked if it was possible to get through to the Chinese frontier. The Rajah answered, it was a very difficult undertaking and in his opinion impossible, as the Khakus were a very wild lot. The Khamtis themselves were afraid of them, and few of them had been more than four days' journey into their hills. They were very numerous, each village had its own headman and was independent of any other, and all would demand tribute. He had heard the Sirkar was very wealthy, and if I had come prepared to spend large sums, it was just possible that I might succeed in getting where I wanted. But then again if it was known that I was in possession of much money, among such a lawless people as the Khakus, he did not see how I was to escape being robbed. There was a powerful Khaku *Ahu* or Chief living four days' journey south of this, his name was Alang Chowtong: it would be absolutely necessary to obtain this man's consent before attempting to enter his country. He advised me to send this man a substantial present, and ask permission to visit him. Beyond Alang Chowtong were numerous other powerful Chiefs, who would also have to be conciliated, but it was imperative that this man should be made friendly to begin with. The Khakus were divided into numerous clans, and the further east you went the more the language changed, until on the east of the Phungmai (eastern branch Irrawaddy), the language was quite distinct and so were the people. In his estimation it would be a very difficult task to reach the Chinese frontier. The Khakus were in a disturbed state at present owing to Chinese emissaries going amongst them, instigating them to combine and fight the English on the Burma frontier. An emissary had only just left Lukkun Rajah's court; he had come to ask the Khamtis to join the Singphos in fighting the English, he had also told them that China had declared war against the English. The Khamtis did not know if he was speaking the truth, and told him they were few in number and their help one way or the other would make no difference against a powerful people like the 'English'. This finished the audience and we returned to camp. In the evening Chownoi Chowsai came over and I gave into his hands the presents I had promised the Rajah earlier in the day.

Before leaving Putou I called upon the Lukkun Rajah with a view of saying 'farewell', and also to thank him for his hospitality to us during the period of our stay at Putou. He was less reserved on this occasion than at any former period I had conversed with him. He is an extremely large-minded man, totally devoid of petty prejudices; his piety is without question and not only makes him slow to take offence, but merciful when offended. He said he was very pleased at my visit, and did not mind telling me that he had formed a great friendship for me. It could not have been a mere matter of chance that had brought me across so many thousand miles of land and water to thus enter into friendly relations with him: we must have met in a former life (Lukkun is a Buddhist) and have been intimate then. This was the only explanation for our meeting now as also for the great pleasure he derived from it. Friends in one existence would be friends in another; though it was not necessary that both should have the same form, for one might be a wild animal, a tiger for instance, and the other a human being (in reference to the transmigration of souls), and if in a previous existence, both of these being then human in shape, had been on friendly terms, they would still remain so. If this were not so how could be accounted for those cases where human beings coming in contact with wild animals had in some instances been killed, and in others left quite unmolested? Lukkun then went on to say that he was an old man now, and in the natural course of things it could not be long before he passed away. He now spent most of his time in religious duties, and in this connexion there were three things he would like to accomplish before he closed his eyes for ever. The first was to build a temple on the Noichenam hill, and plaster it entirely with gold leaf: the second was to raise a pillar in front of the large temple at Kongmulung as high as the temple itself and on its summit to place the gold image of a duck (the Buddhist god in one of his existences is said to have assumed the shape of this bird); the third was to connect Putou with Langtao by a raised road throughout, so far only about two miles having been done. When he had accomplished these three tasks he would be ready to go into his grave. His coffin he had already prepared: he was seated on it now. 'This is it,' he said, tapping with the fingers of his right hand the oblong box on which he was seated, an elaborately ornamented affair, some six feet long and two feet high, studded with small coins, coloured beads and diamond-shaped mirrors, and profusely gilt. He then had brought out for my inspection several small images of Buddha, one cut out of a solid piece of amber the work of his own hands, and another of glass which he had had made to his order in Calcutta a few years ago. He had sent to Calcutta again last December for a similar image but of larger size: he wished to get one three feet high, but the glass-workers had told his people that they could not undertake to make one of that size, saying it was impossible to blow glass to such dimensions. He now asked me if this was a fact, but I was obliged to confess my ignorance on the subject of glass blowing, telling him that though I had often seen glass worked I had never inquired as to the limit to which it could be blown, but that I thought the difficulty could be overcome by moulding. Returning to the subject of my visit, Lukkun said a party of Khamti traders had a few days ago returned from Assam and they had brought a message from Ningro Samon of Borua-pothar to the effect that I was not a representative of the Government but was travelling on my own responsibility, and that it was not necessary to assist me in any way. He did not know why Ningro had sent this message, but he was inclined to think that Ningro was an evil disposed person, as his (Lukkun's) son when on a visit to Assam last year stayed with Ningro for some days, and had brought back very unfavourable reports of him. However he was not to be influenced by what Ningro said, as the letter I had given him from the Burma Government amply proved that I was travelling with the authority of that Government. He would always welcome my countrymen whenever they chose to pay this country a visit. The journey from Assam was a difficult one and not likely to tempt many travellers: the Khamtis had a saying that a man was an old man who had journeyed to Assam three years consecutively, because of the difficult nature of the path and the privations endured en route. The Singphos were also always ready to levy blackmail on traders and others who passed through their villages, or to rob them. This was their greatest complaint in connexion with the Chaukang route. There were two other routes into Assam, via the Phungan pass, and the Mishmi path, but they were so difficult and only open for a few months in the year, and then at unseasonable periods, that as trade routes they were practically useless. With reference to the Chaukang route he wished me to speak a word or two to the authorities in Assam to ask them to interfere in some way so as to prevent traders en route being blackmailed or robbed by the Singphos on the Dehing. I said it was a very difficult matter for us to interfere so far beyond our frontier, but that I would represent it to the authorities. As it was now getting late and our people had been waiting some time to make a start, I rose and took my leave, Lukkun's pony being ready saddled and waiting for me at the stockade gate.

11

HOW TO SMOKE OPIUM

(J. Errol Gray, *Diary of a journey to the Bor Khamti Country, 1892–3*, 1893, p. 40 f.)

EVERY Khamti village has a large extent of poppy cultivation, generally in its immediate vicinity; these fields are carefully and strongly fenced in, as cattle, more especially buffalo, are passionately fond of the plant, and if once they succeed in entering a field it is almost impossible to keep them out afterwards. The poppy is in flower now and the fields look very pretty with their purple, white, and yellow colours. Only a small proportion of the Khamtis are abstainers from this drug. The way they extract it from the plant is as follows: about the latter end or middle of February, according to the season, the capsules, of which there are three or four to a plant, begin to ripen: a small incision is now made with a sharp knife in each capsule, and the sap oozing out is carefully wiped off on a piece of clean cloth; only a single incision is made in each capsule in one day, the following day the plant is given a rest; the third day another incision is made in the capsule and the sap wiped up as before, and this process is continued every alternate day until the capsule is exhausted. The cloth used to wipe up the sap becomes impregnated with it, and is carefully set aside in long strips about three inches wide until required. When required a small piece is cut off this strip and steeped in tepid water which extracts all the drug contained in it; this water being drunk has an intoxicating effect. When wanted for smoking, the water is boiled away until a viscid residue remains: this is mixed with or rather absorbed by very finely cut young plantain leaves that have been dried to crispness at the fire, and the mess is made up into little pellets which are put into the pipe one at a time, and being set alight the smoke inhaled into the lungs and expelled through the nostrils. This smoke invariably passes through water before it is inhaled, on the principle of the Indian hubble-bubble. It requires a greater amount of the drug to intoxicate when smoked than when taken in the liquid form.

12

THE LEGENDARY ORIGIN OF THE KHAMPTIS

(C. R. Macgregor, *Military Report on the Kampti-Singpho Countries*, 1887, p. 69)

In the beginning all was water. Phra (God) placed some earth on a fish's back, and ordered a female to give birth to an egg. God cut the egg in two equal portions, placing one portion on the earth. He, by means of a hill which he constructed, ascended and fixed the other half of the egg above, and this upper part formed the sky.

In the beginning there was a tree. From the berry of this tree grew a flower, and out of this flower came a pair of human beings, a male and a female.

The Rajas are said to have had their origin in the egg which Phra ordered to be produced, and which was the origin of the world.

13

AN ENORMOUS BIRD

(J. Errol Gray, *Diary of a journey to the Bor Khamti Country 1892–3*, 1893, p. 54 f.)

In the evening I went to see a large rock at the mouth of the Nam Yun which was said to have imprinted on it the mark of a child's foot, also that of a bird's claw. This stone was so large that we had to make a rough ladder before we could climb on to it. There were certainly some marks on the stone, but it required a good effort of imagination to find the likeness to either claw or foot. The legend says that in olden days an enormous bird used to haunt this part of the country, preying on children; and that on one occasion it perched on this stone to devour a child it had seized, when the marks alluded to were left. The legend goes on to say that this bird at last grew so rapacious that the whole country took up arms against it, but the more it was hunted the more wary it got, and whenever it seized a child would go off with it to a high hill in the Nam Yun valley called Noi Kham (the golden hill) on which grew an enormous tree whose branches were of silver and gold and which was held sacred by the Khamtis, and there perched on the topmost branches it would devour its prey in safety. No other trees in the country were strong enough to bear the weight of this bird on their branches, so a general consultation being held it was determined to sacrifice the sacred golden tree and cut it down, when the bird finding no resting place would either quit the country–or perching on some stone or rock would afford an opportunity to destroy it. So the tree was cut down and things turned out just as had been calculated: the bird in vain tried to rest on the branches of other trees; they all gave way under its weight: at last in desperation it perched on a huge slab of rock at the mouth of the Sada stream (we had passed this yesterday) where it was killed by four slaves who pierced it through and through with their arrows. The tree of gold disappeared after it was cut down in a small lake which had formed around it. This lake is now overgrown with weeds, and in the cold season when the water dries up these weeds are said annually to take fire by spontaneous combustion. This is the tale as it was told to me by one of our Khamti guides. Khamti means 'place of gold'.

14

THE TREE OF IRON

(J. F. Needham, *Outline Grammar of the Khamti Language*, 1894)

THE Khamtis residing within British territory (chiefly up the Tenga-pani) on our north-east frontier are a small, well-behaved, and industrious community, numbering about 2,000 souls.

They call themselves Tai, and their forefathers came to Assam over 100 years ago from the country known to us as Bor or great Khamti, a valley of considerable extent lying high up the Irrawaddy, in latitude 27° and 28° north eastward of Sadiya.

The Bor Khamtis likewise call themselves Tai, and they are supposed to number about 20,000. They speak of their country as Mung Khamti, 'country of the Khamtis', and two derivations of the word Khamti have been given me: (1) It means 'tied to the spot', from *kham* to stick, adhere to, remain where placed, &c., and *ti*, spot, place. The Bor Khamtis, having numerous slaves who, it is alleged, would bolt *en masse* if an opportunity offered itself, are afraid to move about; (2) Khamti means 'golden locality', from *kham*, gold and *ti* spot, place.

A legend exists that a tree of iron grew in their country which yielded golden fruit; that their enemies fearing they, the Bor Khamtis, would become inordinately rich by means of this tree sent a demon to devour them; that this demon took up his abode in the said gold-yielding tree and as he threatened to annihilate them they were compelled, in self-defence to fell the tree in order to kill him, it being too high to admit of their doing so in any other way. The legend says the tree was felled by fire and the demon was then destroyed.

Chapter XIII

THE SINGPHOS

1

HISTORICAL PRELUDE

(A. Mackenzie, *History*, 1884, pp. 61 ff.)

Of the Singphos we possess an admirable account from the pen of Colonel Hannay, whose knowledge of the North-Eastern Frontier and of Burma was singularly extensive. In giving a general summary of the origin of this people, I cannot do better than follow him, turning to the records for their later history. He considers the Singphos to be identical in race with the Kakus or Kakhyens of Burma, whose chief habitat was on the great eastern branch of the Irrawaddy. They extended nearly as far south as N. lat. 25, while touching on the north and east the borders of China in lat. 27 30. With the break-up of the Northern Shan kingdom, the Kakhyens entered on a career of aggression and conquest, which practically placed in their hands the whole country lying between Upper Assam and Bhamo.

Such is the account of the origin of this people put forward by the best critics; but the Singphos of Assam will by no means allow themselves to be classed as Kakus or Kakhyens, though they do in fact call their eastern and southern brethren by that name, and maintain the same family titles and divisions of clans as prevail among the more remote tribes.The following are the designations of the principal clans: (1) Tesan, (2) Mirip, (3) Lophae, (4) Lutong, and (5) Mayrung. Each clan has a Kaku and a Singpho branch. Besides these there is a clan of Lattora Kakus called Lessoo, on the east of Assam, who originally came direct from the Chinese frontier.

The different members and branches of Singpho clans and families are thus distinguished: *Gam* is the affix indicating the elder branch or member of a family; *Noung*, the second; *La*, the third; *Thu*, the fourth; *Tung*, the fifth, &c. We have thus Beesa Gam, the head of that clan; Ningroo La, the third branch of the Ningroo family; and so on. In Assam (with the exception of the Pisi Gam-Kudjoo, and Jagoon, who appear to be distinct families, and Tang

Jang Tung of the Mayrung clan), the whole of the resident Singphos are of the Tesan division. They are subdivided into three clans, called Tenghai, Mayho, and Nimbrong.

The first appearance of the Singphos in Assam was during the troubles following on the Moamariah rebellion in the reign of Gourinath Sing. They drove out the Khamptis from the lowlands under the Patkoi hills, and settled themselves on the Tengapani east of Sadiya, and on the Upper Booree Dehing, in the tract called Namrup. At first they were welcomed as deliverers by the Assamese peasantry, and, under their Chief Gakhen Thu, restored order to the country devastated by the Moamariahs. But when the Burmese invaded the province in 1817, an era of plunder and misrule supervened, and every petty Chief, who could get together a following, pillaged the Assamese on his own account. Thousands of Assamese cultivators were carried off as slaves; and the whole of East Assam was wellnigh depopulated.

There are no full and authentic accounts of this troublous period in the later history of Assam, and if this is true even of the lower and more civilized portions of the province, it cannot be expected that there should be found in the records of Government any information of value regarding the remote and savage frontier of Sadiya. The first notice of the Singphos as yet brought to light in our records dates only from 1825, when it would appear that a fresh incursion of the tribe from beyond the Patkoi drew the attention of the British Government to the fact of their existence. The Burmese had but lately been expelled from Assam. The Khamptis were still in charge of Sadiya. The Government had not made up its mind as to its future policy in Assam. It was unwilling to undertake the defence of a tract so remote as Sadiya. It shrank from interfering with tribes so uncouth as those of the Patkoi and sub-Himalayan ranges.

At this crisis the Singpho bands, numbering in all about 7,500 men—as frontier rumour reckoned them—shut up the Sadiya Khawa Gohain within his stockades, and attacked the Bor Senapati in his own territory. The Khamptis called in the Abors to their aid, and both Khamptis and Moamariahs sent praying for British assistance, recognizing thereby the position of Government at that time as arbiter of the destinies of Assam. Assistance was given for defensive purposes only, strict injunctions being laid down that no advance was to be made into the country undeniably held by the

Singphos, and that no offensive operations should be attempted against that tribe.

The Singphos seem early to have conceived a respect for the British arms. Very shortly after the issue of the orders above described, they made advances to our local officers, and negotiations were entered upon with the view of inducing them to surrender their Assamese captives, and refrain from plundering the Sadiya villages. Inquiries were also instituted as to whether they would undertake to hold the passes of the Patkoi against the Burmese. The character of their tribal organization, not perhaps at that time fully understood, rendered the ultimate success of any such negotiations very uncertain. They were not ordinarily, or save for combined aggression, a united tribe, but an aggregation of independent petty cantons each under its own Chief, and each jealous of the other, and quite ready to attack its neighbour, if need were or interest prompted. Hence it was almost impossible to deal with them as a whole, though it was by no means difficult to attach temporarily to our interests any individual Chief who thought he saw some advantage to be gained therefrom. They seem to have had serious fears lest the British should proceed to expel them as they had driven out the Burmese. Considerable tracts of land had been occupied by them and were cultivated by slave labour. These they were anxious to retain. They also hoped, it was found, that by being on good terms with the British they would be protected from the Burmese—an expectation which, when known, rendered somewhat futile the proposal that they should themselves shield Assam from the incursions of that power. The main difficulty, however, which lay in the way of a permanent understanding with the Singphos was the uncompromising attitude taken up by Government with regard to the retention by them of captives and plunder.

Early in 1825 the four chief cantons under Luttora Gam, Lattao Gam, Beesa Gam, and Duffa Gam, made definite advances, and were assured of the quiet possession of their lands if they would only restore their Assamese slaves and give up their Assamese booty. We had good reason at this time to encourage their overtures, for the Burmese were expected daily to show themselves on the Patkoi, and early news of their advance could come to us only through the Singphos. No pains were, however, taken to protect them from the invaders, and accordingly they with prudent alacrity made over their stockades to the Burmese forces, when these did appear, and professed to their new allies the most perfect contempt for the far-away English at Sadiya, though they sent at the same time messages to us expressive of their anxiety to be rid of the Burmese. In June Captain Neufville advanced up the Noa Dehing, and by a series of gallant assaults expelled the Burmese from the villages of the Beesa and Duffa Gams, and eventually from the plains altogether. The Singpho Chiefs, doubtful of our intentions, having been unable to resist the temptation of taking an active share in the fighting, and unfortunately for them on the wrong side, fled to the hills. Their villages were therefore destroyed, and 3,000 Assamese captives restored to freedom. Captain Neufville after this set himself to pacify the whole low country round Sadiya. But first he summoned the Bor Senapati, the Khamptis, and the Miris, to aid him in making a progress through the other Singpho villages, in order to release all the Assamese slaves that yet remained there. He was only partially successful. The Singphos of that day did no manual labour, and as their very subsistence depended on their slaves, they made (even the most friendly of them) strenuous exertions to conceal these useful chattels. His operations resulted, however, in the surrender of the Beesa Gam and other Chiefs (September 1825). The Beesa Gam was permitted to move the site of his village from the pass on the Noa Dehing, hitherto occupied by him, to a more accessible place near Borhath, on the Booree Dehing.

In June 1826 Mr Scott, the Governor-General's Agent, visited Sadiya, when sixteen out of twenty-eight Singpho Chiefs entered into engagements with the British Government, agreeing to give up captives and assist the British troops in case of future need, and promising to refer disputes to the arbitrament of the local officers. Hostages were given for the due fulfilment of these engagements.

Altogether Captain Neufville had released 6,000 captives. The loss of this wealth was severely felt by the Singphos, and to give them some equivalent, Mr Scott proposed to create a trade between Assam and the Upper Irrawaddy, which should pass through their hands. It was settled that the Beesa Gam should have a general control over the rest of the tribe who had submitted, and that the twelve Chiefs who still held out should be warned that if they did not come in within two months they would not be allowed to settle in Assam. It does not appear that the idea of opening up a trade across the

Patkoi ever came to anything, or indeed that any active steps were ever taken to develop it. Mr Scott's hands were full, and his letters everywhere teem with large ideas and proposals that he could never himself have hoped to carry out, but which testify to the genius of the man, and have lain many of them in obscurity from that day to this. Four years later, in 1830, an attempt was indeed made to create a trade at Sadiya itself, by the opening of a Government depot, and a Mr Bruce was appointed to the charge of it on a salary of Rs 100 monthly with a share in the profits. The idea was a good one, and, if properly developed, might have had a very marked effect upon our relations with savage tribes all round the frontier. How long the experiment was persevered in it is impossible to say. Like many other points of interest in the older records, it drops out of sight.

The refugee Singphos were in no hurry to come in and respond to our overtures. Perhaps the policy adopted of treating the Beesa Gam as paramount Chief of the tribe tended of itself to keep away the Duffa Gam, his lifelong rival, who took advantage of the disturbed state of the frontier to carry on a continued series of raids out of Burma on the Beesa Gam and his dependent villages. The Duffa Gam indeed seems to have had his hand against every man, for we read of his siding with the Shans against the Burmese, a confederacy which the British officer at Sadiya was at one time invited to join.

In February 1830 the Agent reported the prevalence of rumours that the Khamptis and Singphos would unite with their brethren beyond the frontier to expel us from Sadiya. Nor were the rumours without some basis; for before the month was out, the Beesa Gam reported that large bodies of Singphos and Khamptis had crossed the Booree Dehing and invaded the plains. They made the village of Luttora Gam on the Tengapani their headquarters, and presently set out on rafts down that river for Sadiya. Captain Neufville attacked and dispersed them, and afterwards drove them out of Luttora back to the Bor Khampti Hills. Rumours were current that the invaders had been called in by the Sadiya Khawa Gohain; but Captain Neufville attached no importance to this, holding that such treachery was opposed to that Chief's interests—an argument by no means in itself conclusive, looking to the history of this frontier. Be that as it may, certain members of his family who rendered very efficient aid were rewarded by grants of land, and his own conduct was highly spoken of in the dispatches. The Beesa Gam had throughout these operations shown himself loyal to his engagements.

In 1831 rumours were again afloat that a large Burmese force was about to invade Assam, and every arrangement was made for repelling such an attack, even to calling on Gumbhir Sing, the Raja of Manipur, to hold his levy in readiness to march across the hills.

Notwithstanding all that had been done, we still hear of Assamese slaves among the Singphos in 1833. Some of these were runaways from Burma, and many were released by the exertions of our Native officials at Sadiya. In July 1834, a European officer was posted at Sadiya permanently; and the chances of any Singpho Chief retaining his slaves became smaller than ever.

There was indeed work and anxiety enough at this outpost for a permanent officer of exceptional qualifications. The Duffa Gam by his restless intrigues and constant raids or feints of attack was a standing trouble to us and all the frontier. In 1835 he made a sudden foray from across the Patkoi, and cut up Beesa's village, killing some ninety persons, including women and children. Later in the year, he again appeared, built stockades as though he meant to stay for months, and drew to his side most of the Gams who had been made subordinate to the Beesa Gam in 1829. A party of troops, however, drove him over the hills again, and all the Chiefs save the Luttora Gam returned to their allegiance. We had to treat such defections and resubmissions as things very much of course. It would have been useless resenting them too violently. We gave our subject Chiefs no adequate aid or protection, and could not blame them overmuch for saving themselves from outrage by temporary submission to an invader.

In February 1837, the Luttora Gam, who next to Duffa was the most powerful of the contumacious Chiefs, submitted.

The Government, anxious for a settlement, about this time addressed the Court of Ava, urging it to restrain its subjects (for such the Duffa Gam now claimed to be) from such attacks. After some trouble the British Resident succeeded in getting leave for Captain Hannay to accompany the Burmese Governor of Mogoung to that quarter, there to see what could be done. The Duffa Gam, thus beset as it were behind and before, placed himself in the hands of the Burmese, and it became a question whether we should claim him from them as a recusant British subject, and if we got him, what to do with him. It was determined ultimately to leave him in their hands. The Duffa Gam returned with the Burmese to Ava, where he was received with honours, which gave great umbrage to the Governor-General in Council, who ordered the Resident in Burma to report upon the facts.

The result showed that our representative at Ava had acted weakly at the outset in not pressing on the Burmese Government the correct view of matters, and the Government of India contented itself with urging the dispatch of a second Burmese deputation to the frontier, with a view to making a final settlement of Singpho affairs. To this the Ava Government at last consented.

Mr Bayfield accompanied this embassy, with the Duffa Gam in attendance. It was arranged that an officer from Assam should cross the Patkoi to meet them. Major White, Captain Hannay, and Dr Griffith accordingly proceeded from Sadiya for this purpose. Want of provisions compelled Major White to fall back, but the other two went on and met Mr Bayfield on the Patkoi. While Major White was moving down from the Patkoi, he came across a band of Nigrang Singphos from Burma, who were attacking certain Naga tribes living on the north face of the Patkoi. As all north of this range was British territory, he compelled the Singphos to give up their captives and make peace. After Major White left, the Burmese Governor appeared and advanced a most insolent claim to the whole of Upper Assam as far as Jeypore. Captain Hannay and Mr Bayfield of course treated this demand with ridicule, upon which the Burmese officials set off on their return to Burma.

It would seem that nothing was settled about the Duffa Gam, for, shortly after the termination of this fruitless embassy, it was reported that that Chief was about to make fresh attempts on Assam. A military post on the Booree Dehing was established in consequence, and orders were given to prevent his entering the province on any pretext whatever.

Early in 1838 the Assam Singphos began to quarrel among themselves, the Peeshee Gam attacking the villages of the Lat Gam. The troops went out to restore order, and were opposed by the Peeshee and Luttora Gams, who now again made common cause against us. It was evident to all the local officers that the Singphos were in a most disturbed and discontented state, and that further trouble would yet be given by this tribe. In 1839 we had indeed both Singphos and Khamptis on our hands, and risings of both tribes had to be put down by military force. In suppressing the Khampti rising, a strong body of troops passed through the Singpho country. This had a good effect, for it led apparently to the submission of Ningroola, a Chief of influence, hitherto attached to Duffa Gam. This man was now induced to undertake the cultivation of tea near his villages, where the plant was indigenous. Although his village had been burnt by the troops before his submission, he seemed honestly anxious to behave loyally for the future, and among other proofs of his good faith he revealed the existence of a store of brass cannon of Hindustani make, that had been buried in the jungle in the days of the Mogul invasion of Assam, and never before discovered by the Authorities, though long known to the tribes.

An attempt was made at this time to bring all the Singpho settlements within reach of surveillance, by insisting on their being transferred within the line of our stockades from Ningroo to Chykoa. No information is given as to how far the attempt succeeded; but for a year or two we find very little notice of the Singphos in the records.

In the cold weather of 1841–2, Captain Vetch visited the Singpho and Naga frontier, and found everything quiet; so quiet, that Government transferred the management of the tract from the Political Department to the Revenue and Judicial Departments of the Bengal Government. The slave difficulty had not, however, entirely died out, for it would appear that the local officers had again referred it to Government, which now ordered a neutral course to be observed. The slaves were not to be assisted to run away, but no force was to be used to bring them back if they escaped.

Peace did not last long. On 10th January 1843, a party of Singphos from Burma attacked our outpost at Ningroo in large numbers and killed seven men. A simultaneous and successful attack on the guard at Beesa was reported, and Saikwah was threatened by a large body of combined Khamptis and Singphos. The movement was evidently concerted and extensive. The Tippum Raja from Hookoom was said to be in it, and both the Beesa Gam and Ningroola were suspected of having been accomplices at least. This latter fact was a great surprise and disappointment. All the Singphos on the Noa and Booree Dehing joined in the revolt. No time was lost in marching troops against them. Ningroola surrendered at the outset, and the Beesa Gam soon after. They protested their innocence, and offered to serve against the Burmese Singphos who were under Seroola Sain and the Lat Gam. The remaining Singphos and Nagas of Assam quickly returned to their allegiance, and gave vigorous assistance against the foreign invaders. The Lat Gam was beaten and surrendered. Stockade after stockade was taken; but still the war dragged on for months, as jungle warfare often does.

The end was however from this date certain, and Government appointed a Commission (Colonel Lloyd and Mr Stainforth) to inquire into the causes of the revolt. Both these gentlemen were prevented by delicate health from undertaking such an arduous duty in a bad climate, and the inquiry was eventually entrusted to Captain Jenkins, the Governor-General's Agent on the spot. That officer declared the causes of the rebellion to be three, viz.: (1) encroachments on the lands and privileges of the Singphos; (2) the seizure and punishment by local officers of some members of their tribes; (3) the orders of the Tippum Raja, now Chief of the Hookoom province under Burma. The Governor-General in Council in reviewing the report set aside the last two grounds, as it was certain the orders of Tippum, if ever given, would have had no effect unless they had fallen on willing ears; and as to the second point it was shown that no Singphos had been punished save under the terms of their engagements, and in accordance with established usage. The real cause Government sought in the first point noticed. Although the Singpho agreements made with Mr Scott are personal rather than local, yet it was clear they were meant to apply within certain limits, that is, within the ordinary habitat of the tribe. Unfortunately no such limits were ever regularly defined, and of late the extension of tea cultivation had made this omission of serious consequence. Just eight days before the insurrection broke out, the Deputy Commissioner had submitted a sketch, in which three lines were drawn from a common point at the mouth of the Noa Dehing diverging south. The most westerly was the limit of the Singpho tribes in Scott's time; further east was the limit of their cultivation now; while still further east from the Noa Dehing Mukh to Ningroo was the line to which Captain Vetch in future proposed to limit them. This showed clearly, the Government thought, how the action of the local officers was gradually pushing back these tribes from territories which they once had occupied. (The Beesa Gam had, in 1842, complained bitterly of the loss of lands. The factory of a Mr Bonynge, which had been a prominent object of attack in the late rebellion, actually stood on forfeited Singpho territory.) Add to this the accumulated grievances arising from our forcible release of their original slaves, and our continued care to prevent their acquiring others, and sufficient causes for rebellion seemed to be established, the Singphos being what they were. On these views of Government, the Agent was invited to submit further report. It was proposed to have a line laid down as in Scott's time, on which no encroachment was to be allowed save under definite and fresh concessions. The right of taxing to Government dues Assamese voluntarily resident among the Singphos, which had never been enforced, was to be definitely given up. A new convention was to be made. But all captured rebels were to be brought to trial. The Beesa Gam was found guilty of rebellion, and imprisoned at Debrooghur for life.

The Agent in his final report contended that the main cause of the Singpho insurrection was the loss of their slaves. The Beesa Gam was the Chief who had suffered most by this. He had also been irritated by our communicating with the other Chiefs direct, and not through him; though his own intrigues had rendered this necessary. He had appointed one Seeroo-la-sen to be his successor, and this man was irritated by the imprisonment of a cousin of his for selling an Assamese; so he joined and led the insurrection. A son-in-law of the Beesa's, Jugundoo, had been imprisoned for cattle stealing. He also rebelled. The Lat Gam, a Kaku, was another dependant of Beesa's, and he was afraid of punishment from us for putting slaves to death for witchcraft. In this way the action taken by the Beesa Gam and his family was held to be explained. The rebellion of Ningroola and his sons was less easily accounted for. Probably loss of slaves and temporary irritation caused it. Ruffandoo joined the rebels, because he was not allowed to raid on the Nagas. All the other Chiefs who took part in the outbreak were from Burma. Captain Jenkins was now certain that the loss of lands had nothing to say to it. No lands had ever been granted to the Singphos, or recognized as theirs, or been claimed by any of them till lately, when the Beesa, instigated by Tippum Raja, set up such a notion. The Agent in conclusion held that the loss of their slaves would soon compel the Singphos to settle down and engage personally in cultivation as many of them had already done, and then he said, we could assign them definite lands and limits. Meantime that matter might be left alone. There were possible other minor grievances that had helped to irritate the Singphos, such as demands for forced labour to build stockades for our troops, but, on the whole, the Agent believed that in the slavery question lay the secret of this abortive rebellion.

Government accepted this report, though it is hardly, perhaps, satisfactory upon some points. To educate the Singphos into civilization a school was ordered to be opened at Saikwah. Ningroola and his son were pardoned and released. On the question of slavery the Government was fully committed, and no retrograde policy could be entertained. Nothing was to be done to encourage the Singphos to believe that slavery would ever be winked at. With these orders the memory of the Singpho insurrection was allowed to die away.

The Singphos have of late years given absolutely no trouble. They are indeed of great use to us in restraining and keeping in order the Naga tribes of the Patkoi.

2

THE MOST POWERFUL TRIBE OF SINGPHOS

(W. Robinson, *Descriptive Account of Asam*, 1841, pp. 373 ff.)

THE Singphos are by far the most powerful tribe bordering on the valley. They are also the most numerous, and are scattered over the greatest extent of country. On the north, they are bounded by that branch of the Brahmaputra known as the Lohit; on the east, by the Langtang range, which separates them from the Bor-Khamtis; on the south by the Patkoi range, which divides them from the Burmese Singphos, from whom they derive their descent; and on the west, by an imaginary line drawn south from Sadiya till it meets the last mentioned mountains.

The Singphos have for several generations been the terror of the Asamese. They were in the constant habit of making eruptions into the plains, in conjunction with the Moamarias or Muttuks, by whom they appear to have been first called into Asam. They sometimes proceeded as far as the very capital itself, plundering the temples, laying waste the country, and carrying off the inhabitants into slavery. These several eruptions have won for them the lowlands they now occupy. Since the British troops have had possession of the valley, these inroads have been prevented; but, impatient of such restraint, these wild people have nevertheless occasionally endeavoured to resort to their old habits. The peace of the neighbourhood has constantly been disturbed by deadly feuds amongst themselves. Their principal quarrels have arisen from a feud between the Beesa Gam, on the one side, and the Duffa Gam, now of some political notoriety, on the other. This feud has been the cause of dividing almost all the Singphos on the frontier; and even those Singpho tribes bordering on China have been involved in the hostilities to which this feud has given rise.

Latterly, however, feeling the necessity of submitting to a power which has so nearly approached them, and whose strength they now perceive they cannot resist, they have shewn an inclination to abandon their old habits of lawlessness and rapine, and to turn attention to agriculture, now become necessary for their subsistence. The altered habits of this rude but energetic race may confidently be expected not only to shed its influence on their own commercial resources, but likewise to extend great advantages to the future prospects of Asam. The emigration that may be expected from the misrule now prevailing in the Shyan states of Ava; the opening prospects of abundant comfort to themselves, arising from the protection of a powerful government in Asam; and the means of wealth held out to them, from the fortunate discovery, and the increasing cultivation, of that singular and highly valuable plant, which Providence has been pleased to bestow in such luxuriance on this province, are but a few of the many advantages that may be looked for, from the gradual amelioration of these people.

The Singphos bordering on Asam are said to be divided into twelve principal tribes or clans, designated after the names of their respective Chiefs, or Gams. Every Chieftain maintains his own separate independence, and seldom unites with any other, unless it be to punish some aspiring Chief obnoxious to them all, or to make plundering excursions upon some neighbouring states. The principal clans are the Beesa Gam, Duffa Gam, Luttao Gam, and Luttora Gam; though these can exercise no powerful authority over the other Gams, their influence is acknowledged to be very considerable.

Rude as is the state of society among the Singphos, they are not without a few aristocratical distinctions. The people in general are divided into four classes, called respectively, Shangai, Myung, Lubrung, and Mirip.

The language of the Singphos possesses many words in common with the Abor, the Burmese, and the Manipuri dialects. The intonations are similar to the Burmese, and its grammatical construction is almost precisely the same. It is peculiar for its combination of consonants, many of which would at first sight appear quite unpronounceable to a European. It doubtless belongs to the monosyllabic stock of languages.

The Singphos have no religion properly their own; but have patched up a creed from amongst the superstitions of all their neighbours, and decorated their rude temples with ruder idols of all religions.

It is the custom of the country to bury the dead. Those of the poorer classes are interred soon after death; but the Chiefs and principal individuals are sometimes not buried for years. The reason alleged for this consummation of the funeral rites is, to allow the widely scattered relations of the deceased to have time to attend, who would not fail to take deadly offence at being deprived of an opportunity of paying reverence to the ashes of the head of their family. Not knowing the art of embalming, the body after death is removed to a distance from any habitation, till decomposition is completed; after that, it is deposited in a coffin, and conveyed to the house of a deceased Chief, where it lies in state, surrounded with all the insignia the illustrious individual enjoyed when alive. When all the relatives have assembled, or communicated their not being able to attend, the coffin is committed to the earth, and a mound of clay, surrounded with a curious trellis-work of bamboos, is raised to his memory.[1] If the person has died a violent death, a buffalo is sacrificed as a propitiation to their deities, and the head

[1] 'A Singpho grave is a raised mound surrounded by a circular trench: the size of the mound denoting the rank of the deceased: children and babies have very small mounds.'—Gray, *Diary*, p. 23. See also the extract on p. 421.

of the animal is fixed to two crossed bamboos and placed near the grave; but if he has died in the course of nature, no sacrifice is considered necessary.

Polygamy is admitted by the laws of the country, and every man keeps as many wives as he chooses, free women or slaves; and treats the offspring of both kinds without partiality.

According to the law of inheritance, the patrimony is divided between the eldest and the youngest son; while any children that may intervene, are left to push their own fortunes as they best can. The eldest son succeeds to the title and estate, while the youngest, carrying away all the personal and movable property, goes in quest of a settlement for himself.

3

SINGPHO RELIGION

(J. B. Neufville, *On the Geography and Population of Assam*, 1828)

THE religion of the Sinh-phos appears to be a strange mixture of all the various idolatries and superstitions of the nations with whom they have intercourse, and to have no fixed principles common to the whole tribe. The ostensible worship is that of Gautma, whose temples and priests are found in all their principal villages, and have evidently, as also by their own account, been borrowed from the Shams and Khamtis. They are also in the habit of deifying any Sinh-phos whom they may chance to kill in action, during a fray with some other tribe or village, and of sacrificing to them as their penates; and in every case of emergency, such as famine, pestilence, or danger, they make offerings to the Megh Deota, god of the elements, of clouds and stones, (called also Nigschis), sacrificing buffaloes, hogs, and cocks. The skulls of buffaloes so offered up are, afterwards, hung up in their houses, in memorial of their piety.

Polygamy, without restriction, is followed by the Sinh-phos, and they make no distinction between the children born to them of Assamese or foreign mothers, and those of the pure Sinh-phos. They reject, with horror, the idea of infanticide, under any shape or pretext.

The custom observed in their funerals varies according to the quality of the deceased, and the manner of his death. Those of the lower classes being buried almost immediately, while the Chiefs are generally kept in state for two or more years, the body being removed to some distance during the progress of decomposition, after which it is placed in a coffin, and again restored to the house, where it remains surrounded by the insignia of rank used during life. The body of the Gaum of Gakhind was found by us in this state, on taking possession of the stockade in June last, and had lain there more than two years.

The reason assigned by them for this custom is, to avoid the danger of drawing on them feuds with the more remote branches of the family, spread in different directions, who would consider it a deadly insult, were the corpse to be interred without due intimation being given, and they thus delay performing the final rites until replies shall have been received from every member entitled to that compliment. At the proper time, the corpse is interred, and a monument of earth, confined by bamboo matting, of a peculiar form, erected over it.

If the deceased met his fate by any violent means, they also sacrifice a buffalo, the head of which they fasten as a memorial in the centre of a large cross of wood of the Saint Andrew's form but, if on the contrary, the case is one of natural death, they omit this ceremony, saying, that the gods have voluntarily taken him to themselves.[1]

4

THE SINGPHOS IN 1847

(J. Butler, *A Sketch of Assam*, 1847, pp. 80 ff.)

THE Shan is the written character used by the Singphoos, and their language is distinct from any of the neighbouring tribes: they write

[1] Captain J. B. Neufville's work on the geography and population of Assam was first published in *Asiatic Researches*, Vol. XVI (1828). It was reprinted in *Selections from the Records of the Bengal Government*, No. XIII (1855). Neufville defeated the Burmese who, aided by Singpho insurgents, reached the Noa Dihing in 1825, gaining a decisive victory over a much larger force at Bisa. The Singphos at this time caused much trouble by slave-raids and Neufville made a number of expeditions among them and finally brought about a measure of peace.

on leaves and a peculiar kind of paper. As yet no European has sufficiently studied the language to appreciate justly the Singphoo literature, or to prepare elementary works for the guidance of others. Nor are we aware of there being any written works in the language, either historical or theological. As civil members of society they are anything but good subjects, from their excessive laziness, immoderate addiction to opium, and general uncertainty of character. They are so indolent and improvident, that notwithstanding they have the most fertile soil in Assam, which yields fruit with little labour, and might be made to produce an abundant crop—notwithstanding, too, their freedom from taxation, grain is always so extravagantly dear, that during several months in the year the people are reduced to subsist on yams and other roots found in the jungles. Almost the whole of the field work is performed by the women and slaves, while the men delight in lounging about the villages, and basking in the sun, when not engaged in hunting or war.

The religion of the Singphoos appears to be a mixture of all the various idolatries and superstitions of the natives with whom they have intercourse. They seem to have no fixed principles common to the whole tribe. Their ostensible worship is that of Gautma, whose temples and priests are to be found in all their principal villages. They are also in the habit of deifying any Singphoos who may chance to be killed in action during a foray upon some other tribe or village, and of sacrificing to them as to their penates. On emergencies, such as famine, pestilence, or danger, they make offerings to the 'Ning Deota', God of the Elements, called also 'Ningschees'; sacrificing buffaloes, hogs, and cocks. The skulls of the buffaloes so offered are afterwards hung up in their houses as mementos of their own piety.[1]

Their funeral ceremonies are simple. The poorer classes burn or bury the body, according to the previously expressed wish of the deceased, and invariably make to the deity an offering of a pig, fowl, or fish, through their Deodhies or priests. On the death of a Chief, numerous ceremonies are performed: the body is detained until all the friends of the deceased can be assembled, when buffaloes,

[1] This paragraph is a good example of the way the early writers borrowed from their predecessors. It is taken almost word for word from Neufville (as a glance at the extract on p. 398 will show) and without a hint of acknowledgement!

pigs, and deer are sacrificed, a grand feast is given, and spirituous liquor distributed to the company. The corpse is then committed to the earth, the priest chants a prayer for the deceased, a clay tomb is raised over the remains, and the grave is encircled with a bamboo fence. Sacrifices are always offered up on the death of every Singphoo, according to the means of the surviving relatives; no matter whether death be caused by accident or war, or in the course of nature.

Polygamy, without restriction, prevails among the Singphoos, and they make no distinction between the children born of Singphoo women and those born of foreign or Assamese women. They reject with horror the idea of infanticide, under any shape or pretext. Marriage is only forbidden with a mother or sister: they may marry stepmothers, brothers' widows, or any other relative. In the marriage ceremony the bridegroom has to present the parents of the bride with a Khamtee *Dhao*, or short sword, a velvet jacket, a silk *Dhota*, and a slave; the rich give gold and silver, buffaloes, and as many slaves as the wealth of the bridegroom will permit. The bridegroom has also to furnish a marriage feast to the friends and relations of the bride; and after the Deodhies or priests have performed certain religious ceremony, the bride is delivered over to the bridegroom, and the jewels, &c., which are on her person, are returned to her parents.

If a man commits adultery, he is obliged to pay damages according to the demand of the injured husband, in slaves, buffaloes, *dhoties*, swords, money, or beads; and if he cannot pay the damages, he pays the penalty of his crime in confinement. No damages are demanded for the violation of an unmarried woman or virgin; but in the event of her being found pregnant, the ravisher has to give the parents three slaves and one buffalo, and the issue is claimed by the man. It is optional with himself to marry his victim, or not. Theft is punished by exacting from the thief double the value of the property stolen.

The Singphoos entertain strange ideas of honour and revenge. Compatibly with their customs and rude notions of religion, a Singphoo Chief could not ever abandon, without dishonour, the application of the *lex talionis* to one who had murdered his relative; although, from circumstances of policy, or deficiency of means, he might postpone the gratification of his vengeance to an indefinite period. A mistaken feeling of religion, combined with private affection for the deceased, fully accounts for this perverted state of mind. The Singphoos imagine that the soul of the murdered individual will torment them until his manes are appeased by the death of one of his enemies; and further, that the anger of their deity would be roused should an opportunity of retaliation be neglected. Nor is the retribution to be limited to the actual perpetrator of the homicide. If death be occasioned by violence committed, or supposed to be committed by anyone, the relations are never appeased until they have murdered one of the family to which the murderer belonged. An innocent person is thus often murdered, who is quite ignorant of the injury committed by his tribe or family.

The houses of the Singphoos are generally nothing but long sheds, roofed in with grass or bamboo leaves, and the walls composed of split bamboo. The floor of the dwelling part is raised about four feet from the ground; and the entrance forms an extensive porch, in which are congregated pigs, fowls, household and agricultural implements, and where women may generally be seen pounding rice. These buildings are sometimes one hundred feet long, and divided into compartments allotted to several families. Occasionally immense houses may be seen, which are occupied by powerful Chiefs; the timbers of these buildings being of such enormous size and length as to render it a matter of surprise that they could have been erected by mere manual labour. At the burning of the Ningrang Chief's house, when the village was surprised by our troops in 1843, the officers remarked that the posts were of prodigious diameter and length; and it was regretted that war rendered it necessary to destroy such a magnificent residence. The mansion was entered by a flight of several steps leading up to the floor, and was divided into numerous rooms by partitions of split bamboo.

The Singphoos have nothing approaching to what we call government: each Chief is independent, collecting no revenue, nor directing in person any force, although he may influence the movements of others. The Singphoos are of a tawny complexion, and a cunning expression, with long bodies and short legs. They are implacable, cruel, and treacherous, stealing upon and murdering with the short sword at night those who have offended or injured them; and are ever ready to coalesce for a foray, if there is a prospect of success. Casualties that occur from the contentions of one tribe with another, murders resulting from private jealousy, the difficulty of procuring food, and exposure to the inclemency of the weather, help to keep the population scanty all over the north-east frontier. In fact, the great cause of the thinness of the population is the want of food, arising from the absence of productive industry. The unsettled and lawless state of society among the Burmese and Singphoos appears likewise to operate in retarding the extension of trade; and this evil cannot be rectified until these tribes are brought more completely under subjection to the British Government. That once effected, a mart might be formed at our extreme boundary; though the scantiness of the population in these regions would probably for some time prevent the establishment of a very brisk trade.

Hookoom is distant from Suddeah about 200 miles; a miserable, desolate, backward country intervening: in fact, almost an entire jungle throughout. At Moonkoom there would be a larger field for commerce, as water communication by the Irawaddy is facile. Broadcloths, &c., could probably be conveyed thither cheaper, via Rangoon, than from the Burrampooter. The same obstacles exist to opening a trade between Assam and the provinces of Yunan, owing to the greater proximity of Yunan to the Burmese empire. By all accounts a considerable trade is carried on between the two countries, via Bamow: a Burmese town within twenty miles of the confines of Yunan; and from the facility of transport which the Irawaddy affords, we may infer that British goods could be supplied at a cheaper rate, and with greater safety, from Rangoon or from Moulmein through the Sangha, than could be effected from Assam. The poverty of the people on this part of our frontier is such that scarcely anyone can afford to buy woollens, excepting the Chiefs, and even those persons generally receive them as presents from the officers of Government. It would therefore be desirable to send up articles of less value. The articles chiefly in demand are salt, cloths, tobacco, opium, knives, needles, cups and saucers, basons and plates.

In 1828, by way of experiment, and to test the possibility of reviving trade, a Government investment of woollen goods to the amount of 4,000 rupees was sent up to Suddeah; but it actually took eight years before the whole stock was sold off, and it would not then, probably, have been disposed of, had not the price been reduced thirty per cent below prime cost. It was sold during the first and second years of its appearance in the market, at prime cost;

afterwards at a reduction of ten, twenty, and thirty per cent. Since then, a trade, such as it is, has been established at Suddeah by native merchants, at considerable risk; for the Government will not undertake to give compensation for any losses the traders may sustain, either from sudden attacks or in their transactions with these wild tribes. Notwithstanding the apparently hopeless prospect of any immediate commercial intercourse taking place between Assam and any portion of western China, there can be no doubt that as civilization advances, the intervening tracts will be traversed, and a lucrative trade may then connect districts now separated by dense forests.

5

A FINE ATHLETIC RACE

(E. T. Dalton, *Descriptive Ethnology of Bengal*, 1872, pp. 9 ff.)

THE Singphos, like the Khamtis, have settled in Asam within the memory of man. They are said to have first made their appearance in the valley during the rebellion of the Muttuck or Mahamaria sect against the Rajah Gaurinath Singh, about A.D. 1793.

Their first settlements were on the Tenga-pani, east of Sadiya, and on the Bori-Dihing river in the tract called Namrup, and they not only met with no opposition from the scattered and harassed Asamese population of that tract, but were well received as an element of strength to assist the inhabitants to hold their own. By degrees the Singphos formed large villages under their Chiefs, the Dapha, the Bisa, the Latora, and other Gams (the head of a family is so called, the second branch assuming the affix 'La', and the third 'Thu' or 'Du'), and not only maintained themselves in a state almost independent of the Asam government, but absorbed into their own communities the few Asamese left in that part of the country.

The Singphos are of the race called by the Burmese Kr-Khyen or Kaku, whose original settlements were on the great eastern branches of the Irrawaddy river; they are there in contact with the

Kunungs, with whom they are closely allied in language and origin. They extended east to the confines of Yunan, and west to the valley of the Kyendwyen; but it was only on spreading into the valley of Asam that they assumed the name of Singpho, which in their own language means 'man'.

When Upper Asam came under the rule of the British Government, it was not till after several engagements with our troops that the Singpho settlements were brought into some sort of subjection. It was then found that their villages contained great numbers of Asamese slaves, who, whenever they got the opportunity, left their masters no more to return, and the action of the authorities in refusing to restore them and giving them every possible facility of escaping was a constant grievance to the Singphos,—a wound to their pride which more than once rankled into open insurrection. No fewer than 5,000 are reported to have been released by one officer, the late Captain Neufville.

From the intercourse of the Singphos with their Asamese female slaves, a mongrel race has sprung up, well known in Upper Asam under the denomination Duaniahs. They have been found very useful auxiliaries in frontier wars from their knowledge of the Singpho language and tactics, and from their fidelity to the Government that relieved them from the Singpho yoke.

The Singphos on the frontiers of Asam occupy large villages often in somewhat unassailable positions, consisting of sixty or more large houses, each from eighty to a hundred feet long and about twenty in breadth, with raised floors throughout and open balcony at one end, where the ladies of the family sit and spin, weave and embroider. The house is divided into different apartments on both sides of a long passage open from end to end. There are generally several hearths round which the family sleep, and over the fire-place are large bamboo racks hanging from the roof, on which are placed meat or fish requiring to be smoked.

They are generally a fine athletic race, above the ordinary standard in height, and capable of enduring great fatigue; but their energies are greatly impaired by the use of opium and spirits, in which they freely indulge. The men tie the hair in a large knot on the crown of the head, and wear a jacket of coloured cotton and chequered under-garment of the same material or of silk, or the Burmese *patso*. The respectable Chiefs assume the Shan or Burmese style of dress, and occasionally short smart jackets of China velvet, with gilt or amber buttons. They also wrap themselves in plaids of thick cotton much in the fashion of Scotch Highlanders.

The features are of the Mongolian type, very oblique eyes and eyebrows, mouths wide, cheekbones high, and heavy square jawbones. Their complexion, never ruddy, varies from a tawny yellow or olive to a dark brown. Hard labour tells on the personal appearance of the females, rendering them coarse in feature and awkward in gait, but in the families of the Chiefs light complexions and pleasing features are sometimes seen. Their dress consists of one piece of coloured cotton cloth, often in large broad horizontal bands of red and blue, fastened round the waist, a jacket and a scarf. The married women wear their hair, which is abundant, in a large broad knot on the crown of the head, fastened with silver bodkins with chains and tassels. Maidens wear their hair gathered in a roll resting on the back of the neck and similarly secured. They are fond of a particular enamelled bead called *deo-mani*, and all wear as ornaments bright pieces of amber inserted in the holes in the lobe of the ear. The men tattoo their limbs slightly, and all married women are tattooed on both legs from the ankle to the knee in broad parallel bands.

The national weapons of this tribe are the heavy short sword called *Dao* or *Dha*, so well known in Asam, admirably adapted for close quarters in war, and for clearing jungle and preparing the ground in peace,—the frontier tribes can dispense with the trouble of converting their swords into ploughshares, they use them as they are:—a spear with a short shaft used for thrusting, and a strong cross-bow with bamboo arrows: but they affect the use of the musket whenever they can get one, and are sometimes seen with China matchlocks.

They use shields of buffalo hide, four feet long, and helmets sometimes of that material, sometimes of thick plaited rattan-work, varnished black, decorated with boars' tusks, &c.

In warfare their attacks are confined to night surprises, which are speedily abandoned if they meet with steady opposition. They are skilled in fortifying naturally difficult positions, using freely the *panja*, a bamboo stake of different lengths sharpened at both ends and stuck in the ground, with which the sides of the hills and all approaches to their position are rendered difficult and dangerous.

If they use muskets on these occasions, the weapons are generally fixed in loopholes of breastworks, ready loaded, and the trigger is pulled when the enemy reaches the point of the road (previously ascertained) covered by them. If they fail by such means to beat off the attacks at once, they abandon the position for another behind it.

In travelling the Singphos carry a haversac, of very neat appearance, cleverly adapted to the head and shoulders. It is made of very finely plaited fibre on a frame of wood covered with the skin of the large grey monkey. They are also provided with handsome bags, woven and embroidered by their wives, in which they carry their pipes and tobacco, opium, &c.

The Singphos understand the smelting of iron, and their blacksmiths with no implements but a lump of stone as an anvil, and a rude hammer, forge weapons,—especially *daos*,—which are highly prized all over the frontier for their temper and durability.

The Singphos manufacture their own wearing apparel. The thread is dyed previous to being woven, and thus are produced the checks and coloured garments of which they are so fond. They use as dyes a kind of indigo called 'Rom', 'Seing Lung', or 'Asso Khat', and the bright yellow root of a creeper called 'Khai Khiew'.

The Singphos repudiate all affinity with the Shans, and are not considered by ethnologists to be connected with them except very remotely. Their language is entirely different, approximating more to the Karen, Manipuri, Burmese, Kuki, Naga, and Abor dialects, and their religion is rude paganism, whilst the Shans are most of them Buddhists.

The Singphos have a confused notion of a Supreme Being, but they propitiate only malignant spirits called Nhats, of which there are three,—the Mu Nhat or spirit above, the Ga Nhat or spirit below, and the household Nhat or penate. They sacrifice fowls, pigs, and dogs to the Nhats, and when about to proceed on important expeditions a buffalo is offered, and acceptance of the flesh of the animal, when cut up and distributed amongst the friends of the Chief, is considered as a pledge that binds them to his service on this particular occasion. There is no regular priesthood amongst the Singphos, but they pay great deference to the Pungyes or priests of the Buddhist Shans. Some of them are, however, supposed to possess powers of divination, and Colonel Hannay mentions having witnessed the process. The diviner was seated by himself at some distance from the crowd, and had beside him a small fire and a bundle of common *nul* grass, which grows to a large size in swamps. Taking a piece of *nul* containing several joints he held it over the flame, until by the heat one of the joints burst with a sharp report, the fracture on each side threw out a number of minute hairlike fibres which were carefully examined and put aside. Another piece was then put in the fire and similarly treated. This continued for at least an hour, when the result was disclosed, namely, that a certain Chief, whose arrival was awaited, would make his appearance in three or four days, and so it happened.

Polygamy prevails amongst the Singphos, and Chiefs especially rejoice in a plurality of wives. The girl is bought with a price, and a feast completes the ceremony. As a maiden she is allowed considerable liberty. I have been informed by Duaniahs that the girls of some villages occupy a house appropriated to their use in which, under charge of an old woman, they receive visits from young men, but I have never seen such an institution, and if it exists it is not shown to strangers.

According to Bisa, one of the most influential and intelligent of the Singpho Gams that settled in Asam, the Singphos believe 'they were originally created and established on a plateau called Majai-Singra-Bhum, situated at a distance of two months' journey from Sadiya, washed by a river flowing in a southerly direction to the Irrawaddy. During their sojourn there they were immortal and held celestial intercourse with the planets and all heavenly intelligences, following the pure worship of one Supreme Being'. Why they left this Eden is not stated in connexion with this tradition; but they have another, in which the fall is assigned to an act of disobedience on their part in bathing in interdicted water. On descending to the plains they became mortal, and having imbrued their hands in the blood of men and animals in self-defence and for subsistence, they soon adopted the idolatries and superstitions of the nations around them.

In succession to patrimonial property the Singphos have a peculiar custom. The eldest takes the landed estate with the titles, the youngest the personalities, and remains in attendance on the Chief or head of the family as during the lifetime of their father.

6

CATCHING TURTLES

(R. Wilcox, 'Memoir of a Survey of Assam and the neighbouring Countries, executed in 1825–6–7–8', *Asiatic Researches*, Vol. XVII, 1832)

FISH abound in the rapids of the Tenga, and river turtle of a very large size are occasionally found and eaten by the Singfos with great relish. I witnessed the capture of one of these creatures of the largest size; it was seen entering a little creek formed by a fallen tree, and a canoe, manned by three Singfos, was instantly planted across the opening. One of them, watching his opportunity, suddenly leaped on the back of the animal, which had descended to the bottom of the pool, and a knife being handed to him, he dipped his head and arms under water and cut two large notches in its hinder part and made fast to it a green pliant cane, with which it was easily pulled on shore; but cased in a coat of mail and armed with sharp teeth at least half an inch long, the turtle was not yet mastered, and advantage was taken of its attempts at self-defence to secure its mouth by presenting a large bamboo which it constantly snapped at. A man, sitting on it, next bored the paws, which being bound on the back with cane reduced the poor turtle to a helpless condition, and he was put on board the boat.

7

THE SINGPHO USE OF TEA

(W. Robinson, *Descriptive Account of Asam*, 1841, pp. 133 f.)

TEA has hitherto been the favourite beverage of those hill tribes in whose vicinity the wild plant has been found. The Singphos have long known and drunk the tea. The young and tender leaves are first plucked and dried in the sun; by some they are exposed alternately to the night dews, and the heat of the sun for three successive days; whilst by others they are put into flat hot pans and turned about till quite dry. This done the leaves are placed in the hollow of a bamboo, and driven firmly down by means of a stick, the bamboo being at the same time held in the heat of a fire. When full, the ends of the bamboos are tied up with leaves, and then hung up in places where they may be exposed to the smoke of the fire. Thus prepared, the tea is said to keep good for years.

In other places, the natives have a different mode of manufacture. Holes are dug in the earth, the sides of which are lined with large leaves. The tea is then boiled, the decoction thrown away, and the leaves themselves are buried in the earth. This is done with the view of reducing the leaves to a state of fermentation; and when this has been effected, the leaves are put into hollow bamboos, and thus prepared are taken to market. When intended for use, the leaves are boiled and the infusion is drunk.

The Butias are said to be particularly attached to this beverage. Their supplies are, however, imported overland from Pekin. The liquor they drink is extremely unlike what we are used to under the same name. It is a compound of water, flour, butter, salt, and bohea tea, with some other astringent ingredients, all boiled, beat up, and intimately blended together.

From the well-known fact of tea being the favourite drink of those tribes in whose vicinity it has been found, as well as from the immense quantity expended in the adjacent kingdom of Butan, it would appear far from chimerical to anticipate a very successful result from the general culture of the plant in Asam, were it merely with the view of rendering it a staple article of trade with the regions in which it is so extensively consumed, and where from the peculiar mode of preparing it for use, less skill in its culture would be necessary, than in those varieties intended for European markets.

8

TWO FESTIVALS

('Narrative Report of the Naga Hills and Lakhimpur Expedition Survey Party, by R. G. Woodthorpe, R.E.,[1] Assistant Superintondent in charge', in *General Report on the Topographical Survey of India, 1876–7*, 1878, pp. 59 ff.)

THE Singphos and Khamtis have been repeatedly described, so that it would be merely a vain repetition to do so here. I may however mention a few ceremonies which we witnessed, and make a few remarks on the Nagas we came across.

At Wakidgaon in the early part of March we witnessed a religious ceremony, which was also performed generally among the Singphos at the same season. The day previous, at certain spots near the headman's house, large posts were put up in the shapes of St Andrew's Cross, intersected by an upright cross, having as finials, small funnel-shaped baskets containing leaves. In front of these again were tufts of tall grass planted in a rectangle of about 8 feet by 4 feet. Early on the morning of the ceremony, little platters on curved legs containing offerings of cloths, flowers, fruits, &c., were brought out and arranged alongside the tufts. Then a couple of buffaloes were brought and secured strongly to posts hard by, and finally about 10 o'clock, the celebrants took their places on low stools in front of the grass, and with long green wands in their hands, which they moved about from time to time to attract the attention of their deities, they commenced a chant, with the same intonation as used by Catholic priests in reciting long prayers. This chant, the burden of which is an invocation to their gods to visit them, bless them, their families and villages, and keep all sickness or evil from them, they kept up without ceasing till past noon, when a pig was brought out and its head severed with one blow; then a long string of bamboo was taken from the nearest buffalo to the headman's house and into the innermost recess; this was to intimate to the household god that the sacrifice of the

[1] R. G. Woodthorpe, R.E., was described at this time as 'a young Engineer Officer of great talent and energy'. It is said that 'he was most successful in his intercourse with the wild tribes on the Frontier of Assam'.

buffalo was about to take place and to show him the way out to it. After a few more incantations the officiant threw some powdered ashes out of a leafy funnel on to the animal's neck; the beast was then hobbled and thrown, and its neck being out slightly as a guide, a man with a sharp *dao* severed the head with two strokes. The women then filled some bamboos with blood, and walked in procession to the other cross, where a few prayers were said, the bamboos deposited and they returned. The second buffalo was then speared to death, its agonies being prolonged by the endeavour to send the spear always into the same spot exactly, which could only be done when the poor beast came to a standstill after each effort to break loose. The animals were then cut up, and the flesh thrown into huge cauldrons over blazing fires and cooked, as also an immense quantity of rice. When ready to be eaten, large mats were spread near, and fresh plantain leaves laid over them, in which the contents of the cauldrons were deposited and the meat cut up into convenient-sized pieces; these, with a proper proportion of rice, were then made up into little parcels in green leaves and put into baskets, which were then carried round the village for distribution, all our people coming in for their share, or at least such as would take it. The Singphos were evidently rather hurt by the somewhat contemptuous refusal of our Hindus to accept the proffered food, another instance of the difficulties which caste prejudices among his followers throw in the way of a surveyor among these wild tribes. The headman presented us with a couple of bottles of Singpho liquor (exceedingly like Scotch whiskey in taste and appearance) and some of the young buffalo steaks, and exceedingly good they turned out to be, though we had had our doubts about them at first. This distribution of food took place at about 5 p.m. and after then, contrary to our expectations, although a good deal of liquor was drunk, not the slightest disturbances took place; the women came as usual at dusk to sit round our fire and listen to the musical box (for which the ladies always asked at every village we went to) and imbibe small doses of anisette, a liqueur I had bought especially for such purposes, and which they relished very much. When we went to dinner they left, and after that everything was perfectly quiet.

The other festival we saw was the Khamti celebration of the Behu, which took place at Palumpan and Chaosamgaon while we were at these villages. Over a small well dug in the ground boarding was placed, and on this all their marble and gilt idols were ranged, interspersed with brass vases filled with sprays of leaves. In the centre rose a big bamboo about four feet high, pivoted above and below; from this several small bamboo tubes projected upwards from various points, being connected together at their ends and to the centre bamboo by coloured threads. These small tubes were pierced with holes in several places throughout their length. The well with the idols, &c., were all enclosed and covered in by a pretty ornamental lattice-work of fine bamboo, above which stood beautiful miniature temples made out of the brown pith of some grasses, and at the corners of the enclosure rose coloured umbrellas on tall poles and streamers of red and white cloth, thoroughly Burmese in appearance. Water at times was poured, while reciting prayers, into a trough full of leaves, whence it flowed into the centre bamboo above mentioned, and finding its way out through the holes in the small arms, caused the whole to revolve, on the principle of the turbine, rapidly watering all the gods impartially as they sat calmly beneath. People came at intervals throughout the day to fill the trough. The young women went about with *chungas* full of water, emptying them over all who came in their way, irrespective of age, sex or condition, and groups of both sexes were to be seen in the river all day long, engaged in furious splashing matches. The boys made big bamboo squirts, which they used most effectively whenever opportunity offered. All was done with the most perfect good humour, and not a soul lost his or her temper. At night the youths had an entertainment, in which character-dances found a prominent feature.

The Nagas of Honkap and the neighbourhood all seem to be subject to a certain extent to the Singphos. In almost every village of the latter along the Dihing we saw several Nagas who live with the Singphos for a certain period every year, receiving free quarters and food, for which, in return they go into the jungles and cut rubber for their masters, by whom they are allowed to keep one-third of what they collect. They also help the Singphos in various ways, such as cultivation, &c. The Singphos have several fields of opium along the Dihing, but in the Tenga Pani villages we did not see any; there is a field near Chamang. This village is on the Tenga Pani, I believe, but we did not come across it, and I dare say there are others off the line of survey which we did not see. These Honkap and other Nagas do not differ much in their appearance, dress, style of building, &c., from those we have met further west, except that their villages are small, and they themselves a dirty, poverty-stricken looking race, with little of the fine physique or air of independence seen among their western neighbours.

9

SINGPHO RITES AND CEREMONIES

(C. R. Macgregor, *Military Report on the Kampti-Singpho Countries*, 1887, pp. 70 ff.)

A YOUTH should marry his cousin, his mother's niece if possible. Should a cousin not be available, the maternal uncle should arrange for a girl of his *jat*; if one is not available, the uncle goes to another family, and says: 'If you give me a girl for my nephew, I will pay you back in kind when one of your family requires a bride.' The father of the youth then gives a feast and presents to the girl's family. Should the youth's father not be able to give presents, he gives or sells one of his daughters to the other family, in lieu of presents.

When everything is satisfactorily arranged, a cloth (*pukong megala*) is placed on the ground, and also a *gumbang* (a species of reed grass). The girl is placed on the right hand of the cloth, and the mother of the youth on the left hand. A matron of the village who is with the girl turns the cloth over, and takes her to the side of the youth's mother, who takes the girl by the hand into her house, and all night long the neighbours sing and feast in the house. The bride and bridegroom remain present all the time, and the bride prepares food for the guests. The bride generally gives the singers (of whom in each village there are only two or three) a present of three hats of cloth.

Singpho women are generally tattooed on the calf of the leg, eight bars alternately black and white. Ningro Samon (or more properly Sam Nong, the Singpho Chief of Mung Lung) informed me that it cost him Rs 60 to have his last new wife 'Kai' tattooed. As a rule, unmarried girls are not tattooed.

When a person is very ill, no medicine is given; but 'Shom Nat' (the jungle deity) is invoked. The *Tumsawa* of the village is called in, and he generally orders a pig and six fowls to be killed. Half of this food is consumed by the *Tumsawa* and his friends, and the other half, called *natsan* (flesh for spirits), is placed outside on a *machan* for the spirits to eat. Should the patient not get better at once, the *Tumsawa* is again called in, and he consults a leaf of *tara* (wild cardamom, a food elephants are very partial to, called in Singpho *mogui shat*, elephant's food). Having consulted the leaf, the *Tumsawa* usually says, 'Shom Nat is displeased, and won't help: call in another Nat'. If a man is injured in fighting, Palan Nat is the one to be invoked. If it is a case of bleeding, Shama Nat. For a woman in childbed, Chisam Nat. The god of the sky is called Ningshie Nat. Should rain or sunshine be required, Ningshie is invoked. Should the second ghostly physician prove inefficacious, others are invoked until the *Tumsawa* and his friends have collected enough food or the patient dies, whichever happens first; nothing is done for the real cure or relief of the sufferer. On death happening, the person is burnt; the ashes are usually collected and placed in a circular mound, round which the relations periodically hang clothes.

If a woman dies in childbed it is considered a disgrace, and the body is taken into the jungles, burnt, and the ashes not preserved.

When a notable dies, a coffin is made, generally of *poma* wood, and the corpse is placed in it in a lying down position on the back. A little silver or gold is placed over the eyes, the corpse is washed and dressed in good clothes; and when all the relations have seen it, is burnt and the ashes, *wanga* (fire-earth) are collected and placed in a mound.

When a person dies, the spirit goes back to the birthplace of the deceased. A spirit (Deoda) points out the road and conducts the spirit of the dead person to a river, where he bathes it. The spirits of the ancestors then come and take it to their abode. The spirits fly about in the air like birds. They do not eat, drink, marry, or even sing songs. If the funeral obsequies are not properly performed, the spirits are liable to go into the bodies of animals. The spirits of persons who have behaved well on earth remain in the air, or are born again as Rajas. The spirits of those who have behaved badly are born again as insects and animals.

10

A SLAVE FOR FIFTY YEARS

(J. Errol Gray, *Diary of a journey to the Bor Khamti Country, 1892–3*, 1893, p. 4 f.)

As I was sitting this morning surrounded by the usual crowd of men and children who never seem to have anything to do, but to sit and stare at one from sunrise to sunset, I saw an old woman break through the crowd, while she kept repeating in Assamese—'Make way for an old slave woman who has come to see the sahib!' Though dressed in Singpho costume, and wizened with age (she must have been over sixty), her features were unmistakably Assamese, though her accent from long residence among the people whose dress she wore had lost its original purity. When she had found her way through the crowd, she fell down at my feet, which she seized with both hands, and would not be induced to let go all the time we were conversing together. It appears that about fifty years ago, when she was a young child, her village (its name and situation she had forgotten) was raided by Singphos and all her people taken into slavery. They were taken away to the Khaku country beyond the Nam Kiu and there sold: she was sold separately from her relations and did not know what had become of them. In the course of time a Singpho had married her and by him she had two sons. Her husband had subsequently died, and after his decease she had been kept moving from place to place, until finally she settled at Khagam. Although fifty years had elapsed since her captivity she had managed to retain a knowledge of her mother-tongue, though imperfect and broken; nor had long years effaced the bitterness of her bondage, and the remembrance of her former freedom made her burst into tears. She did not wish to be released however: where would she go, and what would she do at her age? I gave her a small present and sent her away. The system of slavery is still largely practised by both Khamtis and Singphos in the Nam Kiu and Hukong valleys, though of course they have to look further afield than Assam for their slaves.

11

MAN'S FIRST DISOBEDIENCE

(J. B. Neufville, *On the Geography and Population of Assam*, 1828)

By the Bisa Gaom, or Chief of the Sinh-pho clan of Bisa:

In the beginning, the Great Gossein (the Supreme Being) created man, and regarded him with especial kindness and favour. He gave him the whole earth to dwell in and enjoy, but forbade him bathing or washing in the river called Ram Sita, under a threatened penalty of being devoured by the Rakhas (Demon) and totally destroyed as the forfeit of his disobedience. That if, on the contrary, he refrained, Rakhas should have no power over him, and he should inherit the earth eternally.

Mankind, however, soon disobeyed the injunction, and the whole race was devoured by Rakhas, with the exception of a man called Siri Jia and his wife Phaksat.

These were seated under a tree, when the Gossein caused a parrot, perched on a bough, to speak, and give them warning to avoid the north and fly to the southward, by which they would escape from Rakhas's hands. The man, Siri Jia, obeyed, but Phaksat took the other road, and fell into the clutches of Rakhas. When Siri Jia saw Phaksat in the power of the Demon, he was divided from them by the river Ram Sita, the forbidden stream, and forgetting, or disregarding the prohibition, he immediately crossed it to her rescue, and was also taken by Rakhas, who prepared to devour them. In the act, however, of lifting them to his mouth, a flame issued from all parts of his body, and consumed him on the spot, since which time no Rakhases have been seen on the earth, in a palpable shape.

The Great Gossein having then fully instructed Siri Jia and Phaksat in all useful knowledge, placed them on the Mujia Singrabhum hill, and from them the present race of men are descended.

By the Satao Gaom, or Chief of the clan Satao of Sinh-phos:

The Sinh-phos came originally from a place situated two months' journey from Satao Gaom, and peopled the earth.

The race of man having killed and roasted buffaloes and pigs, which they devoured, without offering up the prescribed portions in sacrifice to the gods, the Supreme Being, in his anger, sent an universal deluge, which covered the earth, and destroyed the whole race of man, with the exception of two men called Kung-litang and Kuliyang and their wives, whom he warned to take refuge on the top of the Singrabhum hill, which remained above the waters; from them the present race are descended.

A brother and sister belonging to a race superior to man were also saved. The Supreme Being directed them to conceal themselves under a conical mound of earth, taking with them two cocks and nine spikes of bamboo, the latter they were to stick through the sides of the mound, and pull them out one by one daily. They did so for eight days, but the cocks took no notice. On drawing out the ninth, the light appeared through, and the cocks crew, by which they knew that the waters had subsided. They then went out, and as they were in search of fire, they encountered the old woman belonging to the Demon Rakhas, who endeavoured to seize them: they, however, effected their escape to the ninth heaven, where they were deified, and are sacrificed to by the Sinh-phos with cocks and pigs.

The name of the brother is Kai-jan and the sister Giung.

By the Sadiya Khawa Gohein, the Khamti Prince of Sadiya:

The race of men having fallen into every kind of iniquity, the Supreme Being, 'called by us Soari Mittia, but worshipped by all nations under different names', determined on destroying it, and creating it anew. With this view, he gave warning in a vision to four holy Goheins, directing them to take shelter in the heaven. Meru (called by the Khamtis Noi Sao Pha) had then caused seven suns to appear, which burnt up the whole earth, and destroyed everything on it. After which there came violent rains which washed away all the cinders and ashes, and refreshed and refertilized the earth.

The four Goheins then descended, and re-peopled it with a new race.

12

SINGPHO TRADITIONS OF CREATION

(C. R. Macgregor, *Military Report on the Kampti-Singpho Countries*, 1887, p. 69 f.)

In the beginning there were only two people, one an old man Tingla and the other an old woman Gumgai; in the skies dwelt two Nats, male and female, called respectively Mutum and Muta. The two terrestrial beings had a son and a daughter. The son left his home for some reason not known, and went to another place on the earth, and the Nats Mutum and Muta took the girl up to the skies. A Nat who dwelt on the earth, called Unga Du, adopted the son. The girl was brought down from above by the Nats, and was married to the boy. The result of this union was that two sons and two daughters were born, who intermarried, and hence sprung the race of Singphos (men). The word Singpho means a man. The name of the first man was Goiung and the name of the first woman was Gajam.

In the very beginning there was nothing but water, until Mutum and Muta came from the clouds, and taking a handful of earth from under the water caused it to remain at the top of the water.

The following account of the origin of the Singphos was given me by Ningro Samon:

In the beginning there was a great flood, and all the wicked people who dwelt in the plains were drowned. This flood lasted for the eight ages of a man's life. In the ninth age Chirun and Woisin, two Nats, dried up the flood with their hair, which was very thick and long. Modoi, the eldest son of Mutum, kept one family of seven people on top of a high hill, and they were not drowned.

13

A SINGPHO STORY-TELLER

(J. Errol Gray, *Diary of a journey to the Bor Khamti Country, 1892–3*, 1893, p. 72 f.)

Kumku-la and his son came to our camp in the morning and stayed the greater part of the day. I rewarded him for having looked after our stores, which we found intact, and for having built the cane bridge over the Dapha. The old man has a wonderful memory and good conversational powers, though excessively egotistical; he talked on a variety of subjects, but chiefly relative to the former power of the Singphos, and their intertribal feuds. He told me that the Dapha valley was once peopled by Miris, but that a great flood swept away their villages and drowned all the inhabitants. The story as told by Kumku-la is not the unvarnished tale as I have set it down, and it may not be out of place to relate it in full if only for the purpose of showing how fond these people are of ascribing to supernatural agencies any occurrence out of the ordinary. This is the story as Kumku-la told it. Many ages ago the Dapha valley was inhabited by a race of Miris; there were seven villages in all, and were situated on both banks of the stream. At that time there was no open grass plain as at present, but the forest came right up to the edge of the water. One day a party of Miris while out hunting came upon two strange beings seated on a large stone at the junction of the Dapha with the Dehing, these were two water sprites, father and son, who were sunning themselves in the open on the river's brink; but the Miris were not aware of the nature of these beings, and one of their party putting arrow to bow drew string and pierced the elder sprite through the back, killing him instantly. The younger sprite dived into the water and disappeared. The Miris on coming up to the dead body saw that it was not an ordinary being they had killed, and guessing at its supernatural character, alarmed at what they had done, precipitately fled. The younger sprite who had dived into the water did not stay his course until he reached his mother's abode, when he at once related what had occurred to his remaining parent, who forthwith vowed vengeance. This vengeance she eked out by causing a heavy landslip to occur in a deep and narrow gorge in the hills through which the Dapha flowed, completely damming up its waters for several hours: then suddenly breaking through the obstruction the waters leaped and rushed down the valley in one broad wave sweeping away a whole forest in their course and leaving no vestige of the seven Miri villages that had lined the river's banks. At that time was formed the open grass plain on the site of the former forest, and certainly the appearance of the open plain studded with huge rocks and boulders of various sizes favours the idea of a formation such as would result from an excessively strong and swift rush of water down the valley.

14

SINGPHO COFFINS

(W. Griffith, *Journey from Upper Assam towards Hookhoom, Ava and Rangoon,* 1837)

CLOSE to the village are the burying places of two Singfos. These have the usual structure of the cemeteries of the tribe, the graves being covered by a high conical thatched roof. I find from Bayfield that they first dry their dead, preserving them in odd-shaped coffins, until the drying process is completed. They then burn the body, afterwards collecting the ashes, which are finally deposited in the mounds over which the conical sheds are erected. Between the village and the graves I saw one of these coffins, which, if it contained a full-grown man, must have admitted the remains in a mutilated shape; and close to this were the bones of a corpse lately burnt.

15

A TOUR IN THE SINGPHO COUNTRY

(J. Errol Gray, *Diary of a journey to the Bor Khamti Country, 1892-3,* 1893, pp. 5 f. & 9 f.)

I NOTICE that many of the Singpho women have their legs from the knee downwards tattooed in parallel bars; others again are without mark of any kind. On inquiry I find that only women of the better classes are permitted to tattoo: men do not tattoo except very slightly and then only on the arm or shoulder. The dress of the men is a cloth worn like a kilt, and a short jacket; they tie their hair in a knot on the top of the head, round which they wind a short turban. The jackets are of cotton dyed blue, the kilt and turban of the same material but different colour, always in checks. They carry their *dhas* (a short sword two feet long) in a wooden scabbard slung round the neck, the *dha* lying under the left arm, and wear them continually. The women wear a cloth resembling the Assamese *mekela* in shape: it is in one piece and reaches from the breast to a little below the knee. Maidens invariably cover their breasts, but after marriage and the birth of a child or two, they are not so particular, and the cloth is as frequently tied round the waist as over the breasts. These cloths are of a dark blue colour with parallel bars of red at intervals running horizontally. The women wear large pieces of amber in their ears: the men occasionally small ear-rings, more often nothing. I cannot call them a handsome race, though many of the men have fine physique. The women are decidedly plain, and soon age owing to the hard work they do, the bulk of the labour falling on their shoulders, even to the cutting and carrying in of firewood. The Singphos generally are great opium-eaters, and no doubt this habit is tending to the deterioration of the race. They grow their own opium, every village having a certain amount of poppy cultivation.

As a race the Singphos are extremely superstitious, and have numerous *nats*, and spirits whom they are constantly propitiating by sacrifices of various kinds. Every petty ailment is ascribed to the influence of some evil spirit which has to be propitiated before the sick person can recover. Buffaloes, cows, pigs, fowls and even dogs are used in their sacrifices. In spite of all this superstition I found them very eager to get medicine, and as these people have an idea that all white men are born doctors I was besieged with applicants for medicines for diseases of all descriptions, and some of the most trivial character, such as a stomach-ache, a pain in the leg, and so on. In features the Singphos have little of the Mongolian type, and in this respect differ both from the Khamtis and the Burmese, who are their neighbours to the north and south: their language is also entirely distinct; it has no written character and appears to be very easily learnt. It has not the harsh guttural sound of the Khamti, but on the contrary is not unpleasant to the ear, there being much alliteration of dentals and labials. The Singphos deal largely in slaves, the wealthy among them possessing large numbers; but they do not ill-treat them and as far as I could judge, the slaves have no harder time than the other members of the family; they eat together, work together and sleep together, and to an outsider there is nothing to show their social inferiority. The Singpho men have a particularly loud and haughty way of speaking; it is the reverse with the women. Their accents are mild and gentle and their address to strangers extremely civil and agreeable. This difference of expression was very noticeable and I was much struck by it.

16

POLITICAL PRESENTS

(J. Errol Gray, *Diary of a journey to the Bor Khamti Country, 1892–3*, 1893, pp. 16 ff.)

1st January 1893.—The valley in which the two villages of Tingsa and Bamjan are situated, is a very small one; hardly two miles in length and less than a mile and a half in breadth. It is somewhat in the shape of a triangle with the Dehing river for its base. The lower spurs of the hills which surround it to the north, east and west are clad with a species of sun grass, as is also the valley itself, presenting a very pleasant spectacle after the interminable tree forest we had been marching through ever since we left the Dapha valley. The Singphos living here are of the Kunki clan, which is a subclan of the N'kum sang. They came originally from the Khaku country beyond the Nam Kiu. They live a very isolated life, being many days' journey from any other villages, and in case of failure of crops must have a very hard time of it. They are keen hunters, annually killing a number of elephants and rhinoceros; the tusks of the former and horns of the latter they bring down and sell to the Merwari merchants established in the villages of Borua pothar, and Chonkam, the ivory fetching Rs 10 to Rs 13 per seer, the horn as much as Rs 80 to Rs 100 per seer. I had sent on couriers in advance to advise the headmen of my coming, and asking them to collect a few maunds of rice against my arrival, promising to give them presents when I arrived, but it appears the headmen took no action in the matter, waiting to see the nature and amount of their presents before interesting themselves on my behalf. This morning about 11 o'clock I heard a great firing of guns in the direction of the Tingsa village and was informed that this announced the visit of the headmen of the valley. Some 10 or 15 minutes later a long row of men filed out of the jungle track which led from the village to our camp. On approaching to a distance of 100 yards from my tent the headmen, four in number, separated from their followers, and joining hands with measured steps and stooping gait came forward to where I was sitting. They had somehow learnt the Indian salutation 'salaam', and this they all shouted at the top of their voices, but they apparently did not know the method of raising the hand to the forehead and in giving the salute stretched out their right hands, to the fullest length the forefinger stiffened and pointing upwards, the rest of the fingers closed. The action and tone of the salutation gave one the impression that instead of being an act of politeness it was more one of intimidation, and it was with difficulty that I could prevent a smile from stealing over my face. As they finished their salute, eight guns fired in rapid succession, with charges that nearly upset the firers, made the hills echo again, and nearly deafened me by their close proximity. The headmen were dressed in the usual Singpho style, but wore over their everyday dress, a long Chinese coat of black silk, having loose sleeves, which had an inside lining of the same material, but of a light blue colour. After they had seated themselves on a waterproof sheet which I had spread out for them on the ground in front of my seat, I opened the conversation by explaining the reasons for my visit (it is very necessary to do this the first opportunity as these people are extremely suspicious), telling them that I had been sent by the Maharani to make the acquaintance of the Khaku Chiefs beyond the Nam Kiu, and to get their permission to go through their territories to search for the head waters of a large river which flowed down through Burma east of the Irrawaddy, and came from the direction of China whose borders I wanted to reach. (I had already found that it would be fatal to my enterprise to state that I was a private individual and had come on my own responsibility, this making me a legitimate prey to every Singpho village I entered, whereas by giving out that I was specially authorized by the Maharani to visit them, I was treated with more respect.) I then said that to enable me to reach the Khamti country I must ask them to supply me with a few maunds of rice, also some fowls, eggs, and anything else in that line they might have for sale. I was willing to pay their own prices, as I knew they were so situated that in the event of their running out of any article it was a very difficult matter to replace it. I then presented the headman of each village with a seer of opium, and another seer to be divided among the villagers as an inducement for them to come in with supplies. This opium was placed on the ground in front of the headmen, but by the way they turned their heads away in an opposite direction, as if they never saw the opium, I knew they were not satisfied, and were meditating further demands. Presently one of them spoke and said (his speech being translated to me): 'The Sahib says he comes as a representative of the Maharani, well and good: but his gifts to us are small and not such as might be expected from one in his position. We had heard of your coming ten days before you arrived from people who had come from the west to out rubber up the valley, and we were looking forward to your arrival, expecting to benefit from it as we had benefited on a previous occasion when two of your countrymen had come here on a surveying expedition (Woodthorpe and Macgregor in 1884). They gave us guns and clothes and opium, but you only offer us opium. We certainly expect now what we received before, otherwise we cannot help you.' Now one of my Singpho guides (Bishi gam) had accompanied Woodthorpe here in 1884, and had told me that though three guns had been given as presents to Khomang people, it was only for services rendered in guiding their party through the hills, one to the guide who took them to Bor Khamti, another to the man who showed them the path into the Hukong valley, and a third for services in connexion with the survey, and helping to cut a path up to a high hill (Baibum) behind Khomang; the only present given to the headman was a cloth. Accordingly I brought these facts to their notice, telling them I had obtained them personally from Woodthorpe, for it would not have been judicious to have mentioned their true origin, as my informant might have got into trouble for it. I said the amount of my present was equal to the value of two guns, and I was giving it to them without asking for any return in the way of guides, but merely as a gift to get permission to buy food from their people. They then asked me to take back the opium and give them four guns instead. To this I demurred saying, I had only brought four guns altogether, and if I gave away all four here, what would I do further on? It was not possible to give all four, but if they would take one gun and two seers opium, I would be glad to let them have this. The proposal, however, did not meet with their approval, and they left saying they would come again on the morrow. Ningro's message is evidently the cause of this attempt to bleed me. It appears 120 Khamti traders passed through Khomang last week on their way to Sạdiya. Owing to their having gone the Dehing route we did not meet them. One of their number having hurt his foot remained behind here. From him we heard that they had only found a trace of snow on the pass, but that they had to hurry over owing to a storm threatening.

2nd January.—The headmen turned up again today, but without the formalities of yesterday. They were very obstinate in coming down in their demands, but eventually matters were arranged by my giving them two guns and two seers of opium. This was rather heavy blackmail to pay to one village, but there was no help for it, we being completely dependent on them for provisions. I was rather amused at a reply made by the headman of the Tingsa village. I had said to him, if you bleed us to this extent we will have to return back for want of sufficient means; his answer was, 'The shame of so doing will lie with you, not with us, for people will laugh when they hear that you have turned back because you were unable to pay your way'. After we had handed over the guns and opium to the headmen, they left saying they would send us rice, fowls, &c., in the evening, and sure enough when evening came we were besieged by women of all ages, bringing rice, fowls, eggs and vegetables, to barter for opium chiefly, but in those cases where cash was asked for, the prices were truly formidable, rice five seers for the rupee; fowls of small size 8 and 12 annas each; Rs 8 and 10 for a half-grown pig, and Rs 20 for a full-grown one. I was told these were the usual rates among themselves, and we were not being imposed on in any way. These villages are so isolated and it is so difficult for people to buy anything from outside, that it is only natural they should put high prices on all they sell. Opium is a great medium of barter, and is more useful than cash. Cotton thread is also in much demand, and a maund of this article I had brought with me from Sadiya was quickly taken off my hands, so quickly indeed that I am afraid I was cheated out of several skeins. Owing to the severe cold of winter, this valley being 3,600 feet above sea level, and in close proximity to the snows, opium does not grow well, nor does cotton grow at all, and as the great proportion of Singphos, both men and women, use the drug, it is in much demand.

Chapter XIV

THE AKAS OF KAMENG

1

HISTORICAL PRELUDE

(A. Mackenzie, *History*, 1884, pp. 21 ff. & 367 ff.)

EASTWARD of the Bhutias, and between them and the Bhoroli (or more correctly the Desserai) river, live the Akas or Arkas, known among themselves as Hrusso. The Akas are of two clans: (1) the Hazari-Khawa, or 'eaters at a thousand hearths', and (2) the Kapa-chors, or 'thieves who lurk amid the cotton plants'. These are a most energetic and savage tribe, who for twenty years were the pests of Char Dwar. With the aid of the Migis, a fierce and cognate race in the interior, they long defied the power of the Towang Deo in the hills. Both clans of Akas together did not, however, in 1884 number over 260 families. Of the Migis there were from three to four hundred households. The Hazari-Khawas were the only branch of this tribe to whom the Assamese conceded formally any right to share in the produce of the Dwars. The Kapachors had no such rights, and anything that they received from the cultivators was simply extorted from their fears. To the Hazari-Khawas the Assam Government had granted the right of *posa*, or, as it is often rather inaccurately called, 'blackmail'.

It is a mistake to suppose that the *posa*, which, as we shall see, was paid to most of the hill tribes bordering on the plains, was an uncertain, ill-defined exaction, depending in amount upon the rapacity of the different hordes who might descend to levy it. It was really well-ascertained revenue payment, on account of which a corresponding remission was made in the State demand upon the *ryot* satisfying it. It may have had its origin in encroachment, or it may have been based upon customary and primeval rights asserted by the hillmen; but it was a distinct feature in the revenue system of the country when the British annexed Assam.

According to the records of 1825, it would seem that the Hazari-Khawas were entitled to receive from each house of their allotted *khels* 'one portion of a female dress, one bundle of cotton thread, and one cotton handkerchief'. At this period the Kapachors (or Koppa-turas as the old records style them) were probably not looked upon as a separate clan, for we read that the Hazari-Khawas were expected to give 'a part' of their collections to the Kapachors.

The inconvenience of permitting a horde of savages to descend annually upon the cultivated lands for the purpose of collecting petty dues from each household was very soon felt by the British Government to be unbearable. Quarrels and outrage were the natural concomitants of such a custom, and at a very early period of our management orders were given to invite the hillmen to surrender their right of direct collection for an annual lump payment in lieu. In many instances no difficulty was found in introducing this reform; in others the proposals were looked upon with suspicion. The claims of the Hazari-Khawas were at last commuted for a yearly sum of Rs 175. This, however, they did not long continue to draw, their connexion with the Kapachors having brought them into trouble with Government in 1835. For nine years after that they kept aloof from any intercourse with our officials, and it was not till 1844 that they were finally brought to terms.

The Kapachors under their leader, the Tangi or Taghi Raja, were long the terror of Durrung and of all the neighbouring clans. Although they numbered only about eighty families, they were able, from the nature of the country and their local knowledge, to defy both the Assam and British Governments for many years. Shortly before the annexation the Taghi Raja murdered the native official in charge of Char Dwar, with twenty of his immediate followers. For this the clan was outlawed, and Mr D. Scott, the first Commissioner of Assam, forbade their entering the plains, styling them a set of lawless brigands; but they nevertheless extorted from the *ryots* of Burgong a contribution of cloths year by year, just as though they were legally entitled to *posa*. In 1829 they were worsted in a quarrel with their brethren, the Hazari-Khawas, and their leader fled into Assam, where he was captured and sent to Gowhatty Jail. Here he became devout, and placed himself under the ghostly teachings of a Hindu spiritual guide, on whose security he was somewhat rashly released by the Governor-General's Agent in 1832. Once free he fled to the hills, rallied his broken clan, murdered all who had been in any way concerned in his capture, and brought his career to its climacteric on the 3rd February 1835 by cutting up and burning the Assam Light Infantry outpost at Baleepara, massacring seventeen souls—men, women, and children. In this outrage it was believed that the Taghi Raja had been assisted by the Hazari-Khawas, and there were good reasons for suspecting that his energy and daring had made him at this time virtual Chief of both clans of Akas, and given him influence even over the Duphlas in the neighbouring hills. At any rate the payment made by Government to the Hazari-Khawas was stopped, as already noted. For seven years after the Baleepara affair, this successful brigand haunted the border jungles, evading every effort made for his capture, and leading repeated forays into Char Dwar. In December 1837 he carried off several captives, and outposts of troops had to be moved up into stockades at the very foot of the hills to protect the low country from his depredations. Again in 1838–9, and yet again in March 1841, similar raids took place, and Government was seriously contemplating an expedition in force, when suddenly either weary of a hunted life, or distrustful of his ability in face of a regular attack, he came in and surrendered. It was alleged that offers of pardon had been unauthorizedly held out to him by the Kotokies (an officially recognized class of interpreters and clan-agents), and looking to the bad effect any ostensible breach of faith might have, the Raja was released on his binding himself by solemn oath not to injure our *ryots* again. He gave hostages for his good conduct, the Kotokies on this occasion becoming his formal sureties. He even agreed to live permanently on the plains, and a small allowance of Rs 20 was settled upon him. Through his influence, the other leaders of the Akas came in and accepted stipends, at the same time binding themselves to preserve the peace of Char Dwar.

The whole amount to be disbursed to the Akas was at that time fixed at Rs 360 per annum. The oaths taken by them 'on the skins of a tiger and bear, on elephant's dung, and by killing a fowl', have on the whole been faithfully observed, though they have made several attempts, not always unsuccessful, to get their allowances raised. In April 1857, for instance, it was reported that they had refused to accept their stipends which had gradually been increased to a total of Rs 668. The Taghi Raja was believed to be at the bottom of this combination, the object of which was avowedly to obtain a further increase. Government at once stopped the whole allowances pending further orders, closed the Dwars to trade, and kept a sharp outlook for the first indication of disturbance. These measures had the desired effect: several of the Chiefs were detached from the Taghi Raja's influence, and early in 1859 sued for pardon. In 1860 the Raja himself submitted, and as he had committed no active aggression, he was, almost too considerately, allowed to draw his former pension with all arrears.

The Akas have given no trouble of late years, a fact which may, perhaps, be accepted as proving the success of the policy of Government in dealing with this tribe. Their frontier line was demarcated with those of the tribes west of them in 1872–3; and the Deputy Commissioner of Durrung who carried out this duty reported that both they and the other hillmen came down in considerable numbers to the plains to trade and graze cattle. To this privilege of grazing they all attach cardinal importance, and Sir G. Campbell was of opinion that, if given as a privilege and not allowed as a right, it afforded a valuable means of securing their good behaviour. The Hazari-Khawas took no objections to the boundary; and in 1873 the Government gave them a grant of 49 acres of land in the plains which much gratified them. But the Kapachors refused at first to recognize the line between the Bhoroli and Khari Dikrai rivers, and put forward extravagant claims. Their Chief, Midhi, eventually however gave in, and the line was demarcated in 1874–5: the Chief also agreeing to send two of his relations to the school at Government expense. In March 1878, Midhi's people gave some trouble on their annual visits to the plains, and three of them were whipped for theft. In January 1882, the forest guards reported that a large body of Kapachor Akas and Duphlas had come down and set up boundary marks in the forests at Potashali, Diju, and Naminimukh, declaring that they would allow no one to pass those points which were all within our territory. Midhi was sent for and denied the fact; and as it was afterwards discovered that a number of Nepalese were trying to get passes from our officers permitting them to go into the Aka hills to collect rubber, it was supposed that the movement of the tribesmen was directed against them. The passes desired by the Nepalese were refused. In this year Midhi's brother who had read at Baleepara School since 1876 suddenly left it. The cold season of 1883–4 has witnessed the first Aka raid since our early connexion with the tribe and our first expedition into their hills. There seems to be little doubt that there has been some local misunderstanding in respect of forest matters....

Taghi, the famous Chief of the Kapachors, was succeeded by his son Midhi, who like his father is a convert to Hinduism. When a grant of land was made to the Hazari-Khawas in 1873, a similar grant was made to the Kapachors to be devoted to the maintenance of Cachari priests. The Kapachors were not satisfied with their grant; in 1875 they demanded much more, and this was summarily refused. They have, therefore, never taken possession of their grant. It has already been stated that they objected to the boundary line laid down in 1875, though they afterwards professed to accept it. This boundary line cut them off from a tract of land claimed by them between the hills and the Bhoroli River. Present at the demarcation on behalf of Government was one Lakhidar, the Mouzadar or native Revenue Officer of Baleepara. The tribe has also by the extension of forest reserves been deprived of what it doubtless considers its ancient right to tap rubber trees at pleasure. They had further been forbidden to catch elephants within the reserves, and threatened by the forest officers with the loss of one of their paths to the plains which runs through what is now a Government forest. Such being the state of things, the Deputy Commissioner of Durrung deputed Lakhidar to procure for the Calcutta Exhibition specimens of agricultural and other implements of the Akas, and to persuade some individuals of the tribe to come down to be modelled. Now, hitherto none but the regularly recognized Kotokies or clan-agents had ever sought to penetrate into the Aka Hills. Lakhidar, however, took with him twelve village elders and *ryots* of Baleepara and a private servant, and went straight to Midhi's village. The Akas declare, and the evidence of one of the Mouzadar's companions supports the statement, that Lakhidar said he had been sent to take down to Calcutta a 'Rajah and a Rani with all their ornaments', for which he was ready to pay. The Akas professed to be furious at this demand, alleging that, when they had given ornaments on former occasions, they had only been partly paid; while the idea of sending a 'Rajah and Rani' to the show was intolerable to them. Anyway after some days' palaver, charging the Mouzadar with being the man who had robbed them of their land, they sent him and his servant under guard to another village. The rest of the party they kept for a week, and then let them go. Meantime they had dispatched to the plains Chandi, Midhi's brother, the lad who had been educated at Baleepara School, with a party of over 100 of the young men of the tribe These came down to Baleepara on the 10th November last, and went frolicking about the bazaar and tea gardens, getting liquor and chaffing the shopkeepers in a goodnatured way. In the afternoon, however, they seized the Forest Clerk and the Forest Ranger, two guns and some money, and carried all off to the hills. They plundered none of the shopkeepers, save one opium-seller whose house they ransacked. 'Never,' wrote the local officer, 'was a raid conducted so peaceably.' Unfortunately the Akas were not content with calling attention to their grievances in this emphatic manner. When the return of the captives was demanded, they sent down four very insolent letters in Bengali, dictated to the Forest Ranger, making preposterous demands for miles of land and forest on the plains, and a lakh of rupees compensation, announcing at the same time the death from fever of the Mouzadar. Frontier police were hurried up to the spot, and a military expedition to recover the captives was speedily organized. On the 17th December 1883 an advanced party of the troops crossed the frontier. The Akas had on the 10th declared to a messenger that they would surrender the captives in twelve days; but instead of this, they attacked the advance camp on the night of the 23rd December in great force, killing one sepoy and wounding seven. When the troops advanced to the Tengapani they found it strongly held by the Akas, whose clouds of poisoned arrows the sepoys much dreaded. It was found necessary to wait for the arrival of the main body and mountain guns. On the 8th January Midhi's village, strongly stockaded, was attacked and taken. The Akas could not stand artillery fire and fled. A few days after this the captives were surrendered. The Akas have been told that, if they will come in and submit absolutely, agreeing to pay any fine imposed, their villages will not be destroyed. Their *posa* will probably be kept in suspense for a year or two. The Hazari-Khawa Akas have remained perfectly friendly all through.

The experience of the expedition has shown that the difficulties of the Aka country are enormous. 'All is well that ends well'; and there is of course a strong presumption that an expedition recommended by the local authorities, and carried to a successful issue, was properly undertaken. I cannot, however, for my part lay aside the doubt whether under any circumstances, save to avenge serious and widespread massacre, an expedition into the unexplored and almost impracticable fastnesses of these Sub-Himalayan tribes is a wise or necessary measure. We might possibly effect all our objects by shutting the offending tribe and its neighbours for some distance on either side out from the plains' markets until submission was made. In that case we should probably see the neighbours turning upon the offenders and compelling them to do exactly what we want them to do. On the Seebsaugor frontier we have seen this result follow the adoption of the plan suggested. In any case it appears probable that the Akas have substantial grievances which will doubtless be looked into, and the lesson has been learnt not to send native Assamese officials into the hills to exploit the tribes for Exhibition or any other purposes.

2

A MISSIONARY'S VIEW OF THE AKAS (1867)

(Reverend C. H. Hesselmeyer, 'The Hill-Tribes of the Northern Frontier of Assam', *J.A.S.B.*, 1868, Vol. XXXVII, pp. 192 ff.)

THE Himalaya mountains, so far as they form the northern boundary of Assam, are inhabited by two distinct races of men. Originally probably one and the same race, they seem to have undergone a change sufficiently marked to authorize their being considered at the present moment as two distinct races.

The mountaineers who occupy the eastern half of those frontier hills seem to be original occupants, or first arrivals, and to have retained their original habits and customs. Those who live to the west, appear to belong to a later period of immigration, subsequent to their descent from Central Asia. When they drove out from before them the first occupants, say the Dimasa and Bora, or Lalong, now living in the plains of Assam, they seem to have come in contact with a certain degree of civilization which effected that change both of feature and habits and customs which is so striking to the beholder.

The last mentioned of these two races are the people commonly called Butias or Butanese—this name applying to all the various and numerous tribes who belong to the same race. These, however, having served our purpose thus far, we may leave for the present, while we turn our attention more in particular to their less civilized brethren to the east.

Unlike the Butias, these possess no common name. The region they occupy, is fully as large as Butan, and equally as interesting. Indeed, little as we know of the people, the country they occupy, is still less known: as much a *terra incognita*, in fact, as the interior of Africa. The few Europeans who have crossed the frontier, have barely done more than skirted this unknown region: none have ever penetrated to the snowy range; none ever crossed its entire width from Assam to Tibet proper. All we know about the country and its inhabitants, we have learnt from the latter, who are, however, not in all cases reliable informants. Until, therefore, a Livingstone or a Wilcox will undertake to traverse its cane-bridged mountain torrents, its snow-capped heights, and brave leeches, *dum-dum* and cannibal Abors,[1]—in order to confirm or otherwise, the statements of native informants,—we shall have to rest satisfied with our present stock of information.

From all, then, we have hitherto been able to collect, it would appear, that that portion of the Eastern Himalayas which lies between the 92° 40′ and 95° 30′ East Long., or between the eastern boundary line of the country of the Tauwang and Kampa Butias, and the Dibong river,—having Assam on its south, and Tibet proper on its north side,—constitutes the home of four peoples, known to the inhabitants of Assam by the names of Aka, Miji, Dafla, and Abor.

Three of these tribes, the Aka, Miji and Dafla, occupy the hills on the southern side of the backbone of the Himalayas, the snowy range. The water of their rivers flows down into Assam direct. I make use of the expression direct, because I thereby wish to explain the more immediate proximity of their mountain-homes to Assam; for, properly speaking, the rivers that run down the northern slopes of the snowy range pour their waters likewise into the same big river which passes through Assam, via the Sampo of Tibet. The Abors alone, in some of their northern clans, are said to dwell on both

[1] There is no evidence that the Abors ever took human flesh.

sides of the snowy mountains, and they are thus in intercourse both with Tibet and Assam.

The seats of these four principal tribes may be defined as follows: commencing from the west or the frontier of Butan we come first upon the Akas. Their country is situated so as to have Assam on the south, Butan on the west, the Miji territory on the north, and the Dafla east. The Buruli river forms the boundary of the Aka and Dafla country, or rather hills. The Mijis again have Butan to the east, and probably north, but the Buruli river running round the northern side of their country until it enters Butan, the Daflas to the east, and their friends and neighbours, the Akas to the south.

The Daflas like the Akas have the valley of Assam for their southern limit, the Akas and Mijis, with the Buruli river intervening, on their west, and the Abors both north and east,—the Subonsiri river running up between the hills of the Abors and Daflas. Then the Abors themselves occupy the whole of the remaining extremity of the eastern Himalayas. They inhabit all the country lying between the territories of the Daflas on the southern face of the snowy range, and the Kampo-Butias on the northern face of the same snowy ridge; Tibet on the north, Assam on the south, and the Mishmi tribes on the east, the Dibong river forming the line of demarcation between the villages of the Abors and Mishmis.

Of all the four tribes above enumerated, the Abors are by far the most important, both as to their numerical strength and their warlike propensities, as well as through the extent of their territory.

In the present communication I shall restrict my remarks to one of the tribes only, namely:

The Akas

The Akas or Angkas live on hills of moderate height, the highest probably not exceeding 6,000 feet, in the angle formed, as before mentioned, by Assam and Butan. Three to four days' climbing over thickly wooded hills, nearly pathless, stumbling up the dry bed of the Buruli and other less important watercourses, thickly strewn with large boulders, clambering up the steep faces of rocks, holding on by a cane-rope, bring the traveller to the small settlement of the Akas. The Miri elephant-hunters follow up the bed of the Buruli river, taking a small light boat along with them, which they lift over the waterfalls, and so reach the Aka country. There is, however, a better road but somewhat circuitous. This road takes the traveller first to Butan to the settlement of the Sat Rajas due north, after a march of about four days, and then goes on to the Aka country due east which you reach in another two days. This is a road which the Aka women and children, and their ponies travel.

The name Aka, or Angka, is given to them by their neighbours; they themselves do not use it, but speak of themselves as Hrusso.[1]

The Hrusso do not pretend to be aborigines of the country they now inhabit. They are unable to tell where the real home of their tribe is. They pretend to have been inhabitants of the plains. Our ancestors, they say, lived in Partabgor on the banks of the Giladhari river, north of Bishnath, but were driven out from thence by Krishna and Boloram.[2]

The language of the Aka, however, tells a tale, and so does their national character. Their language contains more words which can be traced to the valleys south of the Patkoi range, joining the Shan and Munipuri countries, than words indicating a closer affinity with the Dafla and Abor tribes. They differ mentally and physically from their mountain neighbours to the same degree.

[1] Kennedy derives the word Aka, which means 'painted' (the Tibetans call this tribe Ka-nag or black-mouthed) from their custom of smearing the face with a mixture of pine-resin and charcoal. 'The women's faces,' he says, 'are tattooed with a very uniform pattern consisting of a line drawn down the middle of the forehead reaching almost to the tip of the nose and a large broad arrow on the chin with the tip corresponding to the centre of the lower lip.'—R. S. Kennedy, *Ethnological Report on the Akas, Khoas and Mijis and the Monbas of Tawang* (1914), p. 7. Captain Kennedy was the Medical Officer who accompanied the Aka Promenade of 1913–14.

[2] Kennedy, however, gives an entirely different account, and quotes an Aka legend as follows: 'Long long ago all men descended from heaven to earth by means of ladders. The Assamese and Akas of the royal blood came down by a golden ladder; the remaining Akas had a silver ladder; the Tibetans and Monbas were given a ladder of iron; the Daflas and Abors had to be satisfied with a bamboo ladder; whilst the Cacharis and Khoas shared a plantain ladder.' All these people came to earth on the Longkapur Hill in the Lohit Valley, whence they scattered in search of land. The Assamese were the first to start and chose the plains. The Akas spent so much time resting and drinking beer that the others got the best land and they had to accept what was left. They first settled near Bhalukpung, where, on the right bank of the Bhoreli River, their two Chiefs, Natapura and Bayu, built their respective capitals. Bayu demanded Natapura's beautiful wife as a sort of tribute and, after a number of adventures the girl with a newly-born child arrived at Bayu's court. The child Arima grew up to be a great warrior and finally killed his own father by mistake. Overcome with remorse he migrated to the present country of the Akas; it is from his children that the present-day Akas are descended.—ibid., p. 1.

The truth seems to be, that the Hrusso entered Assam about the same period when the far more numerous and daring Ahoms burst from their hills into the valley. Probably the Akas preceded them, and having been driven from place to place, they finally settled on the hills where they now still live. As to numerical importance, the Angkas would barely deserve any notice at all. They do not number more than one thousand souls.

This handful of hill people live in two detached villages. The greater one is inhabited by Akas who have earned for themselves the sobriquet of cotton thieves, or Kapas-chor. The smaller is peopled by a less offensive clan called the Hazarikhuka, or breakfast-eaters.[1]

There is a third class of Angkas spoken of by the people of the plains who go by the name of Angka Miris. Old maps have them located beyond the snowy range on the Tibet side. But by all accounts, these Angka Miris live to the east of the Kapas-chor Angkas. The Miris of the plains who are in the habit of hunting for elephants, deny having ever heard of Angka Miris. Further inquiry, however, may enable me to throw more light upon this tribe.

The importance which attaches to the Akas is first the bad name which they bear among the people of the valley who inhabit the tracts of country bordering on the Aka hills. For the Akas, few as they are in number, make up for this deficiency by being bold and daring robbers and cut-throats. Next in importance is their situation between the people of the valley of Assam and the powerful and very numerous clans of the Miji tribe. The Mijis, it would seem, are not in the habit of visiting Assam, except only one small Chief; but they highly prize the silk and cotton cloth the Akas are able to procure from the plains, and for which these demand from the Mijis exorbitant prices. As a third cause of their importance may be adduced the fact that, although powerless themselves, they know how to make themselves formidable through the influence they manage to exercise over the Mijis, whose countless hosts they would be able without much difficulty to lead any day against any foe.

There are about ten clans for which the term households, or families, would be the more appropriate one to use; yet each of these

[1] Their own word for Kapas-chor is Kavatsun and for Hazarikhuka is Kutsun. Hazarikhuka is better translated 'devourer of a thousand hearths'.

petty clans has a Chief whom they style Raja, like their neighbours, the Butias,—not Gam, like their other neighbours, the Daflas.

These clans are so small, that they find room each in a house by themselves. Some clans number only thirty souls, others sixty to one hundred and according to the number of inmates is the size of each house. The most numerous clan boasts of a Chief, who is but too well known among the Assamese, and the neighbouring hillmen, and no doubt the Bengal Government too has learnt to know his name. This is Tagi Raja. This man has succeeded in obtaining the hegemony over all the Kapas-chor Akas, and as he exercises great influence over the Mijis also, he is able to intimidate the rest of the Aka people, and thus may be said to be the head of all the Hrusso.

The Hazarikhuka Akas live in three clans on a separate hill from the Tagi's people.

Internal feuds are numerous. It is a matter of no rare occurrence to see clan against clan, i.e. family against family enlist the aid of the Mijis and carry on a miniature warfare.

The Hrusso use the cross-bow and poisoned arrow,[1] a light spear for the purposes of throwing, and a narrow sword, about four feet long. They manufacture their own arms; the iron and steel, however, they buy in Assam. They use neither shield nor helmet. Their tactics are simple; like all the hill tribes, they rely upon sudden surprise, they lie in ambush and fall upon their foes unawares.

The Assamese Buruas of the days of the native rulers used the Akas for purposes of revenge and intrigue. And it was through the party-spirit of one of the Buruas, or governors of Chardoar in the days of Gaurinath, the last real king of Assam, that the Akas obtained the privilege of levying pieces of Eria silk (Bambyz), and cotton cloth from every household in the Balipara *mehal*, which they continue to do unto this day. The only occasion on which the Akas have come into hostile collision with the present government of Assam, occurred some twenty-five years ago when their daring raids led to the capture of the young Tagi Raja and, after his liberation, to the massacre of the garrison of a stockade close to the pass which leads into their hills.

[1] For the poisoned arrows of the Akas, see an article by L. A. Waddell, 'Note on the Poisoned Arrows of the Akas', *Journal of the Anthropological Institute* (1895), Vol. XXIV, p. 57.

All attempts to punish this bold and blackguardly act remained unsuccessful; at last the little war seems not to have been carried on with much spirit, and matters between the Hrusso and the British Government were left in *status quo*.

Since that revengeful and treacherous act, however, the Akas have been content to levy their silk and cotton pieces, and to accept Rs 860 of blackmail per annum, without any further deeds of robbery and murder.

They now pay their annual visit to Assam in the months of February and March; take their due; make their purchases in iron, steel and brass vessels, in beads and other articles of luxury, and, after the above mentioned levying of cloth, return the way they came.

The Aka, though uncivilized, is not devoid of religious ideas. He has no written castras or religious books of any kind, it is true, he has no system of religion and knows nothing of caste. But the Aka fears the high mountains which tower aloft over his dwelling; and from the snow-clad sides of which leaps the thundering avalanche; he fears the roaring torrents of the deep glen which interposes between him and his friends beyond; and he fears the dark and dense jungles in which his cattle lose their way.

These dark and threatening powers of nature, he invests with supernatural attributes. They are his gods. Thus there is Fuxu, the god of jungle and water; Firan and Siman, the gods of war, and Satu, the god of house and field.

Over all these gods the modern Aka places Hori Deo, a Hindu deity. This is an innovation, introduced by Tagi Raja after his imprisonment. For whilst a captive, he became a disciple, as it were, of a Hindu *guru*, who in his turn obliged Tagi, by giving security for his new convert's future good behaviour.

All these gods have their little temples or rather *puja* huts, which contain representations of them, some are said to be of silver and gold. These latter most probably would turn out to be Buddhist images, obtained from the Butias.

Near the *puja* houses lives the Deori or sacrificing priest. He is always chosen from among the other Akas by divine token, it does not matter whether he is a bachelor or married. This Deori has to perform the daily worship for all the people, and on all special occasions he has to sacrifice the requisite number of *mithuns*, cows, goats, fowls and pigeons. Geese and ducks there are none to be found in all the settlements of either Aka or Miji. The Akas entertain some crude notions of a state of punishment and reward after death.[1]

To follow an Aka through his domestic and public life, I shall have to begin with the erection of the dwelling-house. The Hrusso cannot build a house where he pleases, for the spot on which he intends to erect his future dwelling must first be ascertained to be a lucky spot. The Deori therefore has to be consulted, animals slain as sacrifices, and the place pronounced to be propitious. Then the felling of timber, and the collecting of the other building materials may be proceeded with. All having been collected, Fuxu receives his offerings, part of which consist in a portion of the building materials.

The house itself is generally very substantially constructed. It is built on piles from 5 to 7 feet above the ground; boarded and comfortably walled in, with carefully planed planks, in this respect resembling the houses of the Kassias. The roof is thatched with a kind of broad leaf, and on account of the strong winds, mats are firmly, but neatly, fastened all over it. The houses of the Daflas and Abors including other hill tribes besides, are less substantially constructed.

All the members of one family or clan, including the slaves, live under the same roof. The size of an Aka dwelling varies therefore with the size of the family. The house of Tagi Raja is 200 feet long and 40 feet broad, a long row of separate compartments running the whole length of the building.

No earthen vessels are used by the Aka for household purposes. They possess huge copper jars to hold the water-supplies of the

[1] The chief Aka deity has since been recorded as Pu-mu-sago. Hesselmeyer fails to note the Buddhist element in Aka religion. Of this Kennedy says: 'Their animism has a very appreciable amount of Tibetan Buddhism mixed through it, in fact one might say that as Tibetan Buddhism is to animism, so is Aka animism to Tibetan Buddhism. Near several of their villages are "Cortens"; in every village are numerous prayer flags or wind horses as the Tibetans picturesquely call them; the chants sung by the priests are undoubtedly imitations of lama chants; many of them wear Tibetan charm boxes (*gan*); the prayer-wheel and the rosary are not unknown among them; and last but not least the house of Kalor, the Kavatsun Chief, is a little Buddhist temple or Chakang with an idol in it.... I fancy the Buddhist influence is on the wane, as they indignantly deny all connexion with Buddhism.'—ibid. p. 8.

family, and for cooking and eating, they use the brass pots and plates which they obtain in the Tezpore bazaar.

The copper jars are not procured by them in Assam, but most likely bartered from the Mijis, who again must have brought them from Butan. The granaries and stables are always built at some distance from the dwelling-house for fear of fire.

The Akas are polygamists: they can marry as many wives as their means allow. A marriage among them is contracted in this wise: The parents or relatives select the future wife from among the female friends of the family, those friends may be either Aka or Miji, for Mijis and Hrusso intermarry. On the day appointed for the wedding, the services of the Deori are again called into requisition; partly with a view to obtain the favour of the gods, but chiefly, I guess, in order to provide an abundance of meat for the hundreds of guests who are to partake of the marriage-feast, and for whom great number of *mithuns*, cows, goats and fowls have to be killed. The festivity, i.e. the eating and drinking—for the Akas, like all hill people indulge in ardent spirits—are to last at least five days and nights uninterruptedly.

The nuptials having thus been duly initiated, the bride and bridegroom are placed by the Deori beneath the canopy, formed of a piece of cloth spread out over them; he then winds another piece of cloth round both, thereby indicating their union, and this ceremony over, they are declared to be man and wife.

At the birth of a child, again sacrifices are brought, but no distinction is made between the sexes: a girl is considered as much a blessing as a boy; the murder of female infants, therefore, is fortunately not known amongst them, although they welcome the birth of a son with the same degree of joy with which such an event is hailed among far more civilized nations.

In like manner are the gods to be propitiated when the ground is hoed and the seed sown, and also at harvest-time.

Seasons of sickness too require the services of the Deori, for the Aka is not in the habit of resorting to medicines of any kind to effect a cure. If a Hrusso falls ill, fowls &c. are offered to Fuxu, and the patient is mesmerized; but should this prove unavailing, matters are left to the good pleasure of Fuxu alone.

The dead among the Akas are not burnt, but buried.[1] A grave is dug four to five feet deep and the body reverently deposited therein. Then a share of all his valuables is placed by the side of the dead, including his spear, bow and arrows. Next a platform is raised over the body to keep the earth from falling upon it, and finally the grave is filled in and over it a small stockade of bamboos and sticks erected, and—in Hindu fashion—a piece of cloth is spread out over the whole.

The Aka, although given to loot and robbery, is yet no idler: he is a great agriculturist. Unlike the Butias, the Akas import no grain from Assam, but subsist on the fruits of their own labour. They cultivate the fine plateaux on the backs of their broad hills, and some of those smiling valleys that stretch themselves out between their hills, miles in length and width.

They hoe the ground and beat the surface fine; then pierce holes with a pointed stick, and drop into each hole three to four grains of rice. Their rice-crops they declare to be as good as, if not superior to those of the best parts of Assam. Besides the common kinds of rice, they cultivate a kind of grain, called Dafla-dhan, of a small size but growing in numerous clusters; it is a grain, in fact, resembling millet. Also vegetables of the same description as those which are found in Assam, and pulses of various kinds are cultivated by the Akas.

There are, however, neither cotton, nor hemp and flax plantations to be met with; the only fibre used by them and the Mijis, as well as all the other hill tribes, is that derived from the rind of a tree known in Assam by the name of Odal, and used for nets and ropes. The consequence is that, the women of the Akas neither spin nor weave, but rely for their cotton cloth on the plains, as already mentioned. Nor do they breed the silkworms known to the Assamese. Though they covet the Eria Bor-Kapors of Assam, and the finer silk *dhuties*, yet they have never taken the trouble of introducing the silkworm into their hills.

[1] Hesselmeyer, in his account of Aka burial, misses the interesting and important point that in former times at least the Akas placed the corpse in the grave in a sitting posture, trussing it with the knees bound to its chest. The head is placed towards the south and beams are laid across above to prevent earth falling on it. Finally the grave is filled in and sometimes a stone mound is built above it.—See Kennedy, ibid., p. 7.

The Akas keep large flocks of *mithuns* or *mithans*, and cows—their flesh is eaten, but the milk of *mithuns*, cows and goats they never touch. They breed pigs and rear fowls and pigeons in great numbers, but geese and ducks are forbidden to them by the gods.

The Hrusso pride themselves on being better feeders than any of the other hillmen. They eat the food of civilized people; never touch the flesh of dogs, or elephants, or other objectionable animals. They indulge in the use of opium and tobacco—in fact, the pipe seldom leaves the mouth of an Angka man or woman. Such a pipe is generally a bit of bamboo with a reed inserted into it at a right angle. Now and then, however, Tibetan pipes of composition metal may be seen in use amongst them. They likewise chew betal which they obtain in the plains, but tea as a beverage is not in use among them, although they keep up a constant intercourse with their Butan neighbours. The well-known ardent drink however—a species of beer, called Mod—prepared by all the aborigines of Assam and its frontier hills, the Akas too drink to excess.

The dress of the Aka has nothing national, or nothing that could distinguish them from other hillmen that border on Assam, except the profusion of Eria cloth wound round their bodies in all manner of ways, and a kind of half-trousers which consist in a piece of Eria cloth tied in such a fashion beneath the knee, as to allow the fringes to hang down over the ankles. When they move, the ample folds of this kind of legging keep swinging and flying about their feet, and thus this piece of garment seems to answer admirably the purpose for which it is intended, namely to keep off the leeches and stinging insects, such as the mosquitoes and the *dum-dum*.

As a head-dress the Aka often wears a kind of ring-cap or crown made of cane, three inches high with one or two tall feathers in front. However, the felt caps of the Butias are as commonly met with, while those who claim the rank of a Raja sport rings or crowns such as those alluded to, only made of thin wood instead of cane, and covered with embossed silver. Tagi himself, however, never appears in the plains without his Tibetan hat of japanned wood of a bright yellow with a glass knob, and a blue silk damask robe of state of Chinese manufacture, but rather faded. All are fond of beads, and they wear them in profusion. Thus dressed up, they appear on state occasions only, the long sword at their side, and one or two minor weapons for cutting besides. When at home, the Aka looks more the savage, and dispenses with most of his garments. But winter is severe, and then he appreciates the neighbourhood of Assam, and the cloth of the *rayats* of Balipara.[1]

In appearance, the Aka bears the same family-likeness with the other Turanian hill tribes; he is a well-made and strongly built man, with more of daring and defiance in his look than the Dafla or even the Naga.

He is ignorant of the art of reading and writing, and though he covets the productions of art which Assam and Butan supply, including Tibetan oil-paintings of Buddhist deities, yet does he look down upon books. The offers of opening a school in their villages, have repeatedly been made to Tagi, but as often politely refused. Tagi dreads the approach of the schoolmaster to his hills, for he knows, that with the schoolmaster there would come a different code of morals and ethics; and he fears, that the English will succeed the schoolmaster, and thus put an end to Tagi, and the selfish aims of the Aka people as regards the Mijis and the inhabitants of the Balipara Mehal.

3

A SOLDIER'S VIEW OF THE AKAS (1884)

(C. R. Macgregor, 'Notes on the Akas and Akaland', *Proc. A.S.B.*, 1884, No. XI, pp. 198 ff.)

THE history of the tribes on the north-east frontier is very obscure, and that of the Akas (or Hrusso clan) is no exception; they assert that

[1] Hesselmeyer says nothing of the dress of Aka women, whom perhaps he never saw. Kennedy's description may therefore be used to supplement the above. 'A woman's dress consists of a cloth wound round the body similar to that worn by a man, except that it reaches almost to the ankles and is often of Assamese silk. She wears a jacket of Assamese silk, rather longer than a man's jacket. Her hair is invariably tied at the head. Round her head, a well-to-do Aka woman wears a very striking and pretty fillet of silver chain-work. In her ears are large vase-shaped silver ear-rings, whilst innumerable necklaces of coloured beads encircle her neck. She generally also wears a *gan*. As a rule the women wear gaiters just like those worn by the men. It may not be out of place to mention that all their silver ornaments are made either in Assam or the neighbouring parts of Tawang.'—ibid., p. 5.

they came originally from the south-east of the Assam valley, and this is not improbable, when the fact that their language assimilates more with that of the tribes bordering Manipur than with that of their immediate neighbours, the Dufflas and Bhutias, is taken into consideration. The Akas also assert that they are of noble origin, and every free Aka considers himself more or less a 'Raja'; the manner and bearing of the free Akas is certainly in favour of their claims, as they assume a very bold and dignified air; *noblesse oblige* is clearly marked in their deportment, if not in their conduct.

The Hrusso clan is divided into two sections, and locally called Kapachors (thieves of cotton) and Hazarikhowas (eaters of a thousand hearths): the above-mentioned names were bestowed by the Assamese, and are now adopted by the Akas themselves, who are rather proud than otherwise of the appellations. The Akas, like most of our mountain tribes, delight in terrifying the dwellers in the plains, on whom they look with the greatest contempt. I was informed by an Aka Raja (so called) that the Kapachors had divided the *mouzah* of Balipara among themselves, and to each Raja was apportioned a certain number of houses, the inhabitants of which were bound to give lodging and food gratis to their respective fedual lords (and their followers) whenever it might please them to visit the plains. The inhabitants are also expected to present a yearly tribute in the shape of pigs, fowls, and silk clothes.

About 300 years ago the Akas, under a Raja called Bam, were settled on the right bank of the river Bhoroli near Balak Pung, and to this day there are evidences (in the shape of masonry, &c.), which bear witness to the occupation of that site. In those days the Akas evidently built themselves (or made their slaves build for them) more substantial houses than they do now. The only specimen of a stone house which I have seen in Akaland was one to the west of Laby's village. This house was built at the instigation and for the accommodation of a Buddhist priest from Thibet, who about half a century ago used to pay the Akas yearly visits for the purpose of converting them to Buddhism. I believe that as long as the priest was with them they adopted the tenets of Buddha, but directly the man died they resumed the old demon worship of their fathers.

The Akas are demon worshippers, i.e. they believe in the existence of various good and evil spirits, who, if not propitiated, will harm them. Hunter mentions the names of three gods, Fuxu, jungle god, Feiran, war god, and Situ, household god; but I could get no definite information about these three deities—in fact, an intelligent Aka, whom I interrogated on the subject, said he had not heard of them. Once a year the Akas pay a visit to the Maj-Bhoroli River, and a sacrifice consisting of two *mithun*, two she-goats, two pigs, and two cocks is made to propitiate 'the spirit of the waters'. If a person falls ill, pigs and fowls are sacrificed (and eaten by the relations and friends of the sick person!) and invocations are made. A few simple herbs are used as medicine, and for all stomachic disorders ginger is freely used. The Akas call their principal deity 'Karza', the day god is called 'Ju', i.e. sun, the night god 'Hubee', i.e. moon, the stars, 'Neitzi', are minor deities.... At Khowagaon, a village to the north of Mehdi's, some flags were found, supposed to be relics of Buddhism. The Akas usually consult omens before going on the war-path, &c., and sacrifice pigs, cocks, and goats to propitiate the spirit of war. *Mithun* are but rarely killed on these occasions, as they are considered too valuable. On the capture of the forest Babus by the Akas, the omens were consulted as to their fate. The decision was both for and against their murder; so I imagine that the Akas, like the Nagas, interpret their omens to suit their own purposes, and have no faith whatever in the auguries.

Corpses are buried, not burnt; a small square stone building about 4 feet high is sometimes erected over the body. A species of altar of split wood, streaked with blue dye and smeared with fowl's blood, is placed near the body, which is always interred with the clothes worn by the individual when alive. Brass cooking utensils are (when the deceased was fortunate enough to have possessed them) placed in the grave.

Among the Akas women are respected. The forest Babus who were domiciled during their captivity in an Aka household said that nothing astonished them so much as to see the respect paid to the women. When there are guests of both sexes in the house, the women are served first. The high estimation in which the Aka male is said to hold his better-half does not, however, prevent his using her for all the hard work in the fields, whilst he stays at home and looks after the children. Marriage is a question of mutual liking (men generally select their brides with reference to their physical qualities). The ceremony of marriage generally takes place when the girl has attained her fourteenth year. Should the union not be a fruitful one, the man is at liberty to take another wife. A young girl (*mimsa*) paints her face before she becomes a married woman. A young man (*mim*), who (as is usually the case among hill tribes) is far vainer about his personal appearance than a young woman, also paints his face, mere smudges, not in the artistic manner the Eastern Naga paints. At a marriage, *mithun* are generally killed, and a feast is given. The bridegroom gives *mithun* and pigs to the bride's father as a dowry. After the feast, the young man takes his bride to his father's house, and she becomes an inmate of the common dormitory. Although privacy in the married life of an Aka is unknown, yet the marriage tie is usually kept unbroken. Husband and wife eat from the same plate (a plantain leaf generally) together. Children are fed separately; the mother cooks the food for the household and feeds the children.

In the evenings, when seated round the hearth (which is placed in the centre of the room), young men and girls dance in turn, moving their hands and feet with a kind of cadence, a small drum being beaten by one of the spectators during the performance. At the end of the entertainment the old women dance to the music of a fiddle. The Aka fiddle is a curious kind of instrument, hairs from a *mithun's* tail serve as strings for the bow and a piece of skin, well stretched, covers the bamboo cup which is used for the bowl; the rosin with which the bow is occasionally rubbed is attached in the most convenient manner to the side of the bowl. I must say that the sound produced is of the mildest description, but I am told that the Aka will listen to it for hours with the greatest pleasure. During the dances everyone, down to the smallest child, drinks the rice wine, which is luckily not of an intoxicating nature.

There is very little crime among the Akas; thefts are very rare, there being hardly anything to steal which is not common property. Murders are also of very rare occurrence. Should a man kill another, a punchayat is held in the village, and the punishment awarded is generally that the murderer should pay a fine in *mithun* to the relations of the deceased, and that he (the murderer) should be banished from the village. I was informed that on one occasion a Miji had killed a Kapachor, so three men of the Kapachors went to the Miji village where the murderer dwelt, took him outside the village, and put him to death with their swords, the other inhabitants of the Miji village approving, or at any rate not preventing, the deed.

The Akas are very hospitable, and guests are treated to the best of everything, even children (who are very obedient) are taught to be hospitable. The houses are substantial erections, the sides of which are planked; they vary in size. Laby's house, an average one, was 63 feet long by 15 feet wide, the height the *machan* (i.e. floor) is from the ground, depends on the slope of the ground—it may be 2 feet at one end and 6 feet at the other. One of the houses in Mehdi's village measured 140 feet in length and 22 feet in width. In the large houses there are partitions and swing doors; the fire-places are usually in the middle of the dormitory, and round this all the members of the family, both young and old, sleep. The roofs are formed at a good angle for running the rain off by placing mats over the bamboo framework and covering them with cane leaves; the canes reach to the *machan*. There is very little attempt in decorating the front of the house; a few horns of the *mithun*, &c., are sometimes put up. Pigs and poultry live under the floor. Sanitary ideas do not exist in the Aka mind.

The Akas wear a kind of toga made of rough Assamese silk or of Bhutia blanket cloth. Leggings are also worn; these are tied at the knee and folded round the leg, giving them the appearance of trousers. The arms are bare, and they do not wear shoes. Their head-covering consists of cane hats like those worn by the Daphlas, or rough felt skull caps similar to those used by the Bhutias. Occasionally a three-decked cane hat, like those used in Thibet, is worn; but the use of this hat is, I believe, confined to the Chiefs. Ear-rings and beads, of which the Akas (in common with all the tribes on the north-east frontier) are inordinately fond, complete the costume. A cumerband in which a sword is placed, is usually part of the dress. The women are decently clad, generally in Eria silk clothes; they wear necklaces of beads, and some of them carry about egg-shaped silver cases obtained from Bhutan. These silver ornaments are much valued, and worn only by the wives of Chiefs.

The principal weapon of the Aka is a long sword, the blade being 4 feet long and handle about 4 inches. Near the hilt the sword is not sharpened, and often a piece of cloth is folded round, so as to enable the owner to use the sword in a two-handed fashion, and in this way the weapon is generally used. The bow and arrows constitute, however, the most effective weapon of the Akas; the bow is an ordinary one (I did not observe any cross-bows), the arrows, some of which have iron barbs, are usually poisoned with aconite; the aconite is mixed up with some kind of adhesive substance, and stuck on to the arrow-head. The poison is obtained from the Mijis, who get it from the higher ranges behind them. I was informed by an Aka that it was expensive, a pig being usually the price of a very small piece. Immediately a wound is received, it should be well scoured out with a knife, well washed with water, and if the wound is in a limb, a bandage should be tightly tied above; stimulants should also be given to the wounded man. Some Gurkhas used the bark of a tree, which they first chewed into a pulp. When a man was hit, some of this pulp was given to the man to chew and some forced into the wound. The bark had a smell like lemon. I saw this used in two cases, one of which was fatal and in the other the wounded man recovered—the recovery was, I think, due to the skilful treatment of the wounded man by the surgeon and not to the supposed antidote. I only mention the use of this bark as an antidote believed in by the Gurkhas, as any information bearing on the subject may be useful.

The Akas possessed a few old muskets and a few guns, which they had looted from Balipara (these were, however, all given up before the expedition left the hills).

Panjis (sharp pointed pieces of bamboo hardened by being half burnt), are placed in the ground to retard the advance or stay the pursuit of an enemy. They are very good obstacles against men who are not well booted. A collection of rocks placed upon a kind of scaffolding of bamboos and held in position by single canes, which can be severed at a blow, are, owing to the precipitous nature of the hills, most formidable obstacles. These obstacles, commonly called booby traps, are usually placed so as to command a path ascending a steep hill-side; and as the path generally zigzags, the rocks, when liberated from the cage, strike it in several places before finding a resting-place at the bottom.

The stockades of the Akas are strong and well-built; they are constructed of double rows of bamboos placed upright in the ground. In the middle earth and stones are placed to a height of about 4 feet; the stockades being 10 or 12 feet high, a perfect *chevaux de frise* of pointed bamboos are firmly secured in the stockades (so firmly are the pointed bamboos secured that it takes one a considerable time to cut a way through). These stockades are constructed near the summit of a hill and in such a position that it is almost impossible for a two-legged animal to 'turn' them. The Akas keep a good supply of large stones behind the stockades, to hurl at an advancing foe.

In my opinion the Aka does not take kindly to the war-path. A thieving expedition, where there is a minimum of danger and a maximum of loot, is more in his line. In the late expedition, the Akas relied to a great extent on the (supposed) inaccessibility of their country, and this, combined with their ignorance of the nature of the troops they were to meet, gave them a certain amount of confidence. At the action at the Tenga River on the 8th January, they blew horns and kept up a peculiar kind of war-chant; this was done probably with the object of encouraging each other and of striking terror into the hearts of their foes. This method of fighting is quite opposed to their usual one, which is essentially a system of ambuscades and surprises, and in this system they excel. Small bodies of men will crouch quietly for hours in the jungle, hiding themselves with the aid of leaves and bushes, which they plant in front of them, and wait for the arrival of a convoy, into which they will fire a volley of poisoned arrows and decamp down the hill-side.

The Akas do not, so far as I am aware, mutilate the slain, nor do they torture a prisoner.

When the Aka is on the war-path he must, of course, have his provisions with him; these are generally carried by one of the slaves, and consist of rice (cooked), rice wine, Indian corn, &c. The cooked rice is carried in long bamboo tubes; several of these are placed in a basket and carried on the slave's back; thus one slave can carry the provisions for three men for about a week. Nearly all the inhabitants of Ramdagaon, on the south (right) bank of the Tenga River, are slaves to the Akas. Whenever Mehdi, Chundi and Co. wish to make a raid, the Ramdăgaon men are ordered to send a contingent to act as coolies and fighting men.

Bridges.—These are of two kinds, viz., the cane cradle suspension and the *hako*. The former, which is used when the river is very deep and rapid, is formed by one or more long and strong canes, which are stretched from bank to bank; they are attached at either end to a kind of scaffolding of bamboos, which is kept securely in position by the aid of large stones piled round it. If there is a convenient tree, one end of the cane is attached to it. Round the thick cane three or four thin cane loops are attached, and to this is fastened another cane, which is used as a pulley; the voyager seats himself in the cane loops, throws his head well back, grasps the cane above him, throws his legs over the cane, and allows himself to slide down the cane. Up to his arrival at the centre the work is easy, after that he has to haul himself uphill, using his hands and feet, his body being supported in the small cane loops. This is a very fatiguing process, and a severe strain on the muscles. When women and children are obliged to use the cradle bridge (and all must use it in the rains), they are hauled across by means of the pulley, and in this way nearly all the stores for the advanced party were crossed over the Maj-Bhoroli. A cradle basket capable of holding two maunds was constructed by one of the Survey Officers, and in this provisions and baggage were pulled across. The width of the River Maj-Bhoroli where the Aka cradle bridge is constructed is about 65 yards, and the water rushes below in a regular torrent. The other description of bridge is called by the Assamese a *hako* bridge; it is somewhat like a trestle bridge; the roadway is made of bamboos, and the whole structure, which is rather infirm, is tied together by cane lashings and creepers.

The Akas trade with Bhutan to the north-west, and with the plains of Assam to the south. From Bhutan the following articles, viz., clothing, warm blankets, *daos*, swords, and silver ornaments, are obtained, and rupees, which are got by the sale of rubber to the Kyahs in the plains, are given in exchange.

From Assam the Akas procure rupees, iron, salt, cotton, and silk goods. Rubber is the chief source of wealth of the Akas. Good rubber (i.e. not rubber shells filled up with mud, a common trick of the simple savage) is worth about Rs 60 a maund. At present the rubber supply is large; but the feckless way in which the Akas treat the trees will probably soon lessen their source of supply. The social status of the Aka is generally estimated by the number of *mithun* (semi-domesticated bison) which he is the owner of. The value of these animals averages about Rs 90; they are used only as an article of food, and are not used for agricultural purposes, neither are they milked (the Akas, in common with all the hill tribes on the north-east frontier, look upon milk as an unclean article, and never use it). *Mithun* are given by a bridegroom to the bride's father as a dowry. *Mithun* are killed and eaten at feasts, and sometimes they are killed as a sacrifice. Pigs and fowls are also very largely consumed by the Akas. The chief article of food is, of course, rice; millet, Indian corn, yams, Job's tears, and a large species of bean (which is very palatable when smoked over an aromatic wood fire) supplement the rice supply. Chillies are abundant, and largely used as a condiment. Tobacco is also grown extensively.[1]

[1] We may note that the Akas in later years continued to win the respect of those who visited them. Thus Captain Neufville wrote of them in 1925 that 'these Akas are an excellent and most interesting people, they are much more civilized than the Dufflas and they are capable of great improvement'. Kennedy too observes that 'the Akas are a much more enlightened and civilized people than the other hill tribes further east'.

BIBLIOGRAPHY OF WORKS IN ENGLISH ON THE NORTH-EAST FRONTIER

ALI, S. & RIPLEY, D. S., 'The Birds of the Mishmi Hills', *J. Bombay Nat. Hist. Soc.*, Vol. XLVIII (1948), pp. 1-37

ALLEN, B. C., *Assam District Gazetteers: Lakhimpur* (Shillong, 1906). Contains a useful historical summary of Government's relations with some of the NEFA tribes

ANDERSON, J. D., *Short Vocabulary of the Aka Language* (Shillong, 1896)

AONOK, S. WATI, 'Morung Organization among the Nocte Nagas', *Vanyajati*, Vol. IV, No. 2 (1956)

BADGLEY, W. F., 'Report on the Treacherous Attack made by the Nagas', *General Report on the Topographical Surveys of India for the Season* 1874-5 (Calcutta, 1876). Describes the massacre of a Survey Party by the Wanchos of Ninu

BADGLEY, W. F., 'Extract from the Narrative Report of Capt. W. F. Badgley', *General Report on the Topographical Surveys of India for the Season* 1874-5 (Calcutta, 1876). Gives some account of the Wanchos

BAILEY, F. M., 'Journey through a Portion of South-Eastern Tibet and the Mishmi Hills', *Geographical Journal*, Vol. XXXIX (1912), pp. 334-471

BAILEY, F. M., *China-Tibet-Assam* (London, 1945)

BAILEY, F. M., *No Passport to Tibet* (London, 1957). Descriptions of Mishmis and Monpas

BALFOUR, H., 'Thorn-Lined Traps and their Distribution', *Man* (March, 1925). Gives some examples of Chang and Sangtam traps

BARUA, HEM, *The Red River and the Blue Hill* (Gauhati, 1956). A useful account of the general setting of NEFA in Assam

BARUA, T. K., *The Idu Mishmis* (Shillong, 1961)

BASU, P. C., 'Head-dress of the Hill Tribes of Assam', *J.R.A.S.B.*, Vol. XXV (N.S., 1929), pp. 103-14. Illustrates the cane-work of the Nagas, Miris, Mishmis and Abors

BAVEJA, J. D., *Across the Golden Heights of Assam and NEFA* (Calcutta, 1961)

BEAMES, J., *Outlines of Indian Philology* (Calcutta, 1867). An appendix gives Abor, Miri and Dafla numerals

BEIERWALTES, W. H. & RAMAN, G., 'Endemic Goitre and Cretinism in Michigan and in the North-eastern Frontier Agency Area', *Current Medical Practice*, Vol. 1, No. 11 (1957), pp. 613-18

BENTINCK, A., 'The Abor Expedition: Geographical Results', *Geographical Journal*, Vol. XLI (1913), pp. 97-114

BERESFORD, G. W., *Notes on the North-Eastern Frontier of Assam* (Shillong, 1881; reprinted, 1906)

BETTS, U., 'The Village Duel in Apatani Society', *Man in India*, Vol. XXVIII (1948), pp. 163-9

BETTS, U., 'The Daflas of the Subansiri Area', *R. Cent. Asian Journal*, Vol. XXXVI (1949), pp. 146-54

BHATTACHARJEE, P. N., 'Dermatoglyphics of the Abor People in Assam', *Anthropologist*, Vol. II, No. 2 (1955)

BHATTACHARJEE, P. N., 'Blood Group Investigations in the Abor Tribe', *Bulletin of the Dept. of Anthropology*, Vol. III, No. 1 (Calcutta, 1954)

BHUYAN, S. K., *Anglo-Assamese Relations*, 1771-1826 (Gauhati, 1949). A standard work; describes early policy towards the tribes

BLISS, C., *Report on the Debong Survey and Exploration Mission*, 1912-13 (Shillong, 1914)

BOR, E., *Adventures of a Botanist's Wife* (London, 1955)

BOR, N. L., 'The Daflas and their Oaths', *J.R.A.S.B.*, Vol. II (Third Series, 1936), pp. 27-39

BOR, N. L., 'Yano Dafla Grammar and Vocabulary', *J.R.A.S.B.*, Vol. IV (Third Series, 1938), pp. 217-81

BOR, N. L., 'A Sketch of the Vegetation of the Aka Hills, Assam. A Synecological Study', *Indian Forest Records*, N.S. Botany, Vol. I (1938)

BOWER, U. G., *The Hidden Land* (London, 1953). About the Subansiri area

BROWN, N., 'Comparison of Indo-Chinese Languages', *J.A.S.B.*, Vol. VI (1837), pp. 1023-36. Includes, among others, vocabularies of Aka, Abor, Mishmi and Singpho words

BURRARD, S. G., *Records of the Survey of India, Exploration on the North-East Frontier during* 1911-12-13 (Calcutta, 1914). Geographical observations of the Mishmi, Abor and Miri Surveys by C. P. Gunter, O. H. B. Trenchard and C. G. Lewis

BUTLER, JOHN, *A Sketch of Assam, with Some Account of the Hill Tribes, by an Officer* (London, 1847). Early descriptions of Abors, Akas, Daflas, Khamptis, Mishmis and Singphos

CAMPBELL, G., *Specimens of the Languages of India, including those of the Aboriginal Tribes of Bengal, the Central Provinces and the Eastern Frontier* (Calcutta, 1874). Describes Abor at p. 21, Dafla at p. 35, and gives vocabularies

CHANG, IMLONG, *A Guide Book in Chang Naga Dialect or Anglo-Chang* (Mokokchang, 1956)

CHARI, M. V. (with B. D. Barua & D. Das), *Report on the Investigation of the 'Unknown Fever' in Kimin-Subansiri Area* (Shillong, 1953)

CHATER, A. F., 'Abor-Suspension Bridges', *Royal Engineers Journal*, Vol. XVI (1912), pp. 217-18

CHOUDHURY, P. C., *The History of Civilization of the People of Assam to the Twelfth Century A.D.* (Gauhati, 1959)

CHOUDHURY, U., 'The Role of Women among the Padam Tribe', *March of India*, Vol. VI, No. 2 (1953), pp. 20-3

COOPER, R. E., 'Bhutan: Tailed People "Daktas"—People with a Tail in the East Bhutanese Himalaya', *Man*, Vol. XXXIII, No. 131 (1933). On the Monpas round Tawang who carry a felt sitting-pad attached to their backs

COOPER, T. T., *New Routes for Commerce: The Mishmee Hills: An Account of a Journey made in an Attempt to Penetrate Thibet from Assam to open New Routes for Commerce* (London, 1873)

CROOKE, W., 'Abor, Abor-Miri', *Hastings's Encyclopaedia of Religion and Ethics* (London, 1908), Vol. I, p. 33

CROWE, H. M., *Mr Crowe's Account of a Journey to Apa Tanang Country* (Shillong, 1890)

CUMMING, R. C. R., 'Notes on Certain Frontier Tribes', *Census of India*, 1921 (Shillong, 1923), Vol. III: Assam, Pt. 1, Report, App. B, pp. 13-14. On the Abors and Miris

CUST, R. N., *A Sketch of the Modern Languages of the East Indies* (London, 1879). Some references to the NEFA tribes and languages at pp. 95-102

DALTON, E. T., *Descriptive Ethnology of Bengal* (Calcutta, 1872; German edition: Berlin, 1875). Gives accounts of the Khamptis, pp. 1-9; Singphos, pp. 9-13; Mishmis, pp. 13-21; Abors, pp. 21-35; Daflas, pp. 35-7; Akas, pp. 37-8; Nagas, pp. 38-44

DALTON, E. T., 'Report . . . of his visit to the Hills in the Neighbourhood of the Soobanshiri River', *J.A.S.B.*, Vol. XIV, Pt. 1 (1845), pp. 150-267

DALTON, E. T., 'On the Meris and Abors of Assam', *J.A.S.B.*, Vol. XIV, Pt. 1 (1845), pp. 426-30

DALTON, E. T., 'Correspondence and Journal of Capt. Dalton, Principal Assistant at Luckimpore, of his Progress in a late visit to a Clan of Abors on the Dihong River', *Selections from the Records of the Bengal Government*, No. XXIII (Calcutta, 1855), pp. 151-69

DIXON, H. N., 'Report on the Mosses of the Abor Expedition, 1911-12', *Indian Botanical Survey Records*, Vol. VI (1914), pp. 57-73

DUFF, B., *Report on the Miri Country and the Operations of the Miri Mission* (Simla, 1912)

DUFF-SUTHERLAND-DUNBAR, G. (with J. Coggin Brown & S. W. Kemp), 'Abors and Galongs', *Memoirs of A.S.B.*, Vol. V (1913-17). A full and valuable account

DUN, G. W., *Preliminary Notes on Daphlas* (Simla, 1896)

DUN, G. W., *Preliminary Notes on Miris* (Simla, 1896). The authorship of this and the preceding item is uncertain, but it is generally attributed to G. W. Dun, sometimes spelt Dunne

DUNBAR, G., *Frontiers* (London, 1932)

DUNBAR, G. (Duff-Sutherland-Dunbar), 'Tribes of the Brahmaputra Valley', *J. R. Soc. Arts*, Vol. LXIII (1915), pp. 189-303. Description of the Abors

DUNBAR, G. (Duff-Sutherland-Dunbar), *Other Men's Lives. A Study of Primitive Peoples* (London, 1938). Includes a popular account of Daflas and Abors at pp. 230-4

DUTTA, P., *The Tangsas of the Namchik and Tirap Valleys* (Shillong, 1959)

ELWIN, VERRIER, 'The North-East Frontier Agency of India' *Geographical Magazine*, Vol. XXIX (1956), pp. 405-16

ELWIN, VERRIER, *A Philosophy for NEFA* (Shillong, 1957; 2nd edition 1959)

ELWIN, VERRIER, *Myths of the North-East Frontier of India* (Shillong, 1958)

FORBES, C. J. F. S., 'On Tibeto-Burman Languages', *J.R.A.S.* (1878), pp. 210-27

FURER-HAIMENDORF, C. VON, 'Agriculture and Land Tenure Among the Apa Tanis', *Man in India*, Vol. XXVI (1946), pp. 20-49

FURER-HAIMENDORF, C. VON, 'Culture Types in the Assam Himalayas', *Ind. Geog. Journal*, Vol. XXI (1946), pp. 1-9. Discusses the Sulungs, Daflas and Apa Tanis

FURER-HAIMENDORF, C. VON, *Ethnographic Notes on the Tribes of the Subansiri Region* (Shillong, 1947)

FURER-HAIMENDORF, C. VON, 'The After-Life in Indian Tribal Belief', *J.R.A.I.*, Vol. LXXXIII (1953), Pt. I, pp. 37-49. Discusses the eschatological ideas of Daflas, Apa Tanis and Konyaks among others

FURER-HAIMENDORF, C. VON, 'Religious Beliefs and Ritual Practices of the Minyong Abors', *Anthropos*, Vol. XLIX (1954)

FURER-HAIMENDORF, C. VON, *Himalayan Barbary* (London, 1955). On the author's travels in the Subansiri area

FURER-HAIMENDORF, C. VON & E. VON, 'Notes on Tribal Justice among the Apa Tanis', *Man in India*, Vol. XXVI (1946), pp. 181-95

GAIT, E., *A History of Assam* (Calcutta and Simla, 1926). Brief accounts of the relations of Government with the NEFA tribes

GILLE, A., 'An Account of an Expedition among the Abors in 1853', *J.R.A.S.B.*, Vol. IX (N.S., 1913), pp. 107-22. Describes Father Krick's visit to Membu

GODWIN-AUSTEN, H. H., 'Notes on the Geology of part of the Dafla Hills, Assam', *J.A.S.B.*, Vol. I (1875), pp. 35 & 139

GODWIN-AUSTEN, H. H., 'List of the Birds collected on the expedition into the Dafla Hills, Assam, together with those obtained in the adjacent Darrang Terai', *J.A.S.B.*, Vol. II (1876), p. 64

GODWIN-AUSTEN, H. H., 'Notes on the Wild Tribes Inhabiting the so-called Naga Hills on our N.E. Frontier of India', *J.A.I.*, Vol. XI (1882), pp. 56-73 & 196-214

GOHAIN, B. C., 'Shifting Cultivation among the Abors', *March of India*, Vol. VI, No. 2 (1953), pp. 39-43

GOHAIN, B. C., 'Agricultural Organization among the Abor', *Bulletin of the Dept. of Anthropology*, Vol. III, No. 2 (Calcutta, 1954)

GRAY, J. ERROL, *Diary of a Journey to the Bor Khamti Country and Sources of the Irrawady made by Mr J. Errol Gray, Season* 1892-3, *from Assam* (Simla, 1893)

GRIERSON, G. A., *Linguistic Survey of India*, Vol. III, Tibeto-Burman Family, Pt. I (Calcutta, 1909). Accounts of the Aka, Abor, Miri, Dafla and Mishmi languages

GRIFFITH, W., 'Visit to the Mishmee Hills in Assam', *Asiatic Journal and Monthly Register*, Vol. XXV (1838), pp. 233-44

GRIFFITH, W., *Journals of Travels in Assam, Burma, Bootan, Afghanistan and the Neighbouring Countries.* Arranged by John McClelland (Calcutta, 1847)

GUHA, B. S., 'The Indian Aborigines and their Administration', *J.A.S.*, Vol. XVII (1911), pp. 19-44. Many references to the NEFA tribes

GURDON, P. R. T., 'On the Khamptis', *J.R.A.S.*, Vol. XXVII (1895), pp. 157-64

HALLIDAY, H. I., 'The Abors of Assam', *United Empire*, Vol. XIX (1928), pp. 339-42

HAMILTON, A., *In Abor Jungles* (London, 1912). Describes the Abor Expedition and the Mishmi and Miri Missions

HAMILTON, A., 'The Mishmi Mission', *Fortnightly Review*, Vol. XCI (1912), pp. 552-65

HAMILTON, F., *An Account of Assam, first compiled in* 1807-14. Edited by S. K. Bhuyan (Gauhati, 1940). A few early references to the NEFA tribes

HAMILTON, R. C., *An Outline Grammar of the Dafla Language, as spoken by the Tribes Immediately South of the Apa Tanang Country* (Shillong, 1900)

HANNAY, S. F., *Sketch of the Singphos, or the Kakhyens of Burma, the Position of the Tribe as regards Baumo and the Inland Trade of the Irrawaddy with Yunnan, followed by an Account of the Shans* (Calcutta, 1847)

HARMAN, H. J., 'Narrative Report of Lt. H. J. Harman in charge Daphla Military Expeditionary Survey', *General Report on the Topographical Surveys of India for the Season* 1874-5 (Calcutta, 1876)

HESSELMEYER, C. H., 'The Hill Tribes of the Northern Frontier of Assam', *J.A.S.B.*, Vol. XXXVII (1868), pp. 192-208. On the Akas

HODGSON, B. H., 'On the Aborigines of North Eastern India and Comparative Vocabularies of the Tibetan, Bodo and Garo Tongues', *J.A.S.B.*, Vol. XVIII (1849), pp. 451-60. Vocabularies of 'Namsang', 'Tengsa', and Abor-Miri

HODGSON, B. H., 'On the Aborigines of the Eastern Frontier', *J.A.S.B.*, Vol. XVIII (1849), pp. 967-75

HODGSON, B. H., *Miscellaneous Essays Relating to Indian Subjects* (London, 1880)

HODSON, T. C., 'Head-Hunting Among the Hill Tribes of Assam', *Folklore*, Vol. XX (1909), pp. 132-43

HOLDICH, T. H., 'The North-Eastern Frontier of India', *J. R. Soc. Arts*, Vol. XC (1912), pp. 379-92

HORE, W. B., *Report on the Abor Country* (Simla, 1913)

HOUGHTON, B., 'Outlines of Tibeto-Burman Linguistic Palaeontology', *J.R.A.S.*, (1896), pp. 23-55

HUDDLESTON, P. G., 'Abor Military and Political Mission 1912-15', *R. Engineering Journal*, Vol. XLIV (1930), pp. 253-62

HUNTER, W. W., *A Statistical Account of Assam* (London, 1879)

HUTTON, J. H., *The Angami Nagas* (London, 1921). On Sangtams, pp. 375-7; on Changs, pp. 377-82; on Phoms, pp. 382-3; on Konyaks, pp. 383-7

HUTTON, J. H., *The Sema Nagas* (London, 1921)

HUTTON, J. H., 'A Chang Naga Folk Tale', *Man in India*, Vol. II (1922), pp. 100-3

HUTTON, J. H., 'Note on a Type of Snare from the Phom Country', *Man*, Vol. XXII (1922)

HUTTON, J. H., 'The Disposal of the Dead at Wakching', *Man*, Vol. XXVII (1927). Describes practices similar to those of the Konyaks in Tuensang

HUTTON, J. H., 'Diaries of Two Tours in the Unadministered Area East of the Naga Hills', *Memoirs of A.S.B.*, Vol. XI, No. 1 (1929). The first detailed anthropological account of the Tuensang tribes

HUTTON, J. H., 'A Note on the Method of Skull Ornamentation practised among the Konyak Nagas of Assam', *Man*, Vol. XXIX (1929)

HUTTON, J. H., 'Outline of Chang Grammar', *J.R.A.S.B.*, Vol. XXV (N.S. 1929), pp. 1-101

HUTTON, J. H., 'Headhunters of the North-East Frontier', *J.R. Soc. Arts*, Vol. LXXXV (1936), pp. 134-44

HUTTON, J. H., *A Primitive Philosophy of Life* (Oxford, 1938)

INSPECTOR-GENERAL OF ASSAM RIFLES, *Review of the Work done by Men of the Assam Rifles during the Earthquake*, 15*th August*, 1950, *and Floods* (Shillong, 1951)

IZZARD, R., *The Hunt for the Buru* (London, 1951)

JENKINS, H. L., 'Notes on a Trip across the Patkoi Range from Assam to the Hookoong Valley', *Proc. A.S.B.* (1870), pp. 230-7

KAULBACK, R., *Salween* (London, 1938). A little on the Mishmis

KENNEDY, R. S., *Ethnological Report on the Akas, Khoas and Mijis and the Monbas of Tawang* (Shillong, 1914)

KINGDON-WARD, F., *The Riddle of the Tsangpo Gorges* (London, 1926)

KINGDON-WARD, F., *Plant-Hunting on the Edge of the World* (London, 1930). A little about the Mishmis

KINGDON-WARD, F., 'The Seingkin and Delei Valleys, N.E. Frontier of India', *Geographical Journal*, Vol. LXXV (1930), pp. 412-35. Describes a Mishmi custom of human sacrifice at a funeral

KINGDON-WARD, F., *A Plant Hunter in Tibet* (London, 1934). There are two chapters about the Mishmis

KINGDON-WARD, F., *Assam Adventure* (London, 1941). References to Monpas

KINGDON-WARD, J., *My Hill So Strong* (London, 1952). Contains a vivid account of the 1950 earthquake as it affected the Lohit F.D.

KONOW, STEN, 'Notes on the languages spoken between the Assam Valley and Tibet', *J.R.A.S.*, 1902, pp. 127-37. Notes on Aka, Dafla, Abor and Mishmi

KRICK, N. M., 'An Account of an Expedition among the Abors in 1853', *J.A.S.B.*, Vol. IX (1913), pp. 107-22

KUMAR, N., 'Blood Group and Secretor Frequency among the Galong', *Bulletin of the Dept. of Anthropology*, Vol. III (1954)

KUMAR, N., 'Taste, Middle-Phalangeal Hair and Occipital Hair Whorls among Nokte Naga', *Bulletin of the Dept. of Anthropology*, Vol. IV, No. 2 (Calcutta, 1954)

LA TOUCHE, T. D., 'Notes on the Geology of the Aka Hills', *Rec. Geo. Surv. India*, Vol. XVIII, p. 121

LEACH, E. R., *Political Systems of Highland Burma* (Cambridge, Mass., 1954). Reference to Khamptis and Singphos

LEPPER, C. H., 'Notes on the Singpho and Khampti Country, North-Eastern Frontier', *Proc. A.S.B.* (1882), pp. 64-70

LINDSAY, A. B., 'Expedition against the Abors, 1911-12', *Army Review*, Vol. IV (1913), pp. 343-58

LITTLE, W. R., *Report on the Abor Expedition*, 1894 (Simla, 1895)

LLOYD, G. & HUTTON, J. H., *Report on the Census of Assam*, 1921 (Shillong, 1923). Contains notes on the Frontier tribes by G. A. Nevill (on Akas, Apa Tanis and Daflas); T. P. M. O'Callaghan (on Khamptis, Singphos and Mishmis); R. C. R. Cumming (on Abors and Miris)

LORRAIN, J. H., *A Dictionary of the Abor-Miri Language, with Illustrative Sentences and Notes* (Shillong, 1910)

LUMSDEN, D. M. & WILLIAMSON, N., 'A Journey into the Abor Country, 1909', *Geographical Journal*, Vol. XXXVII (1911), pp. 621-9

MACGREGOR, C. R., 'Notes on Akas and Akaland', *Proc. A.S.B.* (1884), pp. 198-212

MACGREGOR, C. R., 'Journal of the Expedition under Colonel Woodthorpe, R.E., from Upper Assam to the Irawadi, and Return over the Patkoi Range', *Proc. R.C.S.*, Vol. IX (1887), pp. 19-42

MACGREGOR, C. R., *Military Report on the Kampti-Singpho Countries* (Calcutta, 1887)

MACKENZIE, A., *History of the relations of the Government with the Hill Tribes of the North-East Frontier of Bengal* (Calcutta, 1884). Contains in Pt. I a historical account of the dealings of Government with the Akas (pp. 21-6), the Daflas (pp. 27-32), the Abors and Miris (pp. 33-46), the Mishmis (pp. 47-54), the Khamptis (pp. 57-60), and the Singphos (pp. 61-72). Appendix C (pp. 399-404) contains a note by P. T. Carnegy. dated 1873, on the 'Seebsaugor Nagas in 1873', and Appendix J (pp. 537-50) consists of extracts from the Assam Census Report of 1881: this gives some brief notes on the Hill Miris, Abors and Daflas

MACKENZIE, A., *Memorandum on the North-East Frontier of Bengal* (Calcutta, 1869)

M'COSH, J., 'Account of the Mountain Tribes on the Extreme N.E. Frontier of Bengal', *J.A.S.B.*, Vol. V (1836), pp. 193-208. Information about Khamptis, Singphos and Abors

MEHTA, K. L., 'The North-East Frontier Agency Today', *March of India*, Vol. VIII (1956), pp. 8-12

MICHELL, St. JOHN F., *Report of the N.E. Frontier of India* (Calcutta, 1883)

MILLINGTON, P., *On the Track of the Abor* (London, 1912)

MILLS, J. P., 'A Brief Note on Agriculture in the Dirang Dzong Area', *Man in India*, Vol. XXVI (1946), pp. 8-11

MILLS, J. P., 'Tours in the Balipara Frontier Tract, Assam', *Man in India*, Vol. XXVI (1947), pp. 9-35

MILLS, J. P., 'A Preliminary Note on the Senjithongji of the Balipara Frontier Tract, Assam', *J. Ind. Anthrop. Inst.*, Vol. II (1948), pp. 1-8

MILLS, J. P., 'The Sacred Chiefs of Assam', *Man in India*, Vol. XXVIII (1948), pp. 149-51. On the Konyak Angs

MILLS, J. P., 'The Mishmis of the Lohit Valley, Assam', *J.R.A.I.*, Vol. LXXXII (1952)

MOOKERJI, R. R., 'Combined Pattern and Basket Specimens from Upper Assam', *Man* (1940). Singpho and Khampti.

'Narrative of the Route Survey of L. Explorer, from Darjeeling to Shigatze, Chetang and Tawang and from Shigatze back to Darjeeling via Gianche Jong and Phari, in 1875-6', *General Report on the Operations of the Survey of India during* 1878-9 (Calcutta, 1879), App. pp. 8-15. Account of the Tawang area

NEEDHAM, J. F., 'Excursion in the Abor Hills; From Sadiya on the Upper Assam and Rima in South-Eastern Tibet', *R.G.S. Suppl. Papers,* Vol. II (1887-9), pp. 485-555.

NEEDHAM, J. F., *Outline Grammar of the Singpho Language* (Shillong, 1889)

NEEDHAM, J. F., *Outline Grammar of the Khamti Language* (Rangoon, 1894)

NEEDHAM, J. F., *Report of a Trip into the Abor Hills,* 1884 (Shillong, 1895)

NEEDHAM, J. F., *Report of a Visit Paid to the Abor Villages of Padu and Kumku*, 1885 (Shillong, 1895)

NEEDHAM, J. F., *Report on the Bebejiya Mishmi Expedition*, 1899-1900 (Shillong, 1900)

NEEDHAM, J. F., *A Collection of a few Moshang Naga Words* (Shillong, 1897)

NEEDHAM, J. F., 'Report on the Abor Villages beyond the British Frontier (1884)', *Assam Review*, Vol. II, No. 7 (1929), pp. 13-16

NEUFVILLE, J. B., 'On the Geography and Population of Assam, 1823', *Asiatic Researches*, Vol. XVI (1828)

NIGAM, R. C., 'Abors and Myths of their Origin', *March of India*, Vol. VI (1953), pp. 31-3

NIGAM, R. C., 'A Study of Padam (Abor) Phonology', *Bulletin of the Dept. of Anthropology*, Vol. III, No. 2 (Calcutta, 1954)

O'CALLAGHAN, T. P. M., 'Notes on Certain Frontier Tribes', *Census of India*, 1921 (Shillong, 1923), Vol. III: Assam, Pt. 1, Report, App. B, pp. 11-12. On the Khamptis, Singphos and Mishmis

OGLE, M. J., 'Extract from the Narrative Report on the Survey Operations with the Hukong Valley Expedition', *General Report on the Operations of the Survey of India during* 1887-8 (Calcutta, 1888), pp. 42-7. Contains a brief account of a Konyak human sacrifice.

O'NEILL, J. S., 'Native Suspension Bridge over the Dihong', *Geographical Journal*, Vol. XL (1912), pp. 213-15

OWEN, JOHN, *Notes on the Naga Tribes in Communication with Assam* (Calcutta, 1884)

PEAL, S. E., 'Report on a Visit to the Nongyang Lake on the Burma Frontier, February 1879', *J.A.S.B.*, Vol. L, Pt. 2 (1881), pp. 1-30

PEAL, S. E., 'The Communal Barracks of Primitive Races', *J.A.S.B.*, Vol. LXI, Pt. 2 (1892), pp. 168-82

PEAL, S. E., 'On the "Morong" as Possibly a Relic of Pre-Marriage Communism', *J.A.I.*, Vol. XXII (1893), pp. 244-61

PEAL, S. E., 'Eastern Nagas of the Tirap and the Namtsik', *J.A.S.B.*, Vol. LXV, Pt. 3 (1896), pp. 9-17

PEEL, A. C., 'Short Notes of a Trip into the Hills South of Sibsaugor', *Proc. A.S.B.* (1869), pp. 76-9. On the Wanchos

PEMBERTON, R. B., *Report on the Eastern Frontier of British India* (Calcutta, 1835)

PUGH, M., *Tribal Games of NEFA* (Shillong, 1958)

RAMAN, G., and BEIERWALTES, W. H., 'Correlation of Goitre, Deaf-mutism and Mental Retardation with Serum Thyroid Hormone Levels in Non-cretinous Inhabitants of a Severe Endemic Goitre Area in India', *Journal of Clinical Endocrinology and Metabolism*, Vol. XIX, No. 2 (1959), pp. 228-33

READ, C. H., 'Exhibition of Ethnological Objects from the Akas. Northern Assam', *J.A.I.*, Vol. XV (1886), pp. 139-40

REID, R., *History of the Frontier Areas Bordering on Assam, from* 1883-1941 (Shillong, 1942)

RIPLEY, DILLON, 'Exploring the Mishmi Hills', *Natural History*, Vol. LVII (1948), pp. 79-85

ROBINSON, W., *A Descriptive Account of Assam, to which is added a Short Account of Neighbouring Tribes* (London, 1841)

ROBINSON, W., 'Notes on the Dophlas and the peculiarities of their Language', *J.A.S.B.*, Vol. XX (1851), pp. 126-37

ROBINSON, W., 'Notes on the Language spoken by the Mi-Shmis', *J.A.S.B.*, Vol. XXIV (1855), pp. 307-24

ROBINSON, W., 'Notes on the Language spoken by the various tribes inhabiting the valley of Asam and its mountain confines', *J.A.S.B.*, Vol. XVIII (1849), pp. 183-237. Includes an Abor vocabulary

ROWLATT, E. A., 'Report of an Expedition into the Mishmee Hills to the north-east of Sudyah', *J.A.S.B.*, Vol. XIV (1845), pp. 477-95

ROY, NILIMA, 'Habitations of the Adis of the Siang Frontier Division', *Vanyajati*, Vol. V, No. 3 (1957), pp. 125-33

ROY, NILIMA, 'Basketry and Domestic Utensils of the Adi', *Vanyajati*, Vol. V, No. 4 (1957), pp. 170-4

ROY, SACHIN, 'The Body Build of the Abor', *Bulletin of the Dept. of Anthropology*, Vol. II, No. 2 (Calcutta, 1953), pp. 99-104

ROY, SACHIN, 'Abor Weapons of War and Chase', *J.A.S.*, Vol. XXII (1956), pp. 139-59

ROY, SACHIN, 'Rhymes and Rhythms of the Abor', *Indian Folk-lore* (December, 1957), pp. 81-93

ROY, SACHIN, 'Dress, Ornaments and Decoration of the Adis', *Vanyajati*. Vol. VI, No. 1 (1958), pp. 4-19

ROY, SACHIN, 'Hunting and Fishing among the Adis', *Vanyajati*, Vol. VI, No. 2 (1958), pp. 52-60

ROY, SACHIN, *Aspects of Padam-Minyong Culture* (Shillong, 1960)

RUSTOMJI, N. K., 'Tribal Administration in the North-East Frontier Agency', *The Adivasis* (Delhi, 1955), pp. 139-46

Selections from the Records of the Bengal Government, 1851-69, No. XXIII (Calcutta, 1855). Contains papers by Neufville, 'On the Geography and Population of Assam'; Wilcox, 'Memoir of a Survey of Assam and the neighbouring Countries, executed in 1825-6-7-8'; Dalton, 'Correspondence & Journal of his visit to a Clan of Abors on the Dihong River'

Selections of Papers Regarding the Hill Tracts between Assam & Burma & on the Upper Brahmaputra, 1825-70 (Calcutta, 1873). Contains papers by Wilcox, 'Memoir of a Survey of Assam'; Pemberton, 'Abstract of Hannay's Journal'; Griffith, 'Journal of a Trip to the Mishmi Mountains'; Griffith, 'A Journey from Upper Assam towards Hockhoom'; Bayfield, 'Narrative of a Journey from Ava to the Frontiers of Assam and Back'; Jenkins, 'Notes on a Trip across the Patkoi Range'; 'Report of a Visit by Capt. Vetch to the Singpho and Naga Frontier'; Reports of Lt. Brodie's Dealings with the Nagas'; Peal, 'Notes on a visit to the Tribes inhabiting the Hills South of Sibsagar'

SEN GUPTA, P. N., 'Investigation on the Dietary Habits of the Aboriginal Tribes of Abor Hills', *Journal Ind. Med. Res.*, Vol. XL (1952), p. 203

SEN GUPTA, P. N., 'The Dietaries of the Primitive Tribes of India', *March of India*, Vol. VI, No. 2 (1953), pp. 60-6

SEN GUPTA, P. N., 'Population Studies and Living Conditions of the Tribes in the Padam and Minyong Areas of Abor Hills (Assam)', *Bulletin of the Dept. of Anthropology*, Vol. II (Calcutta, 1953), pp. 91-112

SEN GUPTA, P. N., 'Studies in the Vital Capacity of Nocte Nagas of Tirap Frontier Division', *Proc. of the National Institute of Sciences of India*, Vol. XXI B, No. 1 (1955)

SHAFER, R., 'Hruso', *Bulletin of the School of Oriental and African Studies*, Vol. XII (1947), pp. 184-96

SHAFER, R., *Bibliography of Sino-Tibetan Languages* (Wiesbaden, 1957)

SHAKESPEAR, L. W., *History of Upper Assam, Upper Burmah and North-Eastern Frontier* (London, 1914)

SHAKESPEAR, L. W., *History of the Assam Rifles* (London, 1929)

SHUKLA, B. K., *The Daflas of the Subansiri Region* (Shillong, 1959)

STACK, E., 'Miris, Daphlas and Abors', *Report on the Census of India*, 1881, *Assam* (Calcutta, 1883), p. 86

STONOR, C. R., 'The Feasts of Merit among the Northern Sangtam Tribe of Assam', *Anthropos*, Vol. XLV (1950)

Ten Years of Progress in NEFA (Shillong, 1957)

TROTTER, H., 'Account of the Pundit's Journey in Great Thibet from Leh in Ladakh to Lhasa, and of his Return to India via Assam', *J.R.G.S.*, Vol. XLVII (1877), pp. 86-136. A little on the Monpas

VETCH, H., 'Report of a Visit by Capt. Vetch to the Singpho and Naga Frontier in 1842', *Selection of Papers Regarding the Hill Tracts between Assam and Burmah, and on the Upper Brahmaputra* (Calcutta, 1873)

WADDELL, L. A., 'A Note on the derivation of Miri', *Man*, Vol. XI, No. 56 (1911)

WADDELL, L. A., 'Note on the Poisoned Arrows of the Akas', *J.A.I.*, Vol. XXIV (1895), p. 57

WADDELL, L. A., 'The Falls of the Tsang-Po (San-Pu) and the identity of that River with the Brahmaputra', *Geographical Journal*, Vol. V (1895), p. 258

WADE, J. P., 'Geographical Sketch of Assam, 1800', *Asiatic Annual Register* (1805)

WARD, G. L. S., *Military Report on the Mishmi Country* (Simla, 1901)

WILCOX, R., 'Memoir of a Survey of Assam and the neighbouring Countries, executed in 1825-6-7-8', *Asiatic Researches*, Vol. XVII, pp. 314-469

WOODTHORPE, R. G., 'Naga Hills Exploration, Report on the Survey Operations in the Naga Hills, 1875-6', *General Report on the Topographical Surveys of India, for the Season* 1875-6 (Shillong, 1876)

WOODTHORPE, R. G., 'Naga Hills Exploration. A letter to Capt. W. F. Badgley dated June 15th, 1876', *General Report on the Topographical Surveys of India, for the Season* 1875-6 (Calcutta, 1877)

WOODTHORPE, R. G., *Assam Surveys*, 1877-8 (Simla, 1878)

YOUNG, E. C., 'A Journey from Yunnan to Assam', *Geographical Journal*, Vol. XXX (1907), pp. 152-80

INDEX